C000140348

"I especially enjoyed the New Mills (lly. Philip comes alive as a colossus-passionate, visionary, his own person, full of drive and determination bent on the highest standards possible with a capacity to select good staff and to get the best from them and to be challenging but also kind and generous. I loved the reflections from students, especially where it caught their different backgrounds and expectations. The story of Romeo and Juliet in Germany is remarkable – real courage and pioneering for its time and the willingness to respond to any challenge. Another huge strength is the insight into the Comprehensive debate, never, in my view, resolved because governments have not funded them properly and have been ambivalent, preferring to constantly tinker with the system. This is a marvellous case study of the impact on one town, the issues/problems and possible solutions."

Robert Wilson, former Head Teacher and Chief Adviser

"I have read with interest and enjoyment the chapter of Philip's time at East Ham Grammar School. The story takes on a different dimension as soon as Philip enters the scene. It is amazing when all that he did in those brief years are listed and categorised. I especially enjoyed the Drama and the accounts from the performers experiences were very well documented warts and all. The Greek section was exceptional and the catalogue of Shakespeare impressive. The portrait of Philip and his effect on those around him was so true and his pupil's contributions were a testament to his genius. I enjoyed the camping exploits too."

Kay Aldridge, a former Redbridge Primary School Deputy Headmistress.

"The book is a wonderful tribute to a very special man of many talents, high ideals, and inspirational zest, who inspired many and made an enormous contribution to English Education in the twentieth century."

Ronald Impey, former pupil and teacher of Classics in Schools and Universities

A LIFETIME IN ENGLISH EDUCATION

PHILIP VENNIS FROM PUPIL TO PRINCIPAL IN POST-WAR BRITAIN

For Professor Kornicki
I hope you enjoy reading this book.
Kind regards and best wishes,
Diana Vennis.

A LIFETIME IN ENGLISH EDUCATION

PHILIP VENNIS FROM PUPIL TO PRINCIPAL IN POST-WAR BRITAIN

DIANA VENNIS

Matador
9 Priory Business Park,
Wistow Road, Kibworth Beauchamp,
Leicestershire. LE8 0RX
Tel: (+44) 116 279 2299
Fax: (+44) 116 279 2277
Email: books@troubador.co.uk
Web: www.troubador.co.uk/matador

ISBN 9781 780882 963

British Library Cataloguing in Publication Data.
A catalogue record for this book is available from the British Library.

Typeset by Troubador Publishing Ltd, Leicester, UK

Matador is an imprint of Troubador Publishing Ltd

Printed and bound in the UK by TJ International, Padstow, Cornwall

This book is dedicated to Philip, my dear husband, who was a unique husband, father and an exceptional school teacher; to his children – Julian, Melanie and Mark; and to the grandchildren he never knew, loved or enjoyed – Billy, Monique, Ollie, Ella, Nina, Edward and Leah.

CONTENTS

FOREWORD

Philip Vennis: A life led between Idealism and Reality

Every person is the product of the times into which they are born and my father, Philip Vennis, was no exception.

Born on 25 November 1925 into a grocer's family in South London, behind him was the Great War and the Russian Revolution - ahead the Second World War and the Great Depression. A generation before him, the British Empire was at its pinnacle - a generation after, it was unstoppably declining.

Philip was a witness to the struggles of the between the war years, the general strike, the unemployment and the economic ruin. He was bright enough to get a scholarship to one of the finest schools in the country, Dulwich College, and this provided him with a golden opportunity from which he never looked back. That classic rags-to-riches tale, the one that starts with humble beginnings and ends with our hero being top of the greasy pole, was the road upon which he (kind of) travelled. The central tenets of Philip's philosophy on life generally, and education specifically, were borne out of this scholarship. He was now on a level playing field with the great and the good. He believed that education was the key to removing social barriers and creating a meritocratic society and this remained a constant throughout his life. The culmination of these ideals, the point at which his ideas coalesced with his ability to put them into action, occurred when he became Principal of Itchen College in 1971.

The turbulence of that earlier era clearly had a great affect, not just on the young Philip, but on every member of British society. How could it not? Men were called off to fight and die for their country while women took their places on the fields and in the factories. Philip himself, head-hunted from Dulwich at the tender age of eighteen, was sent to Bletchley Park to learn Japanese. He was then seconded to the US Navy in the Pacific to help translate Japanese transmissions. These experiences remained with him, never in a self-aggrandising way – usually in a self-deprecating fashion. His usual crack was that he only knew the Japanese for "Enemy Submarine Sunk" and nothing else so if he ever went to modern day Tokyo he would be completely useless - which of course he would have been...For the sacrifices made by men and women in the war on both fronts, for all the blood and tears, for all the hard graft, there needed to be a light at the end of the tunnel. Britain had to be a country worth fighting for...the status quo was collapsing and the War quickened a social process that had started two decades before with the end of the Great War. Even the usually self-obsessed British ruling class recognised that if all these sacrifices were required so soon after the last war, then the country had to be a place fit for returning heroes in 1945.

Given Philip's admiration for Churchill, the landslide victory of Clement Attlee's Labour Party in 1945 must have been bitter-sweet. Churchill may have been a great war leader but the voters did not trust him to rebuild Britain. A sea change had occurred and the people of Britain did not want a return to the economic dark days of the between the war years. The Beveridge Report of 1942 highlighted all these issues, and formed the basis upon which the new Labour Government governed.

So those vote winning mantras were:
No return to the dole queues of the late twenties and thirties
A health system free at the point of provision, for rich or poor
A cradle-to-grave welfare system and, crucially for Philip,
An education for all provided by the state

It's no surprise that, like a lot of young men when the war finished, Philip wished for a new type of society for Britain. Ever the individualist he was not a card carrying socialist or Labour supporter; more a radical liberal, almost patrician in outlook, who believed in the power of the state to do good things. A state that would protect the vulnerable, provide for you when you're old, level the playing field of class ridden Britain. Philip believed in a society where working class kids had as much of a chance in life as the rich kids; a society where you didn't have to pay for a quality education and which was open to all.

In a contemporary environment, where a brand new private and fee paying university has just been announced by various academic stars and independent schools, all set up by newspaper columnists, these ideas seem like the ravings of a mad leftie. But at the time, before the eighties, they were central ideas in the consensus politics of post-war Britain. In true iconoclastic style, Philip always wanted to go one step further and was arguing that the state should pay working class kids a wage to go into further education at the age of sixteen during the seventies and eighties, right through the culturally shifting tide of Thatcherite

Britain. 'Give them a living wage so that they can afford to go to further education, so they can become important members of our society, so they can reach their full potential', he would thunder at his Annual Speech Days at Itchen College. It was the only way that pupils would transcend their backgrounds...

Unlike the current political orthodoxy which believes that the market will provide all the answers and that the profit motive is the ultimate motivator, Philip was moved by higher ideals. He was a missionary without the religion, an idealist, but also a, sometimes contradictory pragmatist - the ends justified the means. During his Itchen College years he made friends, threw parties and worked the room like a politician looking for votes. What appeared like a form of social hypocrisy when I was younger was a game of 'realpolitik', played because Philip believed in the greater prize.

And that prize...well what was it? Education was a key but to what. A deeper understanding of culture and history enriched one's life and consequently made society more civilised. What differentiates us from animals is that erudition, those plays, that beautiful piece of music and while Philip may not have achieved his dream of a youth education wage for all up to eighteen years and maybe beyond, this is where he had his greatest impact.

Philip had a passionate urge to share the great insights on the human condition highlighted by the master dramatists, in particular William Shakespeare. I remember quite late in his life he took me to see 'Antony & Cleopatra' with Alan Bates and Francis de la Tour at the Barbican (I think) – absolutely mind numbingly boring in my opinion with the worst and longest death scene by Alan Bates...Philip loved it of course. He also took me to see 'Coriolanus' with Charles Dance and the Taming of the Shrew with Jonathan Pryce...and a whole number of other great plays, some of which seemed interminably long, others absolutely brilliant.

During his early teaching years he directed a whole range of plays to some degree of acclaim. Philip had an actor's understanding of showmanship and grandstanding and a director's eye for great drama and storytelling; with, of course, a huge well of sentimentality not uncommon to men of his generation (or do we all end up like that?).

He believed that classical music was one of the highest cultural points of Western society - the beauty that he heard in those melodies, by Mozart or Delius, Mahler or Debussy, Elgar or Beethoven, were the very pinnacle of human achievement. They put feelings that couldn't be expressed in words into a language that we could all understand.

He did all he could to impress his belief in the power of music onto all three of his children. I learned the cello and piano at a young age, my brother the clarinet, and my sister the violin. On social occasions he would call upon us to perform as a trio where, exquisitely embarrassed, we would saw and blew our way through a classic *magnum opus* by a musical deity in front of his very important (and adult!) guests. It still makes me squirm...

Sometimes his beliefs were contradictory and he had the ability to hold two different points at the same time although this was probably an essential characteristic of being English at the time. He believed that the British Empire was an overall force for good - that it brought an essential decency to far-flung (and to his mind uncivilised) places - and that Gandhi was a genius. He believed in teaching me Latin to O Level because the local (comprehensive) school I went to did not teach it. Post-war, with the British Empire collapsing, he believed that Britain should hand the torch of decency and democracy to the Americans – but to the America of Stephen Sondheim and George Gershwin, of Gore Vidal and JFK, and not the America of McCarthy and Hoover, of Vietnam and napalm. Philip loved the idea of the USA, its limitless dream of freedom and landscape, unsullied by the tribulations of British class warfare, where a man stood tall for what he believed in or so he liked to think. Maybe this love affair with the simple myths of America (reflected in a lifelong love of westerns) was really about the desire to cut through all the contradictions, compromises, hypocrisy of the politics that he dealt with everyday within the educational establishment.

And when put in the context of the mid thirties and forties, when Philip was becoming a young man, the beginning of his love for America makes sense. In the right corner we have the unholy trinity and blood drenched hands of Hitler, Mussolini and Franco, and in the opposite corner you have that genocidal Uncle, Joe Stalin, distorting Marxism through a hall of mirrors and poisoning the left for generations (maybe forever?). Who came riding in on their white chargers from across the pond to save us from the Nazi menace? The Seventh Cavalry in the modern and well equipped form of the US Army whistling Yankee doodle dandee as they cleaned up old Europe. No wonder Roosevelt and Churchill looked like angels to Philip. And comparatively I guess they were...He believed that Churchill was without faults because he had led the nation through the war; Philip had all of Churchill's history books, we went to Chartwell as a family and of course to Bleinheim. I remember, at his instigation, watching the film 'Young Winston' by Richard Attenborough (a derring-do, boys' own story of Churchill's early years at the turn of the twentieth century, set against the stirring British music of Edward Elgar) and it having a profound effect on my young and impressionable mind. And yes, Winston is even my middle name.

So Philip's journey began in the economic turbulence of the twenties and thirties and the Second World War, and his career ended almost coincidentally with the toppling of Thatcher (another grocer's child and a near contemporary but what a different path taken). Dying just on the cusp of the new millennium, he missed 9/11, the Iraq war and the banking crisis which precipitated the biggest depression since the thirties. We even have a coalition government that prides itself on the austerity of its policies; how laissez-faire capitalism is going to bring Britain back to health; and of course there is a huge disparity between rich and poor. Looking down he must think that those dark days of the twenties and thirties have returned.

Over five decades Philip dedicated his professional life to a passionate belief in education for all. He was born in an era where public service was an important and central idea to the rebuilding of British society post war. Increasingly with the Thatcher led social changes of the eighties he became a man out of time.

Gradually over the last twenty years the dream of comprehensive, free co-ed education for all has been eroded. The buzz words of the current era have been parental choice, which has hidden an agenda of a two tier education system. One bunch of schools for middle class parents and one for the working class and the great masses; the people, who for one reason or another, were not dealt the best hand. This was anathema to someone like Philip.

The ideas for which he fought and argued all his life now seem like a whisper from a different age. His great dream of education, as the key to a civilised society, seems moribund in the current climate. In my opinion, nobody is discussing education in these terms. The left has given up the fight against the market and we now have a system that helps the haves and turns its back on the have-nots.

Maybe his legacy is not in the big vision he had, but in the minutiae and details of his life. He believed that everyone had something precious to give to society usually creatively or artistically, as well as in the more traditional subjects. The way in which he touched his students with his passion for the arts on a day to day basis or the way his generosity of spirit always encouraged the dreams, hopes and aspirations of others no matter what their background or the way that he related to and understood teenagers in his care, some of whom came from pretty difficult backgrounds.

So Philip Vennis, your professional epitaph:

A man of dedication and commitment
Passionate in his feeling for the arts,
Sometimes contradictory and many times complicated, yet
always steadfast in his absolute belief in the power of education.

Philip carried the torch for his ideals over many years, ideals that may wane and flow through the shifting patterns of modern society but will always have an essential heartfelt decency to them and a belief in the power of human beings to transcend their backgrounds.

This book, by telling his professional journey over almost fifty years, will, I hope, provide inspiration to progressive educationalists in the UK and a salient history lesson on British education in general. Above all else, with his combination of high ideals and hard pragmaticism, it is a testament to the strength of character of my father, the headmaster.

Mark Vennis, June 2012

INTRODUCTION

Philip Harvey Vennis was a man of deep principle and passionate about education. He was an indomitable person who always stood up for his beliefs and idealisms, and was not disconcerted when people disagreed with his views.

He was a man of boundless energy and enthusiasm, who knew from the days of his own privileged education that his life's work would be to educate working class children, open their doors and raise their horizons in the ways in which his own education had successfully achieved.

He was born to a working class family on 25 November 1925. He was the only son and second child of Milton and Nancy Vennis, at the time of his birth his father ran a tobacconist shop and the family lived above the shop. Living in London, where employment was difficult meant that in order to obtain work the family moved frequently and disruption to Philip's schooling inevitably took place. He attended four different junior schools, St.Helen's, Westcliff on Sea; Hamlet Court Road; Derwentwater Acton; and New Park Road School, Brixton, and so lack of continuity of study, friends and routines could have been constantly unsettling. However, even at this young age, nothing deterred this boy's ambition to succeed. He and his father would spend a lot of time studying together, especially looking at maps and studying geography, well before Philip went to Dulwich College. At his last junior elementary school, New Park Road in Brixton, after receiving some initial tuition in French, Philip gained a scholarship to Dulwich College and this is where his educational journey really began.

Many of his own thoughts and philosophy of education are included here, especially in the later chapters. Contributions and quotations are an important part of the book and these are from his ex-pupils, colleagues, educational leaders, friends and press cuttings. This is not a straightforward biography, but an account of the life and times of one very unusual educator who has influenced the progress and direction of the four schools/colleges in which he worked and the many pupils who benefitted from his teaching and leadership. In his life Philip was connected with a range of educational establishments – a London County Council junior elementary school - New Park Road School; a public school – Dulwich College; a boys' grammar school - East Ham Grammar School; an early co-educational comprehensive school – Ounsdale; a co-educational grammar school – New Mills Grammar School; and a sixth form college – Itchen College. Quite a spectrum of the education scene in England from 1935 to 1988.

For over forty years Philip Vennis was in education. His career as a teacher, deputy headmaster, headmaster and college principal spanned two great Education Acts. One of the most important pieces of legislation of twentieth Century education was the Education Act of 1944, also known as the 'Butler Act', and at the end of his career was the Education Reform Act of 1988.

His own education at a London County Council elementary school and then Dulwich College were formative years for his understanding of educational values.

He left Dulwich College in 1944, his education having been interrupted by the Second World War.

He spent eighteen months at Bletchley Park as a sub-lieutenant in the Royal Navy (Special Branch Special Service in Japanese Intelligence) learning Japanese and assisting with the code breaking of Japanese Naval messages.

Degrees in Classics and English from Peterhouse, Cambridge, and then the University of London for a Post Graduate Teaching Diploma enabled him to enter his chosen profession of a teacher.

Initially he taught in the tripartite system (grammar schools, secondary modern schools and secondary technical schools) in a state grammar school.

He spent nine years (1949 to 1958) at East Ham Grammar School for Boys under the leadership of Dr. J. L. Whiteley, who enabled this young, and enthusiastic teacher to have the time and space to develop and expand his ideas, and to channel his energies into helping pupils in the state education system.

Comprehensive schools were just beginning in the middle to late fifties and these schools would take all pupils regardless of ability (except those children with special needs who attended special schools), and would cater for children from a variety of social backgrounds, and there would be no examination or any other selection process for entry. Philip was Deputy headmaster at a rural comprehensive school, Ounsdale School, in Wombourne from 1958 to 1962.

His experience at this Comprehensive School helped very much in getting his first Headship, at New Mills Grammar School. The local press at New Mills noted after Philip's appointment, 'A notable feature about the appointment is that Mr. Vennis is now Deputy headmaster of a comprehensive school which has about 900 pupils.

Roughly, that school is about as big as the two New Mills schools – Grammar and County Secondary – put together. Does Mr. Vennis's appointment mean, as has been thought likely for some time, that Derbyshire Education Committee will decide on the two New Mills secondary schools becoming a comprehensive school, or, at least, joining together in a comprehensive system? It may be that the move to link up will be made in the not too distant future. With his comprehensive school experience, Mr. Vennis should be the right man to see that such a switch would work as smoothly as possible'. (High Peak

Reporter 20 April 1962) He did indeed see through the amalgamation of the Grammar School and the Secondary School in New Mills in 1970.

Having always been a great advocate of sixth form education, for his final post he became Itchen Sixth Form College's Principal. In an article in the Education Magazine,25 December 1970, 'Heading for change – Itchen College – one of Southampton's trio of brave new secondary colleges for the sixteen to nineteens – is to have a new headmaster. He is Mr.Philip Vennis, Head of the New Mills School in Stockport, which recently went comprehensive and his experience there should stand him in very good stead in his new post. For one thing the changeover at New Mills was from grammar to comprehensive – Itchen College, too, has had to cope with a run down of its grammar course in the past four years. For another, New Mills has a Sixth form of nearly 200 which for some years now has been open access. And Itchen College, in common with its sister secondary colleges, works on the open access principle'.

For nearly eighteen years he gave unstinting dedication to every generation of sixth formers and the community in which he served. The effect of his personality upon Itchen was profound. He had a remarkable career, he was passionate about education and many of the quotations from his papers and speeches quoted later in the book reflect such passion. His commitment to education was so strong, with singleness of purpose, passionate idealism and educational vision with nothing being unachievable. Nothing and nobody deflected him from his vision and ideals. He was a remarkable man, inspirational and fearless, very confident with a strong self belief, a powerful ebullient character that had an ability to enrich the lives of all who knew him.'You see good in all of us, you have touched many lives with greatness and lit up mine with the huge courage of your noble convictions, with mighty voice and glorious guffaw, you've thundered out for fairness and fineness, great deeds and great art, Shakespeare and Mozart, Churchill and Dancing at Lughnasa. You have strengthened my timid spirit'. (Gordon Ward. English and Humanities Advisor/Inspector for Hampshire).He has influenced so many young lives, he has made deep impressions on them, and he has widened horizons, he has inspired pupils to be interested in classics, Shakespeare, literature, the theatre, and scouting.

One of his ex-pupils from East Ham Grammar School writes 'Mr.Vennis was a dynamic and demanding teacher who brooked no nonsense but who had a sharp sense of humour. It was always a relief to see his face crack into a broad grin at some inanity. Nevertheless, his influence has remained with me for fifty years, the discipline of Latin is so fundamental to a European language. How on earth do children manage these days?

However I remember him most for the production of Shakespearian plays.'

CHAPTER 1

Dulwich College

"I went to Dulwich in 1937. Before then, owing to the nomadic habits of my family I had been to four state (or state aided) Junior Elementary Schools. I remember my fourth school quite well. It was a London County Council Junior Elementary; the staff were keen and very helpful and were very pleased when I passed the London County Council Junior Scholarship to Dulwich College." (P.H.V. 1948)

In the 1904 Code it was stated what a junior elementary school could be, and in a paragraph directly aimed at Local Education Authorities it insisted that 'it will be an important, though subsidiary object of the school to discover individual children who show promise of exceptional capacity, and to develop their special gifts (so far as this can be done without sacrificing the interests of the majority of the children) so that they may be qualified to pass at the proper age into secondary schools and be able to derive the maximum of benefit there offered to them.' Philip's education at New Park Road School (now Robert Atkins School) in his final year before going to Dulwich College covered most traditional areas of the curriculum in categories such as reading, spelling, composition, handwriting, arithmetic, mental arithmetic, science, geography and history. From his school reports of that era it is evident that he was a high achiever, with the headteacher commenting that he showed considerable promise. Clearly New Park Road was listening and implementing the 1904 Code.

Following the First World War, the 1918 Act was passed and by 1920 the London County Council increased the number of secondary school places available to those children attending Elementary Schools, and proposed nineteen projects for this to happen. They also increased the number of junior county scholarships, which in the first ten years of the twentieth century were only available to less than five per cent of children, and, by the time that Philip sat the Scholarship the London County Council was offering one thousand six hundred scholarships per annum. These scholarships were an examination in arithmetic and English which tested intelligence rather than acquired knowledge. Dulwich College was one of the first fee-paying schools to offer places to scholarship boys.

New Park Road was a typical London Junior Elementary School in a design which was influenced by the Queen Anne style. (Colour photograph 2.); it was designed by T. J. Bailey and built in 1897, with sash windows and the red brick vernacular, with stone dressings. London school designs of the 1890s included classrooms and a large hall which could be used for class teaching; instead of the traditional idea of the 1870s when a single large room would be divided off by the use of curtains. New Park Road is one of London's archetypical 'Three Decker' Schools (colour photograph 1.) which was originally built for use by the infants on the ground floor, boys above and girls on top. The main reasons for building high was the shortage of land and to give the schools a physically important role in the communities in which they served. This is still evident today with New Park Road School being flanked on one side by Victorian terraced houses.

'A Wartime education'- 1937 to 1944

"In my first year at Dulwich I had been among boys from the same sort of home (flats – houses with no gardens – 'street players' all of us). But in the second year 2A was peopled by lads from the various preparatory schools which fed the College, or by colonials, or boys from distant homes who were boarders. Thus began some of the most subtle and complex relationships typical of the modern public school. I, a normal cockney from South London, was amazed to find a boy who had never been on or knew of a 'tram', and he was equally amazed at my lack of experience of the country and my lack of knowledge of the most common wildflowers. This I think was a really valuable contribution to my 'education', and didme more good than my swift progress through the intricacies of the domus declension".
(P.H.V. 1948)

The headmaster for the first part of Philip's schooling at Dulwich College was Walter Booth. Walter Booth, an old boy of Bradford Grammar School was 37 years old when he was appointed in 1928. He had been headmaster of Wolverhampton Grammar School, a scholar of Corpus Christi College, Cambridge, graduating in Natural Sciences and History, and was the first modern Master of Dulwich College who was not a Classicist. Booth was a likeable man, who showed genuine interest in his staff and their families. He was friendly and open and had a passion for riding. This is the characteristic of Booth most remembered by the pre-war boys. He would leave his residence (Bell House) to watch school games on horseback and sometimes trot around the pitches, quite frequently he would be seen around the College in his riding breeches. Booth, in spite of his background was particularly keen to develop Dulwich as a boarding school – of the 600 boys in the College before the Second World War, 112 were boarders. Booth wanted to increase the numbers by 48, thus making 160 boarders. He gave reasons why boys should be boarders: apart from it being the 'most liberal of schools' for the education it offered, it is recorded in the Dulwich College governors' minutes on 14 February1930 – 'The advantages of being actually in the centre of the Empire where all the art and learning of different civilisations of all parts of the world have their witness; where all classes of society come together with understanding and good will; where the conditions of daily life, despite all the advantages of a great city, yet resemble that of the country and where the advantages of both the day boy and the boarding systems are brought together'.One advantage for the boys of witnessing different civilisations in London was going to the cinema and 'a study of public school slang in 1940 reported that Dulwich boys, unlike boys at country boarding schools, relished using many Americanisms learned from the movies' (The Times, 6 April 1940).

As the thirties progressed and Dulwich Estate income improved, the Governors turned more to developing the boarding side than offering free places. In 1927, there were 170 such boys, but the following year the Governors asked the Board of Education to reduce the number of 'free places'. This was taken to Parliament by the M.P. for North Camberwell, Mr. G.C. Ammon who protested that this would 'debar large numbers of boys from L.C.C. (London County Council) elementary schools from places at the College and that it had robbed the poor of this Foundation, just as had happened to the poor in the case of many other Educational institutions in this country'. (Hansard 14 March 1928). At the time the L.C.C. would pay full fees at Dulwich for one of their boys from a family with only the one child and an income of £450, and full fees for boys from a family of eight children with £800 income per annum. It was argued in Parliament that it was a waste of national resources to deprive the country of the very best brains it could get by not sending more South London boys to Dulwich. Lord Eustace Percy who was the President of the Board of Education, however, insisted that 'you have to maintain the character of the school.' 'The governors of Dulwich declared that they would like to cut the entry to fifteen scholars a year' (Daily Mirror 5 June 1928).

However, by 1934, the College's intake was modified as follows – 157 boys from preparatory schools from the age of eleven to fourteen years, 18 from elementary schools and 27 from other public schools and secondary schools from fourteen to sixteen years. At this time Dulwich had about twenty five per cent of its yearly quota of new boys from the L.C.C. (Philip being one of these entrants in 1937). The Council paid their fees (after a means test) to the school Governors. L.C.C. scholars were therefore in the minority, 'but were no different from the rest of the boys – except that sometimes unacceptable colloquialisms were promptly, firmly and kindly corrected'. (Alan Gregory 1937 – 1944)

Philip was one of the 25%
of the entrants in 1937
who arrived at Dulwich
College as a L.C.C.
Scholarship boy.

Some of the most difficult times in the College's history began in 1938 (a year after Philip started at Dulwich). In October, as the international situation deteriorated and following widespread fears of air raids over London with the government drawing up plans for the evacuation of children from London, Booth pre-empted this by evacuating 400 boys and 40 masters to Cinderford in the Forest of Dean. This was an elaborate evacuation. Parents were given three choices, their boys could stay at the College with a very much reduced staff; they could be evacuated privately; or the boys could go to Cinderford, bringing light hand luggage and £3. Seventy two boys set off on bicycles; ten of whom successfully reached Cinderford and eventually back again by bicycle (a round trip of 250 miles), six coaches and cars with mattresses on the roof set off down crammed roads. 250 stayed at a disused fever hospital, which was completely surrounded by corrugated steel fencing. Philip later wrote 'I was never a boarder at Dulwich. But my first experience of living with other boys was Cinderford – I disliked it intensely and it has coloured my attitude to boarding schools, ever since'. This evacuation was said to be a success, although it rained all the time, the hospital had inadequate heating and lessons were few and far between. There was a shortage of basic rations such as bread, tea and jam. The boys returned to London after less than one week, during the false sense of security after Mr. Chamberlain's speech 'Peace in our time'. Staffing replacement became difficult as young Masters joined up and the College suffered acute financial distress. By September 1939, the wartime reduction of the Estates subsidy by £1,000 per annum; the £2,000 cost of the air raid shelter at Tonbridge; and the loss of fees from withdrawing boys put the College £12,000 in the red. Parents preferred a country boarding school during wartime. Mr.Booth, the Master imagined the College buildings as actually under siege and he put to the Governors – only to be declined – 'that boys should dig trenches all round the school grounds against attack.'

In May 1939 arrangements were made for a full evacuation of the College to Tonbridge School. Meanwhile the Barrage Balloon unit, 903 Squadron R.A.F. Balloon Barrage, booked the College fields and premises for June to October whilst the College was in Tonbridge. They took over Barry buildings as their headquarters, and the boarding houses for billets. Costs became too prohibitive for the Squadron who found the College's charges of £100 per week rather expensive, and by November they left, having occupied the College for fifteen weeks. On 1 September 1939, one day after the general evacuation from London of woman and children had begun, around 600 boys were sent to Tonbridge. For the first few nights, the boys had to spend the nights on the Tonbridge School gymnasium floor; but after a few days the College arranged to use large empty houses and the towns people who were willing to give shelter to the boys. Many boys' billets were scattered all over the town. However, the Tonbridge land ladies complained about the low rate of the government allowance, which was six shillings and sixpence for small boys and ten shillings and six pence for those over 16. Philip shared with four other Dulwich boys and one Dulwich Master, the home of the Tonbridge maths master, Mr. (Johnny) and Mrs. Watts, which was only a few minutes' walk from Tonbridge station. Alan Gregory (1937–44), one of the other Dulwich boys who lived with the Watts says that 'he remembers playing chess with Philip much of their time in Tonbridge. However, after a short time Philip left the Watt's house for other accommodation in Tonbridge. I do recall the great kindness shown by Philip's parents in giving my mother a lift in their car from London to Tonbridge'.

Tonbridge and Dulwich took turns in the classrooms, the laboratories, and the fives courts and the armoury. Sir James Cobban's memoir of the evacuations, 'Dulwich goes to War' recalls 'the schoolboy day endured by Dulwich: in the morning the boys played rugger and did their prep; lessons were held in the afternoons, from lunch until 15.40, and again in the evenings. They were split into groups of twenty to thirty boys under 'House Tutors'. The parents objected to their boys being taught at night time and having to 'blunder and grope' their way to evening school through a blacked out Tonbridge from their lodgings.' The evacuation lasted only one term before boys returned to Dulwich. In December 1939, Mr. Booth decided to return from Tonbridge. This return was a relief to all the boys and staff involved. On their return the boys found that during their time in Tonbridge air raid shelters had been built, class rooms had been provided for the junior school, the buttery had been rebuilt and a central heating system installed. This was the term in which Philip entered the senior school, and in his case the classical lower fourth of 1939. By February 1940 seven Masters had left for war service. This is evident in Philip's school report for the Lent term of 1940 'Owing to the recent departure of Mr. Warren on war service reports on English, Divinity, Latin and Greek cannot be given'.

Philip wrote 'The war affected school life only externally. Rules of clothing, of discipline, of punctuality were in no way relaxed. Even being bombed out was not a sufficient excuse for not having a clean white stiff collar the next day.' The playing fields did not witness the usual normal tranquil scenes of the College games, but boys now played cricket below the barrage balloons. In late May and early June Dulwich boys were playing cricket and Philip recalled in 1948 'on that terrible afternoon which I remember so clearly, the trains from Dover (the main line crosses the school grounds) were slowly following one another in, packed inside and out with men in all stages of exhaustion and fatigue, wounded and all but dead, supporting one another at the windows, fixed in an immovable jam – nearly half a million of them – and as they went by us we continued our cricket game and the veterans of Dunkirk cheered us instead of us cheering them!'

These troops trapped in Northern France were rescued from complete defeat by an improvised evacuation – operation Dynamo. 338,000 men had been evacuated, and more than two thirds were British.

In September 1940, after the fall of France in the summer the blitz began on London. Boys arrived at school carrying briefcases and gas masks. Philip writes 'My house in Brixton was damaged and made uninhabitable in September 1940 in a day light raid; I missed one day's school, and turned up the following day hoping to be the centre of attention and sympathy (at the age of fourteen one isn't concerned with broader issues). But our glorious *'Semper Eadem'* demanded otherwise and moreover this was the year of School Certificate; my form master was only concerned that I should get a new set of Latin and Greek books immediately, and make up on my own one missed homework.' Other boys had similar experiences and day boys would frequently be late for school as they had to clear debris from bombing, before they could do their homework. Dulwich had a 'home guard' – two Masters and six boys to look after the defence of the grounds and the buildings and to be on duty as Air Raid Wardens all night. A fire brigade of twenty five was on call day and night, and a team of four Masters and eight boys put out at least nineteen incendiary bombs. Dulwich was the only Public School to remain in London. During the Autumn Term of 1940 London was attacked for ninety one consecutive days and nights, and the number on the roll dropped from 675 to 450 boys in two weeks.

Philip writes 'So we went on, up, down, up, down, all day and every day to the shelters at school, construing Virgil in converted cellars as the guns boomed overhead. It was grand fun – masters with tin helmets and gowns are one of the funniest things you can see!' 'The demoralising effect of the war on Booth and the Masters attempting to carry on with normal life and education can be imagined; the drone of bombers at night, fire bombs, shrapnel on all the rugby pitches, a bomb crater on the First XV pitch, the loss of the ten Fives courts and shattered windows at the College. The great entrance gates to the College were bombed on the night of 28 August 1940, destroying forever the terracotta heraldic beasts and the iron lanterns that crowned them.' (Jan Piggott. Dulwich College, A History 1616 to 2008, by kind permission of the Governors of Dulwich College). Iron railings from the College boundaries had by now been melted down for the 'war effort'. Charles Barry's magnificent iron gates had been removed prior to the bombing and were hidden and therefore saved. A bomb fell in the night of 15 September 1940 shattering windows and collapsing ceilings. Alan Gregory (Dulwich College 1937 – 44) writes, 'From then on the war, was I suppose, a fairly dominant background to life at Dulwich. In daylight raids we left our normal rooms in favour of the strengthened basements; I remember our being a bit slow to get going on one occasion and our form master, who I think had had a bomb near his house previously, suggesting that we remember this was a blitz, not an invitation to go and play cricket or words to that effect. After night raids, some might be late for school. I remember cycling around bomb craters one morning in Lordship Lane. Saddest of all I remember two brothers whose parents were killed in their house on Sydenham Hill'.

From 8 August to 31 October 1940, while boys, including Philip, were sitting at their desks in classrooms at the College, thirteen Old Alleynians who had not long left the College helped fight The Battle of Britain, and like so many pilots displayed skill and courage flying the Spitfires over British and European battlefields; all risking their lives and eight of the thirteen losing their lives trying to save London from the devastating bombing that had flattened Warsaw and Rotterdam. As the bombardment continued the London skies were covered with many vapour trails left by the Spitfires which were viewed over Dulwich. Several of the staff slept in the basement of the north block and some of the boys' lessons took place underground.

'In Goering's first phase of air attacks encounters were at their most intense over and on the borders of the College: above Croydon, Kenley and Biggin Hill; in September, at the climax of the attack, the full force of the Luftwaffe would be launched against London.' (H. Saunders – The Battle of Britain, August – October 1940.) 'At the height of the Blitz in 1940, there were five or six raids on London a day, and boys at the College carried gas masks and identity cards; a bomb fell on the First XI outfield. When two boys who had thrown themselves to the ground in the 'clump' as a bomb fell then ran to the edge of the crater to look for souvenir metal, according to legend, were caned by Trevor Bailey for breaking the College rules by walking on the sacred pitch!' (Jan Piggott. Dulwich College 1616 to 2008. By kind permission of the Governors of Dulwich College).

In December 1940, after three months of bombardment, there was more discussion of evacuation. This did not happen, since the one possible place considered for evacuation was the Royal College of Agriculture at Cirencester was taken by a government department before Dulwich could make a decision. It was thought that Dulwich might be taken over also by the government. In spite of the evacuation to Tonbridge and shortened school hours on return to Dulwich, exam results were good and there were six Awards at Oxford and Cambridge. The boys responded well to all the difficulties.

Early in 1941, the College faced more financial difficulties and despite an increase in pupil numbers from 615 to 640 there was a deficit of £4,000 and loans of £16,000 to repay. Measures to reduce costs included the cutting off of the heating for the swimming pool, reducing music and games and suspending rugby matches. However, the cricket season was a great success, despite the Blitz, and it saw the rise of the young Trevor Bailey (born 1923) who was in the College XI for five years. He also was at Cambridge with Philip. By March 1941 there were fewer air raids.

Mr. Booth, Master of the College, was beginning to show signs of the enormous toll that these war years had taken on him. He was unable to deal adequately with the situation and gave indications that he was losing his control and grip. He himself had had a bad experience during the First World War as a prisoner of war. Booth had arrived at Dulwich with a very good reputation and had demonstrated personality and drive in his Headship at Wolverhampton Grammar School. However, Dulwich was too big for him with major outside factors such as the great depression and Second World War affecting his ability as Master. He began to drink heavily, boys recall that his breath smelt strongly of whisky in the mornings. The governors heard grievances about his condition from individual Masters, and senior staff delivered a 'private and confidential' document, but Booth suddenly resigned on 25 April 1941. An interregnum appointment of Revd. H.H. Dixon was made for the Summer Term and the first part of the Autumn Term. In time of war, Christopher, third son of Arthur Herman Gilkes (Master Dulwich – 1885 – 1914) was about to return to occupy the Master's study and transform the College. Christopher Gilkes 'was a man of courage, iron will, vision, and shrewdness, qualities which were to be of crucial importance in the difficult years to come'. (Sheila Hodges – 'God's Gift. A Living History of Dulwich College). He was himself an Old Alleynian and had become Captain of the School and of boxing. He was an Oxford classicist and had taught at Uppingham before becoming headmaster of Stockport Grammar School. Thus for his last two and a half years at Dulwich, Philip was studying under a new influential Master.

In 1942, after a few months of fewer air raids, when the College life continued more normally, although sporadic raids still made life difficult, the fury of aerial bombardment began again. The Dulwich area became a target area during the latter war years because of the V1 rocket bombs. The College lay on a main flight path of the enemy bombers, and was part of the suburban area where bombs intended for Westminster and the City were ditched on return flights. The German press reported a belief that the College had been evacuated and was being used by the government and that the College was still being used to educate boys was untrue. An Old Alleynian had picked up a German trench newspaper containing this article – 'It is a well known trick that when the English wish to deceive the world about the bombing of school buildings, they try to give the impression that it is still a school. We do not know what staff or department has taken over these buildings, but we have an idea that it is a high department because, amongst other things, the school buildings are near to a golf course on which high British and American Officers must have played with zeal.'

In December 1943 the College opened its doors to the wider stricken community and the ground floor of North Block was used for sheltering local people during air raids. Conditions in the College kitchen deteriorated, with the outbreak of dysentery in March 1943. Despite all these problems and the devastation of war all around and in the College, Dulwich managed to continue the boys' education as far as the interruptions allowed, and such special events such as Founder's Day and Christmas Concerts were held. Founders Day was celebrated in June 1942 and 1943 with Music and Speeches.

DULWICH COLLEGE

FOUNDER'S DAY

Music and Speeches

FRIDAY, JUNE 18TH, 1943

THE FIRST VERSE OF THE SCHOOL SONG.

OVERTURE .. .. "Titus" .. .. *Mozart*

THE ORCHESTRA.

ENGLISH
(a) "1914" .. .. *Rupert Brooke*

B. BARTON-CHAPPLE.

(b) "For the Fallen" .. .. *Lawrence Binyon*

J. W. WATSON.

LATIN .. .. .. from Vergil, Aeneid II
The dead Hector appears in a dream to Aeneas on the night of Troy's fall, and commissions him to found a new Troy overseas.

A. H. MACDONALD

GREEK .. .. .. from Sophocles, Antigone
Antigone, condemned to death, spurns the offer of her sister to share her fate, since she had not shared the heroic deed.

N. J. FRITH, G. L. HOLLIS

A near miss raid on 4 February 1944 left most of the school's windows shattered. Also in 1944, the boys became familiar with the sound of the 'doodle-bug', the VI rocket bomb and its silently sinister 'cutting out' just before striking. They would take shelter under their desks in lessons or under the tables at lunch in the Great Hall. In games lessons or in physical training exercises outdoors boys and Masters lay prone on the ground in cricket flannels or shirt sleeves. The strain on the boys, staff and Master was unrelenting, the boys on roll dipping to 450. Then on the night of 10 July 1944 another disaster struck. 'Ten minutes after the eighty boarders had crossed the grounds to sleep in the shelters in the main building, a flying VI bomb fell on the gravel between the Science Building, the Armoury, Squash and Fives Courts, roughly at the back of the present Edward Alleyn Theatre, destroying half of the old Science Building, the Armoury, several Fives and all four Squash courts, collapsing the roof of the Gym and the Baths, and badly damaging the Engineering Block, the new boiler house, and the roofs of the new Ivyholme and Blew boarding houses; in the Barry buildings every room was damaged in some way, and hardly a single pane of glass was left intact. Miraculously, no one was hurt.' (Jan Piggott. A History of Dulwich College 1616 to 2008. By kind permission of the Governors of Dulwich College.) When Gilkes arrived at the College the next morning he said 'There is not a single room in which we can safely sit''. The College suffered further damage two weeks later when the Chapel and the Picture Gallery were bombed and made unusable. Temporary wooden huts and Science laboratories at James Allen's Girls' School were used as temporary accommodation. Daily life at the College is hard to comprehend, but boys like Philip Vennis and Alan Gregory studied, took examinations and gained entries to Universities. Christopher Gilkes said in 1945: 'The previous two years had been the most dangerous and anxious time in the College's entire history: another direct hit and the school would have 'gone under'. But he went on 'It was our duty, if we claimed to be a great school, to give a lead to London in resisting the attempts of the enemy to paralyse the normal life of the City, and I am proud to be able to say that we were the only school in London which continued its work above ground, in spite of the dangers and difficulties which beset us. At that time the coolness and courage of the Masters and the boys was beyond all praise. I remember many things happened at that time, and some of them stand out in my mind. I remember the prefects coming to me to protest that it was undignified and unmanly to retire into the passage when a flying bomb was going to fall close to us.'

'Gilkes own bravery and moral leadership during this period were unfailing and unshakeable.' (Sheila Hodges – 'God's Gift' A Living History of Dulwich College).

Victory, when it came, was not celebrated with much enthusiasm at the battered and tired College. Shortly after VE Day blast walls in front of the main building were demolished. It was a long time before the damage caused by the war was totally eradicated, but a visit by the King and Queen helped to lift the spirits. The total number of Alleynians who served in the war was 3,320, 330 of these died or were lost at sea and 115 were interned in prison camps.

One member of staff who made an impression on Philip Vennis in the sixth form was Philip H Vellacott (1907 – 1997), who taught him classics. Not only did they possess the same initials – P.H.V., both were classicists and both were interested and active in drama and dramatic productions. On Philip Vennis's report of Summer 1943 – Philip Vellacott wrote 'Classics – His best work is shown in a developing facility for translation. He is a thorough and careful student, but his compositions usually lack inspiration'. (Colour photograph 4.). Of his prose work at the end of Philip Vennis's time at Dulwich, Philip Vellacott wrote 'steady, careful work, occasionally rather good'. Two years after Philip left Dulwich, one of the pupils who had had Philip Vellacott as his form- master in 1945 was Garth Davidson and he recalls 'I clearly remember Philip Vellacott coming into room 45 in the North Block and saying "My name is Vellacott – two 'LL's' and two 'TT's". I came to realise that accuracy in all things was what he always required of us. He was also my Form Master in the Classical Upper Fifth, and taught us in the Sixth Form'. Garth Davidson later became a Classics teacher at Dulwich and recollects another incident which is now in the Dulwich archives. 'The incident of the Greek Prose happened in the sixties. Philip Vellacott had set the Sixth form a passage of English to translate into Greek prose, and one of the boys recognised it as being a direct translation of a passage of one of the Greek orators – Lysias, I think. The boy simply copied out the original Greek, and handed it in as his own work. It came back with a few corrections and suggested improvements in red ink, with a comment something like 'Very commendable!' and given a mark of 8 out of 10! The prose is in the Classical Sixth Memorabilia.' Garth Davidson admired Philip Vellacott greatly and whenever he was using one of his books in his lessons at Dulwich he always took the opportunity to tell the boys about him and his remarkable attributes. 'Philip Vellacott was an enormously influential Master, of exceptional culture and intellect, Vellacott was Head of Classics at Dulwich in 1960 until his retirement in 1967. He possessed a lofty character and was a man who was able to think and speak naturally in Greek; he had earlier in his career worked in East End missions. His reputation as a Classical Scholar and translator of many penguin classics and Greek tragedies was international and he worked hard whilst at the College, giving talks to Societies on such topics as 'Justice and the Gods' and reviving the College's reputation for drama, of which he was placed in charge. This involved the annual school play, which at first he produced himself, and there followed twenty four high standard productions of Shakespeare. His own translation of Euripides 'Ion' was regarded as a significant return to pre-war standards. He founded and directed the Attic Players who put on productions of his translation of Euripides and other classical plays.' (Jan Piggott. Dulwich College. A History 1616 to 2008. By kind permission of the Governors of Dulwich College.) The members of The Attic Players came from outside the College and some were from East Ham Drama Guild. Philip Vennis acted and directed some of these productions whilst he was teaching at East Ham Grammar School and once a year the Attic Players performed there. These productions included Aeschylus 'The Choephori', Aristophanes 'The Clouds,' Sophocles 'Trachiniae' and Euripides 'Helen.'

Two other important Masters at Dulwich as far as Philip was concerned were his form master for the year 1939 to 40 – Frank Bamford (1904 – 1954), Vellacott's predecessor as Head of Classics. Mr.Bamford used to thunder at his class "Don't sit here like so many buckets waiting to be filled". W.S.Wright (1900 – 1998), a great scholar and who was appointed as a classicist in 1924 also Philip's form master, wrote in his summary on his Michaelmas Term 1941 report 'very good – thoughtful work and good interest'. By the end of Philip's time at Dulwich, on his final school report for the Lent term 1944 Wright added ' has worked hard and enjoyed the term. Best wishes for Cambridge and the Navy'. The academic performance of this sixth form was high and the College won seven awards at Oxford and Cambridge in 1944. Many of these were awarded the coveted State Scholarships, that covered both full fees and maintenance at Universities.

When Philip entered Dulwich in 1937, he entered the Junior School to read a largely uniform curriculum, at thirteen entering the Senior School he had to choose either the Classical, History/Modern Languages, Maths or Science side. Alan Gregory (1937- 44), a contemporary of Philip's throughout their time at Dulwich, says, 'When I showed up on my first day in good time in the quad, an enthusiastic fellow nearby said that we all had to assemble in the Lower hall to be told which form we were to join. I had read too many 'Magnet' stories of Billy Bunter and japes at Greyfriars to be willing to believe anything others told me, and took no notice of it. A few moments later, a master appeared to tell new boys to assemble in the Lower hall! I started in the second form and after a year moved into the middle third. In these years I met boys whose friendship has lasted throughout our lives, an inestimable good fortune. I did well enough in these two years for it to be assumed that I would go into the Classical side of the Senior School. I think there was still, in the thirties some degree of presumption that unless a boy had some special reason for wishing to learn Modern Languages (perhaps for a diplomatic future) or science, Classics was the place for the brighter ones. So into the Classical lower fourth (assembled at Tonbridge in September 1939) I duly went'.

Another contemporary of Philip at Dulwich was Peter Edgley and he recalls memories of over seventy years ago the following: 'Philip Vennis and I first encountered each other in September 1939. That was when the newly-minted Classical lower fourth (of which we were members) started learning Greek.

Thereafter we continued to progress up the school together, on the Classical side (though after the evacuation to Tonbridge and the events of 1940 and 41, reduced our numbers). The senior school was divided into Classical, Modern and Science streams. Reflecting educational prejudices dating back to medieval times, we and others tacitly accepted the presumption that the brainiest chaps were to be found where you got a grounding in Latin and Greek. Philip must have left a bit earlier than some of us, as I don't remember him in my last terms at the College. He and I were not especially close. He was in the Scouts, my energies were more concentrated on playing games; he was a keen member of the Sea Cadets, I was an un-keen member of the Junior Training Corps (the Army unit, noticeably less motivated than both the Air Training Corps and the Sea Cadets).

Apart from the pugnacity and cockiness we associate with all bantam-weights (especially the red-haired ones!), the thing I remember most clearly about Philip was his great interest in politics. At that time Britain was concentrating on winning a war, and normal political activity and debate was all but suspended while we were growing up between 1940 and 1945. The great majority of us knew nothing about politics and cared less, until we were suddenly confronted with new ideas as the nation re-opened the conflict of Left and Right at the end of the war. Philip was the exception, and I feel that this knowledge to some extent marked him off from the rest of us.

That assumes of course that his ultra Left wing political stance was genuine. At this distance in time, I find it difficult to recall how much his aggressively Left wing views were genuinely held, and how much they owed to teenage posturing and a desire to *'epater les bourgeois.'* (We were certainly a pretty bourgeois lot, though the climate of opinion after 1941 was a bit more sympathetic to 'our brave Soviet allies' than normal). I think I remember him getting frustrated when we refused to take him seriously – or was he merely irritated that we refused to rise to the bait of his teasing? Better to ask his fellow Scouts, who knew him far better than I did.

Dulwich at that time was a very mixed school – that was one of the best things about it. Then as now, it stands exactly on the boundary between affluent suburbs and some less fortunate parts of inner London. A good scholarship scheme, involving the Inner London Education Authority and other local authorities, provided a leaven to improve the basically middle-class mix, and everyone benefited. I always felt this gave us an opportunity to practice getting on with people from a variety of backgrounds – 'from Dukes to dustmen' is the cliché – not available, I think in the bigger name public schools.

One of my friends, then and later, was a scholarship boy and the son of a sea-cook; he went on to become a director of BP, one of the biggest companies in the world. That brings me on to my other main point, that we were a pretty bright form, even by Dulwich standards; fourteen – more than half of the small boys who formed that 1939 Classical lower fourth – later won open awards to Oxbridge. Philip was one of them.

It is also interesting that two of our number – Rupert Sutton and Philip himself – were part of the super-intellectual workforce based on Bletchley, the hush-hush code-breaking unit whose successes shortened World War II Rupert was quickly taught written Japanese, and worked in Delhi briefly until the two atom bombs ended the war. (I had a mysterious interview in 1943, which I later realized was for Bletchley, but I very rightly got no further). My closest friend in the form, and later my best man (Norman Frith), was taught spoken Japanese at the School of Oriental and African Studies, but he never got the opportunity to exercise his skills, thanks to the tiresome propensity of the Japanese military to die rather than surrender.

Perhaps because of the evacuation in 1939, and wartime experiences we shared subsequently, a collective esprit de corps took root and survived.'

Scouting had been established by the Mathematics Master Mr .H.V. Styler in 1929, and by the time that Philip joined them almost ten years later the scouting philosophy was well embedded at Dulwich. Scouting was an important part of Philip's life at Dulwich and later at East Ham Grammar School. By 1940 the Dulwich Scout Troop in the form of a 'Joint Troop' consisted of fifty five boys. Philip was one of these Scouts in the Swift Patrol, but like most activities during the uncertain and difficult times of the war, scouting activities were affected. The Scouts continued to grow at Dulwich and by 1943 there were six patrols. The Troop helped the war effort by growing vegetables on their recently acquired allotment within the grounds of the College. Camps still took place, but tents had to be camouflaged or pitched under trees in the eastern half of the country. Camps were not allowed near any military establishments and the rationing of food also presented difficulties at camp. Philip became patrol leader in 1943, thus giving him his first experience of leadership. During the wartime, scouting at Dulwich was often good fun and the scouts benefitted from learning a variety of skills such as orienteering, canoeing, rock climbing, forestry and the art of camping. Awhile after the end of the war in 1949, when he had joined the staff at East Ham Grammar School, Philip maintained his links with Dulwich by becoming the Assistant Scout Master of the 25th Camberwell (!st Dulwich College) Group. He kept up the links with Dulwich by arranging joint camps with his newly formed Scout Group at East Ham, more of which is written in chapter five.

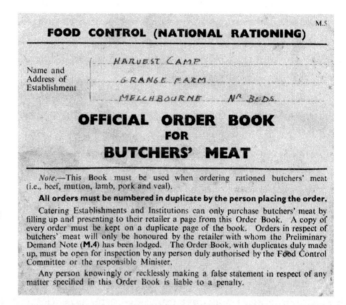

A ration book from a wartime Scout camp in 1943.

Scouts learning different skills during a camp in the 1940s.

The attraction of scouting for boys is difficult to define, but like many things which defy definition it can be described. Many scouts gave little thought to what it was in which they were participating. The principal attributes of scouting are service, training and the outdoor life. Philip took part in several College camps, including one in Broadstone Warren, in the Ashdown Forest in April 1940. For five days the scouts and officers slept in tents hidden in the undergrowth because of the wartime restrictions. Philip's contemporary Alan Gregory recalls their scouting friendship: 'We were both in Troop 1. Philip was not of a build to enjoy sports of any kind, but he was very much a doer and had great character. He had that very necessary thing, a keen sense of humour. I remember his competence at Easter and Summer camps, not least when the latter grew to four weeks, farming at harvest time.'

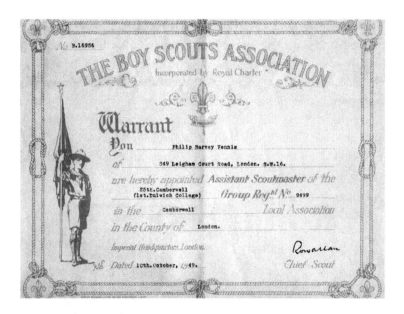

Scouts helping to bring in the harvest in 1941 and 1942.

Philip took School Certificate in July 1941 and gained 'Credits' in English Language, English Literature, Greek, French and Mathematics and 'Very Good' in Latin. The next two years saw him studying for Higher School Certificates, and in 1943 Philip satisfied the examiners in three subjects – Classics, French and English Literature. That summer Philip sat for a Scholarship at Cambridge and gained an Exhibition in Classics to Peterhouse. A letter from London County Council, Education Officers' Department to Philip states that 'he has successfully gained a Senior County Exhibition which is tenable for the necessary period of the course (not exceeding three years) as from 1 August 1944 at a school of a university to enable you to read for a degree in Classics. Senior County Exhibitions are usually held at day colleges but they may be held at residential colleges if the Council is satisfied that the students' resources are sufficient to meet the cost of residence and incidental expenses. The Council considers that a man student at most colleges at Oxford or Cambridge should have at his disposal for the expenses of his course a total amount of £225 per year, and that a woman student at a residential college should possess an aggregate income equivalent to the amount represented by the combined total of £50 and the college fees for board, residence and tuition. The value of a Senior County Exhibition for a resident student will not exceed £40 a year for an arts course or £55 a year for a natural science course.' Philip did not begin at Peterhouse until October 1946.

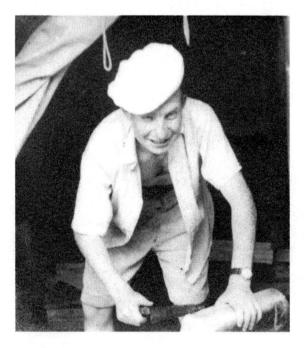

Philip as Quartermaster in the late 1940s.

CHAPTER 2

Bletchley Park 'A small part in a big secret' 1944 to 1946

"Bound by the Official Secrets Act as I am, I can say little of my time at Bletchley Park. There as a young Royal Navy sub-lieutenant, I learnt Japanese; I can only remember the following phrase in Japanese 'enemy submarine sunk'. All of us who worked at Bletchley were forbidden to talk or write about it." (P.H.V. 1970)

Sub-Lieutenant, Philip Vennis, R.N.V.R. (Special Branch, Special Service) in 1945

As he left Dulwich in March 1944, Philip received the following letter from the RNVR Secretary at Naval Gate, Cockspur Street, London SW1. (Philip had already been notified on 9 September 1943 the he had been awarded a Senior County Exhibition to read Classics at Cambridge) "With reference to your application for a university short course, the Admiralty have allocated you Cambridge University to read Classics. This course commences on 11 April 1944". This short course, however, was the sixth Japanese course to be run by Captain Oswald Tuck.

The first courses arranged by Tiltman, who was head of Bletchley Park's military section, began in Bedford on 2 February 1942, and, by the end of the war, eleven of them had taken place under the tutorship of Oswald Tuck. Tiltman, who had consulted the School of Oriental and African Studies, was informed that it took five years to learn Japanese properly and two years to achieve the absolute minimum for any kind of good standard; this, of course, was too long for Tiltman, and so he decided to go ahead with his 'experimental' course of only six months. He chose young men who had potential as code breakers and could learn unusual languages. Advice to Tiltman was that he should recruit classical scholars, aged between eighteen and twenty from Oxford and Cambridge Universities. Therefore, most of these recruits for these courses were Classical scholars, whose names had been put forward by the Classics Tutor at Oxford or Cambridge.

At Bletchley Park in 1944. Philip, back row, first left.

Today the debate still goes on about the influences of learning Latin and in The Times newspaper of November 2011, a letter to the Editor from Ralph Erskine (Co-editor, The Bletchley Park Code breakers) wrote 'The Bletchley Park code breakers could easily have answered the question "What is the point of Latin?" (Times2. 7 November 2011). When they urgently needed a large number of Japanese translators in 1942, The School of Oriental and African Studies told them that no one could learn Japanese in under two years.'

Fortunately, Brigadier John Tiltman disagreed and organised intensive six-month courses in Japanese for Oxford and Cambridge undergraduates reading Latin and Greek. The resulting translators, including John Chadwick (who later collaborated with Michael Ventris on deciphering Linear B, which is an early form of Greek with a syllabic script of about two hundred syllabic signs) were outstandingly successful.

They even handled the most difficult technical topics, such as the construction details of the advanced Type XXIU-boats. These first Japanese courses began after Pearl Harbour and the declaration of war against Japan. There were a few specialists in Bletchley Park working with the 'purple' machine on the Japanese diplomatic codes. There were at this time, only about eleven Japanese linguists completing the language course annually at London University's School of Oriental and African Studies. Although the School of Oriental and African Studies thought that no one could learn useful Japanese in a few months, Tiltman had taught himself in a few months, and young men like Philip Vennis were being taught by Oswald Tuck an elderly Naval Captain. Tuck had been in Naval Intelligence in the First World War and was brought out of retirement to teach enough Japanese to break codes as he was a fluent Japanese speaker. He was an enthusiastic and able teacher, using innovative teaching methods. Every day the students moved back one row, and those on the back row moved to the front. Lessons were intensive – 09.30 to 17.00 on weekdays plus Saturday morning. At first, Tuck had few teaching aids – a grammar book, a book of printed Japanese characters and three Japanese/English dictionaries. There are great difficulties in learning the language, especially with the different writing system. In the seventh and eighth centuries A.D. the Japanese took on the Chinese writing system, but used completely different grammar and construction. Japanese is a most difficult language to learn as its form is so different from most European languages. The most success in learning Japanese was by those recruits that had a good photographic memory.

Michael Loewe, one of the first recruits, in his contribution in the book Codebreakers (By permission of Oxford University Press) says:

'Captain Oswald Tuck had in all probability no more idea than his students of the nature of the work for which they were to be trained or the type of problem that they would be facing. Intended to last six months the course was expected to do no more than leave its students with sufficient command of the language to break ciphers, build up code books, and translate or summarise Japanese signals traffic into service English. It was not expected that after a mere six months the students would be able to read Japanese literature. It remained to be seen how far, at the end of six months, the brightest members of the class would be able to read the Japanese press or handle the correspondence of Japanese diplomats.' Students learned about one thousand two hundred characters during the course, with the vocabulary which they would need for wartime translations. Philip and his co–students used the flash card method – characters with their meaning and pronunciation were written on pieces of card and memorised. Philip's complete set of the one thousand two hundred character cards is still preserved.(Colour photograph 8.) All of the vocabulary learnt was that which would be needed for translating formal military, naval and air force signal and captured documents. The Japanese for 'you', 'me', 'us' and other personal pronouns were never taught, since they were not going to appear in any military or naval document. It is interesting to note from the evidence of Philip's exercise books the order in which he learnt the sequence of words.(Colour photograph 7.) These books are still intact and give a clear picture of the importance of the order of the words that Oswald Tuck taught these young scholars. For example on the first page – KAN – ship, SEN – battle and the compound SENKAN – battleship, KUTIKUKAN – destroyer, KOOGEKI – attack, page fifteen of the book, words such as MUSEN – wireless, DENSIN – telegram/cable, TUUHOO – to report, are evident and at the end of the book KIZAI – equipment, ZIDOOSYA – motor vehicles and KOOHYOO – public announcements. Tuck also taught them something about Japanese life and literature. After four months of the course, Tiltman sent off the students to work for a short time in the Japanese Diplomatic section, where they were to be tested by the long term Japanese interpreters.

Two further students were taken by Tuck to a School of Oriental and African Studies meeting, where the staff gave them a surprise language test. The students more than satisfied the demands of the S.O.A.S. and the Diplomatic section. One of Tiltman's early recruits recalls how Tiltman had explained that he had broken the cipher, but his knowledge of Japanese was not sufficient to take it further forward and it was up to the recruits to do so. Maurice Wiles, the recruit said 'We were pretty ill-equipped. Knowledge of the language was essential to the task assigned to us, but it was no straightforward matter of translation. As yet there were no texts on which to exercise our newly acquired translation skills. None of the thousand or so characters that we had painstakingly learned were there on the page before us. Something much more was needed, for which we had no specialist training – an approach to problem solving that our initial interviewers no doubt hoped had been ingrained in us by our interest in chess and crosswords.' At the end of his course in 1944, Philip went on a month's code breaking exercise, and, as was usual, Tiltman called on him to find out how he was getting on. He was then allocated his place of work at Bletchley Park. The Naval Section, under Hugh Foss, was forty strong and worked on Japanese merchant and naval codes. Hugh Foss was a British cryptographer, who had learnt Japanese as a boy whilst living in Japan (his father was a missionary Bishop there). At Bletchley Park he was head of the Japanese Naval Section. This section in 1942 was originally in Elmer's School, a short distance from Bletchley Park, but by the time Philip joined the Naval Section in 1944, it was in Hut 7 at

Bletchley Park. As the unit expanded it moved to Block B. Photographs of Philip's time in Hut 7 indicate that he was working alongside Angus Wilson and Bentley Bridgewater, as well as other Navy and WRNS personnel.

A group photograph of Section 5 in 1945 with Angus Johnstone-Wilson in the front row, second from right. Other names that are known are on the back row Myfanwy Cornwall-Jones (third left), Graham Summer (fourth right), Philip Vennis (second right), on the middle row John Statham (first left), and on the front row Isobel Sandison (fifth right – next to Angus Wilson).

One of Philip's co workers, Miss Cornwall –Jones recalls of her time in Hut 7:
'Here I was content and in fact happy in my work and working relationships. We collated traffic, noting the names of ships – all merchant vessels, as I recall – and the ports they called at, and the J.N. codes they used. I kept a card index of the ship's names and call signs.

Hours of work were 09.00 – 18.00 (days) and 16.00 – 24.00 (evenings). Occasionally overtime was worked from 18.00 till finished; we could go home on the 22.30 transport.'

Angus Wilson was recruited to Bletchley Park (Colour photograph 5.) by one of his old colleagues from the British Museum. At the beginning of the war he helped towards the safe storage of the British Museum treasures before serving the rest of the war in Naval Intelligence. Accounts vary as to the details of Angus Wilson's working life at Bletchley Park but some records indicate that he sat on a raised platform overlooking a posse of WRNS who were working on an enormous index of naval codes or that he worked in a small office and occasionally went to teach on an induction course in Bedford. Angus Wilson and Bentley Bridgewater are attributed with helping to win the war by some people since Angus Wilson was a 'complete memory bank; an expert on Japanese call signs and he 'had a computer' in his head. Wilson worked with the best brains in the country in a 'rarefied atmosphere'. The 'Boffins' as these young men were known were often eccentric; they were legendary about their absent-mindedness which compensated for their awesome brain power.

Another group photograph of Bletchley Park personnel. Left to right – Willie Ewing, Mary, Gwen, Jo, Philip Vennis and Howard. (some surnames not known.)

Also to help alleviate the shortage of Japanese linguists, in May 1942 the School of Oriental and African Studies (SOAS) began special courses for grammar school boys in their last year at school, who were studying Classics, German, Russian or French. Dulwich College accommodated this war office scheme, in conjunction with the SOAS in the teaching of oriental languages. They taught a select group of grammar and public school boys, who were to be qualified to serve as Intelligence Officers, behind enemy lines. These bright boys, aged seventeen and over, some seventy in total boarded at Dulwich College between 1942 and 1943. Philip was too young to join this group of boys and hence was seconded from the beginning of his Classics degree at Cambridge to learn Japanese in 1944.

Records of Bletchley Park, some of which still have not reached the Public Records Office, indicate that it is difficult to trace even one man's progress through this carefully constructed wartime secret establishment. Philip's own documentation of his Naval career is limited, there is evidence that he had draft orders to join H.M.S. *Ganges* on 28 October 1944 and then on 27 April 1945 – 'The Lord's Commissioners of the Admiralty herby appoint you 'Temporary Midshipman RNVR (Special Branch Special Service) on H.M.S. *Victory* and his last draft was on 1 August 1946 to H.M.S. *Saker,* which was a shore-based transit accommodation of the Royal Navy during the war, located just outside of New York. It was used by crews picking up ships allocated to the Royal Navy. H.M.S. *Saker* went on to become the collective title for Royal Navy personnel serving in the U.S.A. Prior to joining H.M.S. *Saker,* from 4 March 1946, Philip Vennis was 'required for duty in connection with the translation of Japanese documents, reporting to Captain O.T. Tuck at the Royal Naval College, Greenwich'. Oswald Tuck had continued teaching and translating Japanese at the Royal Naval College after the war.

Intelligence Division,
Naval Staff,
Admiralty, S.W.1.

27th February, 1946.

      You are required for duty in connection with the translation of Japanese documents as from Monday, 4th March. Arrangements have been made for this work to be undertaken at Greenwich.

2. You are accordingly to report to Instructor Captain O.T. Tuck at the Royal Naval College, Greenwich, at 1100 on the above date. Accommodation and messing will be provided at the College.

3. You are to acknowledge receipt of these instructions forthwith to the Director of Naval Intelligence (N.I.D.4), Admiralty, Whitehall, S.W.1.

Director of Naval Intelligence

Sub-Lieutenant P.H. Vennis, R.N.V.R.,
349 Leigham Court Road,
London, S.W.16.

Letter requesting Philip to translate Japanese documents at the Royal Naval College.

Bletchley Park and its grounds were taken over as the wartime headquarters of the Government Code and Cypher School in 1938. This organisation controlled all British cryptanalysis and transmitted the resulting intelligence under the 'Ultra' code name to British and American operational headquarters. The number of staff employed at Bletchley Park rose from under 200 in 1939 to nearly 7,000 in 1944. With so many workers, three working shifts were in operation, which impacted on the life of the local community. Many workers were billeted in Bletchley, the whole town had been commandeered, but some workers were accommodated with families and in hotels within a twenty mile radius of Bletchley.

Some of the billets were very near to Bletchley Park, there was a hostel five minutes away that housed about 300 civilians, and Elmer's School provided accommodation for thirty men, whilst nearly 250 women lived in Wilton Avenue, just outside the gates. Margaret Drabble in her biography of Angus Wilson writes 'Angus was billeted a couple of miles outside Bletchley, in the village of Simpson. Simpson lay beyond Fenny Stratford, over the level crossing and under the railway bridge, down by the hump-bridged canal. He was placed with a gardener's widow, Mrs. Emily Hill, who lived with her schoolmistress daughter Nellie in an old cottage in the middle of the village. He slept in the bed vacated by her son Arthur, unfortunately taken prisoner of war by the Japanese: Arthur a regular soldier, had been about to come home when war broke out and caught him in Singapore. Angus felt he was the cuckoo in the nest. (Cuckoos always interested Angus). When Bentley Bridgewater arrived at Bletchley Park he was first placed in a pub, but then managed to find a room in Simpson in a council house with the milkman and his wife.' These sorts of arrangements were typical of the billets that the Bletchley Park workers got used to. Newport Pagnell and Stony Stratford were two other towns used for billets, although they were ten miles from Bletchley Park; some of the accommodation was of a better quality than those nearer to Bletchley, although some were still basic. Other towns used for billets included Wolverton and New Bradwell, which for many of the workers provided a contrast to the life that they were used to in London. At times, the locals felt intimidated by the influx of 'worldly' strangers. However, many families, locals and workers built up fruitful and happy relationships. Milton Keynes village, which was later in 1967 to become a new town – an amalgamation of some thirteen villages, was also used for billets. Again varied accommodation was experienced by the workers; some had no gas or electricity, used oil lamps and cooked on oil heaters, kept warm by paraffin heaters or with a coal fire if there was enough coal, whilst others were lucky enough to be kept warm and to be fed well. The grandest billet of all was Woburn Abbey, ten miles from Bletchley Park, but the young women billeted there lacked hot water, the drainage at times contaminated the drinking water supply and food was terrible!

Whilst some living conditions were poor most of the workers also endured a poor working environment at Bletchley Park. Most of Philip's time at Bletchley Park was spent in Hut 7, which was constructed of Canadian pine with an outside covering of ship lap boarding. Hut 7 does not remain today but its position can be seen on the old plans of Bletchley Park. Huts 1, 3, 4, 6 and 8 still remain. The huts were quickly built on low brick 'sleeper' walls. Local carpenters helped finish the constructions. Some of the remaining huts are looking shabby today. (Colour photograph 6.)

Huts 1, 6 and 3 were protected in the war years by a bomb–blast wall that was built about twenty-four inches from the outside wall of the building. This bomb–blast wall was about nine inches thick. There was not much comfort within the buildings, flexibility was essential and internal partitions were put up and taken down as and when needed. Rooms frequently changed shape. There is no clear record of how many buildings were constructed between 1939 and 1945. Many had functions changed on a regular basis. It was in February 1943 that the Naval Section moved into Hut 7. New staff, including Philip Vennis arrived in late 1944/early 1945, but Hut 7 was cramped and there were limited tools (e.g. indexes).

A shift system was introduced because of the poor accommodation. Shift work was from 09.00 to 16.00, 16.00 to 24.00 and 24.00 to 09.00. Each lasted a working week which was six days long. Many worked for twelve days and then took two days leave to go home. Some found the night shift 'tedious' as most of the traffic was intercepted during the day so there was not a lot for the night workers to do. Others, however, thought that the night shift presented an opportunity to work quietly with nothing to distract them or their concentration. The intelligence workers used the JN4 and JN25 code groups amongst others. JN4 according to Hugh Denham in the Codebreakers (by permission of Oxford University Press) was 'A big code book, used in tactical situations, unreciphered. That is to say, the user looks up in the book the word or phrase which he wishes to encode and finds the assigned arbitrary code group, and so on throughout the message. These code groups without further modification are the text which is sent by the radio operator. The receiver of the message needs the decode version of the code book, sorted in code group order, to decide the text. In the case of JN4, the code groups consisted of four 'kana' (kana syllables are the Japanese equivalent of an alphabet), the fourth syllable being a 'garble check', by tracking the four syllables through a table you could tell whether the group had been transmitted correctly.

There was no easy way of exploiting JN4. The code book was huge. JN25 was the main system, carrying about seventy percent of all Japanese naval communications. JN25 differed from JN4 in that the code groups consisted of five digits, not four, and that the code-groups were reciphered by a 'long additive'. JN25 code groups had an attenuated garble-check – all authentic code-groups were divisible by three.'

As well as these two major codes the workers looked at minor codes, recovering code-group meanings and then spending time on clerical work and indexing. A lot of effort was spent on editing signals from Washington and sending them on to Kilindini (in Kenya).

Hut 7 continued to expand and when staff from the Italian Naval Section moved across to work on Japanese material and new recruits such as the young WRNS, Anne Petrides arrived, accommodation became even more crowded. Anne Petrides worked on an index of merchant shipping movements and recalls in The Emperor's Code by Michael Smith, (reprinted by permission of Peters Fraser and Dunlop on behalf of Michael Smith) 'I joined Naval Section at Bletchley Park the day after my eighteenth birthday 'celebrated' at the WRNS training centre at Mill Hill on 31 May 1944 and was flung into the work of cataloguing ships, entering brief notes on their cards about the decoded signals as they came to us from the translations. Most of their warships had been sunk by then and we were dealing with 'maru' – merchant ships.

The naval officers in my office included Gorley Putt and 'shrimp' Hordern, brother of Michael Hordern, the actor. As a very young girl I was petrified to be left all alone at lunchtime, in four interconnecting rooms – and in fact justifiably so, as a senior officer from the Admiralty phoned and said "Can we go over?", followed by a burble of words. He came back in clear language and was outraged to find that not only had no one seen fit to tell me which button to press for the scrambler but that no 'duty officer' was present. A regular visitor from 'down the passage', usually on quieter night watches, was Angus Wilson. His first book of stories was said to have originated in a series of sessions he had with a psychiatrist. I believed the men cracked more easily under the strain, whereas girls found it easier to have a crying breakdown'. The working environment in all of the huts was difficult – outside it was often very muddy with duck boards being used to help the situation, but everything often felt cold, damp and foggy. One worker said that 'The only room I ever saw in all the two years I spent at Bletchley Park was the one I worked in – Hut 7'. The working environment was utilitarian with little comfort – tables were covered in army blankets with ashtrays, eyebrow tweezers and note pad on top, gritty concrete floors and poor toilets often with wet floors. Many times there was a haze of cigarette smoke trapped in the room and sleeping on duty was deemed a serious crime. Facilities for heating the huts were basic, usually 'pot stoves', and in the summer months the huts were unbearably hot, lighting was poor and windows were covered in mesh to stop people looking in. The physical demands for working in the huts were unremitting.

When all of this came to an end, Philip, like many who had served at Bletchley Park, found it hard to adjust to normal civilian life and to concentrate on studying at Cambridge after the intensity of life in the huts. There was also the added burden of the secrecy, not only was nothing said by Philip, and others, about what they were doing when they were working at Bletchley Park, but they had to remain silent for many years to come.

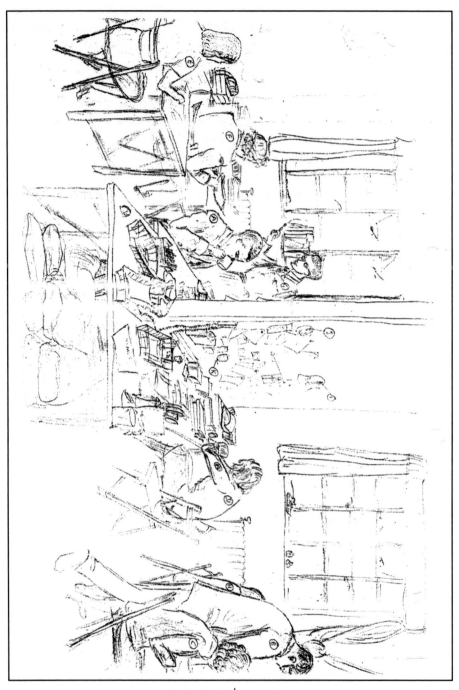

A sketch by
Myfanwy
Cornwall-
Jones of Hut 7
at work and
her descriptions
of the
occupants.

Exhibit A: S/Lt K.R. Howard-Williams, the Fuhrer.

Exhibit B: Mr W.T. Ewing, Deputy Fuhrer. Rather poor likeness; Willie is tall and thin.

Exhibit C: P.O. P.Goatly, WRNS. The hair is remarkably like; but Prue is rather larger altogether.

Exhibit D: P.O. B.M. Godman, WRNS. A very good likeness of Mary at work.

Exhibit E: Miss A.L. Dent. Jill's hair is not really so neat.

Exhibit F: L/W J.Tackerberry, WRCNS. Another good likeness.

Exhibit G: S/Lt P.H.Vennis. Note: red hair and freckles, also younger than drawn. Not a good likeness of Philip, except for the cigarette holder.

Exhibit H: Miss M. Cornwall-Jones. The best likeness of the lot!

Exhibit I: The Fuhrer's thinking cap.

Exhibit J: Hirohito's death mask, carved from a puff ball.

Exhibit K: Ditto, carved from a stale bun.

These were the notes which accompanied Miss Cornwall-Jones' sketches.

CHAPTER 3

Peterhouse, Cambridge University

During the early part of the twentieth century, Cambridge remained a compact built-up area, but pre-1939, the town was becoming suburbanised, with many middle class people moving out to the neighbouring villages or new estates a mile from the town centre. Bicycles were widely used because of the compactness of the town and the flat terrain. Following the war many workers cycled into the centre and when shops closed for lunch, they would cycle home and return after their lunch. However, with the advent of the motor car it became clear to the authorities that the narrow ancient streets were not compatible to motoring, and they tried to find solutions to the traffic problem whilst still preserving the unique ancient features of Cambridge. The population of Cambridge rose from 40,000 in 1900 doubling to about 80,000 in the time when Philip lived there. Likewise the growth of undergraduates increased from just under 3,000 in early in the twentieth century to over 5,000 pre-Second World War. Little development took place in Cambridge during the Second World War, and like most of Britain growth did not really begin until the early fifties. Cambridge was given city status in 1951 for 'exceptional' reasons – it was the only ancient seat of learning in the United Kingdom which was not a city and the status was awarded to coincide with the 750th anniversary of the borough's first charter of incorporation. The City Authorities have striven to maintain the ancient and unique character of the centre of the city, which is still fundamentally medieval with narrow streets.

Peterhouse is the oldest College in Cambridge, having been founded in 1284 by Hugh de Balsham, Bishop of Ely, initially for a Master and fourteen poor fellows, who lived in the College but taught outside. Hugh de Balsham bequeathed money to his scholars who bought land and built a hall in the thirteenth century, which still survives today, although it underwent extensive restoration in the late nineteenth century. (Colour photograph 10.) The restoration included some of the finest pre-Raphaelite stained glass windows in the country by Burne-Jones, Madox-Brown and William Morris. The Tudor fireplace is surrounded by daisy tiles designed by William Morris. Early scholars worshipped in St.Peter's- without- Trumpington-Gate which was rebuilt and renamed St. Mary the Less in 1340. In 1628, whilst Mathew Wren (Sir Christopher Wren's uncle) was Master of Peterhouse the chapel and the library were built, the chapel transformed the appearance of Peterhouse from the street. The architecture of the chapel demonstrates the transition from Gothic to Renaissance architecture that took place in this era under the Stuarts. (Colour photograph 9.) The East window was hidden during the Civil War and therefore was not destroyed. It is based on Rubens 'Le Coup de Lance'. (Colour photograph 11.)

'Classics and English Tripos' 1946 to 1948

"Forests in the lake, high trees, deep water,
Sky above descending, truth everywhere;
No huntin', shootin', fishin', - but foxes
Renewed into life, - birds buoyant now,
And fish playing ball. Green shows
The countryside as England appears
Not knowing herself, but floating again
Away down a new alley – no cul-de-sac
This time. A new hard core revealed,
A kaleidoscope of eternal colours
Appearing beneath an ancient
Tawdriness.
Here let us live –
In a world to win."
(P.H.V. 1947 – On hearing Vaughan Williams Fifth Symphony)

Philip sat his scholarship and exhibition papers for Classics in March 1944, with the expectation that he would be at Peterhouse in October 1944. However, on the application form for admission to the examination for entrance scholarships and exhibitions, there was a proviso 'successful candidates proceeding into national service may expect to have their scholarships and exhibitions reserved until a reasonable time after the cessation of hostilities'. For Philip, 'the hostilities' did not cease until he was released by the Admiralty in October 1946 to rejoin his studies for the Classical Tripos, (he had already undertaken some study at Peterhouse prior to his joining the RNVR).

Although the war had finished, life in England still endured the conditions of war until the early fifties with rationing and controls within society still in existence. Life was dominated by the consequences of war. Few people had cars; Philip owned a car, having learnt to drive naval trucks on Southsea Common whilst at HMS *Victory,* and, in correspondence with Dr.Burkill, who was a Fellow at Peterhouse, Philip asked if he could garage his car in Cambridge.

Dr.Burkill wrote on 2 October 1946 'The restriction on cars to men under twenty two years old applies to keeping a car as well as to using it. The garage space in the town is limited and we do not want it taken up by cars which are not in use, so will you please keep yours at home?'

Already Cambridge had difficulty with traffic management, and clearly tried to restrict car usage in the town.

In many parts of the country including Cambridge re-building was happening, but many materials and foodstuffs were scarcer than they had been during the war. The coal-mining areas became more active during the war, but by 1945 production was low and only reached the pre-war level in 1950. With the war barely over, the greatest freeze for over a century came in the winter of 1946-47, with serious blizzards which were followed by floods. These heavy snow-storms and sub-zero temperatures with the shortage of fuel brought Britain's economy to an almost standstill. Power cuts made over four million workers idle, many coal trains were stuck in drifts up to twenty feet deep and many homes and Cambridge Colleges were without heat or light for long periods of the day. Richard Baker, O.B.E, R.D, (BBC television newsreader for nearly thirty years) was at Peterhouse at the same time as Philip and wrote in the Peterhouse Annual of 1999.'On my return to Peterhouse in October 1946, I found that long hours with medieval history had lost their appeal. The winter was desperately cold; the only means of heating my room was a small coal fire. But there was almost no coal. Like many other commodities, it was severely rationed, and if you managed to keep the fire going a couple of hours a day you were lucky. There was no heating in the bedrooms, and the jug of water in the wash-hand basin regularly froze over. There was a chamber pot, but more serious calls of nature entailed a long freezing walk to the 'Birdwood'. Nights were thus not pleasant, and the start of each day was not promising, as we shivered to the 'Birdwood' for a bath before setting off for breakfast in Hall, clutching our small rations of butter and sugar.'

After the long cold winter, there were still difficulties being encountered. The editor of the Magazine of the Peterhouse Sexcentenary Club wrote in Easter 1946 'The war is now happily over, but its effects linger on in no uncertain fashion. We are plagued with rations, queues, and a shortage of every conceivable commodity, even the mainstay of our very existence – cash. In the midst of all this surrounded by complaints of every sort, shortage of staff and, worst of all, by early breakfast, we seem somehow to carry on in a desultory sort of way; in fact, Cambridge has never been fuller in all its long history. But for all its fullness, it is not what it was'.

In Cambridge student numbers were increasing. At Peterhouse in the latter years of the war there was a stable figure of about ninety students, a third of these were cadets for the services taking six month courses, most of the remainder were scientists or engineers continuing their studies, in order that they might be better qualified for taking part in the war-effort at a later stage. In the first term of peace – Michaelmas 1945, numbers at Peterhouse increased to one hundred and twenty students. The great pressure came in 1946 when the Government's Further Education and Training scheme made it financially possible for any ex-service man whose education had been interrupted by the war to study at any University at which he could gain admission. This resulted in a vast number of applications, with some Cambridge Colleges receiving three thousand applications in one year. Peterhouse was inundated with applications so the Master and Fellows laid down certain principles for priority in dealing with applications. The first preference was given to men who had been in residence at Peterhouse before war service but who had not been able to stay long enough to get a degree. After them, preference was given to elected scholars and exhibitioners and others with clear titles to a place who had not been in residence at all. Philip was one of twelve students in 1946-7 undertaking the classics Tripos. For Peterhouse, as with many Cambridge colleges the provision of rooms for undergraduates was a problem. There were few licensed lodgings available, on account of an increase in the permanent population of the town although some lodging houses increased their capacity and some college rooms were being shared by two men. Philip's first lodgings were in rooms at 8 Brunswick Terrace, but ration supplies for his breakfast were supplied by Peterhouse, as the landlady Mrs Jones did not have any surplus food rations. Tutorial arrangements within Peterhouse were adjusted to take account of the increase in number of students. For his first term Philip's tutor was Dr.Birkill and for the last two terms of his first year Mr.Lubbock was his tutor.

During the war the life of the College had been different to the pre-war days. The rationing system had produced great difficulty for the Peterhouse kitchen, who nevertheless with skill and ingenuity kept the kitchens to a high standard. Limitations on the number of private guests were restricted for both undergraduates and the High Table, but even so there was sometimes insufficient food for the undergraduates. Protests from the university did secure additional rations, from which the public schools had already benefited.

Gradually war time austerities were being relaxed and such things as the College Ball were revived in 1946, and the window-boxes containing a show of pink geraniums were planted for the first time after the war in 1948. In the academic year of 1946-7 the Perne Society was revived and a number of interesting play productions revived an interest in drama, Twelfth Night being performed in the Michaelmas Term 1947.

Philip in his University years, 1946 - 1948

For Philip, like many other undergraduates returning from war service, settling down into academic study and ways of thought made his first term difficult. The cold winter of 1946-47 only added to the discomfort and the adaptation these young men had to make. It was said that the wind blew all the way from the Ural Mountains with nothing stopping it until Cambridge. The Tudor and more recent buildings of Peterhouse certainly necessitated the using of clothes coupons for warmer winter coats and scarves. Often like the rest of the nation, power cuts affected the lighting in Peterhouse. Philip used candlelight for his reading, essay writing and other academic activities, making him appreciate how his early predecessors would probably have studied. Apart from the extreme cold, rations of food were even tighter than they had been during the war, cigarettes were difficult to obtain but one shop in Trumpington Street did have an under the counter supply for regular customers. Entertainment for Philip usually consisted of an occasional trip to the cinema or visiting the local public houses – usually The Little Rose or in the summer months The Anchor and The Mill. Cambridge at this time was often descended upon in the evenings by the American Airmen from nearby airfields and some Polish airmen. Disturbances sometimes occurred with a few fights between the Americans and undergraduates ensuing in one of the pubs. Philip in his spare time frequently visited the bookshops – Heffers in Petty Cury, Bowes and Bowes and the second hand and antiquarian shops, where he used up any spare cash he may have had. Towards the end of the academic year 1946-47, Philip requested that he deferred his degree until June 1948, since he had barely undertaken two years study for the classical Tripos, and, he wished also to undertake a degree in English in his final year. He was however dissuaded from deferring his degree since Mr.Lubbock, his tutor, wanted to make a decision regarding coming up again in 1947-48 when he had the result of the classical tripos. Mr.Lubbock wrote to Philip on 20 June, after his result in Part I of the classical Tripos 'Your request to stay up for a further year has been carefully considered by the Tutors and by the Governing Body and I am sorry to tell you that in the present circumstances they do not feel able to grant it. Pressure on new entries and of men returning after service is, as you know, extremely heavy and it is felt that another year would be of very doubtful advantage to you besides excluding someone else. I think too that you would be well advised to look for a job at once instead of waiting till next year when the competition will be still greater. You need not think that there is anything derogatory in a degree gained in under two years. It is as much as most people have had in the war years; you have passed in an honours examination, and the circumstances are well known.' Of course, Philip being the person that he was did not accept this decision, he responded by replying to Mr.Guthrie, after he had been interviewed by the University Appointments Board – 'The University Appointments Board were not very helpful. They told me that I was too young and had not enough experience for the BBC, The British Council etc; and their only offers were either the Special Departmental Branch of the Civil Service, which doesn't look very promising, or teaching, which is my first choice. They agreed that for the latter, a second part of some Tripos would be most helpful. In view of all this, I am still very eager to return to Peterhouse for another year, and I was wondering if you would have a word with Mr.Lubbock about this. I have only been at Cambridge eighteen months in all, the first six months of which I was on a short-course and had not a lot of time to attend to classics. In any case I was doing only Greek at the time, so that when I came up last October (1946), the Latin I started then was the first since leaving school. I had been demobbed only three days before full term, and so have never had a long vacation or indeed very much time at all to prepare for the Tripos. As you know, had the College let me, I would have taken another year over Part I.

I have been informed that the English Tripos is extremely difficult. I do hope that it isn't putting you to a lot of trouble to ask you to point all the above out to Mr.Lubbock and ask him if I may return to Peterhouse in October (1947)'. Mr.Guthrie spoke to Mr.Lubbock and this was his reply on 12 July 1947 to Philip. 'I have had a talk to Mr.Lubbock on your behalf and suggested that your case might be reconsidered in view of your keen desire for another year here, on the ground that your Cadet course in Latin only ought not to be regarded as the equivalent of a year's work and the Preliminary Examination from the point of preparation for the Tripos. He agreed that this might be allowed to make a difference, and we discussed the possibilities of how you might spend another year with profit. The best possibility seems to be English Part II, and so if you can come to Cambridge again and see Mr.Tompkins at Westcott House, and if after interview he is satisfied that you would be able in the time available to make a reasonable showing in his subject then we are both prepared to recommend to the Governing Body that you come back for another year.

As to Part II Classics, I would advise against that in the interest of your future, since a combination of the two subjects would almost certainly be an advantage'. Philip of course was delighted with this response from Mr.Guthrie and subsequently thanked him for his intervention, but unfortunately Philip was rushed to hospital with the need for an appendectomy at the beginning of August 1947 and was unable to meet with Mr.Tompkins until 26 August. Mr.Tompkin's response to R.G. Heard, a Tutor at Peterhouse states 'I have seen this man Vennis, and perhaps ought to make some report. A factor to consider seemed to me his desire to teach. He would have to teach form subjects in a public school, since he's not good enough to teach at any higher level, and there does seem a good deal to be said for his desirability of combining classics with English for this purpose. The London educational department will not take him without another subject. From the point of view of his own career, therefore, there seems a case for letting him read English. As to what he would get in English it is difficult to say. He doesn't strike me as very bright or to have much background knowledge, but he might gain a 2:1 if he works hard. I don't know if my snappy reactions add anything to your considerations, but I might suggest that it would be a kindness to come to a decision pretty soon so that he may try and get a job or entry into a training college.' Philip received confirmation that he had been accepted by the Governing Body to read Part II of the English Tripos at Peterhouse beginning October 1947. Philip, obviously in his interview with Mr.Tompkins, did not come over as having the potential for the exceptional teacher that he was to become, and presumably by Cambridge standards gaining a 2:1 was considered to be not very 'bright'. The Fellow that most supported Philip's desire to undertake another year at Peterhouse was W.K.C. Guthrie who attended Dulwich College as a boy, obtained a first class degree in both parts of his classical Tripos and became well known for his History of Greek Philosophy, which was published in 1962. Guthrie became the University Orator in 1939, a position he held for eighteen years and in which he was responsible for delivering speeches in Latin in honour of recipients of honorary degrees. He taught Philip both Latin and Greek during the academic year 1946-7 for his classical Tripos.

Philip started part II of his English Tripos in October 1947, living in Fen Court, which was designed by H.C Hughes and P. Bicknell in 1939-41. Fen Court was amongst the earliest buildings in Cambridge in the style of the Modern Movement which was begun by Walter Gropius at the Bauhaus. Above the entrance doorway there is a carved panel by Anthony Foster with an inscription that evokes the mood in Britain as the building was completed. This inscription is *DE PROFUNDIS CLAMA VI MCMXL* – 'out of the depths have I cried out 1940' which are the first words of Psalm 130, one of the Penitential Psalms. Next to the inscription is a depiction of St. Peter being saved from the sea.

It was at the beginning of this academic year that he met an Indian gentleman who was to become his lifelong friend, Soli Mistry. Soli was a little older than Philip as he had already graduated at Bombay University and was coming to Cambridge for his doctorate. At the age of ninety Soli has recalled some of his memories of meeting Philip in his early days at Peterhouse.

'I arrived in Cambridge in September 1947 as a post-graduate student from Bombay. Being of Indian descent I attracted some attention from other students, probably because India had newly become Independent on 14 August 1947 and was in the news at the time. I was on the high seas when the division and separation of India and Pakistan and all the horror that ensued was taking place. Following partition there was a complete breakdown of law and order, many people died in riots, massacres or just from hardship whilst trying to flee to a safe place. About half a million people died and approximately twelve million became homeless.

I came to Cambridge to join Dunn Nutritional Laboratory, which was part of the Medical Research Council of England. In order to be part of the University I had to be affiliated to a College, and at that time those who were not affiliated with a College went to Fitzwilliam House. When I arrived in England the High Commissioner of India suggested Peterhouse, as he was an old Petrian. He wanted me to have the experience of a College in Cambridge especially as Fitzwilliam at that time was not a College.

Philip met me as one of the group of students from Peterhouse. This lively classicist with red hair asked me if I played Bridge, and our friendship began, which lasted for fifty years until his death in 1999. For a year we overlapped at Peterhouse. Philip was living at Fen Court next to the 'Birdwood', and I was living in 'Noah's Ark' – the oldest part of Peterhouse which is in the Courtyard. The accommodation at Fen Court had central heating and was more modern than Noah's Ark. I had two 'gyps' who cared for me in this freezing, old accommodation. Mr. and Mrs. Goose, if I remember correctly, lit fires for me and put hot water bottles ready at bedtime (coming from Bombay I felt the cold!). The winter of 1947 was particularly cold in Britain and as a result of this freezing weather I was transferred to St. Peter's Terrace the next semester – it was luxurious with central heating and an electric fire! The room was larger and warmer than Noah's Ark. When I needed to have a bath or shower I (and other students) had to walk out in the cold weather to the 'Birdwood'. Rations were very short and portions and allowances were less than earlier in the war. However, dinner time at Peterhouse was special. Peterhouse was well known for its good food, they had a farm where most food originated from. In post war Britain food was still rationed, meat was scarce and whale meat and jugged hare were served sometimes at Peterhouse. On these occasions Philip would quip 'we are having Moby Dick for dinner tonight'. We always had to attend the dining room in jacket, tie and gown. The dining room was arranged with the high table (Dons and Fellows) then the semi-high table (postgraduate students) and the undergraduates were on the regular floor. This seating arrangement was the only thing that I remember made a difference to my College life; otherwise my enhanced status as an MA did not affect everyday College life.

A lot of my time and Philip's time was spent playing Bridge and eating cakes (which were on coupons) from 'Fitzbillies'. (Colour photograph 12.) Sometimes I went to Lyons Restaurant for a wonderful lunch for five shillings or a smaller lunch for two shillings and ten pence. When I met Philip, he was known with the rest of the undergraduates that had returned from the Armed Forces war service as the 'Generals', this group of undergraduates outnumbered those who were eighteen and had come straight from school and were the 'schoolboys'. Some of the undergraduates had been in war service for up to six years, others like Philip had done two or three years. Most of these returning war service mature undergraduates worked very hard as they had 'lost' these years in the war and had not come back to Peterhouse, or any other University College, not to achieve the best degree possible.

While at St. Peter's Terrace, which is opposite Addenbrookes Hospital and next to the Fitzwilliam Museum, there was no porter's lodge, so when friends came they could not enter. I remember one Saturday morning Philip and our mutual friend Villicania (graduate student from Mexico) singing at the bottom of the building 'Oh what a beautiful morning' beckoning me to come down and let them into the building! Philip was always singing and he liked these musicals, operas of Gilbert and Sullivan and romantic songs of the day. I, Philip and Villiacania formed a close friendship and spent a lot of time together. Villiacania was a postgraduate student reading English Literature under E.M. Forster and he and Philip conducted deep discussions about literature. I was the science man amongst these literary hotheads and didn't get into these discussions. In summer 1948, Philip, I and two others, went in his small Austin 7 to Europe, arriving in Paris on Bastille Day – 14 July 1948. We went to Switzerland via the St. Gottard pass, which we made nearly all the way up until the last five hundred metres and then the car did not have enough power to get up – so Philip drove in reverse and we made it!' (Emeritus Professor of Bio –Chemistry and Nutritional Sciences Sorab Mistry PhD Cantab. University of Illinois, Champaign Urbana. U.S.A. Peterhouse 1947 -51)

Philip remained in Fen Court until he was requested four weeks before his finals in the English Tripos to vacate his room to another undergraduate who was suffering with medical problems. By taking the English Tripos Philip began his deep intellectual interest in English literature, which remained with him the rest of his life. His love of Shakespeare, D.H. Lawrence, W.H. Auden, G.M. Hopkins, T.S. Elliot, Milton, Byron, Dickens, Hardy, Chaucer, and many others were regularly used in his teaching and his school assemblies. Philip's most influential teacher was Frank Leavis, who was director of studies in English at Downing College for thirty years. Leavis upheld rigorous intellectual standards and he was responsible for raising the profiles of literary figures such as James Joyce, T.S. Eliot, W.B. Yeats, G.M. Hopkins and D.H. Lawrence. Philip attended his open, free tutorials at Downing every week and discovered that Leavis had an instinct for academic democracy. He treated undergraduates as equals or potential equals. This idea grew from his belief that healthy literature nourishes and that 'collaboration between teachers and students are the roots of a sane society'. Leavis revered Shakespeare and was the most creative, serious and influential literary critic since his Victorian model Matthew Arnold.

In April 1948 Philip applied to the University Of London Institute Of Education to undertake the Teacher's Diploma course, commencing in October 1948. His Tutors Mr. Guthrie and Mr. Lubbock gave references for this course. Mr. Guthrie wrote 'Intellectually Vennis is well up to the requirements of the teaching profession. His character is also excellent and he is a conscientious worker. I would not however describe him as a strong personality, and you may find that on this side he is a little colourless and not especially good at arousing interest and enthusiasm in others'. Mr.Lubbock wrote 'He is limited in ability but has developed considerably during the past year, having read English for one year only his results are expected to be entirely creditable'. Philip's tutors were very short in their references and Mr.Guthrie's comments on his personality were absolutely wrong, because there is no doubt that Philip's ability to interest his students and evoke their attention was excellent and to state that he was a little 'colourless' was also a gross understatement, but of course, he may have developed these characteristics after leaving Peterhouse.

CHAPTER 4

University of London Institute of Education

Philip undertook his Post Graduate Certificate of Education at one of the most prestigious Institutes of Education in the country. The London Institute of Education is famous throughout the world for its training of teachers and its educational research. The Institute began in 1902 at the London Day Training College, under the London County Council and the University of London. At the time that Philip was at the Institute it was the University's largest central activity. After he left in 1949, it became a wider Institute and some thirty associated Colleges and Departments of Education were under its auspices. It was initially opened over one hundred years ago, with fifty eight students, to train teachers for the elementary and secondary schools of London, but by the time it transferred to the University of London it developed rapidly. It has a reputation for producing good teachers and today trains 4,400 students. The buildings, because of this expansion, have frequently changed location in London. Originally the London Day Training College was housed at the London School of Economics, but when Philip studied there it was in the heart of the University in the north wing of the Senate House, where it had moved in 1938.

'At last a Teacher' 1948 to 1949

'Human dignity is our goal in education, with the aim of giving the opportunity to live a free and full life. I am not competent to discuss the spiritual side of education, or to attempt to put a child on the right path vis-a-vis his relations with his God. I think it is extremely important, but I do not think it can be done by one or two religious education periods a week. I think it is open to discussion how far it is the teacher's business to attempt to make a child a good Christian and in any case I think it is largely a question of atmosphere; indeed I think all good education a matter of atmosphere. It is not open to question that a child, when he or she comes to adulthood, has to take his or her place as a citizen in the community. And we in the teaching profession hope of course that he or she will be above all things a thinking member of society'. (P.H.V. April 1949)

Philip began at the University of London in September 1948. It had always been his ambition to become a teacher and so this year at the Institute was the beginning of his teaching career. Throughout the year he spent two days a week

43

undertaking teaching practice at Westminster City School and Marylebone Grammar School, teaching English and Greek and three days a week at the Institute studying psychology and the principles of education. As part of these studies he was asked to think about his own education in a critical manner, this is what he wrote in November 1948. (Parts of this study is also to be found in a different context in the Dulwich College chapter).

'Imagine a sausage machine; a machine which produced regularly and without fail a string of excellent sausages every year, and has been doing so for one hundred years. Started originally with the idea of turning meat, left behind by other but or not otherwise to be used, into useful, clean, wholesome food, it had begun, after three or four hundred years, to fail in its purpose, and the supply of meat for it began to falter. So about one hundred years ago, a certain eminent butcher, seeing this situation, decided to remedy it by making the machine up to date, with new equipment and new ideas that it might turn out the sort of sausages people now wanted. His experiment was a huge success; much more meat of all sorts, some much better than before, some much worse, became available to the machine, and his model was taken up and copied all over the country. Many inferior machines were set up, more perfected indeed in their mechanism than his, and therefore turning out sausages more alike in shape, in colour, in taste, and in general content, or more usually in lack of content. Today these machines have more meat available than ever before; meat which might go to other butchers for preparation for fresh salad or tasty roast dishes, goes instead to the sausage machine.

For the English people love sausages: they like to use them for many culinary purposes, some very apt, some less so; they like them peppery, but not too peppery; they like them to be all of the same shape within a reasonable degree and above all, they dislike them intensely if their skins break around them or at the ends. All this the sausage machine now takes care of, and although various suggestions for new skins, or looser fitting skins, (or even horror of horrors, no skin at all) have been made, on the whole the butchers in charge take their stand by the fact of their having survived a hundred years, and, "why shouldn't we then", they say, "survive another hundred years!" and by the nation's general good health which, they say, is their doing; and by the greatness and undoubted foresight of that eminent butcher of one hundred years ago. Furthermore they state that sausages hold the nation together -"No sausages-no Empire", we are told.

For butchers, read - 'public school masters' and 'governors'; for meat, read – 'all boys anywhere'; for sausages, read – 'ex-public school system'; and there you have what seems to me a not unfair description of what that system does, and why and how it does it. I spent seven years at a public school, Dulwich College, a by-no-means inferior or imitative one, but one that was certainly in a bad way at the time of Dr. Arnold's reforms at Rugby, and also certainly one that took up and put into practice the spirit, if not the letter, of those reforms. But I am not a sausage; at least I do not think I am; and I will certainly grant that many of the sausage skins no longer fit, or at any rate are soon burst. The resulting meat-patty is, in small doses, equally (or more?) good for the nation's health. It 'has been through' the machine, and has what advantages are to be derived from that process. But it remains, and always will remain sausage – (i.e. minced) meat. So you see that, although I agree that to start with the country would lose a staple source food from the diet, I do not agree that it would starve if the machines were radically overhauled, and made to turn out rather a different product, a variegated, coloured and high-tasting meat with full protein-content left in it. The people may like English sausages, but have they ever tried American hot-dogs, or Viennese sausages or even French veal? And would they perhaps not like these even more?

I went to Dulwich in 1937 at the age of eleven plus (as the educationalists – and they alone I think – love to call children of this age). Before then, owing to the nomadic habits of my family I had been to four state (or state aided) junior elementary schools. Of the first three I remember very little except that I was sadly disappointed in the first, a Roman Catholic school, which seemed so much more serious place, than I had thought school to be. (Before this, up to the age of five, I had the curious notion that school was a place where I would sit on a high stool and be whirled round in a ring by one older than myself. I cannot trace the origin of this very odd belief.)

I remember my fourth school quite well. It was a L.C.C. junior elementary; and a very good one too. The staff were keen and very helpful. Particularly in Geography, they encouraged me greatly in my only 'aptitude', map drawing and making. This hobby which should have been encouraged throughout my education was to be drowned later at Dulwich in the general morass of mental culture to which we were all submitted. New Park Road School, S.W.2 was very pleased indeed when, on my passing the L.C.C. Junior Scholarship, my parents entered me for Dulwich, or so they seemed to me then; but on looking back now I wonder if some of them really knew what was coming, and were just a little dubious about what it would do to the one productive and creative thing I could do – map-making; - a curious thought. Yet I feel they must have felt some qualm, for they were good men and women who would not like to see a boy who might become a contributor to a living culture turned instead into another culture – dispenser, or worse still (and more likely) into a culture-organiser or administrator. But the ways of the middle-class parent are inscrutable even to the best of men.

And so to Alleyn's College of God's Gift, founded 1616 by one of Shakespeare's actors, Edward Alleyn. My parents chose Dulwich because they quite sincerely thought that I should receive a better (by their standards – those of the shop-keeping middle – class) education than at any other locally available (I never became a boarder) secondary schools. Looking back now I can say that on the whole, and of the choice available, Dulwich was the best. They also had the reason that to have a son at a Public School was in itself no mean thing, and the social prestige of having been there was (and still is even in the most 'enlightened' circles) enormous.

At this time Dulwich took about twenty-five per cent of its yearly quota of new boys from the L.C.C. The council paid their fees (after a means test) to the School governors, who were then free to spend it as they pleased. Furthermore the Council had the right to a nominee on the Board of governors, but this was merely *'a sop to Cerberus'* as it were. My parents were requested to have me taught some French (for which the Council did not pay) before I entered the College, and this was the first cog-wheel of the machine to which I was tied. Latin began immediately (six periods a week), and Latin remained the pivot of the curriculum throughout my seven years. French and Mathematics were our other two main subjects.

English, History and Geography (and this last hurt me at the time most of all, though I see now the lack of English was the real fault) were subsidiary, as they were always to be. Masters were kind, and the discipline was not hard, and, owing to the fact that I took to Latin Grammar like a duck to water, I was put up to the next form, 2A, at the end of the first term. This involved a change of strata among the boys. Hitherto I had been among boys from the same sort of home (flats – houses with no gardens – 'street players' all of us) as myself. But 2A was peopled by lads from the various preparatory schools which fed the College the other seventy- five per cent, or colonials and boys from distant homes who were boarders. Thus began some of the most subtle and complex relationships typical of the modern (particularly in London) public school. I, a normal cockney from South London, was amazed to find a boy who had never been on nor even knew of a 'tram', and he was equally amazed at my lack of experience of the country and my lack of knowledge of the most common wild flowers. This I think was a really valuable contribution to my education, and did me more good than my swift progress through the intricacies of the *'domus'* declension. Dulwich always had a large number of boys who came in daily from the Kent countryside, and they, and we who cycled or bussed on an L.C.C. ticket, formed very separate groups in the junior school. But progress up the school made us very fast friends, although we very rarely went to one another's homes, through either shame, or fear, or both.

At thirteen plus we moved up to the Senior School. This meant in theory a choice of the Classical, Modern or Science sides; in practice this was decided by a combination of circumstances with masters' preferences and parents' near-snobbery. If one were near the top of one's third form, one was thought to be suited to the Classics; my form-master was a 'Classic'; my parents thought a Classical education the 'thing'. They were honestly convinced one would not get on in the world without it. So in September 1939 I was in the Classical Fourth A; and according to all accepted accounts, I was made for life.

I was, as I have said, never a boarder at Dulwich, but the year before this, 'Munich' had sent the school scuttling across the country to the Forest of Dean. Here I had my first experience of living with other boys; I disliked it intensely, and it has coloured my attitude to boarding schools ever since.

The brutality and viciousness of public school boarding life, its accent on a male community living together, almost emphasising and underlining the necessity for homosexuality, are clear to me because of a few weeks of 'boarding'. A school that includes boys up to eighteen and a half years, boys who are put in almost sole and complete charge of children seven or eight years younger than themselves; a school where 'fagging' is yet allowed, and beating by one boy of another legal, a school in which hero-worship is very common and indeed the only outlet of affection for the younger boys – a hero-worship moreover depending on athletics; a school where boys are recognised more for physical than mental powers, and not at all (rather the opposite) for spiritual – such a school, laying as it does far too great an emphasis on the physical, must by its nature and in reality does produce the most extraordinary and unhealthy physical vices. Whatever there is to be said for public schools, is assuredly not to be said for their boarding side. This system must be rooted out and destroyed. The outbreak of war found us billeted on Tonbridge School (we had returned from the Forest of Dean after Mr. Chamberlain's 'Peace in our time' speech). The whole school came back to Dulwich in December 1939, and there we remained through blitz and Baedeker raids, through V.1 and V.2 and all. At one time I believe we were the only major school (never less than 750 boys even at the height of the blitz) left in London, and we were all made very proud of this. 'We never closed' was a motto we shared with the chorus girls of the Windmill Theatre, an institution, not otherwise having much in common with us! The war affected school life only externally. Rules of clothing, of discipline, of punctuality etc were in no way relaxed. Even being bombed out was not a sufficient excuse for not having on a clean white stiff collar the next day. My house in Brixton was damaged and mad uninhabitable in September 1940 in a daylight raid; I missed one day's school, and turned up the following day hoping to be the centre of attention and sympathy (at the age of fourteen one isn't very much concerned with the broader issues). But *'Our glorious Semper Eadem'* demanded otherwise, and moreover this was the year of School Certificate; my form master was only concerned that I should get a new set of Latin and Greek books immediately, and make up my one missed homework. So we went on, up, down, up, down, all day, every day to the shelters at the school, construing Virgil in converted cellars as the guns boomed overhead. It was grand fun – masters with tin helmets and gowns are one of the funniest things you can see. But nothing could shake the machine.

Of course the boys thought it all a huge joke and even hoped each morning as they arrived at school that Hitler might have mistaken it for a different sort of sausage factory. Actually it was bombed three times, but we were never given a holiday on account of this. We had to help put the machine in order.

As regards sport (every Wednesday and Saturday afternoon – compulsory) this too was little affected. Even on that terrible afternoon which I remember so very clearly in the early summer of 1940 when the trains from Dover – for the main line crosses the school grounds – were slowly following one another in, packed inside and out with men in all stages of exhaustion and fatigue, wounded and all but dead, supporting one another at the windows, fixed in an immovable jam, - nearly half a million of them, - as they went by , we continued placidly to play cricket in the fields, and the veterans of Dunkirk cheered us instead of us cheering them. This was the first occasion I remember thinking that mine was at least a curious school. Those in charge cannot stop this machine even if they want to, I thought.

But the war did affect our outlook; impossible to have been born in the 'twenties, and brought up in the thirties and to have seen the resulting upheaval as one was growing to manhood in the forties, and not be affected. Even the sausage machine couldn't alter the world which made its sausage meat. Political clubs flourished; 'second-fronters' were vociferous; democracy in school life was demanded. In some measure these activities began to take the place of the drama clubs etc., more usual at such a school in peace time.

After School Certificate, came another choice of futures; one could change to the Modern or Science sides, or go to the Mathematics form. But here the same three pressures as before were evident. I stayed on the Classical side on the express condition of being able to continue Geography. I was let down in this, and here lies my major grumble at Dulwich. Lower down in the school, I had produced many large maps, and geographical journals and essays, I was very fond of this subject and had hoped to become a cartographer. But Dulwich thought otherwise, and during my next three years, I did sixth form Classical work. This was very well organised and as good as it could be – particularly for verse composition. Ancient History too came my way, but no modern. English remained subsidiary – a few progressive projects (I wrote a Life of Shelley) were

48

included, but on the whole it was merely reading 'King Lear' for Higher Certificate. There was no attempt to correlate English and Classics at all, and no study of our Language and Literature as such. French was continued desultorily – up to a reading of Racine in the dullest possible manner. A year's German (purely to read Professor Willamowitz von Moellendorf's' Prolegomena ad...etc,) was attempted. Russian was introduced but failed. Why? - because Classics took all our time and attention; it was extremely thorough – a typical week would include something like this:

2 periods of Greek Verse Composition
2 periods of Latin Verse Composition
2 periods of Greek Prose Composition
2 periods of Latin Prose Composition
2 periods of Demosthenes
2 periods of Cicero
2 periods of Homer
2 periods of Virgil
1 period each of Aeschylus, Thucydides, Horace, Tacitus
4 periods of Ancient History
4 periods of Classical general
1 period of the New Testament in Greek

In a thirty six period week (we worked Saturday morning but not Wednesday afternoon) this leaves seven for non Classical subjects. From this it is clear that one's Classics were in a sound state when one left Dulwich, and if the times and pupil were normal, a double first in the Classical Tripos at Cambridge should have been well in view; (the school had a preference for Cambridge).

But when one left Dulwich, a young man, one had no idea of the broader outlets of human endeavour; one knew nothing at all of music – and this seems now to me the greatest gap of all in this so called education, for, but for a lucky meeting in the Navy, I might never have known the delights of Mozart, - European civilisation at its highest since the Greeks; this one can say quite honestly. There was little music at Dulwich but, (to be fair the new Master is attempting to remedy this) unless one's parents were themselves educated enough to know the value of music, it was just left aside – (I am only now learning the piano). One knew nothing of the fine arts; of history in the broader sense; of any of the forces at work in our world. Most of all one's knowledge of one's own literature was extremely slight; I had read when I left Dulwich:-

Some pages of Chaucer

5 plays of Shakespeare
1 of Marlow
1 book of Paradise Lost and some poems of Milton
Selected Johnson
Selected Shelley
David Copperfield
Items in various anthologies

This you will see is not a very great deal; I had not heard of Donne and the Metaphysicals; of Hopkins; or of any moderns; of George Eliot or Jane Austen or etc …ad infintum. This was a great gap; for a scholar who had read in the Greek Lyrists, and had translated Juvenal, I was extraordinarily ignorant of my own literature. Was I educated?

My two years doing Classics (broken by two years in the Navy which were highly educative) at Cambridge were a mere continuance – and not a very hard one – of the Dulwich Classical sixth. After the first part of the Tripos, I took my courage in both hands and finally broke with the Classics. I intended reverting to my old love Geography, but owing to a chance meeting with an admirer of Dr. Leavis, who put the case for making English the main Humanity so well, that he won me over completely, I took the English Tripos Part II and in no way regret it. It was already too late for me to be a productive artist as regards map making; but at least I might help to train others to be such. My friends from Dulwich are or will be in the Civil Service, or in big business houses, or in 'Colonies' trade, or what you will. They are sausages, and I am a patty – I am not sorry to have burst my skin.

I do not regret having been at Dulwich College. It was far the best thing available. It laid down a basis for the love and appreciation of man's highest achievement yet, Greek life. It involved me in helping to run, and being trained for responsibility in, the Boy Scouts, and so led to a very fruitful interest in youth clubs. No I do not regret my seven years at the College, but I would ask the authorities there to ask themselves again 'What are we trying to do?'

I suggest that to those teaching the Humanities D.H. Lawrence provides a 'locus classicus' for thought about their work: "One must speak for life and growth, amid all this mass of destruction and disintegration"Let them keep this by for reference when planning their curriculum, and their pupils will not grow up in a world apart, in an oasis amid a general desert; in a school life utterly divorced from home life, will not grow up to wonder when they come to man hood what that very intelligent man, Matthew Arnold, meant in 'Dover Beach' when he said

'Ah Love, let us be true to one another;
For the world which seems to lie before us like a land of dreams,
Hath really neither joy, nor love, nor light,
Nor certitude, nor peace, nor help for pain,
And we are here as on a darkening plain
Swept with confused alarms of struggle and flight
Where ignorant armies clash by night.'

'For, their education has been 'speaking for life' they will surely know, and the greatest of Greek thoughts 'nothing to much, or everything in moderation will be their bible. The Greeks indeed did have sausages, but they did not make them with a machine. Machines, I think, do not 'speak for life'.

Although Philip was disillusioned and to some extent disappointed by his schoolboy education he did up hold values in the education system and during his second term at the Institute wrote in depth about these values, some of which were part of his philosophy when he began teaching and later as a headmaster.

'Unless we agree on what the values of life are, we clearly can have no goal in education, and if we have no goal, the discussion of methods is merely futile'. 'Thus wrote James T. Adams in his book, 'The Epic of America' in 1931. Fifty years ago educated men would have known what he meant without very much need for serious thought about it; but for us the dwellers in the civilisation of 'The Century of the Common Man', the above statement raises some almost unanswerable questions; we certainly agree with the three premises which Adams is using; we can even find a measure of agreement over methods to be used in education, (unless we are completely wedded to certain age-old and very academic educations); as for goals, we seem to find it necessary to split only into two or three major groups at the moment, (I mean the Communists, the Catholics, and what nearly amounts to the rest of us); but on values, we are completely and hopelessly divided. The reasons for these divisions are manifold and complex, and many go back a long way in our history. But in the main it is because a majority of us, at any rate, are lost, and are wandering very much on the by-roads of belief that we do not know which values mean most to us. For we, the men of the mid-twentieth Century, (and that this remarkable century has reached its half-way point; we were recently most vividly reminded by that important speech of Mr. Churchill at the mid-century convocation of the Massachusetts's Institute of Technology, important because of his stress on man's possibilities and not machine's; and the fact that it was held in America at a Technical Institute is very significant; for America is our new 'Mecca', and Technics are what have made it our 'Mecca'), we then, the men of the mid-twentieth Century, find ourselves almost at bay; our old values have disappeared, and we are not at all sure what we ought to put in their place, or if we ought to put anything at all. We, in the West, have defeated tyranny only to find it replaced by another almost as bad; at the moment our answer to this new threat is the atom bomb, rather than an opposing way of life, an answer we do not like but which we think we cannot help; we have lost our religion, and are not sure whether we want to replace it or not; we believe in education but find that the more education we give, the less those educated want to do the non–attractive but nevertheless very necessary jobs of the community. For a time many of us thought that we must concentrate on giving a technical education, but I think we can say we have seen that this, although obviously still needed, by itself would be no solution of our main problem; for this main problem is no less than so to educate our community that it will come to enjoy the very boring jobs that our civilisation has produced and continues to produce in ever increasing quantities, jobs which are necessary to its efficiency, but which in themselves are uninteresting, and give no appearance of becoming interesting in the foreseeable future. This is our problem; how are we to solve it? Technical education is not what is wanted, neither have we either the children or the schools suitable for a mass extension of it. The old grammar school education is even less suited to producing the sort of reasonably intelligent citizen that we need. Of late we gave up, to a certain extent altogether, any hope of making people interested in their work, and concentrated instead on their leisure. This theory is still respected in many educational, and even more in some governmental circles; a major (and to a large extent satisfactory) result of it has been the immense increase since the war in attempts to bring the various arts to the 'man in the street'; the Arts Council, the British Council, the National Theatre, the recent decision to encourage local authorities to set up and aid drama societies, etc, are all part of the drive for what is thought is going to be a 'cultured' nation; that it has had some effect would seem to be proved by attendance at things like the proms in London; the growth in the number of symphony orchestras in the country; the queues at Covent Garden, and for ballet everywhere, and so on; even the institution of the BBC's radio network would seem to be in some measure a reflection of it.

All this activity is by no means a bad thing; quite the contrary; to some extent it will undoubtedly help to make people much more aware of the possibilities inherent in our civilisation, the possibilities for real adult mental pleasure of all kinds; nevertheless what strikes one first about all these various activities is their topsy-turvy ness, almost their cackhandedness; they take people who have been half educated, or mis educated, or not educated at all, and proceed to attempt to add a veneer to them at the adult stage; they are not connected with adult education as such, and it seems likely therefore that what they do can only amount at best to some sort of veneer; the answer usually given to this objection is that all these things are in addition to the education system, not instead of it; these adults either cannot or will not be interested in further education, and therefore these multifarious aids to the Arts can do nothing but good; this is a fair answer, and one cannot, I think, object to it. But what one can and does object to are the two predominant ideas behind all this; the first and most important of these is what I have already referred to as 'Education for Leisure'; obviously it is of some importance in an industrial democracy such as ours has increasingly become, that people should use their leisure hours in pursuits that are not harmful to their fellows and if possible are beneficial to themselves; but the idea that we should concentrate our attention on this in education, and so retreat from even trying to educate them for their work, seems to me wholly a false one; no doubt it would be easier, but it remains a retreat, and so it cannot lead to any healthy improvement in the life of the community for which these children are being educated. This 'Education for Leisure' leads directly to the second idea upon which all this is based; it is more obvious but may not be so harmful in the end; it is the idea that it all amounts to 'culture'; that 'culture' is thus given out, and the customer will become a 'cultured' person. T. S. Eliot has recently written a whole book ('Towards the Definition of Culture') to try to arrive at a definition of culture. I am not clear that he came to any very satisfactory one, but he was quite certain, and he carries his reader with him here, that whatever 'culture' means, it is not this imposition from above of knowledge of the various arts or modern European civilisation. In fact a 'culture' probably adds up to something very like a whole way of life (with everything which appertains to that way of life included) of any people, or more correctly of any ethnic group. The results of this 'Education for Leisure' appear to be of a varying nature; at worst they give us for example the chimney sweep, with less than no interest in his job, hastening through it by day, doing it not at all well, and going home in the evening and on to the queue for the 'prom', there to indulge in the hero worship of some musical artist, with little appreciation of that artist's undoubted talents, and possibly with none at all of the concerto he is playing (which will probably be one that he has listened to many times before, as this method produces no taste for anything new to him, let alone for any contemporary music).

The whole evening will come to an end with an amount of applause that verges on something like a sort of mob frenzy, an insistence that the now tired artist shall play again and again to this over-zealous but probably at heart non-appreciative audience; this sort of result in no way helps to keep alive the vigorous end of this 'culture', the contemporary musician, or his works. But that is not to say that all this has no value at all; it obviously does do something towards making its adherents more appreciative of things well outside their daily routine; we might get the chimney sweep who came home and learnt to play the violin in his leisure time; we might even get one whose actual work, (because of the pleasure he was getting from his new hobby) realises the importance of chimney sweeping and will take an interest or even a delight in doing the job well. And this last point is precisely what an industrial democracy badly needs; and that system of education which will produce such a citizen for us, is the system we must institute and carry out. Such a system will depend in the first place upon the values on which it is based, and the values in life which it most treasures. These are rather difficult to sum up for us in a few words, but can we say something like:

"A belief in the immense innate possibilities of every individual person; a belief in his dignity as a human being; and a belief as far as is consistent with the general good of the community in which he lives, he shall be given every opportunity to develop his powers, spiritual, mental and physical, and live a free and full life".

This may seem to be a series of rather dull platitudes; but because a thing has been said before does not mean that repetition of it is unnecessary; on the contrary, we must sometimes re-examine basic beliefs in the light of the changing conditions of our society.

The above then is our goal in education 'Opportunity to live a free and full life' sums up our aim; and 'human dignity' are our key words, a human dignity which is implied in the 'good-neighbourliness' so essential to a people who live as we do, 50,000,000, on a not very large island.

The full title of this piece of research 'We are all Greeks – values in our education system' may seem not a little presumptuous; if taken literally, it is obviously untrue; if, as is more likely, taken to mean in this context, that all our children should be given the old academic and 'grammar school' classical education, it is obviously ludicrous, and would take little refuting; but I was not intending to offer an untruth, not trying to be ludicrous; rather I was trying to sum up in one phrase what appears to me to be most needed in a general way in education. 'Human dignity' were to be our key words; and the Greeks, of all the peoples the world has known were for 'Humanity'. 'Humanity' combines in a word 'mankind' and his achievement through the ages is something very near to what we need; so I made use of this quotation from a particular context to illustrate my general point. For just what did Shelley mean when he wrote in the preface in his drama 'Hellas'?

'We are all Greeks. Our laws, our literature, our religion, our arts, have their root in Greece. But for Greece – Rome, the instructor, the conqueror, or the metropolis, of our ancestors, would have spread no illumination with her arms, and we might still have been savages and idolaters; or what is worse, might have arrived at such a stagnant and miserablestate of social institutions as China and Japan posses.

The human form and the human mind attained to perfection in Greece which has impressed its image on those faultless productions whose very fragments are the despair of modern art; and has propagated impulses which cannot cease, through a thousand channels of manifest or imperceptible operation, to ennoble and delight mankind until the extinction ofthe race'. P.B.Shelley, Preface to Hellas, a lyrical drama, 1821.The poet is giving his reasons for writing a dramatic poem, based on Greek form, (The Persae of Aeschyius is actually his model, for Shelley saw a close resemblance between the Persian and Turkish invasions), about the liberation of Greece from Turkish rule-a war which seems to us a little remote and of infinitesimal importance. Furthermore even this general preface would seem to be a reflection of Shelley's youthful idealism and not very accurate thinking. Nevertheless to me he seems to have touched on a profound truth which concerns our contemporaries in general and educationists in particular.

A.N.Whitehead in 'The Adventures of Ideas' (published in 1948) has the following remark –'The Greeks and the Romans at their best period have been taken as the standard of civilisation.We have aimed at reproducing the excellences of these societies – preferably the society of Athens in its prime.These standards have served the Western races well. But the procedure has its disadvantages. It is backward looking, and it is limited to one type of social excellence. Today the world is passing into a new stage of its existence..,The particular example of an ancient society sets too static an ideal, and neglects the whole range of opportunity...

Also I suggest that the Greeks themselves were not backward looking, nor static. Compared to their neighbours, they were singularly unhistorical. They were speculative, adventurous, eager for novelty. The most un–Greek thing that we can do is to copy the Greeks. For emphatically they were not copyists.'

If we place alongside this particular quotation, Whitehead's general attitude to the Greek achievement, roughly that we owe both all our methods of thought, and very much of what we think about, to it, and try to make a synthesis of the two, we shall have achieved for ourselves the sort of attitude to the Greeks we want, and the sort of effect that we need them to have on us and on our education at which I am aiming here.

It may seem curious, but it is not to be denied that it would seem to have been the teachers of Classics who have been most 'un-Greek'; for they tried to copy in their educational curricula, in the name of Greece, what they thought to be the most valuable lesson to be learned from it - discipline – the discipline of formal learning, of 'grammar', and they made the 'grammar schools' for their purpose; in these they concentrated on Latin as the prime necessity in the education of any gentleman. They carried out a policy in complete disregard of the major Greek virtues 'nothing too much' and of 'moderation 'or 'temperance'. They were, and are, anything but forward looking, and their general complete insistence on hanging on, as much as they could, wherever they could, as long as they could, to their grasp of the grammar school curriculum brought the Classics as a whole into disrepute from which it is still suffering today. For they were naturally thought to be representative of all classically trained persons, and therefore it was thought the Classics must of their nature be against progress, and forever going to hold up, by their presence, scientific studies. A moment's thought will make it quite apparent that this most un-Greek thing of all… 'They were speculative, eager for novelty' says Whitehead. It is often the case that those who plead and act most virulently for a cause, themselves do it most harm, and here we have a very extreme case of the truth of this saying; one cannot, I find, so much as mention Classics in any general company, particularly scientific, without bringing down upon one's comparatively innocent head a storm of abuse, with mutterings about reactionary, and stick in the mud, and so on; and no amount of explaining ever seems to convince the assembled company that one is really suggesting something quite progressive.

It is still true, I think that Latin, even now a major subject (comprising a third of those taking the General Schools Certificate) on the curriculum is taught in most schools as a 'dead' language; that is to say one never ceases to be aware that it is the language of a civilisation long since passed away. This both because of the methods of teaching it, still predominately what they were fifty years ago, and because Latin was not the language of a people of great intellectual gifts, and did not, I think, produce a literature of the most inspiring kind nor of the highest rank, not compared at any rate with Greek, or English, or indeed of some other modern European languages; this last seems to be a truth that never gets said and needs to be.

Greek always seemed to me to be the more attractive even when taught by the same old academic methods as Latin; and this I take to be a proof of its continuing 'life' as a language. The arguments in favour of keeping Latin, and not replacing it by Greek (where there is room, as on most grammar school curricula, for only one of the two languages), are nearly all founded on our debt to the Roman Empire, i.e. its helping to spread Christianity, its having made Western Europe 'Romance' and so on, arguments which might indeed be used in other ways about Greek too; but they seem to me to be unsound arguments. For we do not learn languages in order to appreciate the empires, or the various

56

influences of those empires, of the peoples who speak them; nor do we learn them for aid with our own or any other language, nor indeed for any of the rest of the very curious and very indirect motives which the defenders of Latin tend to adduce. We do not want to copy the Greeks; still less do we want to copy the Romans, (indeed are we not one up on the latter, for have we not discovered a secret about the long life of empires which they never thought of during their five hundred years of rule, the secret of associating ones former colonies with one as independent nations?) We study the humanities in order to profit by the best of what humanity has written, composed, painted, and, in fact, done; to learn from its mistakes, but above all to benefit from its discovered beauties; we are presented with an immense amount of things to choose from, and we must pick our material with care, and see that we do not waste our time on any of the lesser material; and I am certainly going to suggest that, if we've only time to learn one of the classical languages, as a language, we should choose Greek; and even more, if we've only time to do one in translation, we should make the same choice. However, in order that I might not seem to be unfair to Latin, I have to admit that so esteemed authority as T.S.Eliot has these words in his essay "What is a Classic?" After saying "…The bloodstream of European literature is Latin and Greek – not as two systems of circulation, but one, for it is through Rome that our parentage in Greece must be traced" he goes on "No modern language can hope to produce a classic, in the sense in which I have called Virgil a classic. Our classic, the classic of all Europe is Virgil".

Of course we have to remember that he was addressing the Virgil Society; in any case I do not think even the above, if true, constitutes a reason in itself for learning Latin rather than Greek.

"We shall not cease from exploration
And the end of all our exploring
Will be to arrive where we started
And know the place for the first time".

writes Eliot in 'Four Quartets – Little Gidding'. Can we say that the Greeks are where we started as a civilisation, and that, if we do keep on 'exploring' in Eliot's sense, we shall 'know' them for the first time? At any rate we should keep on trying.

Our educational system consists in the main of four types of school; apart from the many part-time post secondary colleges, institutes, and universities. These are the primary and the three sorts of secondary school. Children as young as five can be introduced to the idea of 'humanity' and certainly by the top of primary school children can be introduced to the Greek myths and some of the many exciting moments in Greek history. The story of all these achievements so long ago and in the dawn of the world, so comparatively early in the history of our civilisation cannot fail to interest them if presented with the right sort of zest.

The secondary technical school does not in the nature of the establishment teach humanities but many technical schools have flourishing drama clubs at the top end of the school; where often a high standard of dramatic production takes place in an attempt to offset the complete technical bias which is very necessary within the school.

The remaining two schools are the secondary moderns and the grammar schools, the one with little in the way of tradition to guide it and with some eighty-five per cent of children over eleven in attendance, the other encumbered by a still strong though dying Latin tradition which has dictated a tendency towards water tightness in the various subjects of the curriculum, allowing little in the way of liaison, and not having heard of the humanities as such. The eighty-five per cent who go to the secondary moderns are obviously going to be the main body of people who will do the jobs we envisaged earlier; they are the heart of the problem; they are often going to do boring and menial work, and we are only just getting round to deciding what we want to do with them in school to prepare them for that work; but even now there seems to have been little real attempt to think out completely a new four year educational course which will produce our much desired intelligent citizen. This is undoubtedly the crux of the whole matter; solve this, the problem of the secondary modern, and we are nearly there.

Now it is straight away obvious that there is no one solution to cover every such school; nor do we want anything so hard and fast. These schools, it is true, should often be a reflection to some extent of local needs and industries, particularly in the country. But in London and the larger towns this scarcely applies, and apart from the little technical work that is done, and the considerable part to be played by physical education, there is nothing that is at all settled about the curriculum. We have, in fact, one half or more of the week to fill. In the grammar school, this is easily settled by splitting it up into four or five main subjects of five or six periods each, French, Latin, History, English, Mathematics and Science or another language. This is not completely desirable for the secondary modern school since it is not a very practical curriculum.

I suggest that the inclusion of Greek Myths, Greek Gods, the story of Troy, elementary history to 500 BC and achievements of the Greeks such as the marathon, democracy etc could be introduced to secondary modern children over their four years in school and could be fitted into lessons in Geography, History and English, supplementing and filling in the background of these humanities, with something about the achievement of the Greeks. It should always be kept in the child's mind that there was a world, a very civilised world before 1945, before 1900, before 1600 or even 1066, in fact before Christ himself, the founder of the religion in which most of them are being brought up during this time. Secondary modern school children leave at the present time at the age of fifteen, and by including some or all of the above mentioned curriculum ideas, one hopes to have stimulated some sort of interest in the ancient world, and its importance to us. Those who go on to part time education (an ever increasing number) could and should be enabled to do something further at the evening technical institutes.

The grammar schools and independent schools have a tradition of their own with which one may or may not disagree. The grammar schools, as we have seen, cannot supply to the community a large proportion numerically, at any rate relative to the secondary moderns; but they do supply many of our leaders. By that I mean all those who administrate the laws at every level, who teach and preach, and judge and heal, and import, and export, and in fact do all the manner of things that need to be done in order to keep the modern nation state on a reasonably even keel. So it would appear even more important that they should have some clear idea of where we are going, and why we want to go there; they must be able to appreciate what we owe to this civilisation and that, and whether we want to go on owing it; above all at the moment, they want to know whether there is a thing called 'democracy', and what it is if there is.

In these schools, Classics have a more difficult problem, if only because they are established; and the established is always hard to move; Latin as a language is predominant, and as I have already suggested, where both are impossible (as in most grammar schools) Greek is preferable in many ways; and where both are possible, Greek should be taught first, as chronology alone would seem to indicate. In fact something like a complete reversal of the present position, with Greek being taken by the A stream and some of the B throughout the school (but never compulsory for all for two years as Latin often is now, as this seems to me to be bad for children, teachers, and the general good health of Classical studies), and Latin for the very few who now learn Greek, or who show special aptitude or interest in it, or are very good at their Greek: or we might try Greek in the A stream and Latin in the B. An experiment of this more general sort would seem to be very well worth carrying out, both for its intrinsic effect, its effect on the general reputation of the Classics, and not least for what may be a very sound effect on the teaching of English. After all nearly all English teachers grumble at one time or another now about the effect of Latin grammar in particular on English lessons and on their children's attitude; but they are not so sure they would like to dispense with the Classics altogether. Would my suggestions be a possible solution of this dilemma?

The effect of the presence of Greek in the curriculum is of some importance, as one does find a rather higher standard generally in those schools where its influence is felt. For if children know if some of their friends are learning a language, they will not find it nearly so strange a phenomenon as those do to whom it is merely a name; further the presence on the staff of someone with a knowledge of Greek, and actually engaged in teaching it, is influential in helping to make the school's life as catholic as possible; in fact one can go as far as to say that all English teachers should attain a knowledge of the Greek alphabet, and even more important, not so much a knowledge, as an appreciation of the Greek achievement; it certainly seems to me to be more to the point for a Humanities teacher than Anglo-Saxon, or old English (I mean pre-Chaucerian), or Beowulf, or any of the more dubious and in many cases compulsory subjects in the present English Honours courses.

This gives you a brief idea of what 'We are all Greeks' might mean to the practice of our education; some of the points mentioned may seem a little far fetched; maybe they are. But it is an idea that I am looking for, the idea of 'Humanity's Adventures in Beauty', for only by studying the beautiful, can we hope to make our own civilisation attain it. I have tried to show that Humanity first found that 'real beauty' in Greece, and that it has scarcely exceeded it since. Two quotations may serve to show something of what I mean; they are, so to speak, on both sides of the main achievement – that of Athens in the Fifth Century – the first a fragment of Sappho from the seventh century BC. (Fragment 4, translated by H. de Vere Stacpoole)

'To Mnasadica who left us to live in Sardis but who
has not forgotten old days and the songs of Atthis'
'Far across the sundering sea
Where in Sardis night is falling,
In her beauty standeth she
Clear across the darkness calling 'Attis'.
Winds of night that blow
Bring no message, waves that fold us
Bear no whisper – yet we know
For the listening night has told us'.

Looking forward, as it were by magic insight to the miracle; and the second from Bion,

(Fragment translated by Andrew Lang), in the second century B.C.

'The wall of Moschus on the mountains crying
    The Muses heard, and loved it long ago;
They heard the hollows of the hills replying,
    They heard the weeping water's overflow
They winged the sacred strain – the song undying,
    The song that all about the world must go –
Where poets for a poet dead are sighing,
    The minstrels for a minstrel friend laid low.
And dirge to dirge that answers, and the weeping
    For Adonais by the summer sea;
The plaints for Lycidas and Thyrsis (sleeping
    Far from the 'forest ground called Thessaly');
These hold thy memory, Bion, in their keeping,
    And are but echoes of the moan for thee.'

(Both these lyrics serve to illustrate incidentally in a small way the possibilities of Greek in translation).

And now to a curious English instance of this 'idea'; Kathleen Freeman prefaces her anthology 'The Greek Way' with the following poem of Robert Browning –

    "By the Fireside"

How well I know what I mean to do
    When the long dark autumn evenings come,
And where, my soul is thy pleasant hue?
    With the music of all thy voices dumb
In life's November too.

I shall be found by the fire, I suppose
    O'er a great wise book as beseemeth age,
While the shutters flap as the cross-wind blows,
    And I turn the page, and I turn the page,
Not verse now, only prose;

Till the young ones whisper, finger on lip,
    "There he is at it, deep in Greek;
Now, then, or never, out we slip
    To cut from the hazels by the creek
A main mast for our ship".

I shall be at indeed, my friends;
    Greek puts already on either side
Such a branch work forth as soon extends
    To a vista opening far and wide,
And I pass out where it ends.'

It seems more appropriate to an end than a beginning; for I want to open the 'vista' at school, and hope the pupil will really 'pass out where it ends'.

We in the West, I said earlier, are at bay, because we are no longer sure of our values; and I have tried to suggest that by looking again at Greece, we shall find out something about values which may help solve our main problem. It will obviously not provide a universal panacea for all our troubles, but it may help. To the Greeks themselves we can address the epigram of their greatest son, Plato – translated by Shelley

'Thou wert the morning star among the living
    Ere thy fair light had fled;-
Now, having died, thou art as Hesperus giving
    New splendour to the dead.'

and decide, not by any means to copy them, but to attempt to bring to life again their achievement in our own time. Now let us hear a Modern Greek on these people, his forbears:

'Everything on which civilisation lives to this day may be said, therefore, to have been potentially implied in the intellectual, aesthetic, moral and social achievements of Athens in the fifth century B.C. That is the Greek miracle.' This may seem a large claim made in understandable pride by a Modern Greek, but even a cursory reading of one book like 'Adventures in Ideas' illustrates the truth of it.

By all these quotations, I have tried to show that many different sorts of men whose judgement we can respect, including the Greeks themselves, think and feel something along the lines on which I have written, and that I am by no means alone in my plea, and I have already shown, that it is a possible and a practical one. I end with a further quotation from T.S. Eliot's 'Little Gidding' which I feel seems to fit exactly into what I am trying to say, the periphrasis in particular, and into the general pattern of the Greek idea.

'What we call the beginning is often the end
And to make an end is to make a beginning.
The end is where we start from. And every phrase
And sentence that is right (where every word is at home

Taking its place to support the others,
The word neither diffident nor ostentatious,
An easy commerce of the old and new,
The common word exact without vulgarity,
The formal word precise but not pedantic,
The complete consort dancing together)
Every phrase and every sentence is an end and a beginning,
Every poem an epitaph. And any action
Is a step to the block, to the fire, down the sea's throat
Or to an illegible stone; and that is where we start.
We die with the dying:
See they return, and bring us with them.
The moment of the rose and the moment of the yew-tree
Are of equal duration.
A people without history
Is not redeemed from time, for history is a pattern
Of timeless moments. So, while the light fails
On a winter's afternoon, in a secluded chapel
History is now and England.'

As deputy headmaster, headmaster or as College Principal, Philip never forgot these early days of his teaching career and where and when possible would implement the Greek 'idea' into the timetable. Ten years after researching 'We are all Greeks' in 1958 whilst timetabling for Ounsdale Comprehensive he included humanities for what would have been the secondary modern children and the curriculum they followed was similar to these early thoughts. He also introduced Greek as the first subject, and Latin as the second, to the more able children who would have gone to a grammar school.

Whilst at London University Institute of Education Philip wrote many poems, here are two of them.

'Je vais dormir'

Je vais dormir we heard
From the voice of our singing bird.
Disembodied – Promethean – a musical shuttle
An Ariel without wings but more than subtle;
The words of her danced in the air,
And I was so glad to be there.
This Joy sent her gleaming knife

And awoke a new life.
As she went up the stair
"Pour dormir, a sa chambre", so rare
A note ebbed over the people
That all heard the peel of this church steeple,
"Clang clang" went the bell
And all men were well
Save me, for I alone heard
"Je vais dormir" from my singing bird.'

'Death of a daughter'

She died in the morning of her life;
Her sun set almost before the East had borne it,
And so she lived, no man's wife
Save death's; but perhaps she did sit
On the right hand? She left a mother
Not unhappy, but wholly broken,
For, though there was another,
Yet here was all her token
Of self-denial, and all joy.
There was a war which passed her by
As swallows pass a bouy,
Having greater objects to fly
Towards over the seas. She stayed with life,
The mother, why or how she never knew,
Putting off the glad day when the strife
Should show 'finis', and the promised rendezvous
Should come in that dream republic
where mothers and daughters again clasp
Hands after long parting, a land where the tick
Of earth's clocks no more intrudes its rasp,
And the sands of time are Saharas, without end:
So often the mother arrives first,
But here it is the daughter they send
To prepare the way, and leave behind a thirst
For death to a parent bereft
Of her only love, sacrificed, like Iphigenia,
To glut by this horrible theft
(In London, spelled "Aulis") something which is higher.

In the Institute of Education classical department production of Euripides 'The Alcestis', which was based on a translation by Gilbert Murray, Philip played 'Death', was the 'Chorus Leader' and helped with the production back stage. He already enjoyed acting and producing and this was the beginning of a long interest in amateur dramatics. Towards the end of the second term Philip and other Teaching Diploma students began applying for teaching posts. Philip's Tutor (A.V.P. Elliott) at the Institute of Education wrote that 'Mr. Vennis is a man of many interests and considerable ability. He is pleasant and co-operative, and has made the most of his opportunities at the Institute, he has a keen and critical mind and a real appreciation of the realities of the work he has chosen. Having taken Classics as well as English at Cambridge, he is particularly interested in the relationship between these two subjects, and has undertaken several teaching experiments in this field. He controls classes well, although he is no martinet; and his relationships with his pupils are easy and friendly. His work is scholarly and thorough and he can get his own enthusiasm across to his classes. He has plenty of energy and has taken a big part in the out of class activities of the Institute, his chief interest of this kind being Drama and Music. He has also done some voluntary work in a Working Men's Institute. He is an exceptionally promising and gifted student, who has a great deal to contribute to the school he serves'. Philip was appointed second classics master at East Ham Grammar School for Boys in July 1949.

CHAPTER 5

East Ham Grammar School for Boys
East Ham, a London Borough

'The most important thing in all this questioning and uncertainty in post war Britain, is to concentrate on the little bit of the world in which one functions and which might conceivably affect the discernible area around one. This is itself not easy in an industrial and indistinct suburb of London, which feels the centripetal of pull of the metropolis in both work and play.' (P.H.V. 1958)

East Ham is about seven miles east of London; today it is part of the Borough of Newham and is principally a dormitory suburb of houses built between 1890 and 1910. The ancient parish of East Ham was rural until about 1850. East Ham grew up around the village church and became a Municipal Borough in 1904 and a County Borough in 1915. In 1965 the County Borough became part of Newham. Although the merger took place many years ago the local people still hold the name East Ham in their memories.

In the middle of the nineteenth century East Ham began to lose its rural character as industrialisation was beginning to be established. Urban development began in 1870 and the transformation of the area was completed with the Albert Dock opening in 1880. Houses built in this era were crowded into long terraces to house families of dock workers and sailors. Some of these houses were later demolished to make way for the building of the King George V Dock, which was built between 1912 and 1921. This area was heavily bombed during the Second World War, and since the war much redevelopment has taken place. In 1891 East Ham was a town of 32,713, and in the following ten years it grew faster than any other place of its size in England to 96,018 in 1901 and by 1921, to 143,246. At the beginning of the twentieth century the population of outer London was just under two million, with the greatest number of people in the east. East London in the twenties saw this huge growth in the population as the London County Council built huge estates in Beacontree and Dagenham, giving the working class Londoners a chance to own a house with electricity and a garden. East Ham contained rows upon rows of red brick terraces housing the lower middle class and skilled working class families. The population decreased after the thirties, partly due to the Second World War bombing; and so subsequently when Philip was there in 1951 the population stood at 120,836.

After the devastation of the bombing in the Blitz in the East End, which was the most heavily bombed district after the City of London, in some areas about one third of the housing was lost. East Ham was severely bombed; this was inevitable given that much of the dockland was within its boundary. Eighty-five per cent of houses were destroyed in the southern part of the docks. Rebuilding was undertaken quickly and cheaply and in twenty five years the architectural look of the borough had changed drastically. Repairs to housing began despite the continuing V1 and V2 bomb attacks and many houses in London had been repaired sufficiently for the inhabitants to move back to their homes by March 1945. By 1947, most of the damaged houses were once again habitable and new homes began to be built in 1948. Immediately following the war, despite the quick repair and rebuilding of houses, London was not a pleasant place to live, the Blitz had made open landscapes and during most of Philip's time at East Ham London remained broken, uncolourful and tired and in many ways still Victorian.

East Ham was to see changes in the demography of its area in the early fifties. In 1951 only one in twenty Londoners had been born outside Britain. In the following years an influx of people from ethnic minority backgrounds was to take place. Since the War many Commonwealth immigrants from India and Pakistan have settled in East Ham. With all these changes East Ham still remained an East End community. East Ham's inhabitants' spirit was tested post war, when so many of their homes lay in rubble, and the high rise flats being built making any type of community difficult to sustain, they overcame this with dogged determination. Philip arrived in East Ham midst all the war devastation and the post war optimism.

A history of East Ham Boys' Grammar School 1905 to 1949

"The English Local Education grammar school post-war was a marvellous place to be as boy and man – and East Ham Grammar School was one of the best of these. When you hear from old boys and learn what they have become; how they have entered and risen in so many professions or risen high in so many places one is continually reminded of the lifting of boys' horizons. The English Boys' Grammar Schools gave chances to boys from poor homes, from families who had not themselves been at a grammar school and to many boys in the Sixth Form. It proved excellent in every way – on the field, on the stage, in music, in uniform, at Speech Day, and, of course, in academic work." (P.H.V. 1955)

Dr. Whiteley who was headmaster of East Ham Grammar School for Boys from 1944 to 1970 (and was the driving force behind the development and expansion of the school in the post-war years), wrote in the Jubilee edition of The Esthameian in 1955 an article for those interested in the development of grammar schools and in East Ham Grammar School in particular. In the article he begins by stating that 'The modern enquirer who is interested in the story of the development of our grammar schools will very quickly find that a hundred years ago there were few grammar schools in the country and that the majority of these, founded in the sixteenth century, were still being managed by the terms of the trust deeds as fixed by their pious founders. The latter were interested in the encouragement of sound learning which in their day and for the next two hundred years meant the study of Latin and Greek, and in the development of true religion. Among such terms, therefore, we find it laid down that the school must be conducted by "one schoolmaster and one usher" or that Greek, Latin and Hebrew were to be the sole subjects of instruction, a diet which we should consider rather ascetic and narrow for the farmers' sons who must have formed the large part of the scholars in many schools, situated as they were in rural areas or small country towns. The State had no supervisory rights, these being entirely in the hands of the Governors, who sometimes forgot that the school existed, sometimes misappropriated the funds, and sometimes were the helpless spectators of incompetent or unscrupulous headmasters. For example, in one grammar school a headmaster had been in charge for thirty years and there had not been a single pupil!

There were, of course, a few good schools and others which at this time were beginning to be influenced by the work of Thomas Arnold of Rugby. On the whole, however, in 1855 the schools were out of touch with the swiftly changing conditions of the century and unable to meet the demand that the rapid increase in the middle classes were about to make upon them.'

Dr. Whiteley continues by stating that 'most of the abuses to which reference had been made were swept away by an important Act, The Endowed Schools Act of 1869. This was only a beginning, for secondary education was still for many years to remain the privilege of the few, either of those who were fortunate enough to live in a town with an Endowed Grammar School and who could secure entry either by payment of fees or by securing a foundation scholarship, or of those whose parents could afford to send their children to the expensive boarding schools, whose numbers increased from seven to twenty in the fifties and sixties of the nineteenth century. All of these schools, however, could do but little to cope with the increasing population, the national birth rate had never been so high as in the period 1860 to 1880, and in any case their fees were well beyond the means of middle and working class parents. There was no State or Local aid which would help the able but poor boy to climb from his National or Board School to the Universities of Oxford or Cambridge. The great Thomas Huxley had spoken with much eloquence of the educational ladder of his day, but on it could climb only the very few who might obtain a foundation scholarship to their local Grammar School and then the necessary tuition to qualify for an Entrance Scholarship or Exhibition in Classics or Mathematics to the Universities. In other words, we are still a long way from 1955, and the educational reformers had to wait impatiently until 1895, when the Bryce Commission reviewed secondary education in this country and made recommendations which were embodied in the great Education Act of 1902. Now the most important item was that which encouraged Local Authorities to build their own secondary (i.e. grammar) schools. In this way our School, one of the first of its kind was established in January 1905 as East Ham Technical College, which was a combination of a boys' and girls' secondary school and classes for evening students – an arrangement which continued until 1932.

In 1907, a free place system was introduced which made it compulsory for grant aided Secondary Schools like ours to award twenty-five per cent of their school places free of cost to children from the elementary schools. At last, the educational ladder was being widened, especially as there had been a big increase in the number of Universities and University Colleges over the last sixty years. It is interesting and thrilling to note that within ten years of the passing of the Balfour Act of 1902 the County and County Borough Council, had founded 330 new secondary schools and had taken over 53 existing ones. The next advance was made in 1918, when the Fisher Act gave great stimulus to the new secondary school, by making financial grants, which enabled them to develop advanced courses in their Sixth forms.

By 1925, the new secondary schools, now all called grammar, had won a well- deserved reputation not only in their own areas but in the country as a whole. Recruited largely from the ablest boys and girls of their district, and staffed by loyal and enthusiastic teachers, they soon showed that they were capable of competing in the fullest sense with the boarding schools and older grammar schools, for they had taken over their long tradition, modified it in the light of modern needs and developments and emphasised the best aspects of our English school life, accurate and sound scholarship, the training of character, and the importance of service in a vigorous and healthy school life. Moreover, the increasing generosity of Local Authorities and the development of Sixth form work slowly enabled gifted, though poor, children to make their way to University and thence to prominent positions in our national life. But perhaps the clearest evidence of the success of the new grammar schools is to be found in the magnificent part played by the Old Boys and Girls in the war effort of 1939-45. In fact, it has been stated by several of those in authority that the expansion of our armed forces could not have been made, had not the grammar schools done such a fine job in the period between the two wars.

But even now our story is not yet complete. As many of the parents of our boys know from experience, even in the thirties, many able children were unable to find admission into a grammar school, either because there were not sufficient places or because their parents could not afford the fees, modest though they were. Again, economic pressure prevented some pupils from completing the course or from going as far academically as they were able. This was especially true for the abler pupil, who still found it difficult to have a University education if his parents could not afford to maintain him. Scholarships were available, but not in sufficient numbers, and competition for the monies available was fierce. In any case, a student who wished to be financially independent of his parents had to secure two, and sometimes three, awards, if he wished to go to Oxford or Cambridge.

Thus in 1944, another Education Act attempted, amongst many other aims, to ensure that entry to a State grammar school should be determined by a pupil's suitability rather, than by his parents' ability to pay fees, and that every pupil who secured entry to a University should receive adequate financial help either from the Local Authority or from the State. Hence fees in State grammar schools were abolished, and thousands of pounds have been spent in helping University students.

Several important results followed, many State grammar schools found that they were receiving a far greater proportion of working class children as against the children of parents who had themselves received a grammar school education and therefore valued it and its traditions for its own sake. It is not surprising, therefore, that during the last ten years (1945-55) some schools failed to win over their new recruits, many of whom soon lose interest and leave at the earliest opportunity at fifteen. On the other hand the generous financial awards given by the Local Authority at eighteen plus for University entrance have encouraged a big expansion in the Sixth Form, and some of the best work in our grammar schools has been done at this level during the last ten years, although this has been a period when there has been much disaffection among the teaching staff as a result of the 1944 Education Act, especially their salary scale. This still does not sufficiently recognise the importance of the Sixth form Master or Mistress, just when the demands of industry and Government Research have almost, but not quite, removed Scientists and Mathematicians from the teaching profession.

And yet, in spite of many difficulties, our School has built up a fine record over the last ten years in the number of boys it has sent on to the Universities – an achievement which succeeding generations may find it difficult to surpass. It can only be hoped that the East Ham boys of the next fifty years will be inspired by the example of those who have gone before them, and, now that the educational facilities are so much easier than in Huxley's time, that educational ladder has become practically a moving staircase, and they will not be lacking in those qualities of character which many of their predecessors have shown in a much more difficult world.

Today the Sixth former has to assume the responsibility of National Service either before he enters his University or begins his career. I am glad to say that this experience, unpopular with some but on the whole cheerfully accepted by most, is generally recognised as giving opportunities, of developing wider contacts and a broader outlook, both which help a young man in achieving a well- balanced maturity. It has been noted that practically all boys benefit from their two years' National Service, although the time may seem a sorry interruption at a critical point in their careers.

Today, however, in the eyes of the general public, the prestige of the grammar school is higher than it has ever been before, and it is to the grammar school that all sections look to provide the boys and girls who seem to be wanted in ever increasing numbers, not only by the professions, but also by the great commercial and industrial concerns, the banks, the Civil Service and the Armed Forces; all of whom seem now to be in cut- throat competition for our boys of seventeen and eighteen.'

Dr. Whiteley concludes his article about grammar school education by saying that 'The curriculum and aims of a grammar school make exacting demands on its pupils. The average pupil will have to face much hard work and mental effort and realise that his character is bred in the way he faces up to his

71

difficulties. If he is to be successful, he must have not only intelligence but also important qualities of character, such as persistence and the willingness to accept grammar school standards, and that, too, in an age when there are more distractions both in and out of the home than ever before. The modern boy has not only to resist the attractions of the wireless and the television, but also the pull of the youth club and, perhaps, the more insidious temptations of the street. He must also have behind him parents who are ready and willing to support the school in encouraging the conscientious performance of homework and his remaining at school until the school course is complete, often in spite of an easy labour market. Pupils must in their own hearts be ready to accept, first the grammar school ethos of hard work, loyalty and *"esprit de corps"* and, secondly, the full responsibilities of school membership which emphasize service to an ideal which is greater than the individual whether it is represented in the Form, the House or the School.'

This school that Dr. Whiteley was rightly proud of began, as he said, as East Ham Technical College and Secondary School for boys and girls and was officially opened in March 1905. The Prince and Princess of Wales, later to become George V and Queen Mary, opened the building which was to take account of the 'phenomenal development of the Borough' which His Worship the Mayor (Alderman J.H. Bethell) referred to in his welcoming of the Royal visitors. He stated that the 'country lanes of ten years ago' and the now jump in population from 6,000 to 115,000 necessitated the building of the College for the provision of Higher Education. This population explosion in the last years of the nineteenth century was due to the flourishing of the docks and people moving out from Hackney, Poplar and Bow. The Balfour Education Act of 1902 required Local Education Authorities to be responsible for providing Secondary Education. East Ham became a Borough in 1904 with the Town Hall being built next to the new College, which was to provide under one roof and one Principal a Grammar School for Boys and Girls (who were not taught together) and an evening technical College. The school already had enrolled 250 boys and girls in January 1905. It was not until 1932 that the three provisions of education were separated when a Girl's Grammar School was built in Plashet Grove. The Boy's Grammar School remained in the 1905 building until 1952. Such was the beginning of East Ham Grammar School, known locally as the 'Tech' (as it was housed in the Technical College in Barking Road and provided both day and evening classes).

In the first years of the Technical College a narrow but excellent education was provided for the young men and women of East Ham. B.G. Payton who was at the Technical College from 1905 to 1909, recalls 'with gratitude to the Tech', where we learned that hard work was the sure way to happiness and success'. He goes on to say that '1903 was an outstanding year for East Ham. The Town Hall was opened and the education committee pushed forward its plans permitted by the 1902 Education Act'. The School was not really ready for occupation when it was officially opened. Mr. Payton recalled he 'was ushered into the main hall. This was very decorative, with large cherubs above the doors, heavily panelled walls and stained- glass lights above in the roof. It was also illuminated by the 'newish' electric light. What a difference there was between this hall and the rooms of the old 'barrack' school, from which I had come! There we had been used to large rooms for sixty or more children with six 'bat wing' gas burners providing very inadequate light during the dark days. The new school was also fitted with a novel system of heating by in-blown hot air apertures in the walls. But, alas, it failed so often to supply anything but air colder than that already in the room! The Principal/headmaster, Mr. W.H. Barker, was a dignified and imposing figure who remained Principal of the dual establishment form 1914 to 1932. He built up from the small school of 1905 a very progressive institute, giving excellent day and evening service to the Borough'. A Chemistry Master A.E. Dunston (1905 to 1915) reinforces B.G. Payton's view of the Principal by saying 'There can be no doubt that the School was fortunate in its Head. Mr. Barker was a fine figure of a man – tall and well-proportioned. He was the picture of dignity, and in the City of London would easily have passed for a prosperous stockbroker. It is not unlikely that East Ham made a singularly happy choice in him. He had been trained at Owen's College, Manchester, and graduated at London.' Although the Technical College was for boys and girls the 'mixing 'was very much controlled, until finally the girls moved to Plashet Grove. Examination results from School Certificate and Matriculation Examinations were very good and gave large numbers of pupils the entry to positions in banks, local government, the civil service, the commerce of the City of London and eventually entry into various professions.

W.E. Huggett was at the school (1916 to 1920) during the First World War, and he is able to recall some of the war years of his education. He had joined the Cadet Corps and late in 1917 he experienced the big daylight raid on London, whilst he was drilling on the old playing fields at Becton. He says 'The raid (which was a new experience for London in those days) grew in fury, while in the next field there was an anti-aircraft gun which blasted forth, making considerably more row than the raiders and probably scared us all rather than the enemy! Armistice Day 1918 stands out in my memory for the excitement, the bonfires and the processions.'

In 1918, after World War One the 1905 secondary schools were encouraged to educate their ablest pupils until eighteen and give them the opportunity to sit the Higher School Certificate – an important passport to University and other professions. During the First and Second World Wars there was a tremendous expansion of secondary education, although it was still confined to a small percentage of the school population, the majority of children leaving at thirteen and later at fourteen from the old Standard VII in the elementary school. This period could be considered the heyday of the secondary school as more and more were built by Local Authorities, more boys and girls stayed on until eighteen plus and the success of the schools increased their prestige and enabled them to claim some parity with the public schools in academic results and in their sporting and cultural life. Out of school activities such as drama, sport, music, debate and clubs flourished, adding a sense of pride to the schools. Old pupil societies were established and a few newly established secondary schools (most now called grammar schools) competed successfully for Open Scholarships at Oxford and Cambridge.

School life was interrupted at the newly named Grammar School for Boys by the Second World War. The Boys' Grammar School was inspected by His Majesty's Inspectors in May 1939 and they commented favourably on academic standards but critically on the buildings. They stated 'The school is doing notably good work in many directions under adverse circumstances. The boys are keen and intelligent and work hard…It would be difficult to find such totally unsatisfactory premises in any maintained secondary school; rebuilding on a more suitable site as soon as circumstances permit is strongly recommended.' There was no hall, the gymnasium had little and poor apparatus, specialist facilities were limited and a playing field some distance away was used for games once a fortnight. Education went on throughout the summer term of 1939 with the exception of a few rehearsals for 'operation evacuation', but by St. Bartholomew's Day radio instructions recalled staff and pupils to await an order to leave London for the 'reception areas'. Parents were given printed instructions (evacuation was voluntary); identification tags were fastened to clothing and gas masks issued. On 31 August 208 boys lined up in the yard in Barking Road. The boys journeyed by train to Swindon and billeting took all evening. The boys soon settled into the routines of their households and as the weeks passed the boys attended three different schools in Swindon and lost their sense of unity. Many pupils and staff returned home at the weekend even when the bombing of London was taking place. The boys worked hard and were very willing to learn whilst in Swindon and much of the credit for this goes to the parents and to the teachers, householders and officials of Swindon. Good results in examinations were achieved in 1939, 1940 and 1941. In 1940 an emergency Grammar School for boys and girls remained in the Girl's Grammar School buildings for those children who were not evacuated. This took a direct bomb hit, which luckily happened on a Saturday. In 1942 the Boys' Grammar School re-opened in East Ham, with the juniors remaining in Swindon until January 1943 when eventually the whole school was reunited. Many old boys entered the forces and as the war continued casualties and fatalities amongst Old Esthameians increased. School life was interrupted by V bomb attacks, many boys and parents escaping with their lives. These deadly V1 and V2's assaults bred an ever present awareness of death and destruction. The school spent much of its time in the basement and in the playground shelters; whilst in class, counting the vast number of planes heading for Europe occupied many hours. When the school was reunited in 1943, E.T. Andrews the headmaster since 1932 was on the point of retirement and in September 1944 his successor J.L. Whiteley took up his post.

When appointed Dr. Whiteley was thirty seven years old. He was an old boy of Manchester Grammar School who did not go to University on account of the death of his father at that time. As a result he had taken B.A., M.A. and PhD degrees at Birkbeck College, University of London, whilst he was teaching. He was a classicist and with a colleague at Selhurst Grammar School he had written a series of Latin text books. Gould and Whiteley were well known to students of Latin. His first battle, as the new headmaster, was to get boys into school uniform including cap and tie. It was to be eight years before the school moved to the new premises at Langdon Crescent. The site in the east of the borough near the Barking boundary was far from ideal, but was the only one available. Much of the land was marshy and covered with watercress beds with the river Back running through the site. The land was often waterlogged despite the culvertisation of the river and the draining of the land. On the forty two acre site the Education Authority built two secondary modern schools (Thomas Lethaby for boys and Burges Manor for girls) as well as the Boys' Grammar School. This campus later became an ideal site for a large comprehensive school in 1972 – Langdon School. Dr. Whiteley was so impressed by the ability and intelligence of the best boys in 5A to whom he taught Latin in his first year as headmaster that he introduced a four year course to School Certificate ('O' level), so that boys could enter the Sixth Form at fifteen plus and if of the right calibre were to be given the chance to compete for Scholarships at Oxbridge.

Thus began the success of the Sixth form, with the unqualified support of the boys and parents and the enthusiasm and teaching power of the staff. The Sixth former exercised a great influence on the school by their maturity, loyalty and sense of responsibility. The qualities that Dr. Whiteley recognised in the boys in 1944 have been maintained throughout the whole history of the school and many Old Esthameians can still be found all over Great Britain and the world in positions of trust and responsibility.

The Boys' Grammar School was built to accommodate 600 boys and opened in 1952, but soon became overcrowded. (Colour photograph 13.) The post war birth rate bulge reached the secondary school in 1957. When Philip left East Ham Grammar School in 1958 there were 898 boys in the school. Dr. Whiteley was a strong believer in grammar schools and would voice his thoughts and convictions at length on any possible occasion. He was an exponent of the meritocracy – the grammar school was the vehicle through which able boys, whatever their background, could better themselves by hard work. His belief was that whatever the boys from the public and direct grant schools could have, so could his East Ham boys. Whiteley took all opportunities to enable boys to experience what he had been unable to experience in his higher education. Dr. Whiteley retired in 1971, just at the Authority was to reorganise into a comprehensive system and the Grammar School he had largely created would disappear. He wrote in the 1965 Esthameian (issue no 108) about his twenty years as headmaster. 'Just before Whitsuntide, 1944, I was appointed headmaster of this school. I consider myself fortunate in having had the experience of working in East Ham. I can remember vividly being impressed by the ability, liveliness and character of 5A whom I taught Latin in my first year, and this impression has been confirmed as the years have gone by. The school is very fortunate in being able to recruit year by year from our excellent Junior Schools a high percentage of able boys who come from homes that have been exceedingly loyal to the school. I want to pay tribute to my colleagues who have been a great source of strength and continuity over the years, especially when all Grammar Schools have found it difficult to recruit staff and hold them once they have been appointed. Since 1944, 130 men have joined the staff of this school. (Dr. Whiteley appointed young men, like Philip, with a career to make, encouraging them to teach creatively and to usefully contribute to out-of-school activities.)

We have expanded the range and scope of the curriculum. It has been an exciting experience to see the development of the school not only in numbers, but also in the opportunity it now gives to all boys in the school to continue their education to the highest level in a wide range of subjects. I remember the old building – the 'Tech' as it was popularly and affectionately known locally, where difficulties of accommodation seemed to bring out the best in boys and staff. Some excellent work was done there between 1944 and 1952 as had been achieved in the previous 39 years the school had occupied the site. It was a great thrill to have the chance to move to our new site at Langdon Crescent with adequate facilities and playing field accommodation. Staff helped at every stage of the planning and we have greatly benefitted from that experience. As I look back I am conscious of the contribution to the success that has been achieved, of an enlightened administration under Mr. Dyer and Mr. W.T. Davies, his successor as Chief Education Officer; the courage of the former who saw that we did get our new school and the guidance of the latter have helped to make my stay in East Ham enjoyable. We have parents whose loyalty to and trust in us are always most moving. Their constant support and their appreciation have always been an important factor in our success. Our Education committee and the governors have played their part. Perhaps I am the only one, who working closely with them at all times, can appreciate their genuine and sincere desire to help and to give the school every support and facility to become what we have consciously endeavoured to be - a lively community where we have had the joy of acquiring and appreciating knowledge, and of learning to grow up and experience the importance of service in the classroom, the playing fields and in the various club activities and societies which are such a feature of our school life. My last word is to the boys of the school themselves from whom I too have learned so much. Each successive year has thrown up a sufficiently large number of boys of ability and character who have been ready to accept the school's aims and ideals and, as they have gone forward, to identify themselves with them. Without their support and help, the school could not have done what it has done in the post-war years. The nature of a headmaster's job is such that there is always a risk that he over estimates his own importance in school life.'

East Ham Grammar School is typical of the grammar school in this country, and it represents the growth of a great idea, and its work is typical of the best work of the best grammar schools.

'A dedicated School master' 1949 to 1958

'What I valued most at East Ham Grammar School could be summed up as follows. The scope the headmaster (Dr. Whiteley) gave young men like me, in their teaching. The door was closed and we were left to teach as we thought proper. The amount of Sixth form teaching which young men were given was most interesting to me. The Headmaster was always willing to encourage us in new methods and new ideas. My interest in Sixth form teaching did not begin at East Ham Grammar School but I was most encouraged by Dr. Whiteley and owe my present position as headmaster of a Sixth Form College directly to him. We were encouraged to take part in as many out of school activities as we could. In my case, the Debating Society, the Library, and the Scouts as the Group Scoutmaster. It was particularly in drama that I was greatly supported. Drama is essential in school life and one of the easiest ways, in my view, by which a young person's personality may be developed outside the classroom. On the other hand, it's a bit of a nuisance to the rest of the school while a production is going on and the producer tends to want his own way and does his best to get it. He's not worried about the interruption of the school for his play!'
(P.H.V. 1971)

Philip recalls 'I was interviewed at the old school (by the town hall) in Dr. Whiteley's room there in early summer 1949. It was my first post, I was at the Institute of Education in London, where Dr. W. had had a notice put up, asking for any keen young men who might wish to teach classics. The interview went well, although I was a worried and apprehensive young man of twenty two; I cannot recall the other candidates for the post. Dr. Whiteley put me completely at ease and I was appointed.

I came to the school, which was then in the old building, in fear and trepidation as a new teacher in September 1949. Many of the staff were quite senior but most were happy to help a junior teacher along. This was particularly true of course of the headmaster, who gave me every encouragement, gave me a fine and interesting timetable, including some General Studies and Classics work with the Third Year Sixth. I was immediately involved and helped with the drama, and if I recall, that winter I co- produced a quite extraordinary production of 'King Lear'.

These early days in September 1949 are recalled by one of Philip's Sixth Form pupils – Bill Hubert, who later became headteacher of Henry Beaufort comprehensive school, Winchester, Hampshire. His recollection tells of a young teacher struggling with some of the boys' pranks in the old building. 'I first met

Mr. P.H. Vennis in early September 1949 when he joined the Classics Department of East Ham Grammar School for Boys (EHGS). We members of the Lower Sixth Arts (6A1) wondered what we were in for in his lessons on Ancient History.

In a short time we had established that in PHV the P was for Phil and that Phil had just completed service in the Royal Navy during which time he had learnt Japanese. Indeed, some of his lessons were on the Japanese language rather than on the history of the Greeks and Romans, but never was there any mention of Bletchley Park.

The EHGS headmaster, recently appointed, was Dr. J.L Whiteley, aka Joe, classicist intent, inter alia, upon spreading the enlightenment of the Classics in that part of London's East End bordering upon Essex.

Most of the annual intake of, at that time, ninety boys into the first year took both French and Latin. At the end of their second year a dozen or so of these boys took Greek in addition to French and Latin and dropped Science. Two years later that is at the end of their fourth year they sat their General Schools Certificate/matriculation exemption exams a year early, with few exceptions successfully, and passed directly into the Sixth Form, then A Levels, followed by University awards and entrance. Shades of Alan Bennett's 'The History Boys!' Such was Dr. Whiteley's commitment to the Classics that the Science Sixth was given minority time experience of the Classics in the shape of reading and discussing the classics in translation. The Science Sixth's reaction was 'You can't be serious!' and they reacted accordingly. These classes were held in small groups and were held in Room 56 – a small seminar room at the top of the school. Phil played his part in selling to the reluctant scientists this, as they saw it, irrelevant and unnecessary exposure to an alien culture.

In the ceiling of Room 56 was a trapdoor which led, according to a rough notice chalked on this flap, to 'Annie's Room'. One day Phil was incautious enough at the beginning of a class with a group of scientists to wonder out loud what was up in Annie's Room. Seizing the opportunity to prolong the digression one of the class suggested that Phil should go up there and find out. Ever helpful the scientists quickly erected a 'ladder' of tables topped with a chair. Never one to shirk a challenge Phil went up the ladder and into Annie's Room. Whereupon the topmost chair was rapidly removed leaving Phil marooned in space.

The Annie's Room happening added to Phil's popularity among the boys as a Master who had a great sense of fun, whose learning they respected and who had their best interests at heart – and not only in class, for Phil threw himself with enthusiasm into the school's drama productions, including the annual school play by The Bard, even to the then unusual initiative of taking the play out into the local community and staging it in the local Central Park. Philip's enthusiasm was inexhaustible. His thirst for culture and learning was lifelong. If his fuse was at times short it was more than counterbalanced by his big heart and his sense of fun and enjoyment'.

Another of Philip's earliest pupils was Christopher France who was head boy in 1952, and later knighted in 1989, who recollects that 'Philip came like a fresh breeze to the school. There were other young masters, of course, but none of them had quite the zest that Philip brought. It was partly that we knew of his Japanese – though not of course its context – and that conjured up images of a war we hardly knew about, as elaborated by Hollywood. Philip was asked to take the combined Sixth Form for General Studies. It was a hard task because we were by this time fixated on Higher School Certificate and beyond. If it wasn't for an exam it didn't count. But my recollections of the sessions are that Philip got us talking about literary and moral issues that we hadn't so far come up against. There was some attempt, fostered by Dr. Whiteley I think, to hi-jack the lessons for Greek Literature in Translation – examinable, and therefore perhaps more acceptable to the clients. But it ran into the sands. The clients detected a double cross, and any way preferred the wider discussions Philip initiated.

The Greek set – 1950 to 51. Left to right Ernie Mott (teacher) Kenneth Davis, Ron Spill, John Moore and Philip Vennis

But many of us enjoyed Greek literature with Philip in another way when he produced 'The Peace' in Greek and English in 1952. Personally, I recall that production as one of the highlights of my school life, and can still remember some of the lines and tunes. My lasting impression is that the production was really something of a triumph for its originality. I still find the words, even the Greek, running through my mind from time to time; he opened my eyes to the world.'

The idea of 'The Peace' according to Philip was unlike any other of Aristophanes' comedies, it is a poetic fantasy, almost idyllic in tone, in favour of the restoration of peace to a war-weary Greece. 'The Peace' demonstrates heart-felt relief by the Greeks at the end of a hated, lengthy and unnecessary war. A greeting from the fifth century BC carries a very full and poignant meaning for the mid-twentieth century AD.

"And your presence will enhance
The growth of vines, and figs, and plants
'Mid joy and laughter, once 'tis known
That you, O Peace, again are home.
And so, our Darling, welcome home
Welcome, welcome, welcome home!"

The Peace of Aristophanes' produced in 1952

Colin Curds, whose career was Keeper of Zoology at the Natural History Museum, and another of Philip's earliest pupils says of Philip's arrival at East Ham. 'I first became aware of the presence of Philip Vennis in September 1950 when he drove through the school gates in an ancient dark brown Austin 7 car which he called Melissa. He parked the car beneath the plane trees (whose fruits were used to make itching powder), and when he got out I immediately noticed his shock of red hair and milk chocolate coloured gabardine suit. I think it was the latter which attracted my attention the most and for the next year I thought of him as the teacher who resembled a choc ice. He did not teach me that year but boys in the A stream classes referred to him as Vennis the menace (it was 1951 before the infamous Dennis the Menace appeared in the Beano comic). I was a soprano in the school choir and Mr. Orchard the music master was asked if we would sing behind the backcloth during the School's

81

production of 'A Midsummer-Night's Dream' in December 1950. So the next occasions I met Phil were during the dress rehearsal and performances in the theatre attached to East Ham Town Hall adjacent to the School. It was very obvious to me that he was in charge from his dynamic approach to directing the actors and the meticulous attention to detail in his instructions. It was nine months later that I actually spoke to him, I was promoted to the A stream in September 1951 and he became my Latin master. I should point out here that if I have any strengths, foreign languages are not included. After a couple of lessons he approached me and said in a pleasant manner '"note that you have been recently been moved up to the A stream, quite obviously this was not on the basis of your Latin". I quickly agreed with him that I was not up to par and that I would at least try to improve. Although I tried, my Latin never did improve and I always lagged behind most of the class. When I eventually failed O level Latin he sought me out and offered his congratulations saying that I had done far better than he had imagined. His approach to teaching was a mix of formality and informality and it was his obvious sense of humour that set him apart from the majority of his colleagues. The headmaster Dr. Whiteley (known by most boys at 'The Old man') had co-authored a Latin primer (Gould and Whiteley) which was used in the school. When setting homework Phil frequently gave us phrases to translate containing the words 'the old man' in ridiculous settings which we thought amusing even though in my case did little to actually improve my grasp of the language. As schoolboys most of us wondered why we should learn a dead language, as it seemed to have little relevance to the modern world. It was only later that I discovered how useful even a feeble grasp of some Latin would be in my career. Much scientific jargon and all animal and plant names are largely based on Latin and Greek roots.'

Colin, has, almost fifty years later, recalled much detail about the day to day running of the school where Philip had his first teaching job. This is how he remembers it as a young boy. 'Admittance to the school was by examination and about twenty per cent of those sitting 'The Scholarship' (later the 11-plus) passed. Borderline cases were re-examined and then interviewed by the headmaster Dr. Joseph Lacey Whiteley. Each year three new classes of around 33 boys were formed and streamed according to their performance in the 11-plus examination. An additional complete class of 30 boys were admitted in the third year to ensure the capture of any late developers. Results of examinations at the end of each school year enabled individuals to rise or fall through the ability streams. A few boys from the C stream were asked to leave at the end of the first year but after that boys were only expelled for reasons other than ability. The total student population was rising to 1,000 boys. No girls were admitted and the only female teacher was the French Assistante who we shared with the Girls' Grammar School.

The school day began with registration. The names of all boys present were taken and if you were absent for a couple of days without informing the school then a man appeared at your front door asking the reason why you were not in attendance. Needless to say it was difficult for truants to escape detection and the only real way was to register and then disappear from the campus. Registration was followed by school assembly which consisted of singing a hymn, prayers and a Sixth former reading from the Bible. There were several Jewish boys in school and they held a short religious service elsewhere and joined the rest of us for any announcements that were made. Immigration had not really started during my time at the school and I can only remember the presence of one non-white boy during the eight years that I attended.

In retrospect the curriculum was quite extensive but strictly followed an academic format. For the first two years all boys followed the same general education classes. All studied French but Latin was introduced to those in the A and B streams during the second year. At the end of the second year those in the A stream had to choose between modern languages or classics. Those who chose modern languages were taught either German or Spanish which alternated on a yearly basis. At the end of the third year, the A stream had to choose between Science, modern languages or classics. All boys in the B or C streams studied eight subjects – English, French, Mathematics, Biology, Chemistry, Physics, History and Geography and probably received a more rounded education than those in the A stream. The sixth form was composed of about 100 boys studying either classics, economics, modern languages or science. The science sixth all studied chemistry and physics but then added both pure and applied mathematics or botany and zoology.

Caning was only metered out by the headmaster but most masters and prefects resorted to corporal punishment of different sorts. Naturally the masters who frequently resorted to this were well known to the boys and we accepted it without a problem. It was never severe and usually took the form of a quick clip around the head. Some masters gave heavier blows than others while some masters resorted to more innovative measures. I remember my French master Mr. Elford-Gulley with some affection; he was a dead shot with chalk and blackboard duster and for some time had a tennis ball lodged in the right hand sleeve of his gown which he used with much effect on those misbehaving in class. The school art master Mr. Spencer had a problem since the art room was built like a university lecture theatre with a bank of benches. If you sat in the back row he could not get within reach to deliver a clout. Naturally those who regularly misbehaved migrated to the far side of the back row. Bert, as he was known, solved the problem by mounting a length of stout rubber tubing to the pole used for opening windows. The back row became less popular after that. We all knew that Phil did not suffer fools gladly and was a strict disciplinarian but I only once remember him clouting a lad. On that occasion a boy was making a racket in the changing rooms during the performance of a play. His noise could easily be heard by the audience and Phil had little choice but to resort to a clout. Most of us realised that the boy deserved it and Phil had little choice since a raised voice – his normal control method – would have added to the problem rather than solving it.

Prefects were selected from the second and third year Sixth form. Their duties usually involved looking after a class before the form-master arrived to take registration. Misbehaviour was rewarded by handing out lines or being put into detention. This meant that the miscreant had to remain in school for about an hour after school on Friday evening. However, most prefects resorted to a quick clip for the most boisterous first and second formers who rarely listened to a prefect. By the third and fourth forms most boys had settled and would talk reasonably amongst themselves without creating havoc. The Prefects were led by the school captain, his deputy, the senior prefect and three others who collectively formed the School council who met with the headmaster on a weekly basis. My recollections of Council meetings are that Dr. Whiteley had already made up his mind on most issues and informed us of his decisions. Theoretically it was supposed to be a two- way discussion but in practice it was difficult to disagree with The Old Man. That is more a reflection on the mood of the mid to late fifties than on Dr. Whiteley – change was in the air but real change was slow. Bullying did not happen at school; certainly I cannot remember a case. Everyone was ragged from time to time but we took it as part of growing up and none became victims for more than a day or two.

The school was divided into four houses (Faraday, Spencer, Gainsborough and Purcell). Competitions included a swimming gala, an athletics sports day and a cross country run (a three mile course in Wanstead Park). Each house had a house captain and a house assembly was held each term. It always seemed to me that the ability to play football was over emphasised at school, and form captains were largely chosen on their in Plashet Grove, opposite the park, some mile or so north. The new school buildings were state of the art. There was a central complex comprising the heating and canteens and an apartment where the site engineer lived. We were very well equipped for the time and all equipment was brand new. For the first time the school had a proper theatre with stage and projection facilities. Each boy had a personal locker and heated cloakrooms dried wet raincoats during inclement weather. We had our own sports grounds with tennis courts instead of travelling a mile south to grounds on the A13 close to Becton. Money ran out towards the end of the build so the promised swimming pool did not materialise. Central kitchens provided lunches for all three schools with waitress service. When we first arrived the quality of food was excellent but did worsen as time went on.'

Another boy from these early days of Philip's time at East Ham was Ronald Impey. He attended the Grammar School from 1949 to 1956 and this is how he recalls Philip as a teacher. 'He was a talented junior member of the Classics department, working with E.V.W. Mott, the Head of Department, and the redoubtable Head Dr. J.L. Whiteley. Apart from his teaching of Latin, Greek and Ancient History, and some English, he threw himself vigorously into the wider life of the school and contributed effectively to the education and enlightenment of many boys of that era.

He taught me Latin from my early years at the school. He had high standards, and combined strictness with a decent humanity which earned him respect. He could be fiery tempered on occasion, both encouraging to the diligent and scathing to the indolent. He told the odd luckless pupil that he could write his entire knowledge of Latin on the back of a postage stamp, and when one lad wrote 'Humanum est errare' at the top of his exam paper, Phil said "but not 444 times, Dickens!" (444 was, I seem to recall, an oddly favourite number with him – and he would sometimes set an imposition of 444 lines!) Once when giving an English – Latin vocabulary test, not having written down or remembered the questions, he said to me "What's number one, Impey?' I politely and innocently replied "Find out, sir" (meaning that 'find out' was the word to be put into Latin) and watched with alarm as his face turned white and he said "What did you say, Impey?"

He gave me great encouragement and help in my studies through the school as I continued with Latin, then took up Greek for O level and later added Ancient History in the Sixth Form, where he was my Form master in the lower Classical Sixth. When I had a long period of absence through pneumonia he even visited me when I was on convalescence in Littlehampton. He gave me great encouragement and support when I was preparing for the Cambridge and Oxford scholarship exams, happily spending extra time with me to go through Greek and Latin verse composition. He certainly made his mark at East Ham Grammar School. He was, I believe, popular, well-respected, and forceful.' (Ronald Impey. Lecturer in Classics, Exeter University.)

Philip arrived in East Ham when it was still recovering from the bombardment of the Second World War, but gradually, although there was still some rationing, there was more optimism in the country after America had ploughed millions of dollars into Britain. This money underwrote the welfare state and the fabulous fifties, under the Prime Ministership of Harold Macmillan who claimed that Britain 'had never had it so good'. As a young schoolmaster Philip asked his pupils in 11A to write about East Ham High Street and this is how two of them found it in 1952:

'Visitors to East Ham cannot remain long in ignorance of one of its main attractions – the High Street. This two and a half mile stretch of road which is crossed by Barking Road at the Town Hall comprises High Street North and South and forms a link between the docks of the East End and the outskirts of Epping Forest.

Whether a person is interested in the ancient Parish church or the seat of local government, the well kept lawns and flower-bedecked beds of Central Park or the commodious swimming pools of Central Baths – High Street South offers them all whilst her tall sister 'North' sweeps sedately towards the Forest and one of the many gateways to the North of England. Known to many shoppers as the 'Oxford Street' of the East End High Street North lends much colour and variety to one of docklands' main thoroughfares bound as it is on both sides with shops of all description. Competition is high here for it is not uncommon to see three or four grocery shops standing side by side each extending a very cordial invitation to one and all to change their registrations for better service and quality. The many house furnishers in the High Street have their salesmen on the spot – in front of the window if you should chance to pause a while in contemplation. Many of the West End shops have their branches in the High Street, amongst them Dolcis for shoes, Richard Shops for coats and gowns and a variety of others which certainly bring West End facilities in style and selection to this Mecca of the East End.

For those who are attracted by the 'Petticoat Lane' types of bargaining there is the Shopping Hall which skirts High Street North and is adjacent to the impressive Marconi International Marine and Wireless company building with its tall aerial masts to call all ships in port and at sea.

This is one of the many 'ports of call' to sailors homeward bound and if they are leaving the East End via East Ham station there are many local pubs which open their doors in welcome as the 'weary traveller homeward plods his way'. Music and sometimes dancing is provided with a game of darts and a snack at the bar thrown in, although if a meal is required there are several restaurants which can provide an excellent bill of fare.

For those who have an hour or two to spare and are fond of films the whole of the High Street provides three cinemas – two in the north and one in the south with the East Ham Palace Theatre for light variety shows (for those in need of relaxation) unless, of course, they prefer the shade of the trees in the park or are interested in tennis, bowls or the putting green, in which case the High Street can still provide these even to the accompaniment of the strains of

Central Park Band, which entertains the public during the summer months. In the winter months there is the Central Library next to the fire station in High Street South where there is an excellent selection of reading matter always available to the public. On the other side of the library is the very core of the High Street – the Town Hall from which local government is administered. Here the Mayor of the Borough entertains his guests in the Mayor's Parlour; justice is administered in the Magistrates Court and the business of the Borough generally conducted – surely one of the main reasons for the attraction of the High Street, East Ham.'

The second account of East Ham in the early fifties by a second year Grammar School pupil has the title of 'Dockland's Oxford Street'.

'Beyond occasional frenzied shopping expeditions on Saturday afternoons, I have hitherto been ill-acquainted with East Ham High Street, so that it was with some surprise, when circumstances recently caused me to spend more than the usual amount of time in my local High Road, that I realised how little of its true life and character is revealed to the casual observer.

Once known as 'White Post Lane', it runs from Manor Park in the north to the Docks in the south. From Manor Way in the northern extremity to the Town Hall is known as High Street North, and this area is primarily the shopping centre.

Dockland in the south, consisting of the King George V Dock and the Royal Albert Dock, is a small colony of its own, harbouring ships from every part of the world, bringing a diversity of goods for the shops, and seamen of all nationalities who will stroll down to the High Road, their Oxford Street, to make their purchases and look at the Town, before they are off to sea again. The Docks, a gateway to the High Road, afford employment to many thousands of the crowds that throng the shopping centre on any Saturday afternoon, and who live in the tributary streets running off High Street North.

The shopping centre, like any other suburban thoroughfare on Saturday afternoon, is crowded with women armed with the inevitable shopping basket, some with children straggling behind sucking lollypops and ice cream cornets. Bright red trolley buses glide smoothly up and down, mingling with the incessant stream of traffic, and bringing yet more people from outlying districts into the town. On their way they pass a myriad of little shops of every kind, until arriving at the junction of Plashet Grove and High Street North, they are forced to move at a slower pace by the traffic congestion, past the fine promenade of large shops until they reach the Station, where the news boys shout outside the entrance, and where one can board a train to the City or West End for a visit to the office or the theatre, or take a trip down to the coast for a glimpse of the sea. Then a gay splash of colour at the foot of the hill – the Borough's 'Palace of

Varieties' – its posters announcing in foot high letters the star of the week. The crowds thin a little as the bus reaches the junction of Barking Road and East Ham High Road, and here is the centre of civic administration around which much of the life of the municipality revolves. Occupying what is an almost ideally central position in the town, and at the corner of the Crossroads to the Town Hall, a fine building with terracotta facings, and embellished with a very fine clock tower, surrounded like a mother hen by her chicks with a number of buildings closely identified with order and good government of the locality. Even the historian is not disappointed, for passing on towards the Docks once more we come upon the ancient Parish Church of St. Mary Magdalene, known to most as 'East Ham Old Church'. It is an early twelfth century edifice, and the local history books tell us that it occupies a spot which was once a remote retreat on the marshes stretching towards the Thames. It has four old Norman windows, and many Roman bricks are incorporated in its battered old walls. Near here too is the old inn 'The Roman Urn', one of the several old establishments with obvious historic associations, and worthy of an evening visit! Evening is not far off, and through the mist of the sunset, looking towards the south, can be discerned huge mounds of unglamorous-looking black coal rising into the sky. They mark the site of the greatest gas works in the world, covering over three hundred and fifty acres of ground. This immense works, in which there are more than ninety miles of railway lines, and where it is necessary when distinguished visitors arrive to employ a special train to take them over the works, employs an enormous staff of manual and office workers who help to turn those great black mounds of coal into light, heat and colour, and so give comfort as well as work to many thousands in this area of the country. And so again to Dockland, as the sky darkens over the now quieter thoroughfare, and the night life in the town begins, as the ships' sirens sound sleepily through the gathering dusk and echo along their own highway, 'Dockland's Oxford Street'.

Philip taught for three years in the old school building and then with the rest of the school moved to Langdon Crescent. Philip was always grateful to Dr. Whiteley for the enormous opportunities he gave him. 'It remains a high honour to have served at East Ham Grammar School in the late forties and fifties. What chances were put in one's way, what high hopes were entertained, what a marvellously involved timetable and what – the crown of perfection in the English grammar school – what a huge array of talent to teach and learn from in the Sixth Form. What a man to argue with as Head, what wit and finesse – what grand openings he offered us- for my part – Drama, Scouts, English for Scientists let alone the classics. We went on to new jobs and used and practised all those ideas of his. Under Dr. Whiteley East Ham Grammar School was a superb example of the English grammar school at its best. It gave chances to boys from poor homes; from families who had not themselves been at a grammar school, it gave chances to the less able at third form level; it gave chances again to very many in the Sixth form; it proved excellent in every way – on the field, on the stage, in music, in style, in uniform, at Speech Days and, of course, in academic work. It opened the doors to thousands of boys so that they had a chance to be leaders in every kind of profession and trade – via Oxbridge and other universities – or by other routes. This is endorsed when you hear from old boys and learn what they have become; how they have entered and risen in so many professions or risen high in so many places – or when you look at the positions to which the staff have risen (Hampshire alone has two sixth form college Principals, two Heads of comprehensive schools, one Professor, one Area Officer, and one Principal of a college of education all from East Ham Grammar School.) One is continually in awe of Dr. Whiteley's huge ability to make the boys have high horizons, his delight in allowing his staff room to grow – he gave us great care and attention; he allowed us to know detail; he gave his great generosity of spirit so that we each could not fail to become the really full men that JLW saw in us when we were all young men. Jokes mattered very much to him. If he could make me laugh or if I could make him laugh – then the day was less weary. He was a big man in every way; he had no envy, bore no grudge and enjoyed his laughter loving life.

East Ham Grammar School for Boys new building in Langdon Crescent. 1952

School mastering, of course, is a sad affair in many ways. It's clearly the passing scene, boys come and go and one rarely sees much of them after they leave, despite their seven years in one's care. Since the late forties, until seventies, teenagers of course have changed a great deal, especially Sixth Formers. Dr. Whiteley, like any great headmaster, changed the school, the subjects, the teaching methods, the atmosphere and himself, with the times. But he kept his sense of humour and his abiding sympathy and patience with the boys growing up.'

Dr. Whiteley gave enormous scope to young, and in this photograph thoughtful teachers like Philip.

The opening quotation of this section of this chapter is included again here in order to keep the flow of Philip's thoughts. 'What I valued most at Langdon could be summed up as follows – (a) the scope Dr. Whiteley gave young men like myself, in their teaching. The door was closed and we were left to teach as we thought proper. (b) The amount of Sixth form teaching which young men were given and which was most interesting to me. He was always willing to encourage us in new methods and new ideas and allow young men to have their place in Sixth form teaching. My interest in Sixth form teaching didn't begin there but certainly it was most encouraged by Dr. Whiteley and I owe my present position as Principal of a Sixth Form College directly to him. (c) We were encouraged of course to take part in as many out of school activities as we could. In my case, the Debating Society, the Library and the Scouts, the latter grew and I became the Group Scoutmaster. Dr. Whiteley came to our camps and our flag days. This supported and encouraged someone like myself who was organising such events. Dr. Whiteley strongly supported and helped the parents' committee; he always attended the Sixth form socials which I organised under his aegis. (d) But it was particularly in Drama that Dr. Whiteley gave the weight of his support. Drama is essential in school life and one of the easiest ways by which a young person's personality may be developed outside the classroom. On the other hand, it's a bit of a nuisance to the rest of the school while it's going on and the producer tends to want his own way and does his best to get it. He's not too worried about the interruption of the school for his play. These were long remembered rehearsals of Shakespeare, and of two Greek plays 'The Cyclops' and Aristophanes' 'Peace', (which we took to Goldsmith's College and University College). Then there were great Shakespeare productions of 'Henry 1V Part 1', 'Coriolanus' and 'Macbeth' and others. Finally I remember JLW giving us his blessing over a fantastic production of 'Journey's End' for the Third Year Sixth and staff. He was always most helpful and nothing was too much trouble for him. He himself took part in 'Captain Carvello' for the Old Esthameians and gave his support to a quite extra-ordinary production of Ibsen's 'Hedda Gabler' for the revived Old Easthameians Dramatic Society. When I was closely engaged in the Shakespearian productions in Central Park for the East Ham County Borough Council, Dr. Whiteley used to give me time for these productions and he always came along to them. What more in fact by way of support from a headmaster could a young teacher ask? All in all then, as a young schoolmaster, I owed a very great deal to Dr. Whiteley. I remember with pleasure many social occasions at his home, I remember no fewer than eight visits to his club in Croydon with parts of our then current Shakespearian productions, which we acted before the club audience. Generosity of spirit, I believe, is essential to the great schoolmaster, and Dr. Whiteley had this. Surely his headship at East Ham from 1944 to 1970 is among the great headships in the post-war years of a grammar school. He always looked forward to the changing scene and could, I have no doubt, have been a great headmaster of a boarding school, a co-educational school or a comprehensive school, had he been a younger man. I am proud and pleased to be able to say how much I owe to him. I remember with pleasure the nine years on which my career and two headships are based and I also remember the many events at East Ham which he and I were both associated with.'

East Ham Grammar School for Boys, the staff in 1955. Philip is in the second row, fifth from the left. Dr. Whiteley is in the middle of the front row, sixth from left.

History was to repeat itself when Philip became Head at New Mills Grammar School in several ways, but in no stronger way than his innate ability (like Dr. Whiteley's) to appoint young teachers/members of staff who not only showed promise as a young teacher (in Dr. Whiteley's case such staff members as Len Moss – who became a headteacher, Peter Kelly who was Professor of Education at Southampton University and Peter Watkins a Sixth Form College Principal), but also were identified by both men as having potential of reaching the top of their chosen career. Philip either observed this talent in Dr. Whiteley or he possessed the intuition needed for choosing potentially ambitious young members of staff, or maybe a combination of both. East Ham Grammar school was modelled on the grammar school ethos which originated in the public schools - as Colin Curds mentioned – a house system used for organising sports activities, the publication of a school magazine in 1915 – The Esthameian, Prefects and an annual Speech Day. When the school celebrated its Golden Jubilee in 1955 a special edition of 'The Esthameian' was published. In this magazine Philip wrote an article about school life in the Grammar School in the fifties called 'This School Today'. He imaginatively sees it through the eyes of an American visitor to the school and this perspective gives an interesting slant on life in a well run, traditional boys' grammar school.

'Distinctly young men' a stranger from America might say, if he saw our Sixth Form; and he would have put his finger on what is undoubtedly the greatest single difference between the school today and its predecessor of fifteen years ago.

For it is the size, variety and vigour of its Sixth Form which chiefly make a Grammar School distinguishable from its Secondary fellows, and under the present headmaster, the Sixth Form at East Ham has indeed achieved these three goals. It numbers well over one hundred with an age range of fifteen to nineteen; it studies the most extraordinary array of subjects, entering for nearly twenty of them at the Advanced Level of GCE; a boy can offer four Natural Sciences, two Sciences and two Mathematics, four Economics subjects, two Modern Languages plus English literature and Latin, or a full Classics course plus History, or some sort of combination of these; additional subjects such as English literature for the scientists, or French and Latin for the economists are regularly being added to the curriculum, as are wireless lessons and various lectures, while the Sixth Former also has his regular doses of religious and physical instruction, and of organised games.

So much for variety; for vigour, we may call to witness a great procession of activities of every sort, run by, and often largely by, the Sixth form whether in school teams, or debates, or drama, or Stamp Club, or Christian Fellowship, or what have you – but more of this later. A great part of this vigour has derived in these last years from the success of the experiment with a third year Sixth form.

This has been achieved by allowing the 'A' stream to go forward from the fourth form straight into the sixth, and by these boys staying on one year after their Advanced Level to take university scholarships and entrances. Academically this has allowed the School to compete with long established Sixth forms with a more reasonable hope of success, and the growing number of Old Esthameians at Oxford and Cambridge bear witness to the success of this venture; in the mean time entrances to London and the provincial Universities have also increased, and in some years as many as twenty five to thirty young men have gone forward from the Sixth form of this school to Universities or university-type colleges to continue their education.

Our stranger from America might well wonder at the standard set by some of our ablest Sixth Formers, and at the leadership they give to the rest of the school in so many spheres of activity. He might be surprised at a community of over seven hundred, which ranges in age from children of eleven to young men of nineteen having any "oneness".

And it is this oneness, the oneness, so to say, of the youngest member of 1E with the School captain, which is, after the Sixth Form, the second major factor which marks out a school. It is a facet of school life sometimes difficult to see perhaps, to those working here, a question of the wood and the trees. I should say that continuity is a part of it –continuity in subjects learned for five or seven years – the A and B streams having Latin, 3A having a third language – German, Spanish or Greek, to deal with – the Ordinary Level of GCE after four or five years, with Advanced two years later, and a scholarship a year after that. School uniform is part of it; cap and blazer do not make a school, but they are a visual reminder of pride in its oneness, and the uniform is now accepted and worn as a normal adjunct of being at the School. Morning assembly is a part of it, and should and does contribute largely to our oneness; and so with School plays, concerts, services, matches and sports. Not all boys can come to everything; and there will always be a few, the square pegs, who will not come to anything; but on the whole it does seem to be true that the boys, before they leave, do begin to have at least a rudimentary impression of the School being one community, with one shared raison d'être.

Were our stranger from America to wander round the School one day in the late afternoon, he might well be surprised to find that a large proportion of staff and boys were still in the building and that they were indulging in the most extraordinary number and variety of usual and less usual out of school activities. And we may put this down as the third major distinctive mark of a grammar school, and in particular, (and to the point) of our School.

As he entered the building he might hear the School orchestra practising its melodious notes, with some aplomb under Mr. Collins, whose advent has brought new vigour to this traditional body; the School's now enormous choir might be rehearsing with it, while from next door the fervent hymn singing of the Christian Fellowship would show that body to have no connection with the choir, and to have more piety than melody. As he passes further down the corridor, he would become aware of the tramp of marching feet, (which could not be the Scout troop as the feet are in time), of much bellowing and some Shakespeare; this would be the Dramatic Society in and around the hall doing its marching and counter-marching, and its little acting; colourful music emanates from the wing, whence every so often a drummer boy emerges, hectic and tearful, to lament to the lighting crew that his gramophone has fused and his drum-stick has broken, while around him numerous boys attempt some rudimentary drama amid a chaos of extras. So much for Shakespeare.

Round to the end of the A block; there lives the Stamp Club sometimes reformed as the Geographical Society – a great many excited youngsters, a few more stern Sixth formers – and Mr.Seidman, a description that might stand for the Photographic Society, that ubiquitous and all pervading body – a trap for the unwary master, or for the Natural History Society, enthusing quietly and omnisciently with Mr. Forrester somewhere over some dubious dead or dying creature. Upstairs in the relaxed atmosphere of C8 – The Memorial Library – the Debating Society learnedly puts forth its views on subjects unknown to its members when they come, and more unknown when they leave. This Society has its junior counterpart when Mr. Moss holds sway, teaching his boys how to debate with parliamentary precision on such supremely important subjects as 'homework' or 'girlfriends'. The Senior Society, putting homework and girlfriends behind it, does indeed debate parliamentary subjects, though whether with precision or relevance is doubtful.

Let us now lead our American through the long B corridor on the first floor whence he may see in the middle distance on green fields of Langdon (when they are visible above the winter's flood), under the gallant, athletic and ever ready supervision of Mr. Mills whence he may see, I say, a great many playing figures: boys at soccer; boys at rugger; boys playing hockey; boys running; boys jumping; boys throwing; boys doing all manner of athletic things; some handball or other training in the School's magnificent gymnasium; if he followed his eye, and went over by the gym, he might pass, where the boys were showering, down to the metal work room where Mr. Spavin spends remarkably little of his time extracting boys from those vast machines in which, I feel sure, anyone else would certainly have caught them. Next door reigns Mr.Handley, in a world of wood, where the boys make for themselves some very useful and beautiful furnishings. Between the gym and the hall lives the Scout Troop, who, with their parents' committee, are (as is right and proper), handymen to the School.

Suppose this American returned in the summer; the overall picture would not be greatly different; less indoor, more outdoor activities; a quiet game of cricket, somehow toning down the industrial background against which it is played – somehow making old this very new building in this very untraditional area.

If he had come back in the last weeks of this Easter term 1955 he would have seen the School at its Jubilee; he would have seen it giving thanks in this County Borough's Parish Church; he would have heard the headmaster telling the Old Boys' Society of the work done here in the last fifty years; he would have seen the School play host to the Borough's officers at a joyful Jubilee Ball; he would have heard a tribute paid to the previous headmaster at a gathering of old pupils now teaching in the Borough; he would have seen some more recent ex-Sixth formers returned to see again and to thank their boyhood mentors, and he would have seen these latter most interested to observe the progress of those they had but recently sent forth; he might have heard a concert of choir and orchestra, or have seen the School's Debating Society play host to numerous Sixth Formers, girls and boys, from surrounding Grammar Schools, in a debate encouraged by, and attended by a representative of 'The Observer' and entitled "This House believes that 1984 is not Far Off", and he might like to think too that the activities of this School help to prove that motion untrue. All this activity gallantly catered for by a few mothers of the Scout group, for a Jubilee which, so to speak, epitomised into one half-term the normal activities of the School over a year.

I personally should also choose to tell our American friend of some other highlights of the School's life in the years since the war; of Greek plays, in Greek and English, on tour and in East Ham; of two plays of Moliere produced exquisitely in French by Mr.Hill; of a large number of staff increasingly engaged in the annual and fruitful production of Shakespeare; of Mr.Payton and his immense undertakings with the costumes; of Mr. Spencer and his décor and his art exhibitions; of the School's contributions to the life of the Borough, whether in an annual drama festival, or verse speaking, or outdoor Shakespeare in the summer, or sports, or art, and so on; of Sixth Form socials, always fun and sometimes, especially the one held at the end of every Summer Term for the leavers, most moving; of concerts, and madrigals round Christmas trees, and of carols; and of… of a never ending procession of things done, of achievements and disappointments, of men and boys.

Or one might rather choose to tell of memorable moments; of Mr. Pain's words to the assembled School, words which will always be remembered by the senior boys present; of Mr. Lock's going – this the staff will remember; of the sad death of Mr.Haslam, so soon after finally leaving us; of the last day of many a

Summer term, when the headmaster tries at the Leavers' service to show what a grammar school is and what it tries to do. And all the time, the normal work of the School goes on, as day by day, the staff here, backed to a great degree by a helpful Council, and led by the unswerving faith of the headmaster in our mission here, fights an unending battle against the slipshod, uneasy, comfort loving tone of this - our civilisation – with its emphasis – all against the grammar school idea – on letting others do rather than on doing, on lack of precision and on lack of learning, on not reading, and on cheapness – against these things we fight in an oasis which frighteningly shrinks before our eyes; I suppose we might even try to carry on in a comprehensive school, but we do not really believe we can, and do not think we should be likely to succeed; as it is we have, I believe, a fighting chance.

Yet our American might be able to tell us that back in his country, a school such as ours would be rare indeed; he could tell us that there the comprehensive egalitarian idea is the normal philosophy behind education; that as a result, they have no Sixth Form, no academic successes, no real "learning", and so on, none of the things which, I and many others here think, make the grammar school tradition worthwhile – and aristocratic, in the proper sense of that much abused word. Let us hope he, this American, will take away with him a proper sense of what we are doing in East Ham; let him not feel that we are snobs, and let him know that we are willing, indeed that we wish, to play our part in the life of the Borough, and are doing so, but that part will only be worth playing as long as we are left to prepare it by ourselves and in our own way. Let our American friend depart finally, accompanied by these three thoughts from us; - if we are not up to expectation,…we say with Cleopatra

> ",,,And when goodwill is showed,
>   Though 't come too short
>   The actor may plead pardon."

>   : - that with T.S.Eliot, we know: -
>   "History is a pattern of timeless moments",
>   And
>   "History is now, and England".

- and finally, that we feel it above all things to be important that this School today Should agree – (as it does agree, I am sure) – and that it should be known to agree – with D.H.Lawrence when he said:"We must stand for life and construction amid all this death and destruction."

Philip was an exceptionally talented young teacher, energetic and unconventional. One of his pupils Donald Martin recalls his time at East Ham Grammar School (1950 to 1957) 'I went straight into the Sixth Form, and did Classics. Phil was the junior Classics teacher and shared the Sixth Form work with the Head of Department Ernie Mott. There was also a third year Sixth doing an extra year after A Levels to try and acquire a State Scholarship, thus I served three years in the Sixth and knew Phil well from the Classics standpoint. I believe he taught Latin further down the school, but I'd never been taught by him until the Sixth. He was also required to teach English literature to the fifth form scientists, supposedly giving them a bit of culture! This led on to Shakespeare plays in which I played a part in 'Henry 1V Part 2' and 'Coriolanus'. This involved after school rehearsals and stays at Debden House, an LEA establishment in Epping Forest. Phil also took pupils to see Greek plays, driving them in his van to Bradfield and taking them by train to Toynbee Hall in London's East End, to see the Attic Players' productions, which either Phil produced or performed in or both. The other main extra curricular activity that Phil was involved with was the Scouts.

Our Sixth form class room was next to Joe Whiteley's study, and Phil would sometimes leave us to have a full and frank discussion next door! On one occasion I remember, while doing some Roman history involving a general Mago, Phil returned, slammed the door, and proclaimed 'May Joe go to hell!' From this we gathered that whatever request he had made had been turned down! On entering the Sixth Form I think I was initially shocked by Phil – he did not appear to do the lesson prep (that, say, Ernie Mott did) but relied on his natural ability to get us through the lesson, e.g. while doing Unseen translation, if we the pupils were stuck on a word, if Phil didn't know it, one of us had to go and get the dictionary from the library! However, I think it did make us the pupils, a bit more self-reliant, and we did argue with him in lessons, which was good preparation for uni tutorials, I later realised. I felt at the time he was not necessarily doing justice to his pupils – years later, when I was pastoral head in another school, I realised that I was also in danger of short-changing my pupils through allowing other matters to take precedence.'

Peter Watkins a member of staff at East Ham Grammar School from 1956 to 1959, who later in his career became Principal of Price's Sixth Form College in Fareham, Hampshire writes in his autobiography 'The man with whom I worked most closely was Philip Vennis who came to East Ham for his first post in 1949 and stayed until 1958, overlapping with my first two years there. He had been a boy at Dulwich College and, after serving in the Navy in the last years of the war, had read Classics and English at Peterhouse, Cambridge. I became a close colleague through helping him with the school Scout group, which he founded. Whiteley had introduced a classic Sixth at East Ham, a highly unusual feature of an east London grammar school, and appointed a Cambridge classicist Vernon Mott to be Head of department. Philip Vennis was the second classics master and taught Latin and Greek. He was a lively and imaginative teacher – there was never a dull moment in his classics though his methods were often self-indulgent. He also produced Greek plays and took parties to classical plays at Cambridge and Bradfield College.

He made an outstanding contribution to school life particularly to its already strong drama tradition, and to that of the Borough. He was a colourful personality with a coherent philosophy of education, which overlapped with Whiteley's though they were not identical. He was a convinced socialist and his views were moving in the direction of comprehensive education while Whiteley remained a firm exponent of grammar schools. Philip Vennis was also mercurial, short tempered and needed to be the centre of attention. He could be difficult to work with – I found this particularly so during Scout camps when we were close colleagues. He left East Ham in July 1958. His swansong was a highly successful production for the Sixth Form Society of 'Journey's End', by R.C.Sherrif in which he played Stanhope. He went to be Deputy Headmaster of Ounsdale Comprehensive School in Staffordshire. In the eighties we were again colleagues as fellow Principals of Hampshire Sixth Form Colleges. I was in touch with him until his death at the age of seventy four in 1999.'

Philip was a great exponent for the learning of Latin and one year after leaving East Ham Grammar School, in his new post as Deputy headmaster at Ounsdale he defended the teaching of Latin following an article written in The Observer newspaper. His argument for Latin is powerful and full of conviction; he responded to the particular points made in the article with the following: 'May I, as a schoolmaster who taught Latin for some years in a grammar school, and am now teaching it in both the 'grammar' and 'modern' streams of a comprehensive, try to reply to last week's article in The Observer curiously entitled "The Latin Obstacle". To what is it supposed to be an obstacle? To the entry of bright young men to Cambridge? On Dr.Lyttleton's own admission, the standard is extremely low; so low in fact that any student of the level accepted by a Cambridge College, could learn and pass inside two months! Latin is dead. Certainly. So is the frog in the Biology laboratory. But by studying the carving up of that frog, children learn about the functions of animal bodies. So with Latin and the functions of the parts of language. Surely it may be permitted to those teaching language subjects to decide the method by which the meaning and use of language in general may be best put over. Latin is useless. But what in education is useful? Algebra? For what? For whom? We are told that children don't open their Latin books again after leaving school; but who apart from Mathematical scholars uses his algebra book? I haven't since I last did Mathematics for School Certificate eighteen years ago.

Latin does not help with French etc. Agreed. Whoever said it was taught merely for this purpose. Children don't arrive within 'a light year' (blinding us with science) of reading Latin literature. Of course not. Nor do those who have O Level mathematics arrive within 'a light year' of understanding Einstein's theory etc. This putting up of mythical hurdles in order to knock them down is an old and rather unscientific game. Does Dr.Lyttleton really think in any case that 'The Aeneid,' or Catullus' Love Poems can be appreciated fully in translation? He drags this point in. Have the private squabbles of the Cambridge Mathematics faculty about their content of their syllabus any relevance to whether the nation's schools should include Latin in their curricula? How do we prove that any single subject of a school's timetable is 'best' for some purpose? It's the total timetable which has its effect.

Of course, there is something to be said for Russian. Still I should have thought that Russian technical treatises (if this is the point) could be more profitably read in English than Virgil. There is something to be said (perhaps more in our future world) for both main forms of Chinese or for Hindi. I have no doubt someone will soon say it! How many languages are set at London O Level? Let Dr .Lyttleton come and make a school timetable and sort out the – is it 80 - claimants to a place. Then let him find the staff, then the room! He says ninety per cent (is this a national figure?) of students (does he mean school children?) take French. What's wrong with that? France is where our greatest single interchange both of ideas and of holidays etc lies and will continue to lie. Dr.Lyttleton says this is not a question of Arts versus Science. But does he really believe that the five periods or so of Latin in the upper streams of schools would give way to Russian – or as has in fact happened already, to the three separate sciences, to mathematics and the practical subjects. If this is what he wants, he should say so. How does Latin (any more than Mathematics or cooking or what have you) "obtrude itself awkwardly in school curriculum"?

"Capacity for learning languages is far greater before fifteen" – this is stated as a fact. Is it? Perhaps then, if Latin is learned before fifteen, Russian may come easier at eighteen. Perhaps the Cambridge Mathematics Faculty could include elementary Russian in its syllabus?

I find it irritating to be told that everything that Oxford and Cambridge decide is later reflected in our schools' curricula. Very few of the children I teach will even try to enter Oxford or Cambridge, or any University. Some will do only two years Latin – five periods in a forty period week for two out of five years. The following is what I hope to achieve by this. A better working

1. *New Park Road School (now the Robert Atkins School), front elevation. An archetypal London three decker school, which dominated the design of schools in the late nineteenth century.*

2. *New Park Road School (now the Robert Atkins School), designed by T.J. Bailey, constructed in 1897, demonstrates the 'Queen Anne' style used in many school buildings.*

3. Front elevation of Dulwich College, which was designed by Charles Barry in the
architectural style of 'thirteenth century North Italian Renaissance',
having its foundation stone laid in 1886.

DULWICH COLLEGE

FORM I.6 *Lower* NAME *Vennis, P.H.*

REPORT for the *Summer* TERM, 194*3*

NUMBER IN FORM *12* AVERAGE AGE OF FORM *17* yrs. *4½* m.

POSITION IN FORM *8* AGE *17* yrs. *8* m.

CLASSICS ..	*His best work is shewn in a developing facility for translation. He is a thorough & careful student, but his compositions usually lack inspiration.* P.H.V. *Latin Prose Good work; just lacks distinction* W.L.W.
HISTORY *and/or* LITERATURE ..	
ENGLISH *and* DIVINITY	*Good work.* W.L.W.
FRENCH *or* GERMAN	*Good keen work.* E.P.

A good term of progress and general development.

W.L. *Wright*
FORM MASTER

CONDUCT *good* DAYS LATE *—*

HOUSE REPORT *Fair* DAYS ABSENT *—*
G.A.W.
G. Good report. *C. N. Gilbey*
W. R. BOOTH,
THE MASTER OF THE COLLEGE

, The School will be re-opened on *Friday*, the *17ᵗʰ* day of *September*
All boys must return punctually on the day named at 9 a.m. Boarders must return to their House by 10 p.m. on the previous
day. The only ground of exemption is sickness; and of this, notice must be sent to the **Master of the College** before term begins.

4.   Philip's lower sixth report
of Summer Term 1943
Remarks are as follows
Classics — His best work is
shown in a developing facility
for translation. He is a
thorough and careful student,
but his compositions usually
lack inspiration. P.H. Vellacott

English — Good work. W.J.
Wright

French — good keen work. E.
Parsley

A good term of progress and
general development.
W.J. Wright —
Form Master

5. *Bletchley Park Mansion which is a mixture of architectural styles dating from the Victorian era is now a grade 2 listed building and was the headquarters of the code breaking operations in the Second world War.*

6. *One of Bletchley Park's wooden huts as it stands today. Hut 7, now demolished, was of a similar construction from Canadian Pine with an outside covering of ship lap boarding.*

CHARACTER		COMPOUNDS
晝 TYUU - daytime 129/5	晝間	TYUUKAN - (during the) day
	晝夜	TYUUYA - night & day. (TYUUSENTAI - day-action unit)
作 SAKU/SA - to make; do. 9/5	作業	SAGYOO - task; operation; work
業 GYOO - business; occupation 7% sude(ni) - already	索敵	SAKUTEKI - to search for the enemy.
倣 HOO; nara(u) - to imitate 9/8 (tni)		(SENTI ITISEIGOO - coordination of plotted positions)
倣 KOO; nara(u) - to imitate 9/8 (tni)	整合	SEIGOO - plotting (course etc)
整 SEI - to adjust; put in order 11/12	艦位	KANI - ship's position
修 SYUU - to practise 9/8	修正	SYUUSEI - to correct
量 RYOO - amount; quantity; volume 72/8	修正量	SYUUSEI RYOO - amount of correction.
表 HYOO - outside; sign; table; to indicate; disclose 145/3 arawa(su) - to show "	表示	HYOOZI - to indicate. (標示)
友 YUU - friendly 24/2	友部隊	YUUBUTAI - allied units. (YUUGUN - our troops)

7. *A page from Philip's Japanese vocabulary book.*

8. *Some of the one thousand two hundred Japanese character flash cards.*

襲 — SYUU; oso(u) - to attack, kasa(naru) - to pile up, tugu) - to inherit. kasane - a suit (of clothes) 212/6

他 — TA; hoka; yoso- other; another; besides 9/3

區 — KU; division; district; boundary; (sub-division of some cities) 173/?

電 — DEN - electricity. inazuma - lightning

終 — SYUU; owari-end; owa(ru); o(eru) - end; finish; tui ni - at last; finally 120/5

振 — SIN; hu(ru) - to shake; huru) - to become active, shake; huri - appearance 66/7

衝 — SYOO - responsible position; tuku) - to strike against. 60/12

識 — SIKI; SI; siru - to know well; discriminate; siru(su) - to write. 149/12

9. *The Chapel built in 1628 during Mathew Wren's (Christopher Wren's Uncle) time as Master of Peterhouse. The Chapel demonstrates the transition from Gothic to Renaissance architecture that took place under the Stuarts.*

10. *The Hall, originally built in 1286, was heightened in the fifteenth century and heavily restored in the nineteenth century, leaving little of the original building. The interior has a tiled fireplace by William Morris and stained glass windows by William Morris, Burne-Jones and Maddox Browne.*

11. *Stained glass in the east window of Peterhouse Chapel. It depicts the Crucifixion based on Rubens 'Le coup de Lance; and was removed and hidden during the Civil War in 1634 thus saving it from being destroyed by the Parliamentarians.*

12. *"A lot of my time and Philip's time was spent eating cakes (which were on ration coupons) from Fitzbillies."*

13. *The Boy's Grammar School was built to accomodate 600 pupils and opened in 1952.*

14. *An illuminated, hand painted, appreciation of Philip's work in the County Borough of East Ham by the Mayor and Education Officers.*

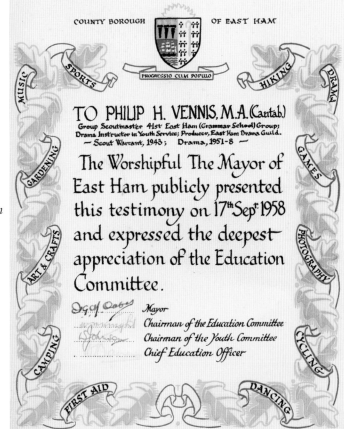

15. *The Parish Church of St. Benedict, built by one of the Priors of Dudley in 1170, had a tower surmounted by a spire in about 1400. The Church is built of pink sandstone.*

16. *The modern village is still centred on the green, the original heart of Wombourne. The village green represents an archetypal 'English Village.'*

knowledge of English; how it works as a language; a more precise use of parts of speech and meaning of words; more interest in the grammar of language; an increased use of the English vocabulary and a regard for the Roman and Greek achievements. I know no better way of doing this, certainly it isn't by increasing the English periods to ten. These I think are not 'old shibboleths', nor are those of us who teach Latin all old fogeys sticking thoughtlessly to a well worn and reactionary groove, because we cannot do anything else. The reaction lies elsewhere. I feel a perfectly progressive teacher.

Dr.Lyttleton say that a 'Liberal Education can't be imposed'. How on earth else can you get it? He implies that learning Latin is horrid for boys and girls; no doubt. He goes on to argue that Russian is very difficult and therefore should replace it! Shall we ask the boys and girls what they would like to learn at the age of eleven? The result might be fun and interesting to a Don but hardly suitable for the timetable!

Greek has almost gone from schools, and Latin is an easy target. I shall be amused to see an article by a Russian Don in some years time proposing to replace the Mathematics in schools by? French Cooking? Criminology?

May I end by saying that in general I find Dr.Lyttleton's article superfluous and really vaguely insulting. We also think sometimes – between lessons. The only statistics that seem to me to be of any value would be the number of borderline children (bottom streams grammar, technical streams and the top streams of modern) who have passed O Level English Language after learning some Latin or without learning any Latin or have failed O Level English Language after learning some Latin or without learning any Latin.

I hope that Cambridge will not give a lead in helping to destroy something established (as Dr.Lyttleton says – yea or nea – it will affect us) without first having studied the whole picture, and not just the tiny percentage which makes up their possible student body.'

Kenneth Harris of The Observer newspaper replied to Philip's responses on 24 February 1959 by saying 'it is an extremely good letter, but unfortunately because of the length of it we are unable to publish it as cutting it would spoil the impact'.

Philip wrote in 1958 after his final production at East Ham Grammar School 'School Drama is only one attempt at a contribution towards living together and making together. It's the making that matters, - not finally what the audiences see. Drama can play a great part in making the school whole, and living; and Shakespeare with his particular all – seeing truth, and his possibilities for expansion in production, and his enormous Elizabethan zest, seems to me the business of schools above all.'

When Philip joined East Ham Grammar School there was already a well-established Dramatic Society. The Dramatic Society began with Dr. Whiteley's appointment as Headmaster in 1944, when he and Mr. Payton jointly produced the first three plays, 'Henry 1V part 1', 'Twelfth Night' and 'Julius Caesar' thereby establishing the 'Shakespearian Tradition'. Whilst the Boys' Grammar School was still in the old building, plays were put on at the hall of the Girls' Grammar School until 1948 and thereafter on the town hall stage. This practice continued with 'King Lear' (1949, co-produced by P.H.V.) and 'A Midsummer-Night's Dream' (1950, co-produced by P.H.V.) and 'Henry V' (1951, in which Philip played the Chorus and co-produced), until the School moved to its new premises and received for the first time, its own hall fully equipped as a theatre. The town hall had had many advantages, chiefly its size and nearness to the school, but a distinct disadvantage was the poor acoustic properties of the hall. At the back of the audience, much of a play was inaudible, not the actors' fault, but the poor acoustics.

Philip started a series of non-Shakespearian productions with two Greek plays, produced in Greek and English – 'The Cyclops of Euripides' (1950) and 'The Peace of Aristophanes' (1952). He produced 'The Cyclops' in the original Greek and English version of Sir J.T. Sheppard who came from Cambridge to see the performances. The Times Educational Supplement on 21 July 1952 wrote in its review 'it has long been recognised that children can learn to appreciate the theatre through acting, also that school performances may bring a remote age to life. Certainly the actors from East Ham Grammar School for Boys, who presented 'The Cyclops of Euripides' in both English and Greek at their sister school last week, seemed on the friendliest terms with the fifth century B.C. Much of the ease of relationship derived from the richly racy English version of Sir J.T. Sheppard. The human taste for sensation is perennial; and his spirited colloquialisms awoke modern echoes in the short Satyr-play which, to bring relief after tragedy, larks around cannibalism. 'The Cyclops', boisterous, gruesome and gay is an excellent play for boys, and the actors treated it with affection.'

After the school moved to its new site in Langdon Crescent, with its magnificent hall fully equipped as a theatre, a greater interest in drama took place and Philip was the main inspiration in this happening.

Philip produced 'Macbeth' in 1953. Geoffrey Whalen who played Donalbain in the production wrote in his review 'Mr. Vennis's production at least prevented the audience from falling asleep. The vigour and enthusiasm which Edwards gave to his portrayal kept the play going with a swing – school productions are so often languid and colourless. The scenery, costumes and lighting added colour and life to the performance, leaving an impression on the play of speed and drive. Mr. Vennis devoted his attention to putting this life and energy into the play.' Colin Davies, a third year Sixth former, and later in his career, headmaster of a comprehensive school in Farnborough, Hampshire, states in his review of 'Macbeth' in which he played Malcolm 'To the cynic, I suppose, the staging of plays by school boys must seem a hopeless waste of everyone's time and trouble from which no ultimate benefit issues, but this is quite a false idea. On the contrary, much is to be gained from taking a part in a play, no matter how small or insignificant that part may be, especially if the play happens to be worthwhile.

The amateur actor learns from experience the technique of acting and producing, and he may, if he is lucky, discover some tricks of the trade. This knowledge, though slight, will help him to understand more clearly and appreciate more fully the ability and skill of the professional actor and dramatist; he will gain much added interest from watching a first class production of a good play.

Yet do not for one moment think that we take a part in a school play because we feel it will do our souls some good (though this of course is an added advantage). There is much more to it than that; we enjoy the play, and everything that goes to make up a play, the greasepaint, the costumes, the lighting, not to mention the producer's tantrums. It is all these things that cause the excitement and enjoyment of taking part in a play, and I myself, whatever in the future I may be lucky enough to see a performance of 'Macbeth' shall recall with great enjoyment the time when, with my school friends, I took a part in our amateur production, though no less enjoyable, version of the play.'

Colin many years later went on to say 'Philip was a major influence and encouragement to me at East Ham Grammar School. He stood out as a new, fresh, young teacher, enthusiastic, generous with his time and really quite inspirational in his love of drama. In that East London school he encouraged us and lifted our horizons so that I among many raised my expectations and dreamed some dreams. He was, as I said, a schoolmaster extraordinary. I am totally grateful that all those years ago he began his teaching career in the school where I was young, eager to learn and looking for someone with a genuine care and concern for his pupils'.

John Edwards who played Macbeth in this production not only recalls the impact of drama 'which was Philip's passion' but years later said 'I know that it is a long time ago, and there must be many pupils since who have reason to be grateful to Philip, but his arrival at East Ham Grammar School was, believe me a breath of fresh air. I don't think we had ever seen a teacher so young for a start – it was still an era of black gowned, stern-faced pre-war types who were rather forbidding. Philip brought fun and enthusiasm into the classroom and, just as important, fun and enthusiasm into activities outside the classroom. As well as drama, I remember, as a non-scout being asked to go along and help one of his summer camps near Wenlock Edge in Shropshire. Not many teachers in those days fraternised with boys outside school or brought their outside interests into school. Philip did and I know my friends at school of that era appreciated it – even more now looking back than perhaps they did at the time. Of course, learning was not forgotten amid all these interests and it amazes me now what a brilliant (and free) education we received. Maybe it is my age but my education, I think, compared with the best schools in the country. There were some wonderful teachers; even some of the old forbidding ones, at East Ham Grammar School, but for me Philip was the teacher who gave us the widest view not just of learning but life. The memories are still vivid – the school Greek play, the Shakespearian school productions and those outside in Central Park, the conversations in his digs about books, plays, productions. School was fun – and much of it was due to Philip.'

The production of 'Henry 1V part 2' followed in 1954, and in this production Philip stepped outside the normal picture frame stage. He used aprons and hall entries and attempted to bring the audience closer to the players, more in line with Shakespeare's own audiences, where the theatre had no proscenium arch. This was his contribution to the new zest of a new Elizabethan age with his highly educative creative production.

Drama as has been said was Philip's passion, and this passion extended outside of the school. He produced and acted with three other groups of amateur dramatists, The Attic Players, The Old Esthameians and The Drama Guild of East Ham Borough. In his nine years in East Ham he was involved in the production of forty plays.(Colour photograph 14.) The Attic Players who were formed by Philip Vellacott from Dulwich College and performed their Greek plays in various venues: in 1950, Euripides' 'Alcestis' was performed in Camberwell; in 1951 Aeschylus' 'Agamemnon' was performed in the Toynbee Hall Theatre; in 1956 'Medea' at the Grammar School; and in 1957 Sophocles' 'Antigone' and Anouilh's 'Antigone' was performed in the Theatre of the City Literary Institute.

These Greek plays were produced in the 'Classical Theatre' idea rather than the 'Romantic Theatre' as is more widely known. The Classical Theatre is different from the Romantic Theatre in that it followed the "unities" – that is the play happened in one place and at one time, and the action lasted for as long as it took to play it; it also used traditional stories, for example the gods and it only had a limited number of actors. The main stumbling block for a producer is that of the character of the Chorus, whose presence must be accepted but can be irritating to the modern ideas of theatre, and who must bring out the beauty of the odes by the timing of their delivery. The two Antigone's were according to The Times Educational Supplement of 15 November 1957, 'an ambitious double bill, linguistically, the contrast was not as pointed as it might have been, because the 'straight' version employed the excellent modern translation by Dudley Fitts and Robert Fitzgerald. The Sophocles was given the conventional Greek drama treatment, in so far as the translation permitted, and incorporated a richly naturalistic study of the Sentry. In Creon we found a character who seemed aware of the changed emphasis in Anouilh's characterisation. Ronald Aldridge, whose inflexibly unimaginative Creon assumed plasticity and sophistication when he changed into modern costume, became the play's true hero.'

Ronald Aldridge who played Creon in this production of 'Antigone', and several other roles in Philip's productions such as in 1953 The Apothecary in 'Romeo and Juliet', Jorgen Tesman in 'Hedda Gabler' also in 1953, Don Pedro, Prince of Arragon in 'Much Ado About Nothing' in 1954 and Octavius Caesar in 'Antony and Cleopatra' in 1955 comments over fifty years later, 'I first met Philip as an adult through amateur drama after he had joined the staff at East Ham Grammar School for Boys. He, like me, in his own schooling had benefited from the 1902 Education Act, in which the initial impulse was to make available education to working class children and to open up opportunities for them, and, subsequently fill the skills gaps in the labour market. At the beginning of the twentieth century labourers were being brought in from parts of Europe to fill these gaps. Philip was aware that he had had a very privileged education at Dulwich and Cambridge and his greatest desire when he arrived at East Ham was to give to working class boys the opportunities he had had.

I attended West Ham Grammar School which was not as traditional as East Ham Grammar School. East Ham under the leadership of Dr. Whiteley, 'aped the public schools' in many ways. Dr. Whiteley always stood by the tripartite system, which had evolved out of the 1944 Education Act, and in which the secondary grammar schools and secondary modern schools grew out of the elementary school system. Philip was not so left wing at this stage and he admired Dr. Whiteley's stance on grammar schools. Dr. Whiteley always supported Philip's often unconventional approach to school life. On one occasion, I recall, Philip used the staff room carpet in his production of 'Hedda Gabbler' without asking anyone's permission!

The other area in which Philip opened doors and new worlds for working class children and (in my case adults) was through drama. For myself, the big door was the 'Greek Theatre', I had learnt a lot about Shakespeare at school and as a regular theatre goer; but it was Philips's taking me to Bradfield and then me subsequently performing in productions of Greek drama that made Greek Theatre "magical", and whenever I watched a Greek tragedy "I was absolutely transported into another world".

Philip's whole career corresponded with current thoughts on education, and in the Late fifties when comprehensive schools were being increased in number his interest in their philosophy became more powerful. He moved with the thinking and his career came full circle when he ran Itchen College; his original ideal of opening doors for working class children was still in the forefront of his thinking. Itchen College was open access and Philip kept absolutely to this ideal. I have to say that at no point did I agree with Philip on his philosophy of Sixth Form Colleges because I am a staunch F.E. man!' (Ronald Aldridge was Principal of City and East London Further Education College, and lifelong friend from 1950 to 1999.)

Trips to Bradfield College to attend Greek plays were a regular feature of Philip's time in East Ham. In June 1952 he took Sixth form boys two weekends running to see Sophocles' 'Antigone' the students were most impressed by the open air theatre, which was as much like the old Greek theatre as possible with its 'orchestra', not as is the normal meaning of the word, but simply a flat, round space where the chorus speak and sing their chants. In July 1955 another trip to Bradfield took place, this time to see Sophocles' 'Oedipus at Colonus'; the Sixth formers enjoyed the atmosphere of a Greek theatre and the play in something like its original surroundings. The auditorium consisted of a semicircular concrete edifice built round a small open space, and, with a number of tiers of step like seats, the actual stage was built in the style of an ancient Greek stage, with its distinctive pediment pillars, which had very simple permanent scenery. On the journey home in Philip's car serious discussions took place about the play, poetry, jazz and music. After the visit to Bradfield Philip wrote in the News Club Newspaper of October 1955, 'Let us not forget the other theatre – the amateur. It is by no means always true that its standards are below those of the professional. At Bradfield College, Berkshire, this summer in the school's open air Greek theatre there was given a near perfect performance with the most remarkable choric movements, of that masterpiece of Sophocles' old age, a play for those who believe in quietude, the Oedipus at Colonus. It was beautifully done by schoolboys in a beautiful setting, if you have a chance, seize it, for they produce triennially.'

The Old Esthameians put on the first dramatic performance in the new school building in November 1952 which was a celebration of their new theatre, in which Dr. Whiteley joined the company as in the role of a bibulous baron. Although Philip produced the play, 'Captain Carvallo', it was a departure for him from Greek Tragedy or Shakespeare. The Times Educational Supplement of 14 November 1952 in its review states 'Mr. Cannan's comedy – to which with some reason, he applies the epithet 'traditional' – might be thought an odd choice for the christening of a school hall. It certainly contains no lack of allusions to facts which every schoolboy, it might once have been argued, should seem not to know. But it is excellent entertainment. The dialogue flashes with popular wisdom, and slapstick and sparkle, cunningly combined, present the company with a constant challenge. Of the two, the slapstick was the better realised.' The other production Philip undertook with the Old Esthameians was 'Hedda Gabler' by Ibsen.

"No. it is only the moral victory I care for." Hedda Gabler by Ibsen with a cast from Old Esthameians, produced in 1952.

This was a bold choice by Philip and an interesting experiment, as it was a long jump after his colourful and rather exciting open air production of 'Romeo and Juliet' (a year previous in June 1953) to the sombre realism of Henrik Ibsen.

By far the biggest out of school productions Philip undertook were for the East Ham County Borough with the East Ham Drama Guild as the main players. These productions usually took place in Central Park in the open air. In June 1952 the Stratford Express newspaper reviewed 'Twelfth Night' by writing 'East Ham can be proud of its Drama Guild. With productions like this it will soon acquire a lustrous reputation. Beauty had been captured, in famous lines triumphantly spoken, in velvet gowns and cloaks of myriad colours, in the Illyrian pastoral background. Comedy was there, in the sparing uproarious buffoons, and philosophy, embedded in lightly sung verses.

"If ever thou shalt love,
In the sweet pangs of it remember me;
For such as I am all true lovers are"

Twelfth Night in East Ham Central Park with the cast from
The Drama Guild of East Ham, produced in 1952.

Shakespeare provided the cloth and Mr. Vennis, with unerring precision, had cut it in vivid fashion.' To celebrate the coronation of Elizabeth II in June 1953 East Ham Drama Guild staged 'Romeo and Juliet'. The Borough had commissioned Philip to be producer, and, despite some inclement weather the cast did not have to withdraw to the marquee. The Times Educational Supplement reviewed this outdoor production in its edition on 19 June 1953 by saying 'It was hard to take East Ham for Italy – though Mr. Philip Vennis the producer of 'Romeo and Juliet' did the best he could to create the illusion by giving the play an operatic treatment. There were drums in the background to mark the brawls, a recorded choir for a moment of poignancy, and the same familiar Tchaikovsky excerpt wafting in on all the love-scenes. Such musical warmth may have cheered the audience, dispirited the damp; but on other grounds it was scarcely more defensible than the floodlit fountain at the back of the stage. How often in productions of this play, must not prettiness have crept in to contaminate passion? There were, however many moments when the authentic notes were touched, especially by Romeo, who felt the beauty of his lines and who spoke the most ardent of them excellently; his scene of despair in the Friar's cell – played, until the proper moment, with a wise economy of means – was particularly effective, and the sincerity of the acting by the company as a whole enabled the tension to be creditably built up.' Brian Wright who played Romeo in this production went on to act professionally, said of Philip 'He was my Latin teacher and form master over forty five years ago at East Ham Grammar School and then through a shared interest in theatre, scouting and all things laughable, my friend. He was also by way of being a mentor, and a powerful influence on my choice of career in theatre and television. In spite of the familiar ups and downs, I have never regretted that choice, and I remain grateful for his encouragement and enthusiasm. I always think of him with great affection, and I know I am not alone in that. I remember our occasional rows. We must both have been very wilful characters. He is a man who lives in many memories, and for me the memory always brings a warm smile.'

"Love, give me strength! and strength Shall help afford. Farewell, dear Father."

Romeo and Juliet in East Ham Central Park with the cast from the Drama Guild of East Ham, produced in 1953

"Friendship is constant in all other things
Save in the office and affairs of love."

Much Ado About Nothing in East Ham Central Park
with the cast from the Drama Guild of East Ham, produced in 1954.

In 1954, Philip produced 'Much Ado about Nothing' with the Drama Guild, which in Philip's own words 'was clearly a success, with a talented cast who responded to the challenge and made this one of the best Shakespearian productions I have done. Much rehearsal was needed, many all day long and it is only then that the play really comes together. I have been accused of having too much atmosphere at my rehearsals, of going on too long, of pushing people too hard – these things in my opinion are essential to a production, and without them people wouldn't and don't play at their peak. The play wouldn't look (and this is most important in Central Park) as it does and should. In any case they are essential parts of the fun; let not the actresses and actors of the Guild come into one of these productions, unprepared to give up time and take trouble even with the smallest Shakespearian roles; he or she would be quite wrong; and let him or her not think that he or she must not act all the time while on the stage, even when not speaking, or even if not speaking throughout the play; there is I think, just that very slight tendency here.' Later on in the same article, which was a report about 'Much Ado about Nothing' to East Ham Borough Council, Philip concludes with 'I believe in Amateur Drama as an education and leisure time activity. As you know, I believe it ranks even above the Boy Scouts, though only just in value. I believe too that Shakespeare is our business, that once a year it is an excellent thing that this Guild come together not to a meeting, but to a production – and that production should be Shakespeare; otherwise he will not be produced here. I believe we have proved that the audience doesn't just want farce. My own preference is for tragedy; and I believe they enjoyed 'Romeo and Juliet', a production of which I am still, against considerable odds, proud. I wonder if people have any proper realisation of the agony of effort and worry, and damage to reputation in the eyes of officialdom, required by the two or three people most closely concerned – and not least the producer – finally to move one of these enormous productions onto the set in the Park; it really is a frantic and fantastic fortnight, and it leaves us very weary men. It's worth it only because the final picture on the set is Shakespeare – one of the great works of man – and Shakespeare, I repeat – his poetry, his prose, his wit, his learning, his beauties, his philosophies, his everything – these are our business.'

One of Philip's last productions for East Ham Borough with the Drama Guild was in 1955 'Antony and Cleopatra'. The school was very closely connected with this production, not just with Philip as the producer but with three other members of staff and many members of the school taking part. The News Club newspaper in its Theatre section in October 1955 published an article written by Philip about 'Antony and Cleopatra'. 'In East Ham, the Drama Guild has the excellent custom of producing Shakespeare with financial aid from the Council in one of the Borough's Parks. This year they attempted 'Antony and Cleopatra', surely one of the most ambitious of Shakespeare's plays for amateurs to perform, and incidentally one of the most worthwhile.

There production was ambitious – a cast of 50, music by Antony Hopkins borrowed from the Redgrave-Ashcroft Stratford production; an Antony by R.A.D.A. student Michael Reed who had the voice and delivery and manner of a professional Antony, the Cleopatra, a local schoolteacher Dorrie Hamilton who had the delivery and caught the fickleness and perpetual change of Cleopatra. Caesar and Enobarbus, both schoolmasters, were outstanding: Ronald Aldridge's Caesar proved a perfectly calculated foil to Antony, spoke the verse beautifully and had clearly studied and was well inside this extraordinary character, who has been called "the oddest fish in Shakespeare, neither hero or villain". Frederick Waterson's Enobarbus reflected the plain man's view of these two lovers: he had vigour and bluntness, giving the play, as is surely intended, certain back bone. The whole production was very worthy of the amateur tradition in England and distinctly of the sort of standard, if I may say so as one involved, that amateurs should wish to aim for. It is also the sort of play the amateurs should want to produce and they should not be afraid of performing 'Antony and Cleopatra'. It is standards that matter in the theatre and standards come in the first place from the choice of play, and in the second, through thoroughness and length of preparation and rehearsal. Those concerned must be able to say with Charmian at the moment of Cleopatra's death, when she is asked by Caesar's guard 'Is this well done?' 'It is well done and fitting.' The Stratford Express in its edition published on 8 July 1955 said of the production 'Mr. Philip Vennis's production was ever dramatic, virile and dynamic. Over 700 hours had been spent in preparing the play. The professional veneer of the finished product, showed unmistakably the value of this company's patience.'

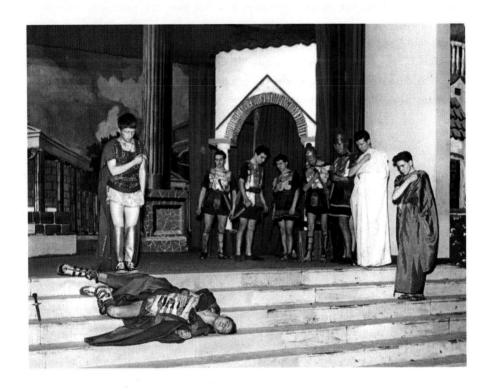

"Bear from hence his body; And morn you for him.
Let him be regarded as the most noble corse that ever herald did follow to his urn."

Coriolanus with a cast from East Ham Grammar School for Boys, produced in 1956.

'Coriolanus' was to be the last Shakespeare play that Philip produced at East Ham Grammar School in December 1956. Both press reviews in the Stratford Express and The Times Educational supplement praised the production. The Stratford Express in its edition 21 December 1956 stated 'Mr. Vennis's production came off best as a pageant. His grouping was always neat, and, with the Senators excellent. Making good use of his various platform levels, he achieved plenty of depth on the big stage. Music was used to good effect and lightening was sometimes inspired – as with a spotlight playing on an eagle over the proscenium arch before and after acts.' The Times Educational Supplement of 21 December 1956 commented that 'Coriolanus is an excellent choice for a school play. Its argument is straightforward and topical; it throws less responsibility on the central character than the better-known tragedies, and its crowd scenes enable many less confident boys to take part in the corporate activity of 'making a play'. In the production at the East Ham Grammar School for Boys the large and boisterous crowd, often entering through the auditorium and usually in full voice, successfully reproduced the fickleness, humour and cowardliness of Shakespeare's 'beast with many heads'. This production was notable throughout for its thorough use of the generous resources of the school; with elaborate lighting, colourful costumes for a cast of over 70 and ominously repetitive music. Much of the action took place on the rostra in front of the proscenium, extending the acting area to the entire width of the hall; the set was ambitious. The producer achieved some striking dramatic moments; notably the carrying of Coriolanus's body in slow procession, picked out in a single horizontal shaft of light, and Coriolanus' walk to exile through the audience with all Rome ranged on the stage waving and saluting.'

"You think there is no limit to what a man can bear?:

Journey's End, a joint staff and sixth form production from East Ham Grammar School for Boys. Produced in 1958.

Philip chose, as his swan song, at East Ham to produce R.C.Sheriff's 'Journey's End'. Members of the Staff and Sixth Form made up the cast. Philip said 'A staff and boys' play, often a dream, became a reality. Six of the third year Sixth and five members of staff are going to do their best with Sheriff's 'Journey' End'. It's a play about the 'the heartbreak in the heart of things', about the waste of war, and the deterioration in a group of men, doomed (as they all know) never to come away from the trenches they hate. 'Journey's End' is no masterpiece like 'Coriolanus', but still a well written and most moving play – "There's a long long trail a winding" 'Journey's End' is a straightforward war play about English soldiers in the front-line trench, waiting for an overwhelming enemy attack from which they know they will not emerge. The characters of the play, typed and unsubtle, show the different possible reactions to such a situation: fortitude, resignation, panic. The mood changes from sentimentality unchecked to sentimentality controlled with a stiff upper lip. It is eminently playable as a tear-jerker, with much atmosphere and action and with some comic relief'. Philip produced it at this level, attempting at Wilfred Owen's statement 'My theme is war and the pity of war. The poetry is the pity'. He directed the cast to interpret their parts and interpolated the action with some of the finest World War One poems. Thus all sorts of emotions were struck: Gracie Fields singing 'There's a long long trail a winding' against 'Does it matter if they lose their legs?' of '... .that old lie, Dulce et decorum est pro patria mori' against The Last Post. Philip, in his role of Stanhope dominated, as it must, and doubling with his role as producer and first lead he demonstrated enormous stamina. The Times Educational Supplement reviewed the production in its edition of 18 July 1958 by commenting 'At East Ham Grammar School the production of R.C.Sheriff's Journey's End was an intelligent performance. The production was the work of Mr. Philip Vennis and the influence of his experience was obvious, especially in the imaginative use of the poems of Owen and Sassoon as a commentary on the action. The play itself is good enough to leave a strong impression on the audience, even though there is very little development of character.'

As has been mentioned, apart from drama Philip's other passion and out of school activity was the Boy Scouts. Philip began the 41st East Ham Group and recalls in 1958, his doubts about beginning a troop, 'Nine years ago, the one thing I was most wary of starting was a Scout group here. Two years later however, with the District Commissioner's agreement, we began as the 41st Troop in the Borough; with the help of the boys in the School who were already Scouts, we managed some four patrols of six; we met in the gym in the old School, and for a time merely survived. One of the original Scouts, Colin Curds remembers the beginning. 'During school assembly in October 1951, at the beginning of my third year at secondary school, the formation of a school scout troop was announced by the headmaster, who said it would be led by Mr. Vennis and would be held on Thursday evenings in the school gymnasium. At the time, none of us were aware of Phil's interest in scouting, which began during his own school days at Dulwich College nor of his expertise as an experienced quarter-master for large scout camps. I learned later that there had been some opposition to Phil's proposed troop by the local scout association who were worried that we might poach scouts from other troops when they were admitted to the Grammar School. This was the time of the Scholarship Examination (later the 11-plus) and I suspect that this was part of the anti-grammar school feelings that many of us experienced to some degree. I certainly experienced sarcastic jibes from some of my more distant relatives. Luckily the local District Commissioner supported the idea after Phil assured the local association that we would not poach recruits from other troops.

A few years earlier I had been a recruit at my local church troop for a short time which did not come up to my expectations. I still maintained a residual interest and along with about fifteen other boys attended the first meeting. From the beginning Phil began to teach us how to tie knots, talk about camping and the sorts of activities in which we could take part. To my relief British Bulldog did not appear on his agenda, and I became a regular member of the 41st East Ham (East Ham Grammar School for Boys) Scout Troop. As word got around more boys joined and we quickly formed into four patrols of six boys which Phil said should be named after British wild animals. We chose Squirrels, Peewits, Otters and Eagles and a further couple were added as others joined in later years. By January 1952 most recruits had acquired uniforms and four of us, John Wilkins, George Wombwell, James Campbell and myself had passed our tenderfoot badge tests and were invested. A few weeks later George V1 died and we attended the announcement given on the steps of East Ham Town Hall which was adjacent to the school. This meant we had to wear black arm bands for several months when in uniform.'

At Easter 1952 a camp was held with Dulwich Group who acted as 'foster-parents' to the fledgling Group from East Ham, and Philip recalls that 'we would not have survived without them. We learned from each other.' Colin Curds continues 'By Easter 1952 Phil decided that we were ready to send a patrol on the first camp. None of those attending had any experience of camping so he arranged that we join the 25th Camberwell (1st Dulwich College) Scout Group at their annual Easter camp in Broadstone Warren, Wych Cross, East Sussex. An experimental patrol comprised of a selection of six boys from East Ham were welcomed at Dulwich College and travelled to Broadstone by lorry. Although the Easter of 1952 came late in the season the weather was cold and we found that there had been a six inch snowfall at the campsite.

Philip as Quatermaster. Easter 1952, with a fledgling Group from East Ham Boys Grammar School and a Dulwich College Group.

So we cleared the snow and pitched our tent adjacent to a Dulwich patrol under the leadership of a boy called John Faulkner who was to be our mentor. The presence of snow on the ground and our total lack of experience led Phil to insist that we spend the first night in a hut rather than under canvas. We were appalled by the idea but after a night in the hut our continual protests finally won the day and Phil allowed us to spend the next four nights under canvas. Camping in the fifties was not quite as we know it now. None of us could afford sleeping bags so we had to rely on blankets sealed with large blanket pins and to make things worse tents did not have sewn-in groundsheets. Each boy had his own 6' x 2'6 groundsheet so that the wind and rain came whistling under the tent brailings. It was a miserable experience, everything was cold and damp, the snow melted and the ground turned to mud but we were kept very busy lighting fires and cooking so that time passed quickly enough. At the weekend we were visited by Dr. Whiteley, his wife and sons. This was rather an occasion for us since most of us had had little direct contact with him at this point in our school life. In the lower school only those with a history of persistent misbehaviour would have spoken to him directly.

It was at this first camp that we saw Phil outside the confines of formal school life. All the Dulwich boys called him Phil while we of course continued with Sir for the first few days. He was kept busy with organising the catering for the whole camp of around fifty boys something we never suspected he could or would do. Furthermore it was he who instructed us on how to cook meals with the raw ingredients that he had purchased. He came to our patrol to eat and somehow we all survived. On our last night there was a campfire organised by the older Dulwich boys but it was Phil who led most of the singing. Campfires ended by drinking cocoa and singing insulting lyrics to the song 'In the Quarter Master's Store' which seemed largely aimed at Phil who was obviously popular with the Dulwich crew. We East Ham boys joined in and added another verse about Phil – we waited for a reaction, but he just laughed with everyone else. That night we said 'Goodnight Phil' for the first time and from then on he was 'Sir' at school but 'Phil' in camp.

Summer Camp, Wenlock Edge, Shropshire

It is now almost the norm for schools to have a parent/teacher association but that was not the case in the early fifties. As a new troop we had virtually no equipment and had borrowed a tent from Dulwich for the first Easter camp. We needed money fast and a reluctant headmaster agreed to allow Phil to set up a scout parents' committee as a way of raising funds. They immediately began organising jumble sales and a local childrens' dance school put on a show to raise funds for us. The parent's committee was an immediate success and we began to purchase equipment seeking rock bottom prices at many ex-army supply shops that sprang up after the war ended. Somehow enough money was raised to purchase sufficient equipment for four patrols to attend the Dulwich scout group's summer camp at Tiverton. We were dwarfed by the Dulwich contingent who boasted three troops, a senior scout troop, and several old boys. By this time John Wilkins and I were ready to be taught how to fell a tree and a Mr. Gipson (but only known as Gippo) who organised all the Dulwich equipment and professed to be an expert axe man agreed to teach us. Unfortunately in spite of our expert's aid (though my memory tells me it was because of his aid) the tree fell the wrong way blocking the private road of the Minister of Food and Fisheries and severing its telephone line in the process. Phil thought it highly amusing and told us not to worry as Gippo was well known for his misplaced tree fellings.'

A member of the Dulwich College troop remembers a different incident from the Tiverton camp, Garth Davidson recalls – 'Surreptitious biscuits were a feature of my final scout camp in 1952. The camp was near Tiverton, with John Cottle as Scout leader. Philip and I were among the HQ members, and we all felt a bit hungry at times! We would steal into Food Stores when nobody, we hoped, was looking, and help ourselves to a biscuit or two from the appropriate tin. Thus was the term 'surreptitious biscuit' born, and from then on it became part of the Davidson family vocabulary – and still is!' Another member of the Dulwich troop was Hector McLean and he says of his dealings with Philip at the Tiverton camp, 'I remember Philip very well in the scouting context, always cheerful, encouraging and practical, all of which were very important when it came to camping. I cannot recall him ever being put out of his stride by problems and having a great capacity for dealing effectively with youngsters.' Colin continues 'The troop began to expand and while we gathered experience and continued to camp with Dulwich College, we joined as I said at Broadstone Warren (Easter), and Blockley (Summer 1952) but Easter 1953 was something different.

The Peewit Patrol – summer Camp, Blockley 1952.

After summer camp in Blockley Phil spent his own summer holiday in France. So at the beginning of the new term he proposed that we spend ten days camping in the Loire valley visiting the chateaux. None of us had been abroad before and this immediately caught our imagination. So in Easter 1953 nine of us departed for Newhaven to meet Phil in Rouen. We camped just outside the town overnight and then split into two groups, the cyclists led by John Wilkins took off for Amboise while the hikers caught a train to Tours and then made for some destination on foot along the north bank of the Loire. Although Amboise was our base camp Phil took us out on daily or overnight trips to visit many chateaux. On one such visit one of the cyclists from Dulwich lost an argument with a lorry and was rushed to hospital. The other cyclists were not involved in the accident and after contacting the emergency services continued to the next campsite. It was rather different for us hikers who then had a long trek ahead of them since Phil was naturally attending to the injured lad in hospital. Furthermore, Phil had all the equipment in his vehicle so the cyclists could do little when they arrived. However, when Phil and the hikers arrived late at night the cyclists had got some fires going and they had charmed the maids of a small chateaux in whose grounds we were camping to supply us with some food. They gave us eggs, olive oil, an enormous frying pan and a keg of red wine. That was a memorable meal. Luckily the injured boy was not too bad and he returned to the base camp a couple of days later. After visiting Amboise, Blois, Chambord, Montmajour, Azay-le-Rideau, Villandry and Chenonceaux we left for a couple of nights in a hostel just outside Paris.' John Wilkins wrote a report about this camp in The Esthameian and mentions Phil's idea of enjoyment 'Having settled ourselves in camp, we set about the grim task of enjoying ourselves. It appears Phil's idea of enjoyment and ours did not meet anywhere along the line. Our conception of a luxurious French holiday was to stretch out on the grass under the hot sun and peacefully to go to sleep, to awaken to the gentle clanging of a frying pan with a ladle by the duty cooks to announce a meal. Did P.H.V. think that? No. Our enjoyment was to be touring chateaux, whether we liked it or not! Accordingly, we started upon a weary slog of the Loire valley, some 'a pied', some 'a velo' and some with P.H.V. a la carte. As for the Scouting side of this camp, the standard was rather higher than was expected. Several Venturer hikes were done and the efficiency with which a one night camp was pitched was surprising.'

Over the next few years the troop attracted new boys as they joined the school, this meant that there was a much wider and better balance of age range. One of these recruits was Tony Prince (EHGS 1953 – 1958) and he said 'I first had dealings with Phil as the school scoutmaster. To an eleven year old Phil was a pretty fierce character and ruled the troop with a rod of iron. He took the job very seriously and he had a funny way of raising one eyebrow above his horn-rimmed glasses when giving you an angry look. I imagine that quite a fiery temper went with his ginger hair. As the years progressed, and we became more mature, we got to know a lighter side of Phil at the summer scout camps, which he seemed to love. He must have had something, as I always went to those camps, rather than going away to the seaside with my parents! Phil was well respected by all of us, and he taught me a lot.'

Colin Curds continues, 'A group of the original recruits were getting older and Phil decided it was time to form a Senior Scout Troop. However, Phil had a busy life running school plays as well as the scouts so he sought assistance with a new member of staff Mr.Barnes taking over troop One and I, now in the Sixth form, formed troop Two with Phil becoming Group Scout Master. In Easter 1955 around a dozen of the Senior Scouts went to Provence in Southern France with a base camp just outside Arles.'

Colin says that, 'scouting under Phil's leadership had a great beneficial effect on him. He was one of the first patrol leaders, was Troop leader for a short time and held an assistant Scout Master's warrant in the Sixth form.' He goes on to say 'although I did not realise it at the time I learnt leadership and management skills over a period of about six years which became vital in my career as Keeper of Zoology at the Natural History Museum. My first two visits to France also had a great influence on me.'

St George's Day Parade, circa 1954. Colin Curds (second in right column) and John Wilkins (second in left column).

Another pupil Ronald Impey, who was not a scout himself, but did go to the South of France says 'I was given a grant to go on a scout trip to Southern France while in the Sixth form. We teamed up with a group of scouts from Dulwich College led by John Cottle. This trip was a most memorable experience for me, particularly as I came from a poor family with an invalid father and would never have been in a position to travel like that. Some of the lads travelled by cycle but I was in the small dormobile party and became accustomed to

Phil's declaiming speeches from 'Henry V' *en route.*'

Philip wrote of the camp in Southern France 'The idea was a Senior Scout camp in the grounds of the Abbaye de Montmajour near Arles in Provence. We were going to have a look at the great Roman ruins at Nimes, at the Pont du Gard, at the medieval cities of les Baux and Beaucaire, at the Pont St. Benezet and the Palais des Papes at Avignon, at paintings, sculptures, and above all at the way the Provencals live in Arles. We were thirty, from East Ham Grammar School and Dulwich. We put our gear, all eighteen hundredweight of it, aboard my dormobile, which with four of the party preceded by three days the main group on the trains through France.

We really were encamped behind Van Gogh's Abbaye de Montmajour; our hosts were very charming and the local 'Scouts de France' helpful and good fun. Apart from one damaged knee gained in falling off a French train, we arrived safely. However, the Mistral blew - a very cold 40 to 50 miles per hour gale – down the Rhone Valley and camping became a perilous business and cycling more so.

We pressed on with the programme and having with us several members of Biology Sixths decided to investigate the curious delta area of the Rhone – home ground of the Gipsies – breeding place for bulls – the great isolated 'ile de la Camargue' which contains the Reserve Zoologique de France' in the Etang de Vaccares. Unfortunately Senior Scouts though we were, we were unable to cope with the local detailed maps, and all attempts to find the entrance to the Digue, the famous wall-road across the sea, which encloses for 40 kilometres the Etang on its southern side, only resulted in our getting more and more lost in the flooded, road less, pathless marshlands, inhabited by a great many flamingos and one or two not very exotic jackdaws. The occasional paysan from the local 'mas', the great bull ranches or 'manades', always suggested a return round the north, prophesying the loss of one dormobile and thirty boys in the floods if we continued.

But a sense of adventure was now with us. We mounted the Digue, the car being now further loaded with one broken cycle as well as fourteen boys and of course, all the gear. Three hours later the car party, having struggled against the Mistral across this extraordinary road, arrived at 22.00 on the sands of the tiny town of Saintes Maries de la Mar. We cooked on the sands, the cyclists eventually arrived, and all endured a very windy night. Next morning the hardier members bathed in the Mediterranean and came out looking bluer than that famous blue sea. The enchantments of Saintes Maries, the centre of Gypsy pilgrimage, were not too easily obvious.

Back in camp cycling became an impossibility and the boys were ferried in two parties to Avignon, where we danced on the Bridge, to the Pont du Gard off which we were nearly blown and to Nimes where we saw a very gory bull-fight.

The camp ended with a three day hike and cycle to Fontains de Vaucluse, where the great river rushes from the mountain, to the imposing new French barrage on the Rhone at Donzere, and to those fantastic caves on the edge of the Massif Central, beautifully opened up and organised by the French, at Aven d'Orgnac. The Dormobile was by now in an unhappy state, for she had been much overloaded. Nevertheless both she and the boys managed to get back and we began the summer term feeling very much the adventurers; a great deal of planning had been necessary – the complete cost of the camp including transport, was £20 for the two weeks; the base camp was 900 miles from London and we had travelled 1,000 miles in and around Provence; on the whole the dormobile had proved the right vehicle in the right place and the extraordinary bounce and zest of the boys, and particularly of Senior Scouts, had done the rest. Their training had served them well, and they can now add to it a further knowledge of the French, and of the ebullience of France, its gaiety and its variety – particularly in Arles, surely one of the loveliest little towns anywhere.'
Peter Watkins joined East Ham Grammar School staff in 1956 and as he says in his autobiography 'I undertook to help with the Scouts out of a sense of guilt at my incapacity at team games though I was no more a natural Scout than a natural games player. There were about fifty boys in the Scouts when I joined, organised in two troops and a small senior Scout group. For adult help Philip had depended on a small group of Old Boys. The troop still met on Thursday evenings. There were a variety of related activities including the parents' committee concerned mostly with fund raising.

Summer camp was the high point of the year. In 1957 we went to Beaminster in Dorset and Philip and I did a recce, during the Whitsun holiday. In Easter 1958 we took a party of Senior Scouts to camp in Brittany. Philip Vennis crossed the channel with his Dormobile and drove through Northern France to meet us at St. Malo. Meanwhile I accompanied the main party from London to Southampton and thence via Jersey to St. Malo. We established a camp overlooking the Gulf of Morbihan on the south coast of Brittany. We visited Vannes, Carnac – the most prehistoric site in Western Europe and the Quiberon peninsular. On our return journey we spent a day in Paris. In the summer of 1958 we camped near Pewsey in Wiltshire in what turned out to be one of the wettest weeks of that or any other summer. Philip Vennis and I had visited Pewsey on a glorious Sunday in May and chosen a site 900 feet up on the edge of Salisbury Plain. It rained almost every day of the camp. The ground became waterlogged, and the road up to the site accessible only with difficulty. Activities were inevitably curtailed and the week turned into an endurance test for all concerned.'

One of the young scouts was Martin Rooke-Matthews who remembers that 'the summer camps were some of the happiest times of my life. Phil was an absolutely no nonsense type, but totally fair and respected by us. I remember at my first camp in Wiltshire in 1958 we had all gone for a long day's hike, in the process of which I was playing with matches and accidentally set fire to a disused lock gate on the local canal, which was itself fairly disused at the time. I didn't notice that I had done it, but luckily Phil and some of the seniors caught and extinguished the fire before too much damage was done. Later that evening he asked for the culprit to own up discreetly, which I did. He was totally restrained, and I went away feeling much better. Phil was, as has been said, very much into drama, and at the same camp he and one of the senior boys did a scene from 'Journey's End', which had been the big play at school at the end of the term. It was very intense and realistic. Then he did a satirical reworking of the scene set in the scout camp instead of the trenches, which restored the warmth of the evening beautifully. The gist of the scene was that the junior officer was being rebuked by his senior for eating some of the privates' meagre rations while he was visiting them.'

Philip's contribution to scouting at East Ham was a formidable one and he recalls what he has undertaken in the seven years of running the troop 'For history there have been: Queen's Scouts (Curds, Ogram, Powell and Allen); The Jamboree in Canada (Curds); to France thrice (Loire, Provence, Brittany; to the Lakes; and to Summer camp seven times;) Christmas parties; Open days and numberless Thursday evenings – all with song and some with sunshine. Jumbles have been run. Teas made and dances catered for – boys could never have had their equipment paid for by a stauncher band of people.

For memories: The loyalties of young men like Colin Curds and John Wilkins – through thick and sometimes very thin times; much camaraderie at home and abroad; 20 boys on board, cyclists all around, and driving in the Mistral across the Carmague to apparently nowhere and Peter Watkins in a high wind in Brittany loyally choking back an acid reply to the five hundred and fifth order of that day.

It's the mystique that counts; it's for insiders only; in twenty one years in Scouting no dull moments, - only small and not so small boys – crises in the rain – early morning rescues; laughter and song and camp cooking. "With the scent of wood-smoke …"

These are the days I shall dream about.' Phil.

When Philip left East Ham after seven years with the Scouts there, Peter Watkins said this of him. 'There are two things that characterise P.H.V.'s scouting. First, his conviction that camping as Scouts do it – disciplined, organised and adventurous - is supremely worthwhile. The school troop has been abroad three times and each time the burden of organisational detail, which has given us an outstanding safety record and made possible the maximum use of the minimum time and money, has been tremendous. Only one who has watched it all happen can imagine how large a burden it is. Second, P.H.V. has persevered endlessly with those who would have left but are now deeply grateful that they didn't. This is part of his conviction that in scouting ordinary boys get their first experience of leadership and responsibility. Throughout, Scouting has been part of P.H.V.s conviction about life and never a chore unwillingly undertaken.' Philip left East Ham Grammar School for boys in August 1958, writing his farewell in the Old Esthameian, an article called 'I like it here – 1949-58' says 'Schools are notoriously difficult to play in terms of sentiment and feeling. Their unity between men and boys, between conflicting interests and temporary gains, is only occasional and never lasting. Still there is or can be an esprit, and here at E.H.G.S. we have sometimes had it.

There have been great changes these nine years. Where we were an average grammar school in an old building with a known purpose, we are now an enormous agglomeration of differing purposes, in an ultra-modern building, with our attitudes questioned and our aims dispersed. This is a move with the times. In 1948, it was still legitimate to hope that, once the post war crises were finally over and the Welfare State in place, the Education Act of 1944 would give this country a unified people with a unified outlook, and with opportunity for each according to his own abilities. 1958 knows better. The second half of our uneasy twentieth century fifties has 'Lucky Jim' as its epitome and a 'pulled-up ladder' for its symbol. We are all either too angry or not angry enough.

The important thing to my mind, in all this hubbub of questioning and uncertainty, is to concentrate on the little bit of the world in which one functions and which one might conceivably affect – on the discernible area around one. This is itself not easy in an industrial and indistinct suburb of London, which feels the centripetal of pull of the metropolis in both work and play.

East Ham, with its 1910 red-brick streets - mile upon endless mile of uninteresting dormitory - may seem to the uninitiated no fit subject of romantic yearnings for roots. Yet roots you have to sink here. Unless you sink them, or grow them - unless you begin to feel that the streets are made up of homes not houses, that Beckton contains men not gases, that the docks are more than a myriad silent cranes, that the flats are for children to play on, and the parks for people to walk in, that the schools are beautiful when noisy in term-time, - unless you feel some of these things, you will never feel the pulse of this place as a pulse that matters separately from elsewhere, as the pulse in fact of home. I have lived many years now in what might be called the 'Poets Corner' of the

Borough. I used to think Shakespeare Crescent always inapt, till I realised the ordinarinesses are what matter most in the make-up of a country, and that William Shakespeare knew this above all; their watching telly, the Hammers, the Pubs and so on constitutes England '58, High Street North, with its thousand thousand shoppers on a Saturday, each threading his or her way down a bargaining hour, epitomises the shape of our time; from railway to town-hall, it contains the threads of ordinariness, '58. As Eliza sings in 'My Fair Lady', summing up the private longings of almost all of our shop-gazers here, "Wouldn't it Be Luvverly?"

Within all this, the grammar school has to have a function. I once called it an oasis; this I think is not quite correct; rather a peninsula of learning, apart but still a part, taking the sons of citizens and giving them back later in life as leaders in every best sense. This is what at best, as has happened here from time to time, the headmaster and staff must try to do; at all costs they must avoid the pulled-up ladder, and if they succeed, then their school will be a microcosm at the summit of the mixed ordinarinesses of our day.

Today a grammar school is on the defensive. It has a defence – that it produces an intellectual elite whose learning makes them more, not less, a part of their age and people; that only in this way can real learning (which still matters) still be taught to those really able to absorb it. The comprehensive experiment will undoubtedly go on, for the mood of the people demands it; but the grammar schools will go on too if they can prove their point - if in fact they stand by their own standards.

There is a song the leavers sing at their social every summer "This is our final day, this is the day we shall remember...", this is the place too; for all leavers, it's only 'Au Revoir', and after "The in-between years", as the popular song goes, they may be back.

To have arrived as a very young man, - a stranger here from Dulwich and Cambridge - to have found a home, to have made many, many friends, to have been accepted as a person, to have met many minds - this has been my experience in East Ham; to apply literature, whether Greek or English, to life, has been a great purpose; to help make Shakespeare and to do a little camping, has passed for creation; and to feel that people matter, has been a final lesson. Every age has put these answers in its own way - from Sophocles at the height of Athens' humanism, when he wrote

"Numberless are the world's wonders,
But none more wonderful than man"

Through Hamlet's searching Renaissance plea: "What a piece of work man is"-

to our own Jimmy Porter, the ordinary man in the ordinary man's age with an extraordinary feeling for our more complex dilemma, crying out with compassion for all mankind.

"Poor squirrels, poor bears."

CHAPTER 6

Ounsdale Comprehensive School
Early beginnings of Ounsdale, Wombourne

'A Comprehensive School is and should be an optimistic affair, bursting its seams with new ideas in every direction, a combination of men and women and adolescents and children of every sort and background and ability who have been brought together into what I believe to be one of the greatest single steps forward ever taken in English education. For every boy and girl here 'Opportunity Knocks', and we should, and are, trying to stretch each separately according to his or her ability, aptitude and age. Largely I think we are succeeding, and chances are being offered to the most academic and to the least, to the oldest and the youngest to play their proper part in the community of the school in preparation for their part in adult life'. (P.H.V. 1962)

In 1958, Wombourne was a growing rural village with a culture and outlook on life very different from the ones which Philip knew in London. Wombourne or Wombourn, is a large village and civil parish located in the district of South Staffordshire in the county of Staffordshire, four miles south south west of Wolverhampton. At the census in 2001 it had a population of 13,691. Wombourne is just outside the West Midlands conurbation and the West Midlands metropolitan county. Today it is to some extent a dormitory village, where many of the residents commute to the larger West Midlands towns and cities, such as Wolverhampton, Dudley, Stourbridge, Telford and Birmingham. It is therefore a popular place to live, a village with a long history, within easy access to the Black Country and to the west the Shropshire hills and Wales. The modern village is still centred on the green, the original heart of Wombourne. The village green resembles an archetypal 'English Village' with the church adjacent, a few half-timbered small independent shops and cottages, and cricket since 1909, with the green being the headquarters of the Wombourne cricket, tennis and bowling club.(Colour photograph 16.) The village's commercial and cultural life revolved around the green. The Parish Church, St. Benedict, was built about 1170 by one of the Priors of Dudley, and has a tower surmounted by a spire, dating from about 1400. However, in 1866-7 the church was largely rebuilt in a late thirteenth century style. The spire was partially taken down and was rebuilt four foot higher; the dragon on the top being replaced by a cross. It is built of pink sandstone.

(Colour photograph 15.) Wombourne is also home to several other Christian churches of varying denominations but, despite its proximity to the diverse West Midlands conurbation, there are no places of worship for other religions.

Wombourne grew from a mainly agricultural village which had developed because of its easily worked soil, to a light industrial one in the Middle Ages. Small iron forges which used the local resources of charcoal and water remained in existence when in the industrial revolution iron production was moved to the coal fired furnaces of the Black Country. With the smithies remaining in production, and the arrival of the Staffordshire and Worcestershire Canal, which integrated the area more fully into industrial Britain, Wombourne became a centre for nail-making. In 1616 the industry was concentrated in and around the village centre. The population of Wombourne in 1841 was 1,220 and in 1861, 1,530. By 1851, Wombourne was a large village with many of the population involved with nail-making. Nail-making remained important into the twentieth century. The village remained quite small and was essentially confined to the area around the present village green until the early fifties when houses were built to accommodate families from slum clearance sites in Wolverhampton. In 1951, Wombourne's population was 3,838, but with all the post war development between1951 to 1960 the population rose to 9,974, and with further dwellings being built the population reached 12,068 in 1971. Development in the village then slowed down and by the 2001 census the population had only increased by 1,622 inhabitants in thirty years.

In 1953, Staffordshire had been planning for some years to provide secondary education throughout the County with small comprehensives. The Director of Education, J.H.P. Oxspring, set out two principles to guide the planning. Much of Staffordshire was a rural area and rural children, he stated and therefore should be educated as far as possible in a rural environment. He also stated that what were then called multi-lateral schools providing academic, technical and practical courses were the best educational solutions for the development of education in Staffordshire. Plans for Staffordshire secondary education were imaginative and controversial. In November 1953, Oxspring reiterated his vision for Staffordshire education, 'We have three comprehensive schools planned, two of them being built and one almost ready to build. Personally I am an advocate for these smaller schools. They (the Conservative Government) have allowed us three only, as an experiment (Willenhall, Tettenhall and Tividale) and a fourth one in Wombourne to be built as a secondary modern with a view to it becoming comprehensive within two years of opening.' Oxspring knew that in many areas of Staffordshire the number of secondary aged children was to increase within the next twenty years. He believed that these numbers leading to a school of between 450 and 800 pupils was an ideal size for a comprehensive school.

Oxspring wrote a memorandum to a sceptical Ministry of Education (David Eccles) in the defence of small comprehensive schools rather than the tripartite system. As a result of this memorandum Staffordshire Education Authority was permitted to plan their system of comprehensive schools on a minimum basis of a five form entry i.e. 150 pupils per year for the four years terminating at the compulsory age of school attendance (fifteen). It was maintained that during these first four years adequate alternative courses should be provided to cater for a varied range of pupils such as now exist in the grammar and secondary modern school, without recourse to extravagant staffing. Remarkable foresight was shown by Staffordshire Education Authority with the planning of schools for pupils that had a wide range of educational needs and that schools should be planned to meet these needs.

It was recorded in The New Secondary Education that 'Small rural comprehensives with about eight hundred pupils (as proposed in Staffordshire) were, it will be remembered, officially regarded as potentially acceptable from the early forties. Partial acceptance of the Staffordshire Plan was a breakthrough. Putting the Plan into practice proved slower than was forseen. The first comprehensives sanctioned by the Minister as an experiment were built in 1955 and Ounsdale originally built as a secondary modern in 1956 became comprehensive in 1958.

By the mid fifties Staffordshire had already built four comprehensive schools on the edge of the Black Country, and planned two more. Staffordshire and Oxspring's plan originally was to admit up to 150 children a year and to have a school no larger than 800 children. The idea was that in order to provide among them a wide range of sixth form courses, each school was to specialise in the rarer subjects, with pupils transferring as and when necessary. This was not a popular idea amongst the teachers and pupils and so Staffordshire increased the number of pupils being admitted to 200 per year and each school was to increase to about 1,000 pupils. The transferring of sixth form students never materialised. The Ministry's insistence on very large comprehensive schools stemmed from the need to keep sixth forms of a size where a variety of course was possible without extravagant use of highly qualified specialist teachers. As a proportion of pupils remaining at school over the age of sixteen increased, smaller comprehensive schools became possible and by the early sixties the Ministry was talking about 1,500 pupils rather than 2,500 pupils as the ideal. Staffordshire Education Authority was therefore able to make progress towards a comprehensive system of secondary education.

Ounsdale in its booklet to parents called 'Opportunity Ounsdale' reflects on the early beginnings of the sixth form, in 1960, with eight pupils and its subsequent expansion. It states that a corresponding development in its range of courses is 'of particular importance for pupils who normally would not be considered for sixth form education. A comprehensive school has a special responsibility to develop such courses, as, if it is to be true to its name, its sixth form must be as comprehensive as the other part of the school.'

Tony Unwin, the rural science teacher and one of Ounsdale's original members of staff recalls the early beginnings of comprehensive education in Staffordshire and Ounsdale in particular.

'Due to the post war 'baby-boom', the 1944 'Butler' Education Act and the egalitarian principles of the Labour government the southern part of Staffordshire – which included Wolverhampton and most of 'The Black Country', there was a great shortage of secondary education accommodation. The County Council, then dominated by the Conservative party, surprisingly decided to build four comprehensive schools to accommodate no more than 450 pupils. The schools built were Willenhall, Tividale, Tettenhall and Ounsdale. A fifth 'Smestow' at Castlecroft, was added some time later, but almost as soon as it opened was lost to Wolverhampton due to the boundary changes of 1966. Highfields, built by Wolverhampton as a separate authority, on the Staffs/Wolverhampton border was originally termed 'bi-lateral'.(A bi-lateral school was officially defined in 1947 as 'one which is organised to provide for any two of the three elements of secondary education – i.e. modern, technical or grammar, organised in clearly defined sides.) It became properly comprehensive some time later. All four original comprehensives were built to the same plans and proved, early on, as 'not fit for purpose'.

Wombourne village expanded in the early fifties due to two large council house estates, Bull Meadow and Giggetty, built to accommodate families from slum clearance sites in Wolverhampton. Private developers, principally William Whittingham then built several estates centred on Orton Lane, Common Road and Planks Lane. Later Sytch Lane and Greenhills were added and finally the Poolhouse estate. Meanwhile there were several small estates 'shoehorned' into any available space such as the wilderness – now known as Ounsdale Crescent. The Local Authority, still Conservative, finally agreed that the new schools could take 550 pupils – but by then Ounsdale's roll was far in excess of that number – indeed the school was still classified by the authority as five form entry, when it had ten form entry. No wonder the school was always short of money. The educational authorities had no idea how to run a comprehensive school as there were very few in the country.

Crown Woods, in London was a large comprehensive where money was no problem. There were one or two comprehensive schools elsewhere, including the Isle of Man, where the headteacher of the Regis School in Tettenhall (one of the original four comprehensives in Staffordshire) came from. Meanwhile Ounsdale, set up a Comprehensive Schools' forum with the original four Staffordshire comprehensives, which later included schools from other authorities'.

'A Deputy Headmaster in Rural Staffordshire' 1958 to 1962

'I arrived here a stranger from London, I have been accepted by many friends and parents, I have helped form some minds and formulate rules, I have given a helpful shove to the beginnings of a big school, I have applied literature, Shakespeare or classical, to life – these have been some of my achievements in Wombourne; and compassion for people is the only final lesson. The formulas of education are many, the achievements rare, and often disappointing. We live by the images we leave.

Every age has put these answers in its own way, from Sophocles at the height of Athens' humanism when he wrote –

'Numberless are the world's wonders, but none more wonderful than man' through Hamlet's surging Renaissance belief - 'What a piece of work is man' – to Jimmy Porter in 'Look Back in Anger,' the ordinary man in an Ordinary Man's age with an extraordinary feeling for our more complex dilemmas, crying out with compassion for all mankind –

'Poor squirrels – poor bears... Teach them to be people who can feel
"the heartbreak in the heart of things", and they'll be good people'. (P.H. V. 1962)

September 1956 saw the opening of a new school in the village of Wombourne. It opened as a secondary modern school but it was obvious from the type of staff and headmaster that had been appointed that this was not its long term intentions. The headmaster Harold Holroyde had an M.A. – 'he was a mixture of orthodox, conservative views on education and very liberal, egalitarian principles, coloured by his non-conformist upbringing and experiences as a non-commission officer in the 1939-45 war' recalls Tony Unwin, one of the original members of Ounsdale's teaching staff. Tony continues, 'A large majority of the then small teaching staff had degrees and were in general much better qualified than what one normally would find in a Secondary Modern School. Mr. Holroyde's liberal ideals were offset by the Senior Mistress's formidable presence and her ultra orthodox and conservative views'. Ounsdale was originally planned as a comprehensive school but opened as a secondary modern. The Staffordshire County Council who approved the building of a comprehensive school in the village were solidly conservative. The actual building of such a school did not conflict with conservative policy because it was a comprehensive serving a rural area which was not directly served by an existing grammar school. However, before the school was actually opened the Government of that time withdrew their support for any new comprehensives.

132

Ounsdale Comprehensive School from the air in 1958.

The buildings were similar to the other Staffordshire comprehensive schools that opened at the same time. (Colour photographs 17. & 18.) There was a three storey block of twelve rooms for the academic teaching block. A separate block of twelve rooms for practical subjects, such as Domestic science, Needlework, Woodwork and Metal work, as well as laboratories for Chemistry and Physics, was constructed directly opposite the academic block. There was also a third block completed in this first phase of building which included the offices, hall, library, gymnasium and dining room.

Children living in and around Wombourne before the opening of Ounsdale were scattered around numerous secondary schools in the area. The 11-plus selection rate for Grammar School in 1955 for this area was about seven per cent with the majority of the selected children being boys. These selected children had several choices of schools – Wolverhampton with four grammar schools, Stourbridge and Bilston with two and Brierley Hill with one. The choice was not as great as it may seem as perhaps only one child would go to a certain school in any one year. The majority of non-selected children went to Kingswinford Secondary Modern, which is about three miles from Wombourne. A few of the children who lived at the south end of the village could go to another similar school at Kinver, about seven miles away – a school bus was provided for these children.

With such large buildings available at Ounsdale the County did not want to have just the first year intake from its defined catchment area so it transferred the second and third year pupils from Kingswinford, and pupils at Kinver, who lived in Ounsdale's catchment area, could also ask to be transferred. The school opened with approximately 180 non – selected pupils.

In September 1957 another intake of 113 non-selected pupils joined Ounsdale and thus the school had pupils from the first year to the fourth year as a normal secondary modern. The staff consisted of twelve teachers offering a variety of subjects.

In 1958, Staffordshire County Council was in a position to change its attitude to comprehensive schools and in September 1958 Ounsdale opened as a comprehensive, with a first year intake of 185 children. An 11-plus examination had been taken by the children but the results were never disclosed to them. The range of ability of these 185 children was from an IQ of 130 (2 children) to 65 (1 child), the largest groups of children being in the middle of the range. Thus the school developed with a gradual building up from the bottom and it was not completely full until September 1964, with just over a 1,000 pupils. As part of the development in going comprehensive the second phase of building saw an increase in classrooms and practical rooms, extensions to the offices and dining room and the addition of an indoor heated swimming pool.

Another change from a secondary modern to comprehensive school was the appointment of new staff. Philip recalls: 'On a murky snowy day in February 1958, Mr. Holroyde, H.H. as I was later to call him, greeted me in Wombourne. After my appointment as Deputy headmaster of Ounsdale he knew, with his proper second sight, that I should get over being a Londoner, and see things – especially a sense of humour – more the Northern way very quickly!.' Philip had great regard for Harold Holroyde; like Joe Whiteley at East Ham Philip was given the time and space to develop his own ideas and use his dynamic personality for the good of the school. On Harold Holroyde's retirement in March 1975 Philip paid tribute to this first headteacher of Ounsdale School. He writes – 'Seventeen years ago Ounsdale became comprehensive, and in the snows of February 1958 H.H. had the temerity to appoint me straight from the 'smoke' in my second post as Deputy headmaster. Four lovely years then ensued of the most extraordinary fermentation of ideas, buildings, courses, arguments and above all – fun. I remember H.H. best for two or three reasons: he'd back you when you made one of your many mistakes, especially if you were me; he was devoted to seeing the best in all children – a real liberal, he brought the best of the grammar school tradition; he had an ability to see something funny at crucial points in difficult meetings; and his Congregational Christianity gave his inner life a sense of meaningfulness which provided the needful resilience against all the variety of changes that the English education scene presented and presents to any teaching career in the second half of our century. It is this Christian forbearance – the combination of a belief in a liberal secular domain, with a belief in the need for Dissent – underlying a Nonconformist conscience which keeps the way ahead reasonably clear and not too narrow, and which has allowed so many Englishmen to decide amid great difficulties on what may be more nearly right and what may be more nearly wrong, thus being enabled to carry through decisions made because of a back bone of real belief.

Many will know that he once commented that he lived life on the boundary – in cricketing terms; ready to bat if necessary, ready to catch if necessary, between the game and the spectator – with a joke to the stand or a joke to the Umpire, between belief and disbelief, ready to turn an arm for a couple of overs, ready to bat at number nine for half a dozen runs – it's a strong, long, real, true English tradition, no flaring suddenness, no *'gloire'* as the French would say, no glamour, but always supportive.

He would ask, as is right, why should we change and will it be better if we do? During my years at Ounsdale we went through the second and third phases of the building programme.

He kept us going during these many invasions of school life by workmen and their machinery which would have taxed the heart of the stoutest 'cortez'. H.H. provided at the beginning, when Ounsdale was a small secondary modern, through the changes that I saw, the inclusion as it were, of the would have been grammar school unit, and then through the long sixties and seventies – he provided a pillar of the radical and questioning establishment.

It is not given to everyone to have the guts enough to ask the right question at the right time of the right people, and English education is the worse for that. H.H. asked those questions.

We had some great days – long before comprehensive schools became part of the political see-saw. We were comprehensive because it suited the rural area and because it worked. H.H. in English education was certainly a pathfinder, and when you think back to Ounsdale's history these seventeen years, you think how comic the now overtly political debate over comprehensives is – comic and sad. H.H. destroyed nothing – no grammar school – no tradition – no anything – he has only founded 'an enduring monument!' Since I left Ounsdale I have been eight years as a Grammar School Head, one year as a Comprehensive Head and four years as a Sixth Form College Principal. But being four years as Deputy headmaster to H.H. remains a highlight, left to myself, but guided and hinted at, rescued, and with behind me his great ongoing deep seated far seeing liberal philosophy – "a man's a man for all that".' Heads have to know all, but not show it – or they have not to show that they don't know all.'

Arriving in this different part of the country, Philip was a stranger with a new job and nowhere to live. Coming from 'the smoke' as West Midlanders called London, Philip was viewed as someone from that 'naughty city', which the locals in Wombourne saw as having a different culture and different morals to their post-war rural village. Wombourne was a fairly parochial village in the late fifties with Wolverhampton or Stourbridge being the furthest some of the residents might have travelled.

Philip found lodgings at 'The Coach and Horses' at Brickbridge with the Godwin family. He drove a Bedford Dormobile called 'Daphne' and was often a figure of curiosity. His acceptance in Wombourne took some time, but eventually, partially as a result of his forward thinking ideas at Ounsdale, and, his outgoing personality he made many friends, and especially amongst the teaching staff some lifelong friends – such as Geoff Morris and Tony Unwin. Geoff and his wife Julie often listened with a sympathetic ear to this young bachelor and on some occasions he would 'crash' out on their lounge settee through sheer exhaustion from not knowing when to stop working or when to eat a meal. His friends supported him through difficult early days; these were made more difficult with the death of his father at the end of his first term at Ounsdale in December 1958. Philip was absolutely devastated by his father's death and had seriously contemplated returning to London to help his grieving mother. He wrote 'On the death of a parent, one suddenly changes. One becomes aware of all sorts of duties one owes. In Ancient Greece it was the custom for sons to give an oration for their fathers. This I did. I summed up his life and achievements. He was a brilliant and remarkable man. Had <u>he</u> had the chances he gave <u>me</u> he might have achieved great things. I recited two verses of a Gerard Manley Hopkin's (1844 – 1889) poem – the last line but one worries me most.

> Bad I am, but yet thy child.
> Father, be thou reconciled,
> Spare thou me, since I see
> With thy might that thou art mild.
> I have life before me still
> And thy purpose to fulfil,
> Yea a debt to pay thee yet:
> Help me, sir, and so I will.

I then went on to read this speech from Shakespeare's Antony and Cleopatra – this play is the height of his belief that 'man' has <u>all</u> the powers inside him for complete fulfilment. Cleopatra is speaking over Antony's dead body.

> "The Crown o'the earth doth melt My lord!
> O wither'd is the garland of the war,
> The soldier's pole is fall'n; young boys and girls
> Are level now with men; The odds is gone,
> And there is nothing left remarkable
> Beneath the visiting moon.

Later on she dreams –

> "I dream'd there was an Emperor Antony:
> O! such another sleep, that I might see
> But such another man.
> His face was as the heavens, and therein stuck
> A Sun and Moon, Which kept their course and lighted
> The little O, the earth.
> His legs bestrid the ocean his rear'd arm
> Crested the world; his voice was propertied
> As all the turned spheres, and that to friends:
> But when he meant to quail and shake the orb
> He was as rattling thunder. For his bounty,

There was no winter in't
In his livery walk'd crowns and crownets; realms and islands
Were as plates dropp'd from his pockets.
Think you there was, or might be, such a man
As this I dreamed of?
For, if there be, or ever were, one such
It's past the size of dreaming."

This I think is the greatest speech in English literature.'

However, the lure and challenge of the job at Ounsdale, kept him in Wombourne. Many of his pupils who were at Ounsdale in 1958 – 59 may recall that for twelve months after his father's death, as part of his father's will and wishes, Philip had to wear a bowler hat on every occasion he went out: this added further to the local belief that he was an eccentric young man. When Philip joined the staff in September 1958 as Deputy headmaster, he found several radical thinkers – Ron Lewis, David Harvey and Nigel Sidaway. Tony Unwin did not see himself as a radical but, having fallen into education thanks to the Suez crisis of 1956, he was determined not to inflict a replica of his own grammar school days, or the deadly dull menu handed out to the pupils in his previous secondary modern school. He continues 'I was appointed to teach Rural Science to a school population that appeared to have a large proportion of country children. My interview was with Mr. Holroyde and Mr. Lamb, a retired, very active and very gentlemanly farmer. He and I talked at length about farming practices some very old, some very new, and my practical experience with livestock. It soon became apparent that the job was mine if I wished (I did) and the possibilities of rearing livestock (calves, sheep, pigs and poultry) in the farm unit that was to be built at the end of the field where the school garden shed was later sited. Then I joined the staff and in September 1958 I was visited by the County's Rural Science Advisor/Inspector who brought a load of flower pots for me to use. When I protested I was not a gardener but was expecting to be supplied with small animals, and the wherewithal to house and feed them, I was told I would have to wait as there was no money available at the present and the project was 'on hold'. In the following months it became clear I was not going to get a small farm – no money forthcoming. This was at a time when Selwyn Lloyds 'Stop Go' financial policy was in place. Indeed Ounsdale always appeared to be affected by the 'Stop' part and never the 'Go'. The corridors in the teaching block were always inadequate because the original costs for the school had to be cut and that was done by cutting the ground square footage of the buildings – hence the narrow corridors. Much of the building material was of inferior quality – for example the tiles in the entrance hall, which soon became very pitted. In 1962 P.H.V. said "you've got a biology degree?" Me "well yes, sort of, B.Sc. Agric". P.H.V. responded "Well you can start a biology department, no more money at present but good experience!"

One of the first and major tasks for Philip was the construction of a timetable for a rapidly growing and changing school. This he did with the aid of a peg board and multi- coloured pegs. Until his arrival no one had formulated any principles for the collation of staff available, subject time required/desirable, suitable accommodation – especially for practical subjects and fitting in with the current educational ethos. The first timetables were a matter of trial and error and the rules for completion derived from the finished article, to be used the following year. Philip said in his *'Ave atque vale'* (hail and farewell) article in 1962, 'In trying to erect a truly educational timetable, which would push out, so to say, opportunities in all directions, we have uncovered an unlooked for array of unusual talents and interests. The timetable is the servant of the school, and it should, in my belief, stand on its head, if necessary, to make 'Abyssinian', so to say, available for the one child that wants to study it. The timetable brings, too, memories of evenings spent, often among good friends, in good fun, with an immense feeling of accomplishment, and out of it grows, as well as 40 periods a week, the houses and the sports and the swimming and the games and form relationships and form teacher relationships, all of which are some of the marks of a good school.' Pupils could leave school as soon as they reached the age of fifteen years, and so there were leavers at Christmas, Easter and in the summer. A night mare to staff, timetable and provide interest, 'No wonder PHV used to wave his hands and puff more vigorously at his cigar!' remembers Tony Unwin. On arrival at Ounsdale Philip revised the school's whole curriculum, since many specialist teachers had been appointed and the first intake of unselected pupils joined the school. Full academic subjects were introduced – Latin, Greek, French, German, Spanish, Physics, Chemistry and Biology. At the other end of the spectrum a specialised remedial department was formed. There was a large variety of courses offered and children at some stage of their days at Ounsdale had to make certain choices and their aptitude and aspirations would be taken into account. No rigid vocational courses were offered but the basic principle of a good all round 'liberal' education was adhered to. All pupils must take English, Mathematics, and a language if possible, a science, a practical subject and one of the humanities. Within this framework plus two other subjects pupils were guided into taking a combination of subjects to fit a particular vocation e.g. engineering, nursing, office work, retail distribution etc. The choice by the child with guidance from the teacher and parents was made in the third year. A careers master and mistress and a complete careers library were used to make informed decisions. The curriculum that was offered to the fourth year was divided into the leavers and the non-leavers.

Leavers had a specially arranged course which introduced them to a number of practical skills such as painting and decorating, car maintenance, photography, woodwork for girls, cookery for boys and first aid. The children did real jobs with real materials and developed knowledge and practical ability. The other part of their timetable included lessons on dealing with aspects of the 'outside world', such as industry, farming, and food. health and leisure.

For the non-leavers twenty six courses were planned out, indicating the ultimate type of job that each course would be most suitable for. The first seventeen courses were aimed at GCE. O level and the remainder are aimed at CSE. There was pupil cross over in one particular subject if necessary. These courses varied from the purely academic to technical and commercial and were continuous over the fourth and fifth years.

The Sixth form did not cater solely for those pupils who were working towards a university or college place, but had in its first year Sixth courses for commerce, taking or re-taking O level and trying for better qualifications. The sixth form also had pupils who were taking two or three A level GCE. In the sixth form not all time was spent on examination work, twelve lessons a week were spent on minority time subjects.

Of the children who attended Ounsdale Comprehensive School about half of them lived outside the village of Wombourne. These children used a system of school buses to bring them into school, but this system made out of school activities a little difficult, but staff at the school usually helped to transport children as necessary. There were no connecting bus services between villages, the only ones that existed were those radially outwards from Wolverhampton. There was always a problem of getting children and parents to return to the school out of school hours. If there is a special concert or drama production in the evening then sometimes special buses were run.

Ounsdale had a wider range of children from different social classes than most schools. The backgrounds from which the children came were not restricted either to the working or middle class but the whole range seemed to be included. In this area the population could roughly be divided into three types:

(a) The people who were born and bred in the country. These people usually either worked on or owned land or more frequently travelled into town to work there.

(b) The over-spill population who were forced by economic reasons to move out from the towns and cities yet still work there.

(c) The middle and upper class people who found it pleasant to live in the country away from their business.

The whole range of children could be found at Ounsdale. Colin Appleby, one of the first intake of pupils in1956 writes 'I guess my parents hoped that I would make it to grammar school. I felt hopelessly unprepared for our 11-plus day at Codsall Secondary Modern. In the top 5 of 46 at Castlecroft Primary, my secondary was to be Ounsdale, some three miles from my home village of Lower Penn. There was no transport in my first year and my recollection is that there were only eight teachers at Ounsdale in 1956. We were streamed into three forms and enjoyed our early experience at the school with Mr. Foster an excellent Maths teacher. My days were governed by the three mile cycle ride from home and back, particularly the long hill back into Lower Penn up Dene's Road. My own family was heavily into West Midlands engineering. My uncles often helped with Mr. Foster's maths homework. I was often complimented at the different and novel ways 'I' was able to find the right answer! My father was employed at Fafnir Bearings in Wolverhampton as Chief Maintenance Engineer. He joined the company in 1939, worked a seven day week and was often 'on call' during holidays. When not at work we would all be at Stratton Street Chapel on the other side of the town (Wolverhampton) or at Barmouth on the Welsh coast for family holidays. Dad's only career advice to me was 'don't work in a factory' We were 'bussed' by coach from the second year ('Noakes Coaches') but this led to more inflexibility for after school sports and drama. Often I would miss the bus and walk three miles back home across canals and railway lines. How I envied my classmates who lived 'up the road' from the school. Our year was one of the early cohorts scheduled for GCEs. Mr. Vennis thought I should include Latin as one of my 8 O levels. I received tuition on a one to one basis and passed in two years. He taught from his office with a typical sixties panoramic plate glass window. On one memorable occasion when explaining the 'ablative absolute' he spotted some loiterers in the playground and banged hard on the window to get their attention. Needless to say the window smashed! More repair work for Mr. Grimshaw our caretaker. The school was an odd mix of rural 'secondary modern', not unlike a similar school in Kinver, and a highly academic input led by Philip Vennis. We did not believe in ourselves but he believed in us. Reasonable O and A levels were followed by university entrance in times when it was highly competitive. The label of 'comprehensive' was unusual and perhaps held a certain cachet for progressive, liberal, 'pink brick' universities. There was also an element of 'public school' discipline and leadership at Ounsdale imported (I guess) from PHV's own experience at East Ham and Dulwich College. I now feel embarrassed at the way in which we dressed down

141

and humiliated fellow pupils in the 'Prefects' council'. At a recent funeral a fellow former Ounsdale pupil reminded me of the times she had appeared in my Prefect's book!

School plays were an important part of school life for staff and pupils. As Sergeant of Marines I can still sing extracts from 'HMS Pinafore' where Philip served as one of my mariners. 'I polished up that handle so carefully, that now I am the ruler of the Queen's Navy' still seems so appropriate as a critique of British leadership, management and culture. PHV was a convinced believer in the more able pupils taking academic routes. I think he saw this as a confirmation of achievement in the new sector and great for the pupils who succeeded. It did not always work. I remember him trying to persuade a highly able friend of mine to stay on for A levels. They walked across the playground in deep conversation as we played football. My friend did not stay on. He left to work for an engineering company in the holidays, founded his own company which still survives, and became a millionaire in the process. Philip I know would have approved of this engineering, entrepreneurial route.

Many of us had read Pedley and were much enthused by the comprehensive ideal. PHV used to complain at the way in which the grammar school system used to waste two thirds of its highly talented intake by focusing attention on Oxbridge entry for the elite top third and labelling others as failures. Equality of opportunity was our mantra and 'as far as who goes farthest'. (Colin Appleby, pupil at Ounsdale 1956 to 1963, Professor in Industrial Studies at the University of Wolverhampton 1989 to 1998 and Professor for the Open University 1999 to 2010.)

At the opening of Ounsdale many of the pupils came from working class families, the remainder, a small proportion came from middle class families with aspirations towards learning and culture. According to Tony Unwin there was a 'Wombourne' disease and he says 'Philip Vennis used to fulminate against the Wombourne disease and its unwillingness to participate in any cultural event.' He continues 'The ambition of the majority was to get through school with as little effort as possible and get a job in a local factory.' He remembers urging pupils to work harder to enable them to get a better job and the answer would be 'Me dad will get me a job at The Morlock'- and so often he did. The 'Wombourne disease' did not affect all the pupils, who, from the earliest days of Ounsdale, were willing to grasp whatever opportunities were given them for mental and spiritual enrichment. This is evident in Colin Appleby's recollection of his early days at Ounsdale. Many of these pupils have said to Tony Unwin, fifty years later, 'that they were very grateful for the opportunities offered and how proud they were to have been amongst the first pupils in a pioneering comprehensive school'.

The administration of the school was mostly undertaken in the administration block with the exception of the Deputy head's office which was based in the main academic block. Administrative duties were influenced by the three separate buildings of the school, two of the blocks connected but the third separated by a playground. There was consequently therefore a lot of movement between blocks with the crossing outdoors often difficult in winter time. The academic block of eighteen classrooms had no connecting corridors across the three storey block and so children, for example, could be at the top of one staircase and may have to go down and up twelve flights of stairs to get to their next lesson!

When Philip joined Ounsdale in 1958 the school was run as one large unit and so he introduced a house system to allow for every boy and girl to take part in the house system via some activity or other. The original house names were Darwin, Elgar, Shakespeare and Wedgwood, with Fry and Priestley being added two years later. The house system had no bearing on the administration of the school except that it affected internal games and competitions such as drama, verse, music and public speaking. The size of the teaching staff increased from at the opening of the school in 1956 with twelve members of staff to when Philip left in 1962 to fifty full time teaching staff. The Headmaster, Deputy Headmaster and Senior Mistress would meet regularly and Philip usually took the weekly staff meeting. One of his main roles was being in charge of boy's discipline, and this often meant administering corporal punishment to the more unruly boys. One of his pupils who joined Ounsdale in 1960 was Linda Fletcher (nee Hoyle) who recalls Philip's role as disciplinarian 'On one occasion Mr. Vennis was sitting in the office near the front gate, twitching his cane and looking at everyone to check that we all had our correct uniform and hats on – how times have changed!' In most comprehensives of this era various methods such as streaming or parallel banding were used in order to break down the mass of children into workable units. Ounsdale did not single out one of these methods but used them all to a varying degree. In the first year when the children enter the school they were placed in one of four bands; this placement was according to the information supplied by the primary school and the Local Education Authority, together with the 11-plus examination, which, although a comprehensive system existed, had not been abolished. A pupil who entered the school in 1958, and would have gone to a grammar school is Phil Bodley, who fifty years later recalls after having met friends from Ounsdale that there was 'A spectrum of opinions regarding how much they as pupils owed the school. These opinions ranged from those who considered that they had benefitted more from Ounsdale than if they had attended alternative schools; to at least one person, who is known to think that the school failed to bring out the best in them. Most seem to recognise the value of resources available – the laboratories and workshops in the Practical block, the gym, the library, the playing fields and the swimming pool. Several have happy memories of being involved in school theatrical productions.

Personally, I regard any shortcomings as primarily being my own fault, particularly my relative lack of commitment, attention and application and the ease with which I could be distracted (especially at an impressionable age in a mixed school!). Years later I wished I'd been much more focussed. If I had to nominate one aspect of the academic curriculum that had the most lasting benefit and which I feel most privileged to have been taught, it is Latin. There must have been countless occasions over the years when the meaning or origin of an English word takes me back to the Latin. There is no certainty that another comparable school would have taught us Latin. I am not saying this because Philip was our Latin teacher, nor is it a comment on the quality of teaching in any of our subjects.

A slight tongue- in-cheek observation is that the comprehensive system at Ounsdale afforded my brother the opportunity to enter near the top and leave near the bottom!

Whenever any of our 1958-1964 class get together it's rare that PHV doesn't get a mention. David Burton's infamous encounter with PHV's wrath is often recalled. We were all in the Art room working with clay when Mr. Tonks (the Art master) went out for a while. Two or three boys started tossing up their balls of soft clay. Unfortunately for David, he tossed too high and it stuck to the ceiling. Frantic attempts to dislodge it with the window pole failed. Mr. Tonks returned. PHV was summoned. Big trouble!' (Phil Bodley, pupil 1958-1964). The bands were given labels C.O.M.P. – C refers to an academic course with one modern and one classical language, O refers to a course with one language only, M refers to a general course with particular attention to English and Mathematics and P forms are the responsibility of the remedial department. Within these bands, also continued throughout the second year, the children were streamed in the C and O bands but not in the M and P bands. In the third year children were streamed throughout the whole ability range. The fourth year was divided into leavers and non-leavers, those staying to the fifth form to take public examinations were arranged in forms according to their ability in basic subjects and in their chosen subjects they were placed in teaching groups according to specific ability in those subjects. The leavers were divided into forms according to their vocation and the sixth form was arranged in small sets in the conventional manner used in a grammar school.

In 1956 when the school opened, one of the masters, besides specialising in history, was also qualified in remedial teaching. He was able to cope with any specific disabilities that the children had, but apart from this they had no special treatment. As the school increased in size the need for more specialized remedial teachers became apparent. In 1959 a remedial department was established with two specialist teachers. In these early days of the school's formation, some of the staff had not previously taught their subjects to A level and some of the early results for A level were perhaps not as good as they could have been.

A prefect system was established in these early days at Ounsdale. Prefects were empowered to 'book' pupils for misbehaviour and such pupils were brought before a 'Prefect's council' presided over by one of the senior prefects and at least one senior member of staff; they had the power to award some minor punishments. Philip introduced this type of Prefect Council as well as the School Parliament. The School Parliament consisted of an elected member from each form, and the meetings were run by prefects and held every other week. Complaints, suggestions and questions were the form of the parliament, with a vote taken on every motion. The prefects then referred back to the Headmaster the relevant points and various points and bills that had been passed. The following passage was written by a Sixth former, in the first edition of the school magazine 'Omnibus', about the introduction of the school parliament. 'Amongst the experiments which Mr. Vennis has attempted to popularise at Ounsdale, his latest, the School Parliament, has been the bravest and most ambitious.

The idea being conceived, the Head Boy, in his first 'address' acted as an excellent mouthpiece in delivering to a suspicious school the plans for, and the importance of, making this democratic institution a successful one. From the first, our fortnightly meetings have had an air of formality about them which is right if we are to imitate a parliamentary tradition long since established since Elizabethan times. In the same instance questions have covered an unlimited scope from problems of discontent over uniform to the lack of soap in the boys' toilets; problems which have encouraged enthusiastic debate from the majority of our fifty members. Naturally not all of the discussions have had a decisive answer and only a few, such as our fight to wear our choice of dress at the Film Society have had a material result. Furthermore we have heard, on occasions, rather more of some voices than others, and would be pleased to hear as much from everyone.

Nevertheless, despite minor problems the Parliament has achieved its main aim – to present a number of pupils with the choice to exercise not only their own but also the opinions of their forms, as a collective debating institution. This alone must be enough reason to ensure a fruitful future for the Parliament, and surely, the success of these initial months will lead to a tradition which Ounsdale will be proud to call individually, her own.'

This dynamic and progressive idea from Philip lasted for many years after his departure from Ounsdale. Many other innovations took place during his time at Ounsdale and the school flourished with extra curriculum activities. Philip was instrumental in introducing the school magazine, whose first edition came out in July 1962 and recalls many of the innovations, activities and drama productions over the first four years of the school being comprehensive. On the opening page Philip quotes in his article 'Thoughts for a beginning' from 'The Antigone' by Jean Anouilh. This reflects his approach to the teaching of young people.

'Be happy. Life flows like water, and you young people let it run away through your fingers. Shut your hands: hold onto it. Life is not what you think it is. Life is a child playing round your feet, a tool you hold firmly in your grip, a bench you sit down upon in the evening, in your garden. People will tell you that that's not life, that life is something else. They will tell you that because they need your strength and your fire, and they will want to make use of you. Don't listen to them. Believe me, the only poor consolation that we have in our old age is to discover that what I have just said to you is true. Life is nothing more than the happiness that you get out of it.'

The appearance of a school magazine was a sign of maturity and growth of the school, with events and achievements being recorded. 1962 was the founding edition of Omnibus, which presented and furthered the school's unity and gave a kaleidoscopic picture of the school. Articles in the magazine included reports on the official opening of the school, visits to Austria, Warwick Castle, Worcester Cathedral, Coalbrookdale, the many House drama evenings, the House music, speaking and arts evening, Speech Days, the film society and other school clubs and drama reports.

Philip did a lot less drama than he had done at East Ham Grammar School. At Ounsdale, although he was involved in helping with the House drama evenings and trained the speakers for Speech Day and other formal evenings, he only managed time to do one major production - 'Twelfth Night' in December 1960, and a short extract from ' A Midsummer-Night's dream' with 4B. In this production of Shakespeare's 'Dream', the children involved were in the remedial form for English and so consequently Philip taped the text since they were mostly non-literate and they learned in their local accent, their parts in the "Bottom" parts of the play – a most interesting performance. With the production of 'Twelfth Night' Philip brought to the audience this play of laughter and tears – the laughter predominating. The production had a resemblance to the Elizabethan drama as Shakespeare had known it – the use of a permanent set, no curtains and the use of an extended apron.

'Tis beauty truly blent, whose red and white
Nature's own sweet and cunning hand laid on;
Lady you are the cruell'st she alive
If you will lead these graces to the grave
And leave the world no copy."

Twelfth Night, Ounsdale School Production in 1960

Philip wrote about the production 'We have stepped outside the usual picture frame stage and attempted to use a permanent set, a little in the manner of Shakespeare's own plays. No curtains are used at any stage of the play. We have attempted to interpret the alternating types of comedy and types of sadness as emphatically as possible; music has been used to underline feeling and character by means of two themes from the text. School plays cannot do more than point a finger towards what might be, but the particular value of a great play on actors, stage- team and audience lies in the drawing together of all in the enjoyment of an entertainment in the truest sense – the meeting of minds – Shakespeare's, the cast's and the audience's.' Philip used his experience from previous productions and the play was a great success, despite the fact that the majority of the cast were the first lower sixth and that this included only two boys – so finding a twin for Viola was difficult!

"I would I had bestowed in the tongues that I have in fencing,
Dancing, and bear baiting. O! had I but followed the arts!

Twelfth Night, Ounsdale School Production in 1960.

One of the members of the cast of 'Twelfth Night', Jennifer Piper, who played Sir Toby Belch, was also Head Girl from 1958 to 1960 and Head of the School from 1960 to 1962 and she writes about her personal experience as a school girl at Ounsdale.

'My first two years at Ounsdale were only different from the secondary modern that I had attended in that there seemed to be more academic work to be done. There was some vague mention of one or two of us sitting for O level but it seemed in the dim and distant future and not really relevant to us. However, in 1958 when we became comprehensive, the appointment of a specialist staff not only affected the first year unselected intake but also the rest of the school then up to fourth year stage.

The appointment of Mr.Vennis as Deputy headmaster had considerable influence on the following four years that he was there. He made definite planned courses leading to O level for my own form and the two corresponding ones in the second and third years. Everyone who had the faintest hope of passing an examination was entered for it. He took particular interest in improving the cultural and out of school life at Ounsdale and in every aspect had, whether one believed in his point of view or not, a dynamic personality. Being a bachelor, he perhaps did more than a man with a family could have done. He was at the school continuously from morning to evening, and besides his Deputy headship he was the Head of the Evening Institute.

I remember that when in the fifth form Mr. Vennis became our form master he continually encouraged us into working. He was interested in us personally and often 'popped' round to our individual homes to have a chat and presumably to see that we were working. Work was paramount and even when we went to Stratford to the theatre as we quite often did, we would have to take our Latin books with us. I have recollections of once when we had to queue for tickets on a Saturday morning and then spend the rest of the day in Stratford. We, or should I say Mr. Vennis found a convenient coffee house and 'did' orally two chapters of Dr. Whiteley's Latin book. This keen non-stop interest in our working habits was not popular I must admit, but in view of the fact that we did not start GCE work until late, we perhaps needed some pushing.

To anyone who has been to an established grammar school all the traditions and modes of behaviour are there readymade but at a new school there is nothing, just the bare minimum of children, staff and a building. Rules had to be made, put into practice, and then evaluated and either accepted or rejected, and as much responsibility as possible for this was left to the prefects and the Prefects' Council. Should we try and conform to the grammar school image or should we try and put our own individual image forward? The popular vote amongst the parents, especially those of the children who might have gone to the local grammar schools, was that we should try and ape the grammar schools as much as possible. Some of the less informed or superior people in the village I have often heard say 'Well of course it's not as good as the grammar schools in Wolverhampton'.

The majority of people around the school I have found, it may be just a generalised impression, criticise so easily. Since leaving Ounsdale I have been a little critical of myself on certain points but at times, especially when I was there, I was always on the defensive and justifying our position.

Being a new comprehensive built at a time when there were very few, we had frequent visitors to the school. One felt that we were continually on show. My form was at the top of the school for four years and was quite a small group, especially in the Sixth form when we were ten in the lower Sixth and eight in the upper Sixth. Consequently we had almost individual attention. This was good from the academic point of view but all of us had to do a great deal of readjusting when we went to colleges and found that we were on the bottom rung and just one of the masses.' (Jennifer Cornes, nee Piper, former Assistant Principal Bilston Community College).

At the official Opening of Ounsdale Comprehensive School in 1961 Philip was responsible for organising 'The Order of Ceremony' for the handing over of the school from Staffordshire County Council and for the 'Service of Dedication' programme that followed. In this programme one of his favourite and most moving poem was recited by a Sixth former 'We are the Music Makers'. Philip felt this was a fitting tribute to the efforts being made at Ounsdale, especially the line 'or one that is coming to birth'. He also identified with the sentiments of the Victorian poet – Arthur William Edgar O'Shaughnessy, (1844-1881), where in this poem he offers for consideration the idea that artists are the real creators and inspiration for mankind and the true makers of history and society. O'Shaughnessy was born in London of Irish parents and had his first collection of poems published in 1870, with two more in 1872 and 1874. 'We are the Music Makers' is the most noted of any of his works and comes from a collection from his book 'Music and Moonlight' published in 1874. Here are the first four verses of 'Ode' which were recited in 1961. Philip later used the latter verses at his first Speech day at New Mills Grammar School in 1962, which are quoted in the New Mills chapter.

We are the music makers,
And we are the dreamers of dreams,
Wandering by lone sea-breakers,
And sitting by desolate streams;-
World-losers and world-forsakers,
On whom the pale moon gleams:
Yet we are the movers and shakers
Of the world for ever, it seems.

With wonderful deathless ditties
We build up the world's great cities,
And out of a fabulous story
We fashion an empire's glory:
One man with a dream, at pleasure,
Shall go forth and conquer a crown;
And three with a song's new measure
Can trample an empire down.

We, in the ages lying
In the buried past of the earth,
Built Nineveh with our sighing,
And Babel itself with our mirth;
And o'erthrew them with prophesying
To the old of the new world's worth
Each age is a dream that is dying,
Or one that is coming to birth.

A breath of our inspiration
Is the life of each generation;
A wondrous thing of our dreaming
Unearthly, impossible seeming –
The soldier, the king, and the peasant
Are working together in one,
Till our dream shall become their present,
And their work in the world be done.

Earlier in the chapter there is a passage that Philip wrote on Mr.Holroyde's retirement in 1975; the following is an article written in July 1962 by Mr.Holroyde in which he pays tribute to Philip and his time at Ounsdale.

'I should like to pay tribute to Mr.P.H.Vennis for the great service which he has rendered to this school over the last four years, and who will be leaving to take up the post of headmaster of the New Mills Grammar School; few promotions could have been better earned.

It is now over four years since we first met at his Appointments interview, and the impression which he made upon me then of a man of boundless energy and a real insight into the development of progressive education, has proved to be a true one. Perhaps his greatest contribution to this school has been in the realm of ideas. He has played a leading part in the development of the non-athletic side of our House activities, and you have all seen the masterly way he has presided over the ceremonies at the various House Festivals. Three years ago he produced scenes from 'A Midsummer-Night's Dream', and just over a year ago he was responsible for a performance of 'Twelfth Night'. He has been the moving spirit behind this, the first number of our School Magazine.

Those who have been fortunate enough to have been his pupils in the fifth and sixth forms can testify to the infinite care he has taken over their careers. He has spent infinite time and energy over college and university entry and providing the leavers with worth-while jobs. In the School generally he has worked indefatigably to make it an orderly and hard-working place, and to 'sell' the idea of a longer school life. He has never spared time or energy, and to the compilation of the School's timetable he has brought a careful attention to detail and an infinite concern over making it fit the requirements of as many pupils as possible.

Three years ago he became Headmaster and Secretary of the Wombourne Evening Institute held on our premises, and during this time it has been built up to an enrolment of some 800 class registrations. It plays an invaluable part in the life of our community. He was also President of the National Union of Teachers, Tettenhall and Seisdon branch, from 1961 to 1962, attending many conferences on members' behalf.

151

Although living as a bachelor, he has been the hub of the School social life, and both the staff and the Sixth form will miss very much the festive occasions which have been so frequent at 'The Croft', where he has so often been the life and soul of the party and the dispenser of refreshments of varying kinds and surpassing quality. I did hear a little bird whisper that on one occasion when he opened a cupboard door there the sausage rolls he had forgotten to produce at the previous party! His unique and famous automobiles, 'Daphne' (who died on the M1 after having passed her seven-year test) and 'Rene' have conveyed many parties of staff and pupils to theatre shows, films and concerts all round the West Midlands, being in fact almost an unofficial school bus. I know that a great share of his affection will remain with this school and with its development, and all of us here wish him every success in the development of his new school. He has much to give and it will be offered unstintingly'.

Many of his pupils wrote to him after he left Ounsdale to thank him for the part he played in their development, here are extracts from two pupils who would have gone to a Grammar School before the opening of Ounsdale. 'I don't think you realise how much you influenced me. You were the most dominant character in my life at a time when I was most impressionable, when I was beginning to think about problems that I had hardly realised existed before. Rightly or wrongly, your ideas, thoughts, philosophies supplied at this time, become in the main, mine.

Do you remember in our Latin lessons you would put forward some idea – which we found outrageous. We would put forward every argument we could think of; then I'd go away and think about it, and I'd invariably conclude by deciding 'He's right you know'. Then I'd practice my newly acquired theories on Mom and Dad, using Vennis arguments as they raised the objections I had raised to you.

When I really think about it, I feel that everything in me that I am proud of, that is my aims and ambitions and outlook for life, I owe to you.' The other pupil reflects two months after Philip's leaving Ounsdale: 'The school is very much the same as ever: I thought it would fall to pieces or at least be very different when you and the Upper Sixth left: it hasn't fallen down and, as I said, it is the same as ever, fortunately or unfortunately! It is so true what you have often said; 'Life still goes on in its same old pattern, regardless of what changes are made'. In spite of it all, what I do know is that what you did for Ounsdale and separate individuals, will never be forgotten by those who knew you. I know you did a lot for me personally – my whole attitude to life and people is a result of the part you played as a teacher, adviser and a friend of the Sixth form. I think I appreciate most deeply the fact that you were always prepared to discuss real and difficult problems about work and life with us – much more as a friend than a teacher. I think the real reason that, I, like the others, often felt indignant and tried to deny things, was because you put into words what we all, deep down, felt and thought but we were not prepared to admit it. Thank you for everything.'

In the first edition of Omnibus Philip wrote his memories of the four years as Deputy headmaster and it is in this article that his empathy with his experiences at Ounsdale are written. The article is titled *'Ave atque vale* – hail and farewell'. "As far as who goes farthest" – and we have come a long way. Many things stick in my memory over four years here. Schools present an endless succession of ending relationships between men and women, boys and girls, teaching and taught, parent and teacher, governors and staff, office and school. They are, as a Greek philosopher said, "Always in a state of flux"; just when you think some permanent relationship is struck, some valuable point really driven home, something you have said remembered for ever, you must stop, and look around, and realise that these things are not so. The whole underlying sadness of school life lies right here in the impermanency of things said and friendships made. Ghosts in fact are everywhere. All you can hope is that out of five million and two seeds sown, two at any rate will germinate – and that is something. Wombourne is essentially a brand new suburb imposed upon an age-old village, having as yet no real *'esprit'* or at least an *'esprit'* in parts of it – and this School is even newer. It has neither the drawbacks not the advantages of traditional things, and every step we have taken, has been taken with one eye to what the grammar school tradition before us, has said 'shall be' and one eye on the sixties and what is varied and valuable and new in our time.

A comprehensive school is and should be an optimistic affair, bursting its seams with new ideas in every direction, a combination of men and women and adolescents and children of every sort and background and ability who have been brought together into what I believe to be one of the greatest single steps forward ever taken in English education. For every boy and girl here 'Opportunity Knocks' and we should, and are, trying to stretch each separately according to his or her ability, aptitude and age. Largely I think we are succeeding, and chances are being offered to the most academic and to the least, to the oldest and to the youngest to play their proper part in adult life. We can only be judged by the next generation, whose parents these will be. We have no answers for twenty years. We can only try experimenting in this direction or in that with the utmost persistence and patience, making allowances at every turn for all that immense number of minor irritants that crop up when human beings live together and the minor impatiences that are the mark of growing up. For the record, as they say - I remember not being accepted, and near fights, and a feeling that too great reservoirs of persistence were called for – and tough, and not so tough boys; I remember nerves at the 'mock' and the first GCE. I remember having to soothe this girl or that boy. I remember feeling personally hurt by the immense savagery of our system which makes so much of life apparently dependent upon certificates – when the results came out, - and some had some, and some had none – the latest version of 'the haves' and 'the have nots'. I remember dreaming again of the Sixth form and their work, and their fun – to me in my more limited moments, the teenagers I most enjoy – sharp minds getting sharper, being sharpened – 'diamond cut diamond!' all the day through. I remember a small office, whose walls contracted as the night wore on, till helping to run a school seemed a long, long nightmare of a fight against time. I remember 4B and 'The Dream' and a Lower Gornal Bottom and that very odd lion and so on. Shakespeare would have understood: and I remember 'Twelfth Night' and a Feste beautifully lit beneath an immense figure above, singing her sadness to Viola and Orsino – a moment of truth in a school hall – and there were Sir Toby, Sir Andrew, Maria and Fabian with their immense zest – bringing in their combination with Olivia and Viola and so on pensiveness rare among schoolgirl actresses. If they did not already know the truth of Feste's lines, they surely one day will: -

"Then come kiss me, sweet and twenty
Youth's a stuff will not endure."

One could go on remembering, for souvenirs are without end. The first two years were an attempt really to build via a limited number of boys and girls, that age old top that I believe secondary schools need for a lead, for an example, for attribute. Perhaps one tried with too few, too soon, but educational change demands hurry and results. We had to have a Sixth out of somewhere, or even out of nowhere. The second two years have been spent in an attempt to make live very quickly some of the more useful traditions of English education in our modern atmosphere. Through all this the Comprehensive School has had its first four years, - led, I should say valiantly, by boys and girls who perhaps have felt they have gained most, and therefore have given most to leading children quite unlike them whom they would not otherwise have met. So the memories that stay make it all appear worthwhile. Life in a big school is often funny, often sad, and always worthwhile. If you do not have your joke at the office, you have your joke in a classroom or at Assembly, or in the staff room, and by these means, not least by the jokes, corners are rounded, edges softened. Remembering is a tearful game, and not to be indulged often. One must look forward, not back, so that these moments that stay will have their main use in being the heart of that cushion on which Ounsdale will now sit under innumerable other cushions, until in fifty years time some child will say, pointing at a greying photograph,

"Look at him; he was the first Deputy headmaster. Doesn't he look old fashioned – Look at them, the first Sixth form – don't they look a lot of old frumps. Still, I suppose they started it all, and that's something."

So, to end at Wombourne is to leave behind only a beginning and out of beginnings come home tides of differing sorts of results. We live in the sixties in the teenage era – of teenagers very much misunderstood, but really almost all very good people, with immense potentialities for good and largely wanting to do well and be good. Schools (allied with parents) must not become a shrinking oasis, only to direct useless disciplines at those not really wanting them. They must advance into the society in which they function, connected at every level with the good things in it, and yet not being afraid to stand up for their own standards and to fight against the slipshod, uneasy, comfort loving atmosphere of the society in which we live. Our business in schools is with standards at every level, and we must not be ashamed to make our fight for them. Our business is with discipline, and with friendship. Our business is the totality of life. Schools, I suppose, are always slightly behind the times, and therefore always appear to have rules not of their day. Perhaps one of their functions is to drag their feet before the oncoming tide of so called progress, to doubt and to be sceptical, and perhaps this is good. To be a centre of our not very interesting dormitory, this perhaps, too, is what we should work for – a place to which boys and girls want to come because learning can and should be fun.

When we began, the school was in the throes of its second building revolution, and the noise and dust round us as we tried to work and embarked upon what more organised societies might have called 'Our Four Year Plan', was excessive, even though relations with the builders were always good.

We were studying 'Great Expectations' which they had and I had, and which we all might reasonably feel have been fulfilled to an extent far greater than expectations then might have been supposed.

Perhaps finally we need only look back and remember what Joe the blacksmith said to his own Pip, looking back on the life they had spent together when Pip was a teenager –

"Cor, what larks, eh, Pip? Cor, what larks!'

I commend them to you.

" As far as who goes farthest." '

Philip left Ounsdale with the full knowledge that he had done an excellent job. Philip also left Ounsdale a married man; he had fallen in love with Diana and made her his wife in July 1962.

Diana, was in many ways opposite to Philip. She came from a rural background, her parents were market gardeners, vegetarians and ran their household with Quaker beliefs. Philip was some years older than Diana, yet their marriage was one of love and devotion, lasting with very few disagreements for nearly forty years until his death in 1999. Calmly supporting Philip when the going was tough in his job, Diana had insight and understanding of the dilemmas in which he sometimes found himself. She had different strengths from Philip and was much more practical, quieter and less extrovert and possibly because of these contrasts the marriage succeeded.

A passionate, romantic and sentimental man he adored, loved and respected Diana for the rest of his life and she gave him the secure home life and the support for the challenges ahead. He was as enthusiastic with his marriage as he was in his career.

CHAPTER 7

New Mills Grammar School
New Mills Derbyshire

New Mills is a town of the Industrial Revolution that sprawls across the hills of the western Peak District. Today, the hillsides are covered by rows of nineteenth century terraces; many of which were built on steep gradients and the skyline is still dominated by the spires of the Anglican and Roman Catholic Churches. It is eight miles south east of Stockport and fifteen miles from Manchester. The town is built in the lower valley of the River Goyt and in the tributary valley of the River Sett, in the north west of Derbyshire, but very close to the Cheshire boarder. There is a seventy foot gorge – the Torrs, which the town stands above. The town people look out on to the moorland hills all around them.

Between 1500 and 1750, before industrialisation and the coming of the textile mills, the area consisted of small hamlets, cottages and hillside farms. Around 1700 the population of the four hamlets which eventually were to makeup the township of New Mills was about 400 people. The slow growth of the population reflected the hardness of life on the valley and hillside farms, the high rate of fatal diseases and the shortage of food in the event of two successive failing harvests. Most of the population were farmers, but there was a growing domestic industry of carpentry, tanning, spinning and weaving in the cottages. Linen and wool were spun on hand wheels and woven into cloth in the cottages and farms. Cotton had arrived in New Mills at the beginning of the eighteenth century and local weavers began to make mixed fabrics in which a strong woollen or linen warp was combined with a cotton weft. The cloth was taken to Stockport market to be sold on for the London markets. It remained a cottage industry with many families living entirely by their weaving for some time, but with the invention of the 'spinning jenny' in 1764, the 'water frame' in 1769 and the 'mule' in 1779, revolution came to the industry and to the people of New Mills. Water- powered spinning mills were opened and the 'water frame' introduced the factory system into the cotton industry.

The industrial Revolution saw rapid and fundamental changes for the manufacture of cotton in the eighteenth century. The Torrs gorge saw development on the banks of the two rivers, the Sett and the Goyt, of water powered mills. (Colour photograph 23.) The Torrs provided the waterfalls and cascades, and with the addition of man-made weirs, there was a regular supply of water for the mills that had developed on the rocky terraces above the water. New Mills developed and quickly spread up what is now the High street and over the fields to Torr Top estate. (Colour photograph 19.) The town became an important centre for cotton spinning, bleaching, dyeing, and calico printing. By 1819 there were eight spinning mills, two print works and two bleach works and the inevitable growth in population that these industries brought. By 1871 the population was 5,028.

New Mills did not develop on easy terrain, many houses were built on steep slopes and as a result often had two storeys on one side and three or four storeys on the other side. New Mills was a new town in the nineteenth century, and today there is a contrast evident in the building styles with the newer brick houses of the twentieth century on the outskirts of the town and the town centre mostly consisting of older houses with flag or blue slate roofs.

The modern stages of the town's history were helped through by development of an urban authority and the process of municipalisation, firstly by local Boards and then by elected Councils. The town hall was built at the end of the nineteenth century in a prominent position in the town and was opened by the Duke of Devonshire in 1871. The tower and the clock were added later, along with an extension which was used as a reading room for the Free Library, which is now the Council chamber. The Carnegie Free Library was added to the town hall with a donation from Andrew Carnegie, a cotton industrialist and steel magnate, who donated much of his money to the buildings of such libraries across the United Kingdom and the United States of America. It is now the New Mills Public Library.

In the early and mid twentieth century redundant mills were sold off. One Victorian wick mill was purchased by Swizzels Matlow, who transferred their confectionary business from London to New Mills in the Blitz. Swizzels Matlow are the largest remaining independant, family owned confectionary company in England. They have a thriving business and they respect the valuable skill based employees and today are the largest employer in the town.

Today New Mills is a designated conservation area, with the High Peak Borough Council justifying the reasons for this designation in its document on the town by saying 'New Mills is a town of dramatic topography and origins that date back to the fourteenth century. Its topography and its supply of fast flowing waters led to its development as a thriving mill town and important centre for the textile industry. Its impressive landscape developed much of its developed form and the townscape that we still see today.'_

'*East Ham and New Mills Grammar Schools came into existence largely through the 1902 Education Act, which represented one of the greatest single steps forward in education, enabling children to go into secondary schools, as they were then called.*' *(P.H.V. 1962)*

The Education Act of 1902, passed by the Balfour government, abolished School Boards. Local Education Authorities were established and Board Schools became Council Schools. The powers given to Local Authorities by the act included that of providing funds from rates to develop secondary education. New Mills town in the form of its Science School, which had been developed at Spring Bank by the Headmaster Mr. Nichols, already possessed this as a secondary school. In May 1908 the Council Log Book has the following entry from Mr.Nichols 'A few months ago the Board of Education insisted upon the termination of the dual headmastership of the Council and Secondary School. As a consequence of this decision my engagement as master of this school which I have had since 1 January 1878 ends today'. The Inspector, in the same year, says in his report 'With the beginning of the next school year the Elementary School will have its own headmaster. The present headmaster has been here many years during which the school has done good work. It was largely due to him that the upper classes were gradually developed into secondary schools of which he will continue to be headmaster'.

As a consequence of the 1902 Education Act, Derbyshire Education Committee proposed in 1904 that New Mills did not need a secondary school and recommended 'a well planned higher grade elementary school.' There was great opposition to this proposal, led by Mr.Nichols and Edward Godward, and they successfully opposed it. Mr.Nichols remained headmaster of the Elementary School and the County Secondary School until 1908 when he was appointed solely headmaster of the County Secondary School.

Mr.Nichols had the foresight to write on parchment the early beginnings of the school; this scroll was placed in the cavity beneath the corner stone of the present building when it was laid by the then Chairman of Governors, Mr. L.J. Hall, J.P. C.C. on 14 December 1912.

The school was designed by the architect, George Widdows, who was responsible for the design of over one hundred schools in Derbyshire. He was the County Architect from 1905 to 1936 and he frequently incorporated advanced, influential and sometimes controversial, innovative designs. (Colour photographs 21. & 22.)

At the beginning of the twentieth century Derbyshire's population increased more than any other county of England, much of this increase was on its eastern boundary because of the expansion and development of the coal fields. This growth in population urgently required more schools and coincided with a revolution in school design during what was termed the 'Healthy schools crusade', which started in 1902 and so building regulations for that year from the Board of Education suggested that 'the best plan for secondary schools is that of a central hall around which other rooms are arranged and from which they are entered by doors, the upper portion of which are glazed!' New Mills is an outstanding example of a George Widdows secondary school where he displayed a great degree of architectural style and ornamentation with generous amounts of stained glass, oak panelling, carved stonework and wrought iron work. New Mills School building is now a Grade II listed building because 'it is considered to be of special architectural interest in a national context and is listed for the following reasons. It is a notable example of the work of George Widdows, who is nationally acknowledged as a leading designer of schools in the early twentieth century and an exponent of advanced ideas on school planning and hygiene. This school is one of only two known examples of a Widdows quadrangular design. Its original plan form remains clearly legible and has not undergone significant alteration. It retains all of the notable elements of its original design and is relatively unaltered. The later enclosure of the quadrangle corridors has not materially affected the legibility of the original plan, and has not significantly affected the buildings' special architectural interest. The exterior is of distinctive and consistently high architectural quality and displays the well-crafted use of locally won gritstone. The interior retains a number of original fixtures and fittings of special interest, including window and door joinery, fire places, and, in the central hall, a set of stained glass windows representative of the Arts and Sciences.' (New Mills Local History Society)

It was not until 1925 that the content of Mr. Nichol's parchment was made public. He wrote after his retirement in the School Magazine a series of articles about the beginnings of the school. This is some of what he wrote. 'I remembered that about twelve years ago I had written a history of the School. It was compiled at the request of the Governors or the architect Mr. Widdows, at the date of the laying of the foundation stone of the new building in 1912. It was engrossed on parchment, and now lies with some other mementos in a cavity under the foundation stone at the east corner of the building. Presumably, these objects are placed there for the information to some future generation when the ordinary records are lost.

I wonder whether, when that day comes, education will be so different from what it is now, that the people will look with amusement on the antiquated system of the early part of the twentieth century, or, whether, in the age of decadence, they will marvel at the excellence of our schools, as we admire those of ancient Greece or Alexandria, always providing that in the event of another great world war, or other catastrophe, there will be any civilisation left to trouble itself about such matters.

It cannot be stated concerning this School that it was at any time founded, established, endowed or even formally opened. By a slow process it has emerged from other institutions, and even the premises in which it is now being carried on were mainly designed and constructed for other purposes. The process of development is the history of higher education in New Mills, and extends without break of continuity over thirty years.

Between 1879 and 1889 the centre of all educational work, outside the elementary schools, was the Mechanics' Institute, which having taken its origin in a house in Market Street quite twenty years earlier was at this time located in the Public Hall with a library, reading room and class room. It was supported entirely by voluntary subscriptions out of which it paid an annual rent of about £10 to the trustees of the Hall.

The President of the Institute from 1874 up to the time of his death in 1890 was Alderman John Mackie J.P, and it was largely due to his far-sightedness, liberality and public spirit that the Institute was enabled to lay the foundations of higher education in New Mills. In 1879, the committee invited me to take up a chemistry class which had been in abeyance for two years, owing to the expense of carrying it on. Some apparatus was bought by Mr. Mackie, and the class was opened under the regulations of the Science and Art Department. In this class during the first session, there were 24 students, whose ages varied from thirteen to fifty two. Next year additional classes were opened in Mathematics and Human physiology. In 1888, a cottage in High Street was rented, and the upper and lower floors fitted with benches and the apparatus for practical work in Chemistry. The cost of the fittings amounted to about £80, to which Mr. Mackie contributed £50.

The School Board, having given to the committee the free use of classrooms at the School on Spring Bank, agreed that other subjects should be taken up, and in 1885 the prospectus contained the following :- Mathematics, Drawing, Physiology, Organic Chemistry, Inorganic Chemistry, theoretical and practical Organic Chemistry, theoretical and practical Calico bleaching, Printing and Dyeing, Geometry, Machine Construction and Building Construction. The teachers were Mr. J.A. Nichols and Mr .J. Stott. The financial arrangements for carrying on the work were simple. The rent of the cottage, the cost of chemicals, and other regular expenses were paid out of the income, consisting of the students' fees and the grants from the Science and Art Department, the balance being paid to the teachers at the end of the session. The system was continued for ten years.

In 1887 the cottage laboratory was condemned by an Inspector of the Science and Art Department, whose duties compelled him to spend an evening in its atmosphere during working hours. In a subsequent interview with the committee he likened it to 'the Black Hole of Calcutta'. After this it was agreed that something ought to be done at once to enable the work to go on, and out of this arose the movement for 'the Jubilee Extension of the Public Hall', to include a lecture room, chemical laboratory and other additions. Subscriptions to the extent of some hundreds of pounds were immediately promised, but the scheme never matured. It was felt that the work was outgrowing the bounds of voluntary effort, and it was finally decided to invite the School Board to carry it on.

Next year this body, having obtained a loan of £836 for the purpose, began an extension of the Board School by the erection of a chemical laboratory, and lecture room. This was intended at first for use as a higher grade day school and the evening technical classes. In 1889 the Technical Institution Act was passed, and adopted by the Urban District Council. They delegated their powers, except that of rating, to the School Board. In the same year the New Mills Mechanics' Institute held its last annual public meeting, and formally transferred its classes to the School Board.

The history of this period illustrates at once the force and the limits of voluntary effort. It was a time marked by great enthusiasm and vitality. Every townsman of any influence or distinction took part in the work. The students were eager for knowledge and zealous in their work. Over 600 individuals had received instruction in the school, and the moral and material results measured by any standard that can be applied, have not been surpassed by any of the succeeding generation of students.

The New Mills School Board decided on the advice of the Science and Art Department to open an organised science day school instead of a higher grade school. It began in 1890 with seven students from the higher classes in the elementary school, but the number had grown to twenty by the end of the first year.

Henry Barber, Esq, J.P. succeeded Alderman Mackie as the representative of the district on the County Council, and very greatly assisted the School Board in developing the school. In 1892 the school was affiliated with the Derbyshire Technical Education Committee as a district technical school. The benefits of the grants from the County Council under the Technical Institute Act now began to be felt and appreciated. At the request of the Science and Art Department more class rooms, a physical laboratory, and a room for woodwork were added, and at the same time, Mrs. Mackie gave to the school a library in memory of her late husband, and she has maintained it ever since.

In 1898 there was a further extension. New laboratories and classrooms were added, partly to satisfy the growing demands of the Department in respect of the day school, and partly to provide for the growing evening technical classes, especially chemistry.

The Organised Science School had now become a school of science under the altered regulations, and the curriculum was modified and extended. The extension of the school was opened in September, 1899, by the Duke of Devonshire.

The Education Act, 1902 made the County Council responsible for education within their area, and as a result the New Mills School Board was dissolved in 1903. The staff at the School at this time consisted of J.A. Nichols, two assistants, and two visiting teachers. The grant earned from the Board of Education in 1903 was £310 on 57 pupils.

During this period the School Board was engaged in a continual effort to comply with the increasing demands of the science and art department in regard to the accommodation, staffing and equipment of the school. 'Loss of recognition', so often threatened, would have crippled the school by the loss of substantial grants, and it was through the efforts of the Board that the building took its present form by repeated additions and alterations.

Through its most critical period the school had a most faithful and determined supporter in the late Councillor Edward Godward, who, first as clerk to the School Board and afterwards as a member of the Derbyshire Education Committee, devoted himself to the work. His lifelong connection with education enabled him to grasp the difficulties in all their bearings, and to give the most valuable guidance in the work he so zealously supported. The headmaster is especially grateful for his help and encouragement during this period of difficulty.

In 1903 the school now became a 'County Secondary School', and the curriculum underwent a considerable change. Science teaching no longer predominated, and the school was organised to provide the elements of a more liberal education. The result of the change was soon manifest. The numbers, practically stationary for some years, increased at an average rate of fifteen scholars per annum during the eight years up to 1911, when the school became full, many children since then been refused admission. The Derbyshire Education Committee made the school one of their pupil-teacher centres in 1905. In 1908 the County Council purchased a site for the erection of a secondary school, the present premises having been declared unsuitable by the Board of Education. The same year Councillor Godward gave £1,000 to provide a trust for scholarships in secondary schools, and 13 scholars are now attending the New Mills School under that trust.

Up to June, 1908, being under the same roof, the two schools had been controlled by the same headmaster. During the earlier developments there had been many advantages in such an arrangement between two schools so closely related, but the rapid growth of the Secondary School made a change imperative, and the headmaster was relieved of the responsibility of the elementary school. The change has been of great advantage to both schools. During this period the school has been financed by the Derbyshire County Council, and its proficiency greatly improved through the provision of a more adequate staff.

The school has now 163 scholars, 76 boys and 87 girls. Of the latter nine are pupil teachers. There are seven forms. In the lower the average age of the pupils is twelve years, and in the highest seventeen years and two months. The staff consisted of seven teachers, one visiting teacher and the headmaster.'

This is the story as told by Mr. Nichols; to whom so much is owed for the work he did in establishing New Mills Secondary School, later in 1945 to become a grammar school. The new school building was never formally opened, preparations were underway for the formal opening of the building, but the outbreak of war in 1914 put an end to them and the school moved from Spring Bank without a ceremony. Mr Nichols continued as Headmaster until 1921, his educational work improving the lives of so many families in New Mills. 'John Nichols is the history of education in New Mills for fifty years.' said Reverend Lauckner who goes on to say 'He had only one sphere of educational service and that was in New Mills. He came here from his college and was a headmaster all his teaching days, over forty years. That in itself is a wonderful achievement. He saw a vision of a splendid educational centre at New Mills. The present educational position and the splendid secondary school have justified the vision, courage and spirit of progressiveness which were marks of his character.'

The newly built accommodation soon to be proved inadequate, considering children, even in the early days of the school, travelled long distances; there were insufficient facilities for dinners. In 1920, a temporary dining room, constructed from three army huts, was erected. This temporary building remained in use for over thirty years.

Mr. W.A .Whitton succeeded Mr. Nichols as headmaster of the County Secondary School in 1921. Although Mr. Whitton was the headmaster, Mr. Nichols kept close contact with the school as he remained President of the Old Scholars Association until 1925, and on the Board of Governors for several years where he continued to give to the school the enthusiasm that founded it.

William Alexander Whitton was born in Leicester where his father was a nonconformist minister and as a boy he attended Colerham School. After school he first went to Liverpool University where he took a first class honours degree in chemistry. Before commencing his teaching career Mr .Whitton spent some time at Bangor University College, and prior to taking up the headship at New Mills he taught at Brigend Grammar School in South Wales, Royal Holloway School, London and was Headmaster at Ross on Wye School. Mr .Whitton was a considerable sportsman, he captained the Rest of Wales at hockey and entered many well known tennis tournaments. On the academic side he wrote papers on the flora and fauna of Hampshire and published several scientific textbooks. Following his appointment as headmaster of New Mills School, and during the next twenty years he devoted himself to developing a Grammar School of which parents and children of North West Derbyshire had every reason to be proud. The school was only six years old when Mr .Whitton became headmaster and during his twenty years service at the school, there was the aftermath of the First World War, the industrial depression of the thirties and the upset of the first years of the Second World War. Against this back ground, and with few resources Mr .Whitton laid the formation for the School which enabled it to subsequently develop into an excellent grammar school, which later generations have appreciated. It was during Mr .Whitton's headship that the school field was converted from a ploughed field to a respectably level and drained playing pitch.

Mr .Whitton's life was built on simplicity, sincerity, friendship and devotion to his School. He knew the value of hard work, but he realised the need for relaxation — such as his hiring a conjuror to amuse the School at the end of term. His school reports were his own and designed to encourage the weakest to make an effort. He played games hard; he viewed corporal punishment with disfavour, but when he called a boy or a girl a Gormeril they knew he was angry and the wrong-doer felt guilty; he believed in allowing boys and girls to have a say in school affairs — for example the house names were the choice of the pupils.

In the school magazine of 1927, now called NeMeSiS (New Mills Secondary School) one of the upper fifth pupils, G. Dodd, describes 'New Mills as I see it' in the following way. 'Not being a native of New Mills, perhaps I have the advantage of seeing it with an unprejudiced eye. It is certainly not one of nature's beauty spots, though, like the curates' egg, 'parts of it are excellent'.

As its name implies, there are numerous mills, and several other important buildings. The majority of the inhabitants are, no doubt, justly proud of the possession of a town hall.

To my mind, by far the most important edifice is that 'Palace of Industry' – New Mills County Secondary School. The journey from the L.M. & S. railway station to the aforementioned school has its monotony relieved by one or two shops. The glaring posters of the latest sensational pictures of the cinema also provide a little variety. We become quite familiar with the ruins of an old mill en route, but it requires rather more imagination than we possess to regard them as picturesque. Though familiarity is supposed to breed contempt, it is not always so, for the School daily strikes one as a fine, up to date, building. The sight of the playing field from the terrace is pleasantly stimulating. The position is such that its occupants are subjected to the minimum of smuts which pervade the atmosphere of the town itself'.

Another pupil during Mr. Whitton's time was Geoff Heath who in his book 'A Mellor Boyhood' about life in a Derbyshire village between two World Wars, says this: 'The headmaster was W.A. Whitton – known to all, staff and scholars alike – as 'Boss'. He was everything that a head should be: kindly, even jocular, towards those who kept the rules, but a blustering, irascible figure, swearing (it was said) in his native Welsh to those who put one foot wrong.' Geoff Heath describes in his book his time at New Mills County Secondary School from his arrival in September 1934. 'Early in September of that year I was found to be waiting for the 0914 train at Marple station wearing my new green school cap – the only compulsory item of uniform for boys. Girls had to have the full outfit of gymslip and blouse, hat and coat in the winter and a regulation dress as an alternative in the summer. For both sexes, there was an optional blazer. The girl's uniform seemed to change from year to year, and could be obtained from only one supplier, who was rather expensive.

The timetable at New Mills was governed by the railway services. Children from the two outlying catchment areas – Mellor and Ludworth to the west, and Chinley and the Hope Valley to the east - had no other means but the train by which to reach New Mills. School could not start until they arrived, and so the first lesson did not begin until 0940. Assembly was at 0930, but was only attended by those from New Mills and its immediate environs – the rest of us attended only on special occasions.

The end of the day was also arranged to fit in with the railway timetable. Lessons ended at 15.55 so that we could catch the 16.17 to Marple. Those from Chinley and Edale were less fortunate. Their train did not leave until around 17.00 hours, and they did their homework under supervision until it was time to walk across the town to the station.

When I was thirteen I got my first bicycle. It was obviously quicker to cycle to school – a distance of three miles – than to set off in the opposite direction for Marple station, ending up with another half mile walk across New Mills. So I abandoned the train. Now I could arrive at school in time for assembly, and I was able to join the local children for morning prayers in the hall.

166

The hall was octagonal, with a domed roof which is still a local landmark. It also doubled as the gymnasium, and the prefects, who occupied the back row during assembly, could loll against the wall bars. Around six of the walls was inscribed the motto: Great works / are performed / not by / strength / but by / perseverance.

The school had only 300 pupils. Life at New Mills was totally different from the council school at Mellor. There was a different teacher for each subject; there was a gymnasium, a dining hall, craft rooms, playing fields, changing rooms. The day was broken into periods by the bells which rang every thirty five minutes. Running in the corridors was forbidden, and outdoor shoes had to be changed to plimsolls before one could venture beyond the cloakroom – rules strictly enforced by the lordly prefects. Homework, too, distinguished the secondary from the primary.

The routine of lessons was relieved towards the end of term by an afternoon of music or theatricals given by a visiting company of players. These were regarded as occasions requiring a few surreptitious sweets to make them really enjoyable, and friends who lived in New Mills would be given a list of our requirements when they went home to lunch. I thus associate 'A Midsummer-Night's Dream' not only with the actor Donald Wolfit, but also with slabs of 'palm' toffee. New Mills was a great school.'

In the same year that Geoff Heath started at New Mills County Secondary School there was written an article in the school magazine about the school life which existed at that time, the article is anonymous but comments ' The greater part of our time at school is taken up with lessons. They are not equally interesting. Homework is less interesting than class work. It is compulsory, so you have to resign yourself to it. I begrudge the hours I devote to it, because there are other and more enjoyable ways of spending time. It is true that homework is not so disagreeable on rainy winter nights because there is not the same desire for amusement. But in summer I find it more pleasant to go out doors and play.

Next to lessons and homework, the prefects are encountered most. They have their advantages and disadvantages. They give an added zest to the commission of minor offences, such as running in the corridors, throwing pumps in the cloakroom, and running down the banks, but on the other hand they restrict your liberty and I think the punishment they mete out is often heavier than befits the crime.

A more agreeable aspect of school life is the playing of games, which range from noughts and crosses in the classroom to the playing of organised games on the field. I like form matches both in cricket and football, but House matches and practice at the nets is quite another matter. I do not like these because in the

House matches the slightest slip is considered a crime, and in the nets people will simply not bowl properly when they have had their innings.

Only the teachers remain to be considered. They enter largely into everybody's life and therefore everyone has definite impressions of them, but on this point silence is golden!'

After twenty years in the school Mr. Whitton retired and Mr. Norman Taylor was appointed headmaster in September 1941. Mr. Taylor was educated at Oldham Hulme Grammar School and the University of Manchester, gaining a B.Sc in Metallurgy. Later he went to the University of London where he gained a first class honours degree in Chemistry and proceeding to M.Sc. Before coming to New Mills he was headmaster of the Queen Elizabeth Grammar School, Atherstone, Warwickshire.

The first four years of Mr. Taylor's headship were spent in the unusually difficult war years. Just previous to his appointment another school evacuated from Southend had shared the building and a number of evacuees still attended the School. The total number of boys and girls in the School was about four hundred.

Conditions were not ideal for learning. Boys and girls had to bring gas masks in containers every day, from time to time air raid practices were held when the School filed out into the air raid shelters, the cadet force was an important part of school life, and every evening a member of the staff slept in the School to report possible fire damage! Sometimes books were unobtainable because stocks had been burnt in raids. Throughout these years Mr. Taylor maintained as high a standard of scholastic achievement as was possible. At that time a holiday was awarded for the achievement of a State Scholarship and these holidays became an annual event.

After the War came a re-building on firmer foundations. Mr. Taylor with the Old Millonian's support organised a scheme to make a suitable memorial to the old boys and one girl who were killed in the war. This entailed a lot of organisation for him and his presence at events for raising money. The electronic organ and the oak panel carved by Hunstones of Tideswell were dedicated in April 1951.

Mr. Taylor held the first full scale speech day since the war, in 1947 in the Art Cinema, not in its usual venue, the Town Hall, because of the great increase in the numbers of pupils. He said that recruiting and retaining science teachers was particularly difficult since they were being attracted to industry with larger salaries. He continued by saying that his aim was to provide on the one side a sound academic education, and on the other side a moral and physical education. He did not wish to make success in either of these an excuse for failure in the other one, nor did he think an excuse was necessary. Mr. Taylor continued to hold Speech Days on an annual basis. In 1948 he talks about the increase in numbers of scholarships and awards, and the fact that it was becoming financially easier to enter University, but this advantage was offset by the vast number of applicants for entry. Speech Day in 1949 saw the emphasis move to the pressing accommodation needs, especially for a gymnasium and a new dining hall.

By this time the School had gained a reputation for the high standard of its scholarship. Over sixty University, State and Major Scholarships were gained by Sixth Formers during Mr. Taylor's headship.

The School was growing in numbers and it was realised that some of the accommodation was inadequate. In 1949 a library, science laboratory and two classrooms were built. But even with these additions the school accommodation was still inadequate as there was no gymnasium, no stage and no facilities for drama, no offices or medical room and the open corridors were not suitable for the harsh climate of the Peak District.

In his subsequent annual speech day reports Mr. Taylor covered such topics as the change from School Certificate and Higher School Certificate, to the O and A level examinations which 'would permit all entrants to take individual subjects, and this would mean a change in the school curriculum so that a pupil's education would not be completed until they reached eighteen, and therefore pupils of ability could not afford to break their education at sixteen'. By 1953 Mr. Taylor was talking about University grants and 'that they were not going to be so easily obtained as in the past.' 'This was', he said, 'to perhaps set a judicious and thoroughly justifiable limit on University entrants although the need for science graduates was still particularly pressing especially in the applied sciences.' By 1954 he talked about staying at school until the age of eighteen and that 'Boys and girls should not worry about the future, whether or not a university entrance was gained, so long as good use was made of the time spent in the Sixth Form. Quite suddenly', he continued, 'the grammar schools find themselves in a seller's market in good sixth form pupils. It is very clear that at the present time what counts is that a course of advanced education has been pursued.' This growing demand for Sixth Formers was reiterated in 1955, and Mr. Taylor went on to say that 'the opportunities for the well-trained person were greater than ever, particularly if that training had given a balanced outlook on life, and was not only training in some particular technique.' He continued with this theme in the following two years' speech days and by 1960 was reporting on the building of an extension to the school and alterations to the existing building, as well as the visit by Her Majesty's School Inspectors who had given an excellent report on the school. The new science laboratories were formally opened in September 1961. These buildings owed much to the forethought and guidance of Mr. Taylor and provided amenities which would help to cultivate the high standard of accuracy and measurement needed by the modern scientist and technician. The school corridors, for long open to the constant changes of wind and weather were glassed in during spring 1961.

Mr. Taylor led the school Jubilee celebrations in March 1961. He said on that occasion 'This is a memorable day in the history of the school. It is very pleasant indeed that we should not only have with us the School's second headmaster, Mr. Whitton but also the son of its first headmaster, Victor Nichols, so that there is an unbroken link from our birth to the present day'

When Mr. Taylor retired in 1962 he was held in high regard for his considerable achievements in such an extensive period. His personal insistence on high academic standards, his constant encouragement of any activity which promoted the educational welfare of the School, his readiness to help especially the boy or girl who needed particular help because of untoward circumstances, his personal and kindly interest in the welfare and later achievements of his pupils made him respected by them.

The change from one headmaster to another is always an important, and sometimes significant, event in the history of a school. At the end of the summer term Mr. Taylor retired from the headmastership of the School, and at the beginning of the autumn term Philip Vennis succeeded him.

New Mills showing Grammar School. 1962

'Challenges of being a headmaster' 1962 to 1971

'We live in the 1960's in the Teenage era – of teenagers very much misunderstood, but really almost all very good people, with immense potentialities for good and largely waiting to do good and be good. Schools (allied with parents) must not become a shrinking oasis, only to direct useless disciplines at those not really wanting them. They must advance into the Society in which they function, connected at every level with the good things in it, and yet not being afraid to stand up for their own standards, and to fight against the slipshod, uneasy, comfort-loving atmosphere of the Society in which we live. Our business in schools is with standards at every level, and we must not be ashamed to make our fight for them. Our business is with discipline, and with friendship. Our business is the totality of life. Schools, I suppose, are always slightly behind the times, and therefore always appear to have rules not of their day. Perhaps one of their functions is to drag their feet before the oncoming tide of so called progress, to doubt and to be sceptical, and perhaps this is good.' (P.H.V. 1962)

Philip on arrival at New Mills Grammar School, 1962.

'The choice of Mr. P.H. Vennis to succeed Mr. Norman Taylor as headmaster of New Mills Grammar School has two unusual features.

For the first time since the school was built in 1912 (and, even before that, when it was housed on Spring Bank), it is to have an 'arts man' as headmaster. Mr. Vennis holds a degree in Classics and English.

Mr. Taylor, like his two predecessors, holds science degrees, and, from the birth of the school, it has always been said to have had a 'science bias'.

After so many years it is perhaps not inopportune that an 'arts man' should take over. Some schools alternate between the two when filling headmasterships.

The second notable feature about the appointment is that Mr. Vennis is now deputy headmaster of a comprehensive school which has about 900 pupils. Roughly, that school is about as big as the two New Mills Schools – grammar and Spring Bank Secondary – put together.

Does Mr. Vennis's appointment mean, as has been likely for some time that Derbyshire Education Committee will decide on the two New Mills secondary schools becoming a comprehensive school, or at least, joining together in a comprehensive system?

It may well be that the move to link up will be made in the not too distant future. With his comprehensive school experience, Mr. Vennis should be the right man to see that such a switch would work as smoothly as possible.

There are, of course, divided views on the question of comprehensive schools. But that's another story.' – The Reporter, 20 April 1962.

So already before Philip's arrival at New Mills the comprehensive debate was started. Going comprehensive was the largest and most complex task Philip had to undertake in his nine years at New Mills. At his first Speech Evening in November 1962, the main speaker was Mr. J.K. Owens Deputy Director of Education for Derbyshire, who allayed any fears about comprehensive education in the New Mills area by stating that there was 'no decision on the school's future'. He said that 'he had been interested to hear that quite a lot of things were being said about the future of the school – 'extraordinary rumours' he called them. But whatever the rumours, no decision at all had been taken about the school's future. Of course, the general policy of the Derbyshire Education Committee was to reorganise secondary education on comprehensive lines. But that was an enormous scheme and would take a long time.' Mr Owens continued 'Comprehensive lines covered all sorts of varieties in the organisation of schools. Before any decisions are made there would be full consultation with the governing bodies of all of the schools affected and that in itself must take time. There will be in time discussions about the future, but at this moment I think there is need for us to keep a very open mind on what is meant by 'comprehensive education'.

Philip's first Speech Evening was different from any previous Speech Day held at the School. He made two important changes, firstly by holding the event in the evening, instead of the afternoon, and secondly all the speeches took place in the first half, allowing the rest of the evening to be devoted to a concert by pupils. The Reporter of 23 November 1962 goes on to state 'Both changes were worthwhile. The concert was highly enjoyable and because speech day was in the evening more parents were able to attend the event in the Art Theatre. Even so, not all pupils could attend, because of shortage of accommodation.' Philip, in the presence of Mr. Owens and 'glancing smilingly at him said 'unless the Deputy Director can build us an assembly hall of our own.' Qualifying by saying that 'it is a pity that New Mills has not a hall big enough to meet the speech day needs, but it would also be a pity if a New Mills speech day had to take place outside New Mills. Ideally, of course, all pupils and parents should be able to attend, so that all of us in this great school, perhaps, 1,700 people, can get together.'

Speech Day 1963, with Philip standing, then left to right, Jeffrey Wilkinson (Area Education Officer), Dave Swinburn, vice Chairman of Governors and Lillian Weston, Chairman of the Governors.

Philip began his speech by saying 'I would not be human if I did not feel a little nervous on this first occasion, particularly as there seems so much to say and so little time to say it. I am not, in fact, promising to be brief. Normally', he continued, 'the headmaster gives a report on Speech Day on the successes of the previous year, but I want to speak mostly about the future.' He did, however, pay tribute to his teaching staff – 'I sometimes think that far too little is ever said about how much a school owes to the persistence and real guts of the teaching profession. Sometimes, I think, boys and girls, and their parents, think we are bound to do the large number of out of school activities (on the field or in the building) and even on a Saturday morning, that we do do. Certainly it is because the staff enjoy the company of your children, but also they are filled with that tremendous age old tradition of British education which believes that what we do in the classroom is only a small proportion of the whole picture. In order to produce a real person we must have and take part in, our sports, our many crafts, our drama, societies and, above all in the Sixth form, that to and fro of debate and discussion, which should be a pleasure for a Sixth former and a pride to their tutors.' Philip goes on to pay tribute to Mr. Taylor by saying that 'he brought to his school mastering many of the assets which many of us believe are essential to the success of this profession. He was persistent, and the fact that the school's corridors are now windowed against the Derbyshire winter and above all his beautiful science block is now erected is permanent witness to his persistence. He had a sense of humour, which I believe you need to hold the attention or affection of the children and staff and if you cannot laugh at the many minor crises of school life and if you cannot make your jokes in Assembly or somewhere and laugh with the school at yourself, what can you do? I know Mr. Taylor had this asset. He held a deep regard for the value of discipline and real academic work, he loved all sports which enabled him to have a happy relationship with many pupils who were perhaps less academically successful than others. He felt that the school should be a community of people which is a real unity. I cannot hope to be like him, because I am quite a different person, and his first words to me were that a new headmaster means changes. He was, of course, right and it had to be so. Most of the changes that we have had so far are not in themselves important, but I am hoping they will in the end add up to changing certain emphases within the school in the direction I feel the sixties demand.' Philip goes on to talk about some of the changes he is hoping to make – the Prefect's system, where he saw the prefects as performing services to their younger brethren and at the same time training themselves to be leaders in every sense, thus giving their personalities more room to develop and their abilities that edge which makes for decision and not hesitation. A School Parliament, which will represent to the Prefects' Council the opinions and feelings of all children, Philip thought this as 'a preparation for life in a democracy – training in choice and in decision and in government, and if our democracy as we know it is to survive, a training in choice is surely most important to it and to us.' Another non-academic change is the formation of a Sixth form Society, which he saw as 'a society through which the Sixth former can debate, and lecture and be lectured to, and dance and have social activities of every sort, so that they can learn from one another as young adults should, and have the rough edges worn off them – a sort of pre-university – university, so that even the Sixth formers who do not go to college will have a taste of the sort of things that go on in them.' Other changes connected with school work included the 'need to face up to the eighteen plus rat race into which we are forced and which has become a major part of our business. We have 84 in the Sixth this year and will probably have 120 next year. This vast increase in potential students is going to produce a log jam at the top end of the school. They not only need two or three A levels but it appears they are going to need a large number of other assets. Minority time is becoming the *Cri de Coeur* of many grammar and comprehensive headmasters. We are going to go onto a (40 period) new timetable- nearly a third of the week on this is to be used on English – some Logic and Training in Logical Thought, and Science for Art students. Russian for Scientists and Social Studies – all adding up to A level General Studies and more importantly to a general education. We are going to persuade our Sixth formers that Colleges of Advanced Technology and the Diploma in Technology are perfectly good alternatives to a university degree, especially in all forms of engineering. Another change to take place is the introduction of a four year course to O level for our top stream – thus enabling them to have three years in the Sixth for advanced level work and thus facing university entrance with their A levels already taken. Greek will be added in the top stream leading to a full classics course in the Sixth form.'

Philip then began his speech about the future of the school by saying 'So much for the present changes, I am now going to speak about the future. I hope I am not going to be misunderstood. To illustrate my point, may I tell you a joke about the Archbishop, which many of you probably know, who arrived in New York and was pestered by a large number of bright journalists in the usual way, and he would not answer any of their questions and was extremely non committal as Archbishops are. Finally one very impertinent young reporter asked "Say Archbishop are you visiting any night clubs whilst you are in New York?" The Archbishop shaking his head with surprise said slowly, "Are there any night clubs in New York?" The next day the headline in a newspaper was "Archbishop's first words – Are there any night clubs in New York?" So unlike the Archbishop, I hope I won't be misunderstood.

The greatest dilemma in which we are involved is the series of tests and selections from the Primary stage to the Secondary, which is the 11-plus, and which certainly involves a percentage of errors for us. It involves the primary schools in getting ready for examinations, involves parents in a great deal of anxiety and children in at least disappointment and even bitterness. We must find, by an absolutely flexible system of transfer between us and other secondary schools (at every age range of the secondary system) – an answer to this near tragedy of the 11-plus. Boys and girls who are lucky enough – if it is luck – at the moment to get into a grammar school should remember throughout their careers here and afterwards that luck at the age of ten is what they have had, and they must not translate this into any sort of feeling of superiority, or even a feeling of charity, but only a feeling of service and justice. The school's motto is 'Let right be done' and we must make every effort, as far as we can, in the changing educational scene, to see that this, in fact, is happening. Transfers, I think must be two way traffic, and so must the use of facilities. We have got to use the facilities of all for the benefit of all and we must not pretend we are an island. It seems certain that if we do, we shall not play the great and valuable part which our talents and experience indicate we could play in an education that is more and more offering opportunities to the highest level to boys and girls who before, it was thought, could not benefit from these opportunities. We must, in fact, hold out our hands for some sort of partnership and at the same time we need to watch our own academic standards (we certainly must not move into a situation where we think academic a dirty word) and we must see that we keep them high. The levelling, in fact, must not be downwards. Thus we shall be able to meet with optimism and easy acceptance the whole trend of English education for the sixties and seventies – with a viable modern minded education, that is able to embrace and, give chance, and find a place for every secondary child of whatever age, ability and aptitude. I used to be a Scout Master and carved into my memory are the various mottos of the parts of it. The Boy Scouts – "Be prepared" – The Senior Scouts – "Look wide" – The Rovers – "Service". These seem very apt for us as we prepare to meet the situation into which, on the whole, national public opinion demands that we move.

I think the American educational philosopher – John Dewey, made one of the best remarks on these aspects of our situation when he said "What the best parent wants for his child, the whole community wants for all its children". Our lead here in Britain in technology is certainly no longer a lead, as the 'sputnik' and 'lunik' and Cape Canaveral show; we need to use and train the skills of all our children in order to recapture it. After all an army needs not only trained generals but also trained lieutenants and NCOs and even, dare I say, a trained PBI. We can afford to neglect no one or only at our very great peril.'

The quotation at the beginning of this chapter was written by Philip as part of a leaving article in the Ounsdale magazine. He believed these words applied equally well to the beginning of his time at New Mills. He felt that 'We teach amidst a welter of comments about teenagers being this or that, about them marrying or not marrying, or being delinquents or being over-paid or being a nuisance or being violent or being something or other. Now I wonder if the people who make all these comments stop to think of the immense pressures that our day puts upon these young people - and even if they stay at school there are pressures – for example, homework which may seem minor, but is very necessary and is one of those pressures which staying at school exaggerates – another one is wearing uniform – but these are minor compared to outside pressures – often of a titillating sort; the fact is that society through its progress has made puberty earlier, and society through its progress has made the age of school leaving later, and we stretch them and stretch them through the period when they feel adult but are treated as children and are not yet responsible, and then we grouse when under this stretching a few snap and some mutter. It really is, in my belief, too hard on them. They want to leave earlier because they feel adults; they have to leave later because they need certificates.

I do not find that these comments of people about teenagers fit in with my experience with any type of teenager, and I think, that largely (though of course there are always exceptions), they are most unselfish, generous minded, interesting and vivacious young people; and sometimes I think, it is time that as a nation we stood still for a moment and lifted our hands and called for three cheers, for a change, for our teenagers. We have to show them that education is something that goes on all our lives; as the Scottish report on 'Education in Scotland' said 'even after eighteen education continues; school teachers should make clear that their pupils should not mistake the prelude for the play'. Given any clear and reasonable lead they will largely come along and live up to expectations - the higher - the more they will rise to them. There is a poem, a nineteenth century one, corny in its way, called the "Music Makers". Sometimes I think it suits us as a profession and certainly I think it has several apt verses if slight alterations are made to the original. May I end with them? (The first four verses in the chapter on Ounsdale Comprehensive School.)

'You have no vision amazing
Of the goodly house you are raising;
You have no divine foreknowing
Of the land to which you are going:
But on some men's souls it hath broken,
A light that shall not yet depart;
And their look, or some words they have spoken,
Wrought flame in other men's hearts.

177

And therefore, today is thrilling
With a past day's late fulfilling;
And you multitudes are enlisted
In the faith that your fathers resisted,
And, scorning the dream of tomorrow,
Are bringing to pass, as you may,
In this world, for its joy or its sorrow,
The dream that was scorned yesterday.

For we, are afar with the dawning
And your sons that are not yet high,
And out of this infinite morning
Intrepid you hear us cry –
How, spite of your human scorning,
Once more God's future draws nigh,
And already goes forth the warning
That we of the past must die.

Great hail! We cry to the comers
From this dazzling unknown shore;
Bring us hither your sons and your summers,
And renew our world as of yore;
We shall teach them our song's new numbers,
And things that they dreamed not before;
Yea, in spite of those dreamers who slumber
And those singers who sing no more.

Changes in any school sometimes bring an uneasiness, and certainly the pupils who had been under Mr .Taylor for most of their time in the school found some of the changes difficult to support and were a little apprehensive of them. Rosemary Simpson, who was head of the school in Philip's first year, writes in the School magazine 'As you will have realised many changes have been made in the school since the advent of Mr.Vennis. Over the years the School has built up an enviable reputation for academic and athletic prowess and also, equally important for the kind of person produced by the school. No-one, however, should be content to remain complacently in a fixed routine, never witnessing any changes, and to prevent this Mr. Vennis decided to make alterations and shake us out of (dare I say) our rut. As a result of this new outlook, many boys and girls who knew the school in former years have been given cause to think about the different facets of education and to appreciate some of the necessary possessions in life – a well developed sense of humour, for example.' In the same school magazine, the Head Boy, Nicholas Broadhurst writes 'New Mills Grammar School is a school of great traditions, of which each member can be proud. Throughout its history it has steadily grown, and under each headmaster has gone from strength to strength. I entered the school when Mr. Taylor was headmaster, and although I have only been here for a short time, I recognised in him a deep sense of loyalty to our old traditions, which he carefully encouraged. Mr. Taylor left a happy and united school to the care of our new headmaster and already it is possible to see that the aim of Mr. Vennis is to carry on the good work of his predecessors. Mr. Vennis believes that this can best be done by giving us a greater say in running the School. I call on all members of the School to support us in our efforts to ensure the smooth running of the School, and to give Mr. Vennis the loyalty, respect and affection which he so justly deserves.'

Fifty years later, Christine Ely (nee Worthington), who was a pupil at the school from 1958 to 1965 writes 'Mr. Vennis is well remembered by me. I will always be grateful to his appointment as headmaster as he opened up the Sixth form and enabled the likes of me – not a high flyer but conscientious and not wanting to end up as a secretary! I took and passed three A levels and went on to Teacher Training in Bath. I taught for thirty years. I was a prefect and on the School Council and remember the regular meetings held in his office. I also remember a special assembly we had when Winston Churchill died. Mr. Vennis was a breath of fresh air for the school – it was a happier place, still strict and with lots of brilliant traditions which I value to this day – Speech Day was transformed and I think he introduced Jerusalem as our school anthem? I am grateful to him that I achieved a career which I loved and benefitted from for my whole life. I would not have been able to do that under any other headmaster.'

Heather Govier (nee Swinburn) also recalls fifty years later 'I was a great admirer of P.H.V. and his whole approach to education. His arrival made a huge difference as the previous head was old school and sleepily heading to retirement.' Heather kept day to day diaries of her time at New Mills Grammar School and here are some of the snippets she recorded 'P.H.V. came into the school like a new broom. The previous head had been in post for 21 years and was pretty set in his ways. Philip must have announced lots of changes at the first assembly on the first day of term for my diary reads: Tuesday 4 September 1962 –
The new Head's nice – he's going to make a lot of changes. One early development was the introduction of the School Parliament and my diary entries about this include – Tuesday 25 September 1962 – Mr. Vennis announced that it was time we chose the School Parliament. There are one girl and one boy from each class. I was nominated as the one girl candidate. Tonight I prepared a speech that I have got to make tomorrow. Wednesday 26 September 1962 – I won the election so I am the

girl representative for form 3G. Derek Martin is the boy. Tuesday 16 October 1962 – It was the meeting of the school parliament today. I asked for a dancing class. They said that we could have one if we could find a member of staff to take us. (I followed up on that by asking the PE mistress to take the class, which she agreed to do – but the scheme came to nought when no boys would participate!) There is also a Prefects' Council – a disciplinary board consisting of the nine most senior members of the Sixth form set up to deal with minor offenders. I did not fall foul of them but my diary reports that my boyfriend did! At half term P.H.V. created a new post of Head of the School – the most senior pupil who could be a boy or girl. The main purpose, I think, was to give girls a chance to be top dog as with the old Head Boy/Head Girl arrangement the boy was usually seen as the senior position. The first HoS was Rosemary Simpson.' Heather kept all her old school reports and comments 'Another of P.H.V.s innovations is that he clearly read all school reports. The previous head had just signed but P.H.V. wrote a comment on every one. That reflected his interest in getting to know every child in the school personally – again a big change from the previous head who would certainly not have known the younger pupils.'

A girl who transferred to the Grammar School at the age of 13, Elaine Stratton (nee Robinson) identifies one of Philip's ideologies as a teacher 'I joined the Grammar School at thirteen; it was my second chance after failing the 11-plus. Although I was doing well at Secondary School he said it was because I was a Robinson that made him decide to take me on. I came from a big family which was money poor, Mr. Vennis had a lot of respect for my family because it did not stop us getting into grammar school and pursuing our dreams. I have just retired after 35 years teaching in primary schools. I remember one incident that is still in my mind today, and is the bedrock of some of my beliefs on life. He said to me, never mind the Sir, just get the s on the end of yes! He helped to instil in me not to be ashamed of my roots and know when to use formal and informal behaviours and speech. I was one of many who was frightened of him but liked and respected him. I remember him as Vennman with his Venmobile (Batman and his Bat mobile) mainly because when he swooped down the corridor, into assembly or the classroom his gown billowed behind him. I remember his passion for Shakespeare.'

1962 was a big year of change for New Mills Grammar School and it is very evident from minutes of the Governors' meetings, not only in 1962, but throughout his nine years at New Mills Philip pushed through and fought for many improvements to the school. As early as 20 September 1962 he highlighted the urgent need for further accommodation. He informed the Governors that there 'were now over 500 on the school roll, that there were 85 in the sixth and over 115 in the fifth forms. In view of the tremendous growth in the upper school, and the desirability of introducing other advanced level subjects, the need for further accommodation was extremely urgent.' The Governors supported Philip's need for this accommodation and recommended two mobile classrooms and further small room accommodation for the Sixth form groups. Staffing was another issue which Philip put before the Governors who again supported his request, and they informed the Authority of the school's requirements and to sought permission to appoint some extra staff as soon as possible. Accommodation and staffing were almost always on the agenda at governors' meetings, and gradually Philip gained extra accommodation and new members of staff.

The changes that took place in the School were considerable, but they bore little relation to the even greater, more numerous and far reaching changes in education that the sixties imposed on a school like New Mills Grammar School. It was not only the new headmaster that meant change but so did Crowther, the CSE (Certificate in Secondary Education), Newsom and Robbins. There was a whole new set of attitudes to education that affected the School.

There were not only changes taking place in the school for Philip, his home life took on another dimension when his first son was born in April 1963. Heather Govier recorded in her diary on Monday 29 April 'Yesterday Mr. Vennis had a baby son. At dinnertime he was wetting the baby's head with the Masters and Mistresses!'

At the beginning of the academic year 1963/64 Philip introduced a new timetable, which altered the old one of thirty five lessons to a forty period week, eight lessons a day. This change was largely to give a greater flexibility in the timetable such as the introduction of new subjects like Classical Greek, Spanish, Engineering, Drawing and Russian. This new timetable was able to include a great deal more minority time both for educational reasons, and to suit the interests of Sixth formers and also to lead to Advanced Level General Studies. All this was an answer to the Crowther Report's plea for minority time which was reflected in the new universities' form which all entrants had to complete. The minority time was twelve lessons a week, which also included games and physical education. Philip believed that A level General Studies was a real test of intelligence and personality and not of knowledge, since it could not be swotted for, and a real educational force and a liberalising one as well. Advanced level Economics was introduced for the first time at the beginning of the academic year, with a view to introducing A level British Constitution and Economic History in the near future.

Again at the beginning of the academic year a technical stream was formed – not just a new name for the third stream, but one to which boys and girls after their second year at school might want to join. This initiative grew out of the need for more technologists and a consideration for the minority of children. This stream in the third and fourth years would take six or seven academic subjects and two or three craft subjects. Domestic Science, Needlework, Art, Engineering Drawing, Engineering Science and Physics with Chemistry are all possible subjects to be studied.

Reflected in his speech at Speech Day 1963 were some of these changes and Philip related the 'present ferment in secondary education brought about by recent Government reports to the changes which had gone on in the school in the past year. The accent was for more universities and people of university calibre, so grammar schools would almost be top heavy with Sixth formers. Yet as recommended in the Crowther Report, which related the education of young people from fifteen to eighteen to changing social and industrial needs; minority interest must be met. The school had done this. The Robbins Report, which dealt with post school advanced education, clearly envisages the opportunities which will be offered in a few years to our young people; laid out 'the motorways of learning in the future' and Philip stated that, 'he intended, and had begun to make every effort to travel on the recommended lines. Yet Robbins and the universities created great pressures on young people.' Philip continued by saying 'The syllabus and examinations tended to 'squash our children flat' and make them sponges who merely absorbed dictated knowledge. The opposite pressure also applied. This was from outside school society which tempted away from academic study and restricted it to school time only. This would lead to shallow knowledge, and was not desirable. It was the job of the school to act as a buffer between the pressures and the children. "You cannot fight against the future, time is on our side"- Gladstone. The school's duty is to maintain the true discipline of learning, of searching for truth and the function of the school is to resist, with parents' help, undue outside pressures so that the child's interest in learning may be protected.'

The changes embodied in these reports - The Newsom Report, 'Half our Future', considered the educational needs of early teenagers of average and less than average ability, will result in fewer children leaving after the fifth form and most Sixth formers proceeding to higher education. The shape of the school will change.'

Not content with coping with all of these changes in the running of the school, Philip began in the Autumn Term 1963 to produce Shakespeare's 'Romeo and Juliet', to be performed 11-14 December in the Art Theatre, New Mills and then in the summer of 1964 for Shakespeare's Quatercentenary in Alsfeld, Germany. (New Mills 'twin town.) Philip's production embodied his belief 'That opportunities to take part in drama and music, however small a part, must be given to every boy and girl. It is not important that only those obviously able to do this should take part; what is important is that those less able to do so should learn by taking part. 'Romeo and Juliet' presented a fact which many of us in education knew to be true – only ten or so of the boys and girls in it could act in any real sense, the other sixty were learning to put forward their personalities, to imagine themselves in the part, to do some deportment, to react in a certain kind of way to situations, - and these are marvellously educative. I think that drama is the easiest single way to give boys and girls and opportunity to create and develop their personalities as fully as they can. It seems to me that in education we are short of ways in which we might do this and we certainly cannot easily do them in the classroom, or not if our teaching is directed all the time towards examinations. In the classroom we need to try to get children to be as inter-active as possible. This is real education for children, by any means that is creative, and their examination results almost certainly follow.' In his production of 'Romeo and Juliet' Philip tried to emphasise the ribaldry and violence of Verona, against this he set the love story with its real purity, amid this violence and ribaldry, the heartbreak. He used music from Tchaikovsky, Delius and Faure and he mingled with these the beautiful final tune of 'West Side Story', underlining the atmosphere of the play. He stepped outside the picture-frame stage and used a permanent set in the manner of Shakespeare's theatre.

"Come, come with me, and we will make short work;
For by your leaves, you shall not stay alone
Till holy church incorporate two in one."

Romeo and Juliet produced in 1963 and in Alsfeld 1964

Before this full scale production could be taken to Alsfeld, where six performances – some open air, some indoor, some morning and some evening were to take place, money for the venture had to be raised. Although the German hosts were being most generous with the production and set, their time, their money and their finding lodgings for the seventy boys and girls, a total of £2,000 was needed. Most of this money was raised by the Parent Teacher Association, much of it at the annual Garden Party, thus enabling every boy and girl in the production to have the tremendous double experience of acting Shakespeare abroad and living with a German family for a fortnight. Donald Rolls who played Friar Lawrence in the production wrote in the school magazine about his 'Experience of a Lifetime'. 'The idea behind the production of 'Romeo and Juliet' by New Mills Grammar School was to celebrate the Quatercentenary of Shakespeare. (1564-1964). The parts were chosen by our headmaster and practising for short times took place before the end of the summer term 1963. During the summer holidays many of the cast endeavoured to learn their numerous lines of blank verse or prose, as the case may be, but most met with little success. However, on return to school in September, the number of rehearsals increased by leaps and bounds, so that, after a while, the words came naturally, and the texts were discarded. It must not be thought that everything went smoothly; many things went wrong in the course of the rehearsal, but, owing to the experience and brilliance of our producer, we always managed to come out on top in the end.

After all, this constant and tiring work had to end sometime, and it was realised that it had all been worthwhile, when the performances went off without a hitch. The Art Theatre was filled every evening, and it was most rewarding to feel that the audiences followed the play with interest, and because of this, the cast were able to convey the atmosphere of the various scenes, effectively.

After the December performances, the end to practising gave one a rather unusual feeling, that after so much hard 'graft'; it was all over in so short a period of time. However, we were fortunate, because we had not seen the end of 'Romeo and Juliet' yet.

Between Christmas and June, practising was suspended, so that the Upper Sixth Form could have time to study for their approaching Advanced Level examinations. But, as soon as these were over, the hard work began all over again, perhaps in a more concentrated form because we had the knowledge that we could be performing in front of people, who, even though they spoke a different language, were conversant with most of Shakespeare's plays, not least 'Romeo and Juliet'. The text had eluded our minds to some extent, but it was surprising how quickly it came to the forefront of our memories again.

At the annual Garden Party excerpts were performed on a temporary stage outside the front entrance of the school.

During the afternoon of 8 August this year, the BBC Television unit arrived at the Art Theatre to film a scene for "Look North", and, after this rather gruelling experience which lasted for about three hours we gave a farewell performance which was attended by many distinguished guests connected with drama and education for the Derbyshire area.

Eventually, the moment for which all the cast was waiting arrived – the departure from New Mills for our destination, Alsfeld, which was a journey lasting three days. After a great send off, we all settled down until our arrival in Alsfeld.

As we drove into this picturesque little town, crowds of people gathered, and in the 'Marketplatz' there were hundreds of unknown faces, with which we were to become acquainted in a very short time. A band played a medley of English tunes and concluded its programme with the national anthems of England and Germany. After various speeches of welcome, each member of the cast was introduced to his or her respective host, and then taken 'home' for lunch.

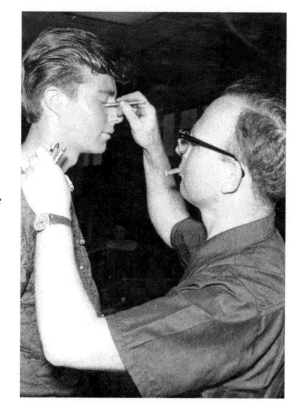

Make up being applied for a performance of Romeo and Juliet in the Klostergarten, Alsfeld, August 1964.

The first performance on unknown ground took place three days after our arrival, but the time which should have been used for catching up with lost sleep, was used instead for 'doing' the town, and viewing the places where the play was to be given, and where scenery was already being constructed and erected – in the *Deutsheshaus*, a large hotel with a theatre on the top floor, and in the *Klostergarten* (a ruined monastery) for open air performances.

Owing to the bad weather, the first performance was given inside. The stage was much smaller than the one we had been used to, but with a curtailing of the actions, we managed with ease. The nerves amongst the cast were prominent, as no one could actually tell how the audience would be affected by the play, but all this nervousness need not have been endured, because, after the finish, Herr Kratz, the *Burgomeister*, gave a lengthy speech, which we presumed to be complimentary even though it was extremely difficult for us to follow. The producer was not excluded, and Herr Kratz presented him with a bouquet of roses which took him by surprise. However, never stuck for a word, Mr. Vennis was able to make an apt quotation from the play in reply "a rose by any name would smell as sweet" concluding with his favourite German words "Danke Schon".

Cover of the programme for Romeo and Juliet performed in Alsfeld, Germany in August 1964.

William Shakespeare 1564–1964

19. bis 23. August 1964

10.00 Uhr und 19.30 Uhr

ROMEO

NEW MILLS GRAMMAR SCHOOL

UND

JULIA

"Hang up Philosophy Unless Philosophy can make a Juliet"

Klostergarten oder Deutsches Haus
in Alsfeld (Oberhessen)

In the *Klostergarten,* even though the raised stone stage was extensive, the cast thoroughly enjoyed performing, especially in the evening when the lighting proved to be most effective. Everyone realised how true Professor Hunt had been when he told the players at the farewell performance, that they would be performing to people who knew a great deal about Shakespeare, and who also produced his plays as well. The audiences were most attentive, and because of this, the cast had an added incentive to do perhaps a little better than their previous best.

Behind the scenes a great deal of work was going on – the making sure that properties were in the right place at the right time, and the sewing of clips onto costumes which had been ripped in the course of rough crowd scenes. After performances, receptions were held which lasted until the early (or should I say late) hours of the morning! It was here, and after the performances as well, that our interpreter, the German Master was indispensible. After the final performance, he was interpreting all the thanks from Mr. Vennis to all those who had made the venture possible, and at one juncture the audience burst into laughter, the cause of which we could not glean. Afterwards we heard that a slip had been made, for in thanking one gentleman for doing so much work in arranging hospitality, it had been said that, "We thank Herr Muller very much for making so much work!"

At the end of the holiday, the whole cast was tired out, but everyone had enjoyed this unique experience. But all the credit must go to the producer, Mr. Vennis, and to Mr. Collins who assisted him. Both of them gave up an extremely large amount of time which they devoted entirely to rehearsals. Even though Mr. Vennis had produced 'Romeo and Juliet' before, he was still enthusiastic, and although harassed at times, he could still crack the joke which broke the tension and cleared the air, especially when the time for public productions was approaching. May I, on behalf of the whole cast, say thank you to Mr. Vennis and all his helpers for giving us this opportunity of a lifetime.'

Philip saw the Alsfeld trip as 'one of the most worthwhile things in which I, as a producer and as a school master, have ever taken part. It was a great pleasure. We certainly became very tired, and we all have a great many tales to tell, but in general, on looking back, we remember how marvellously we were treated, and in return what fine performances our boys and girls gave, and how they proved that our standards are high. The German audiences were disciplined and large and appreciative, and they all but drowned us in their generosity as hosts on numerous occasions. To the boys and girls in minor parts who came largely because they wanted to take part in the twinning scheme, I would say that I would hope that you will always look back on this unique experience. You had the pleasure of being in the German homes of very generous hosts, who helped you with your time and their money and their food when you were needed at rehearsals. To the leading actors I would say that you had an experience that will always be valuable. The extraordinary business of living in Germany with people who rapidly became your friends, and of putting over these parts in a Shakespeare tragedy to audiences, will always remain with you as a memorable venture. The whole thing was well done by all of you, and I hope you will carry its memories along the road of life.'

John Worthington, a pupil at New Mills Grammar School – 1960 to 1967, who later became a G.P. recalls that 'I was in the production of Romeo and Juliet that went to Alsfeld, it was all very memorable'. John goes onto say that 'Philip and Diana were kind to me and this included them inviting me and no doubt other awkward teenagers to their home. Initially I was under Norman Taylor as headmaster, who was a science teacher of the old school, but I did benefit from his legacy of the new science block where I spent most of my time doing the A Levels for Medical School. The School Council was innovative and gave us responsibility and input. I feel very lucky indeed to have gone to such a school with very high teaching standards. I think one of the things about Philip was his enthusiasm and injecting new ideas into the school. We lived in a sort of golden age re schooling I think. To get that quality of schooling now it would have to be private I suppose, a relatively small number of pupils, quiet discipline and respect.'

Speech Day in November 1964 of course, reflected the success of 'Romeo and Juliet' in Alsfeld, but it also heralded the fact that more changes in the school would have to take place. The report of the speech in the local press headlined the 'School may face big changes'. 'Big changes may be in store for New Mills Grammar School', said the Headmaster, Mr. P.H. Vennis at the school's annual speech day. 'This may not matter if we can succeed, as I believe we can, in carrying on those things in a grammar school's tradition and this school's tradition in particular, which matters most, and continue to stand for standards and to see that they don't slip. In fact, to sum it up, we must see, and I think we can, that levelling up is what happens in every kind of way. For the moment, as the answer to the question 'what is education? we have to escape the outside pressures as much and as often as we can. We need to establish finally in our minds that we are not a place to be judged by examination results. Though it is very nice to get good results and it is very nice to be congratulated by lots of people, it would be a pity if our kind of school, and New Mills Grammar School in particular were judged by the A and O levels. We do not want to be in any league in this matter – either at the top or the bottom.' Mr. Vennis went on to say 'Such results would have no final purpose if in order to get them the school had to lose such things as a sense of moral purpose, a sense of community, a sense of service, an integration of the personality, a growing up amongst the boys and girls which enabled them to become quite adult people and individuals and questioners in the community.

In the near future they would have to face a new kind of exam, the CSE, which is supposed to be based more on what children were really able to do in terms of activities and creation rather than on purely academic work. In congratulating us on our exam results, people forget that the major things that matter in a child's education and a young person education too, cannot easily be tested in exams. I would like to be congratulated because our school is great and famous and stands up for standards and does well in art and music and drama and sports and exhibitions of every kind. I think in the last year we made a move in this direction and a very successful one.

The fact is, of course, that English grammar school education has, for a great many years, neglected art, music and drama, and is in some danger of neglecting its sports. The school has had tremendous successes in those obvious things by which people judge a school. They had good O levels, a remarkable success with the new fourth form entry at Ordinary Level and good results from all the fifths. At Advanced level, despite the many other preoccupations of the Upper Sixth the results were really outstanding. They all gained deserved success in entries to universities, colleges and many other courses. They also gained seven county awards with distinction, which is a remarkable number for a school of our size.'

In December 1964 the school was forecasting an increased number of pupils, Philip in his report to governors said 'that next year there would be about 460 pupils below the Sixth Form and 155 in the Sixth Form, making a total of 615 pupils overall. Two new permanent staff would be needed and he named English, Classics, and boy's Technical subjects, Music, Art and Scripture Knowledge as some of the gaps.' By March 1965, Philip was given permission to appoint three more members of staff, provided some of the part-time teaching would be dispensed with. At the governors' meeting in June 1965 he confirmed the new staff members who were to join the school in September 1965, this included R.C. Wilson and A.M. Sheldon who later contribute to this chapter with their personal recollections of time at New Mills.

The end of January 1965 saw the death of Sir Winston Churchill. Philip was a great proponent of Churchill and defends why he celebrated his life throughout the school. 'During this present term we, as a school, like everyone else in the nation, felt the loss of Sir Winston Churchill, and, for two weeks, Assemblies were devoted to trying to remember some of the many facets of this great man. His life should be an inspiration to all of you; its many sidedness, its sheer length of effort for England, and its extraordinary achievements should be the kind of things that every boy and girl will want to admire. No boy or girl will want to forget that but for him in 1940, their lives would have been quite different, and the freedom they enjoy to learn the things they do learn at this school might really not have existed at all. I am sure that no one of you fails to appreciate this extraordinary debt that you owe to England's greatest son in this century.' He goes on to say that 'at the end of the Summer Term the school will host some of the boys and girls of the *Gymnasium* at Alsfeld, who were such generous hosts to us last summer. The parents of many boys and girls at the school may want to have a German boy or girl in their homes, and the reconciliation on which Sir Winston Churchill set his heart after the war will show for us in a continued growth of the twinning scheme.'

In June 1965, Philip became a father for the second time; his daughter's birth was one of the highlights of his life. Philip's life at home and at school was very busy, but he never failed to make time for his children; he was an emotional man, capable of giving much love, compassion and devotion to his family.

July 1965 saw the introduction of a scheme for Sixth form boys and girls to undertake a month's social and community service after the completion of their examinations. Philip wrote to three local councils and he hoped that the councils would support the idea. New Mills council was very keen for the scheme to start that summer. Philip's letter stated that 'I have seventy Upper Sixth formers this year, probably the biggest we shall have because of the birth rate bulge 18 years ago. In addition it seems to be the first occasion where GCE Advanced levels will end early – largely by the middle of June. Then the Upper Sixth Formers will have about four weeks of term left. I would very much like to occupy them in some form of social service in the townships where they live. I do not want them to do any kind of work for which other people are paid, but I feel strongly that these seventy intelligent and able young people should occupy the month in some constructive way.' Philip was keen that 'we should get rid of any kind of 'Jack' mentality, which some young people of this kind may have these days. They will learn about life by cleaning up rubbish, doing gardening work for pensioners, doing domestic chores for old people, help with the meals on wheels service and assist old people shopping.' The councils recorded the highest praise for the scheme and endorsed it as an excellent idea. Following the completion of the scheme the school received many letters thanking the hard working pupils for the thorough way they completed the tasks in hand.

Alan Sheldon, who joined the school in September 1965, recalls over forty five years later 'I went to New Mills Grammar School, straight from North Manchester Grammar School, as second in the Languages Department. The contrast could hardly have been greater – from the old fashioned old worldly corridors of the very traditional grammar school with the most scholarly type of

190

staff and staffroom and with the most dignified and solemn headmaster (R.M. Sibson) – truly of the 'old school' and always to be seen in mortarboard and gown, - to the most amazingly friendly and open atmosphere of New Mills Grammar School where P.H.V. showed a good sense of humour, treated you as a friend, and even called you by your first name! What a difference, but what a good learning atmosphere.

Not only did he create the good learning atmosphere among the pupils, but, as far as I was concerned, he brought out the best in the staff also. He showed me that I was capable of things that I had never realised before – simply by expecting that they could be done, for example, producing a short play for the inter-form end of term performance, and, even more terrifying at the time, asking me – without warning – to do an on the spot translation of his welcoming speech to the French party from Strasbourg, when they arrived in New Mills – something I had never faced before and would not have considered myself capable of doing without P.H.V.s expectation.

I would describe my feelings about P.H.V. as enormous respect and admiration – tinged from time to time with some irritation and the occasional annoyance, but nothing more. I learnt that it was possible to have an argument – even a shouting match on one occasion (something that I would never before have considered possible with someone so high as a headmaster) and for it to be over with as quickly as it started, without any hard feelings, and to be immediately forgotten, and this of course, in itself, was another reason to feel respect for him.

My time at New Mills Grammar School was very happy and it was only because of the need to find promotion elsewhere – so common at that time, before the expansion of so many comprehensive schools, thus allowing much more internal promotion – that I had to leave, with regret, after two and a half years. Both then, when I became Head of Department, and later, when I became a Deputy headmaster, P.H.V. gave me the fullest and warmest support for which I was, and remain, very grateful.'

Philip, as was said in chapter 5, had this ability to choose young members of staff who showed potential for progressing, often to the top, of their chosen career, and no one epitomizes this more than Robert Wilson. New Mills became a hot bed of potential leaders and Robert Wilson acknowledges this by saying that Philip 'had a real skill in appointing good, enthusiastic young staff giving them a real role and letting them get on with it. He allowed us to take risks within sensible bounds, supported and encouraged us and gave us new opportunities when we had proved ourselves. I was at New Mills from September 1965 to December 1972, it was my first post. I went on to be Deputy headmaster in Lichfield, for which Philip wrote a reference and when re-reading it some years later I was reminded how rapidly I progressed through with Philip's support and encouragement. Within a year I was second in charge of the Sixth form, the Head of Department in Classics and by my third year at New Mills I became Head of the Sixth Form. I do remember Philip spending time with me, teaching me all about UCCA and FE entry, encouraging me to visit universities, and later, before he left, showing me how to do a timetable, a skill which I am sure helped me get my next post. My next post was to a Headship - Weston Road School in Stafford, where I remained for ten years before taking up a senior advisory post in Hertford from 1992 to 1997 and as Chief Advisor I had a team of over 100, serving 90 secondary schools, 440 primaries and 30 special schools. Then for the last eight years before retirement I was a lead trainer in the East Region, based in Cambridge, for the National Professional Qualification for Headship (I don't think Philip would have conformed!). Philip launched a group of us with passion, values, imagination and a sense of fun and enjoyment. He gave us the conviction that we could and should 'make a difference to children's' lives. I look back with a strong sense of privilege and joy and I am deeply grateful.'

Robert goes on to recall four stories about his time in New Mills. The first story is as follows 'At the end of my first term, when everyone was tired, Philip held a staff meeting when he had a real go at us. "I'm the only one who does anything here", I started to protest and was shushed by those around me, partly because I was a new boy and partly because those around me knew it would only prolong the meeting. Better to assent in silence. But I did go and see him afterwards (I've always been a little precious about what I see as justice). I started to list all the extra things I was doing. Philip interrupted "I know you are. So are XYZ. I like a good shout sometimes" I said I thought that not everyone should be tarred with the same brush. "If the cap fits wear it" he said. We ended by agreeing it had been splendid theatre. I discovered very early on that if you were contributing you always got a hearing and that he knew his staff.'

The second anecdote states that 'once I needed to see him and discovered from the secretary that he was on the phone but she thought he had just about finished. "I'm on the phone to Jack Longland (Director of Education)" he whispered, then loudly into the phone "You lot created this school across the valley, you give me the three extra staff I need" and went on for a while longer giving reasons. "That will show them", he said as he came off the phone. When I told the story to the Friday night gang (we met in a public house in New Mills Friday evenings and swapped the week's experiences with colleagues from Marple Hall Grammar School), one cynic suggested there was no one on the other end but it was for my benefit or it was, to the Divisional Office in Buxton. He got the three extra staff!

The third memory of New Mills recites 'As the staff numbers increased we got two big new mobiles as the new staff room. I had been elected Chairman of the Common Room. One lunch time Philip gathered a small group of staff to discuss pastoral matters in one year group. Those of us relaxing, drinking tea or coffee were as considerate as possible but there was some conversational noise level. Philip twice shushed people. The second time I said quietly 'Mr. Vennis, colleagues are trying to be as quiet as possible but it is their lunch time and this is the Common Room. In fact we're a little surprised the meeting for only a few isn't in your room'. He stood up, furious, slammed his papers down on the table. "I moved heaven and earth to get this staff room for you all but now that it's Mr. Wilson's and Mr. Wilson does not want us here we'll leave." Later in the afternoon a boy interrupted my lesson. "Please sir, Mr. Vennis wants to see you and now". I had been anxious about a summons but he started with an abject apology before I could express my regrets – "quite right –I shouldn't have been there in the first place", while I was repeating our deep gratitude for our new facilities.'

The last story recalls 'Philip had felt some staff were leaving too soon at the end of the day – not pulling their weight. He issued a diktat that no one should leave before 16.10. A day or two later he spotted Alan Sheldon driving very slowly down the main drive at 16.00 amongst the crowd of pupils. Up shot his window followed by a huge bellow. "Mr Sheldon, I thought I said no member of staff could leave before...and before he could finish Alan had wound down his car window and shouted "Mr. Vennis, I will be here all evening helping with your bxxxxx play. I'm going to get a sandwich so that I don't starve, if that is allowed". The pupils loved it and it was one of our favourite episodes ever. Of course they made it up. Our lasting memory is that life was never dull, that he could have a short fuse, that he cared passionately and that he could apologise and was, in turn, forgiving. I personally owed him a great deal.' One of Robert's colleagues, Ian Stuart who was to join the school in 1967, says complimentary of Robert 'he was Head of the Sixth form, - a high flyer - dizzyingly clever – very gentle and quiet. He and P.H.V. had plenty of frank discussions and yet they made a good pair.'

The Speech day held in November 1965, apart from the annual review of the school's year, contained some of Philip's philosophy on comprehensive education; the debate had begun after his appointment and was to continue for another five years. He said 'I ought to make clear that I am personally in favour of comprehensive schools, and think that very probably in doing away with the 11-plus they will make a very great contribution to English education. In New Mills we shall have a very fine comprehensive school. I think this because I believe that the grammar school will be a central and complete unit in it. A comprehensive school must make sure that the efficiency and continuity of the grammar school on which it is built is unimpaired, and that our particular work can go on as before. Then, of course, even for the boys and girls of the grammar school there will be great advantages in mixing with their secondary fellows, and for those secondary fellows there will be even greater advantages in the courses open to them. This is for the future – it remains to say that at the moment we at the Grammar School have nothing to fear provided we see to it that the School goes on as an efficient working unit. We produce an education here which we hope to extend to others, and that education is a very fine one. The state grammar schools have stood England well in the 50 or 60 years of their existence. They have produced a whole class of people who are now leaders – technologists, foremen and so on – leaders in every kind of sphere. As Sir Winston once said during the war it is the grammar schools that produced the men and women who largely led the country during it. We must not exaggerate this, but for the sake of England we must make sure that the continuity is there. We have here an education we want to extend to as many others as possible, though we must not pretend, that there is a grammar school education for all. A comprehensive school will have all kinds of courses to suit all kinds of children at all kinds of paces, ages and abilities. The best of each side will go on. So we have nothing to fear, and I do not think that we shall in any way be destroyed – indeed we may enter on a new and more flexible life, nor shall we lose the important things in our education – the standing up for standards, the respect for English culture, the important education of the able, and of the above average child, the Sixth Form tradition, a respect for hard work and the discipline of academic learning. But we have many other things to contribute – the out of school activities, the sports – and a general set of attitudes which I think are important to us and to the country.

We can honestly say that we have an education that belongs to everybody and we want to share it provided we are allowed to do so on terms that will not spoil our own work. We are, in the Grammar School, prisoners of our own success, and there is no reasonable doubt that we should feel honoured that people wish to imitate us and share what we have done so successfully these fifty years. Clearly we ought not to be unwilling to share all this provided our own work will continue unaffected. In fact, however, I strongly believe that here in New Mills we shall have an education which will suit each boy and girl according to his or her abilities, interests, age and aptitude. We are proud of the school; we have no fears for its future. We can say and we want to continue to be able to say – indeed I hope that perhaps these words will finally become our school motto – we will carry each boy and girl along on our tide, as Casca says in Julius Caesar "as far as who goes farthest".

The debate over going comprehensive dominated much of Philip's and the governing body's time. Philip's response to a scheme that had been proposed by Derbyshire Education Committee, for comprehensive education in New Mills, and about which he felt had been produced without any kind of consultation and was quite destructive of the Grammar School, begins –

'When I came here, I was told that the school would eventually become a comprehensive school. By definition, to my mind, a comprehensive school must include a complete Grammar School, i.e. at least a three stream Grammar. With this in view, I have changed this school so that it is more ready to become the central unit of a large comprehensive. I have broken up the third stream into two technical streams, and allowed able children to go into it. It is therefore, not a proper third stream. I have started, or vastly increased the practical subject's side of the school, so that boys and girls might have a proper practical and technical course to follow to O level. These courses would be vastly extended in a comprehensive to include a great many children now at Secondary Moderns. I have made a great turnabout in the School's life so that the attention of the staff is continually focussed on the third stream. This I consider to be a proper comprehensive mood, and in line with what I was told when I came here, that this school would, in the reasonably near future, become comprehensive.

I, myself, have always believed in comprehensive education. It must clearly, however, mean that children of all abilities come into one school, and there must be enough academic children to make sure there is a 'levelling up' and not a 'levelling down'. It is vital that these children be at least a third to a half of the whole school, and not merely in the Sixth Form.

Because of pressure from a number of sources I decided to abandon French as the permanent first language in the first years and alternate yearly, with the whole year group, between French and German. This seemed the best way of adopting the view taken in the last Government Circular on Modern Languages in the Grammar School that German should be an equal first language with French. Latin is introduced in the second year in two streams, and this is continued up to O level in two streams. I have done this because I think Latin has a value as such, and, for almost all Arts degree in England, O level Latin is still necessary for university entrance. In many cases A level Latin is desirable.

In the third year, in the second stream, children can opt for a third language, Spanish, so they are then doing French or German plus Latin and Spanish, or, alternatively, and do the Science course. Roughly a third do Spanish and two thirds do the Science. If they do Spanish they continue with Physics with Chemistry to O level, if they do sciences they do Physics and Chemistry. The whole school does Biology to O level except a few children in the third stream. In the third year, in the top stream, a very few do Classical Greek, about ten children opt for Russian if their first language is French or French possibly if their first language is German, and the rest (about two thirds of the form) do the separate Sciences, the linguists do Physics with Chemistry. By these means I have been able to introduce a great deal more Latin, a great deal of Spanish, Russian and Classical Greek in the main school.

In the Sixth form we now have twenty two A level subjects, including Advanced Level General Studies. We have three minority time afternoons a week, constituting twelve periods. These are not particularly directed towards General Studies, they include Drama or Art or Music, changing by term, Social Studies, History of Science or Science, changing by term, Logic, Use of English, Religious Knowledge, Games, Current Affairs and a minority time language chosen from Russian, German, Spanish or French. This scheme has given many average boys and girls who came into the Sixth form from the third stream a very greatly increased interest in the Sixth form, and I think it is most successful. We now have a large Sixth and fifth form leaving has been cut to a small minority. I think we have had very great success in selling a longer school life, which I consider to be one of the most important jobs we are doing. This is, however, a wholly academic Sixth form; everybody does at least two A levels, plus A level General – most do three plus A level General. We have been in the position to absorb a small group of people of less than average academic ability from Chapel and Spring Bank who have done well here. They have, however, been absorbed into the Sixth form easily because they have been a very small minority. The following A levels depend upon work done by the specialist Staff from the fifths down; - all the languages – Latin, Greek, French, German, Russian and Spanish, Mathematics, Further Mathematics, Physics, Chemistry and Biology – and probably several of the rest of the twenty two A level subjects we are doing. I think this proves that we are an active and efficient Grammar School, modern minded and looking to its ablest, its average and its less able children. We are in a position to extend nearly all these courses with great flexibility in a big comprehensive school.

If the scheme that has been presented to the Governors were, in fact, to be passed the following, in my opinion would be the results. This Grammar School would be halved and, therefore, truncated, and to put it mildly, destroyed. At the moment half our children come from Buxworth, Chapel en le Frith, Chinley, Edale, Castleton and Whaley Bridge. The four year course would be destroyed and could not be run either here or at Chapel. Over fifty per cent of our top third and fourth formers would not be at this school. Since the top stream runs at an average of 25 to 28 pupils, clearly a four year course for those left would not be viable, nor could one easily staff it, still less could one split it, so to speak, into Greek, Russian or Science groups. Children who wanted to do these subjects, or who wanted a four year course would, therefore, suffer greatly.

A comprehensive must mean that every child is able to work at his or her own level or his or her own pace - some take O level in four years, some in five, some in six, some CSE. in five and O level in six, some just C.S.E. and some no public examination at all. If we are not in position to do this, we may as well not change.

The school suggested at Chapel would contain no Sixth Form. It follows that it would shed its Sixth Formers to this Sixth Form at sixteen plus. I calculate that 60 of the present Sixth Form here, of 150, would therefore, have come in at sixteen plus. It would be quite impossible to absorb them into the school in terms of esprit or leadership. By the time one had succeeded, they would already be on the point of leaving or so busy with A level they would not feel involved. It is, of course, possible to absorb into a Sixth form of nearly two hundred a minority group of up to perhaps a quarter, but not, I think, much more than this. There is no point in imposing a kind of Sixth Form College on a small comprehensive school underneath it. These boys and girls who came into the Sixth would not have, as I will show later, the range of subjects to choose among our twenty two A levels. We would be forced to cut those Advanced Levels down. Many of them, as I showed above, are not viable in a Sixth form only. We would have the sort of scheme where we would be chasing around teaching a few people O level Latin just because they wanted to go to university. Such a course would be un-educational, wasteful, and in my opinion, not very practical.

The course, however, that is very important, indeed key nowadays in the Sixth Form, and that would suffer most, would be the Mathematics, Further Mathematics and Physics course. This produces for our university faculties all our Honours Mathematicians, all our Honours Physicists and all our Engineers except Chemical Engineers. The Mechanical, Civil, Electrical, Production, Structural and many other Engineering groups come from this set up. It would be quite impossible for the Senior Maths man to teach Further Mathematics, to boys and girls who had not been in any sense under the supervision of him or his Staff, or even in the same school, up to O level. There are very great difficulties here which should not be glossed over. This seems to me a key group, one open to both the brightest and the less bright pupil, and one that we should be very eager to observe survive. Since the school at Chapel would contain no Sixth form it would be unlikely to attract specialist Staff in any case. If they went there specialisms e.g. Classics or Russian would scarcely have enough candidates to present them with a timetable, nor, on the other hand, would we have enough candidates for such subjects here. We should thus be ruining the chance for boys and girls to do subjects of this kind in the school. I do not, myself, think it practical to envisage a set up where staff have to meet so often in schools six miles apart in order to co-operate in their timetables that a fortnightly staff meeting becomes a trial.

The comprehensive school envisaged at New Mills would have a narrow social base. The Government Circular comes out against this. It would be based on the Urban District of New Mills very largely, and would probably contain greater social problems then need be. Such a school would have even greater difficulty in persuading them to any kind of learning or academic work. The larger the academic minority the easier this becomes, or to put it in its simplest – the presence of two children doing Classical Greek in the top third has some kind of influence which permeates to the least able children academically who know of that going on. The best way I know of working a comprehensive so that the tougher and less social elements are easily contained, and so that we move a step towards comprehensives being one of the methods of cutting down on juvenile delinquency, is via boy/girl leadership in the Upper Sixth. It is vital for this that these boys and girls will have been through the school – they will, so to speak, be in the fourth when others enter in the firsts so that when these, the leaders, are in the Upper Sixth and some less easily disciplined or more easily bored children are in the fourth, these will have known them for four years and will present a real lead to them. It seems an obvious truth to me that those who feel 'cock 'o the walk' in a leading fourth form may not feel so much so when they have over their heads 150 fifth formers and 200 Sixth formers. It is easier to sell a longer school life when there are clearly present successes of all kinds from a great many children who are enjoying that longer life.

The school proposed at New Mills would be less than good enough for children now at Spring Bank or children who would be going there. They would not have their full comprehensive, they would not be meeting as many academically able children as they ought to be, nor as many courses. Flexibility would be cut down.

The numbers anticipated include continual reference to 'by 1981'. In fact, at the moment, this Grammar School is three form entry and so is Spring Bank. This Grammar School would be halved so that the resulting comprehensive would be four and a half form entry. I cannot think this either viable or useful. To be seven form entry by 1981 and this can be by no means certain, it means that for twelve years or so the school would go on as a four and a half form entry. There are, in addition, three forms at Chapel. The three schools added together at the moment make a nine form entry school. I do not consider by any means this too large, or even, I would say, large enough, for a full comprehensive. Arguments against the size of comprehensives seem to me not to be very proper. Roughly, speaking the larger the better. It is not proper to break this staff, who work together as a team, and I think it would be very wrong to do so. No arguments about their leaving the school in two or three years can possibly hide the fact that such a scheme as has been put forward would not use their talents while they are here. Nor would it be easy to shift some of them to Chapel – they may not wish to do so. They certainly will not wish to go where there is no Sixth form. Even worse is the faint suggestion of a Sixth form at Chapel en le Frith Secondary. This would be even less viable than the suggestions already made.

In almost every sense, therefore, as comprehensives have been seen in England at least since the first London plan in 1947, the two comprehensives suggested are lame in most senses – Chapel rather more than New Mills because of the lack of a Sixth Form. It cannot honestly be said that a fair deal can be made in these circumstances, either by the less academically able, now at secondary moderns, who would not get a fair comprehensive in any sense at all in either town, and still less do they present a fair opening for the children of grammar school ability who would be normally at this Grammar School. They would not be able to do a number of subjects that academic education ought to offer them; they would not be able to take O level in four years; they would not, in either half of the set up, be able to meet the specialist staff they ought to, they would not, in either half, be taught in the kind of groups they have been and should be used to. A glance at the UCCA entrance booklet for this year will show that a school of our kind should be, and is, aiming its children at a vast variety of new degree courses in nearly one hundred degree giving places.

It seems to me unlikely, therefore, that honours graduates will, in future, be produced in this corner of Derbyshire. I say this in all seriousness. Unless we look after the skills and carefully educate the minds of the top twelve per cent of the population, we shall surely be doing a considerable disservice to England and, of course, particularly, to this area. We cannot produce honours graduates unless they are educated in those subjects properly to O level. Their work must be guided and looked after by specialists and the senior men and women in the subjects who are teaching the subject to Advanced and Special Level and who know the ins and outs of university entrance. This seems to me a most important point. Indeed it could be argued that children in the Junior School gain more if they are taught by people, who, they know, are teaching the Upper Sixth at Special Level. This question of specialists applies throughout, but particularly too in the Sciences and Mathematics, and even English in the first year.

There is a long and permanent connection between this School and Whaley Bridge and I strongly believe it should be maintained. There is no point in breaking traditions of this kind in order to become comprehensive. The best comprehensives arise where it can be shown clearly that the previous traditions of the central school, i.e. the Grammar School in this case, continue. The same applies to Chapel en le Frith where again there is a strong connection. This school has already lost its Hope Valley contingent of able children and I would strongly deprecate its being truncated further.

I think it can be reasonably shown, therefore, that the two comprehensive schools envisaged in the plan are neither of them really viable. In particular New Mills Grammar School's fine work is going to be stopped. This work extends to all subjects at all levels of ability and ages. The whole tradition of this school, which has grown up over many years before the war and since the war, and then more recently under my Headship, is going to be spoilt. I fear it could be truly said that under this scheme this is a Grammar School that will be, as the opponents of comprehensives delight in saying, destroyed. This is quite wrong, and its work should be positively improved, both academically, in spread of subjects, and by the very fact of able children meeting less able children. I cannot emphasise too strongly that what is proposed is entirely retrograde and retrogressive, in my opinion.

Here are some suggestions for other possible schemes. There could be a through comprehensive for the whole area (pupils from eleven to eighteen years), based on New Mills Grammar School, which would undoubtedly be the best, and this would assume that the buildings at Chapel en le Frith would not be used as a Secondary School. But if, as it seems likely, it must be used as a secondary school then, clearly we must have a compromise.

The compromise envisaged is one which destroys the Grammar School, and does not cope with the needs of the able children. Is this a better compromise than leaving things as they are, or roughly so, i.e. the Grammar School absorbing Spring Bank at the right moment, retaining its present area, and some selection going on in the Chapel area? Is some selection necessarily worse, as a compromise, than what is proposed in the plan? The Government Circular suggests that a comprehensive scheme that is damaging should not be envisaged. This presumably means that, if necessary, selection should be kept. This would, in fact, mean a secondary school at Chapel going on to sixteen plus. A comprehensive school in New Mills, including the Moderns from Chapel and the present New Mills Grammar area would, it is said, leave a non viable secondary at Chapel.

May I suggest that a possible scheme would be for the boys and girls from Chapel, Chinley and Buxworth, who now come here and more or less congregate in my third stream, to be left at Chapel Secondary thus strengthening the GCE element there by about fifteen children a year. The Headmaster at Chapel believes that I get nearly forty per cent from the Chapel area in most year groups.

If, therefore, we could have a scheme whereby the top twenty per cent only came to New Mills and the rest stayed at Chapel Secondary then, in fact, Chapel's G.C.E. and fifth form element would be strengthened. Such boys and girls would not include those who would need those extra options I have suggested in my top two streams. In my opinion they would still lose as we are doing so much for the third stream here now.

Cannot parental choice be used? If, in fact, New Mills Comprehensive included the present Spring Bank, the present moderns from Whaley Bridge and the present grammar school area, could not those who go to New Mills Comprehensive from Chapel, Chinley and Buxworth be those whose parents choose for them and sign a document to the effect that they would stay at school until eighteen plus, or alternatively choose University. Parental choice is not the same as selection, and might very well be a suitable way out. Perhaps this parental choice, where parents were hesitant, could be guided by the primary Headteacher. If this did not work then they could have a diagnostic year at Chapel before coming on here, but one year is the maximum and they would clearly have to learn the foreign language being taught at New Mills. It seems to me parental choice for eighteen plus or university seems a suitable way out and at eleven plus it seems unlikely that parents would sign a document that they would keep their children at school until eighteen plus unless they really meant it. Eighteen plus is too far ahead for most parents unless they really feel that university honours degree was what their children were going to get. Such a scheme would leave Chapel en le Frith Secondary with about 400 children, including a reasonable GCE.'

Philip then summarised by stating ' I do not honestly and sincerely think that the scheme put forward is workable and I do not really see myself trying to work it. I have a strong believe in comprehensive education, but it includes a belief in the power and need for academic learning. I believe that the people who have the academic learning must be the leaders and, therefore, a school must have enough. There are, in my belief, enough lame comprehensive schools in the country without adding to them. A comprehensive school must not be a gigantic secondary modern with a goodish GCE stream and some kind of Sixth form which is not truly and properly academic. It is the leaders of wit and learning and ability who do so much for the others in such a school. It may seem a 'public school' view but I think it is the only proper one to entertain when embarking on a comprehensive experiment. We must not experiment in such a way that more children are damaged than helped by the reorganisation in question. I believe that the scheme put forward by the Authority is of such a kind. It is the kind of error made in Liverpool which has been so damaging to the picture of comprehensive education in the country, and it is the kind of thing now being put forward in Manchester city. If a grammar school is to be the central unit then you must clearly start with the grammar school as a unit and add to it. The only other proper way to start a comprehensive is where you have a new town or some such entity and no schools of any kind to begin with. Then you can begin a proper comprehensive from scratch. It is certainly my experience in a Staffordshire comprehensive school, set in the country, that it was lame from the start because it had scarcely one grammar school stream. It was, therefore, always dominated by the need for fourth year leaving courses, and never enough attention was paid to the academic children. It was always a fight to get staff and to get their attention, and it was almost impossible to make the Sixth Form work properly. All my contacts with it still show this to be the case. In my opinion such a school can never be a happy, working and successful unit and I cannot say this too strongly. It always will spend its energies teaching in corners to odd groups to make up for their losses on the timetable and their losses in numbers, and it will never be able to absorb very fully its new Sixth Formers. I ought to make the further point that, in my opinion, it is a great error continually to shift children about during their puberty. It seems to me important that you should get them somewhere at eleven and leave them there absolutely as long as possible, preferably until nineteen.. Any kind of system which continually moves children around after they have done two years here or there is not at all satisfactory. Once we ought to consider whether what we are going to have is, in any true sense, better than what we have now. Although I believe in comprehensive education and comprehensive schools, I cannot think that any old compromise is necessarily better than the present system of the Grammar School fed at the Sixth form level by two Secondary Moderns. And, in so far as it is a comparatively easy move to absorb Spring Bank in the years to come, then there would seem to be even less of a problem than is currently thought.

The staff here are of course, becoming disaffected. The 'close and genuine' consultation envisaged in the Government Circular does not appear to be forthcoming. They have distinct and intelligent views which are not to be denied. They are, after all, professional people doing their job. I think it unfair and improper that their future should be decided without consulting them, and this present scheme certainly does decide it for several of them.

As a result of this, this Grammar School in the next few years will itself suffer as a Grammar School. Uncertainty is not good in education either for the Staff or the children. Stability is everything. Children particularly need to feel that what happens this year will be so next year. Pattern is essential. We have already had big changes and have now settled into a mould and it seems to me important that the reorganisation takes place smoothly and with as little upset as possible to this major unit in it.

I do therefore, most sincerely and humbly, beg the Authority to think again about what the scheme they have put forward may do to the children of this area, particularly the able children upon whom so much in the future depends. They will not want it said, I think, that they have ruined a fine Grammar School in searching for the will 'o the wisp currently entertained of the neighbourhood idea - that all children in one place shall go to one school. This may not, in the end, turn out to be at all an improvement on what they have now. Clearly any reorganisation must be shown to be an improvement for the vast majority of the children involved'.

A statement was put out by the governors following Philip's response to the Authority's scheme for reorganisation in the area and this stated that 'The governors disapprove of any scheme which involves a two-tier system of comprehensive education' and that they 'are in favour of the merging of Spring Bank School with the Grammar School, with, as an interim solution, selection at 11-plus of those children from the Chapel catchment area thought suitable for a Sixth form course' and that 'they felt no long term decision could be recommended because they consider the catchment areas for Chapel, New Mills and Buxton should be reviewed.'

The following governors' meeting in December 1965 approved several joint recommendations which were to be submitted on behalf of the three schools concerned. These included long term plans that the Authority should look again at the catchment areas of the secondary schools in Buxton, New Mills and Chapel en le Frith and that the short term plans should allow a maximum of freedom for the Local Authority and governing bodies over the long term, so that the final solution may be made in the light of future educational thought and local development. Other recommendations submitted included that the New Mills Grammar and Spring Bank Secondary become one school, and buildings be expedited. That this New Mills School include the present 'non-selected' children from Furness Vale. That the element in this New Mills School from the Chapel Secondary catchment area be not more than twenty-five per cent of the total in that Chapel catchment area. That this top twenty-five per cent from the Chapel catchment area be directed to the New Mills School. That Chapel Secondary School retains its present intake, plus the differential between about twenty-five per cent and the percentage that now goes to New Mills Grammar School from the Chapel School catchment area. That this twenty-five per cent in the Chapel catchment area should be in accordance with parental choice where possible – the parents to choose New Mills if they desire an academic Sixth form course for their child. And the final recommendation was that Spring Bank should keep its present intake until reorganisation. The New Mills Grammar School Governing Body took these recommendations to Derbyshire Education Committee shortly after the meeting, so that the difficult question of publicity in the New Mills area could be decided upon.

By the summer of 1966, Derbyshire Education Committee brought out new plans for the reorganisation of its schools in North West Derbyshire; these came about by the holding of many more meetings with negotiations taking place. They had listened and taken on board many of the suggestions on offer. An agreement was reached which the New Mills Grammar School Governors felt was very satisfactory for the school; it meant that as far as one could see into the future that the Grammar School would remain itself, whatever additions were made to it and that its traditions and its work would carry on and that it would include a sufficient number of able children for the Grammar School work (even below the Sixth form) to have the right number of options, and that it would be viable not only in the Sixth Form, but below it. The governors, the headmaster, the School staff and the PTA put in a lot of extra work on the school's behalf to secure the agreement for the comprehensive reorganisation. No dates for the changeover were given by Derbyshire Education Committee, but the proposal was that New Mills Grammar School was to be extended to an eight form entry comprehensive school, for the age span eleven to eighteen years, and to provide Sixth form facilities for the whole area, with 1,200 pupils, plus 200 in the Sixth form. Chapel en le Frith County Secondary School would be extended to a six form entry providing for the age span eleven to sixteen years for 900 pupils. The gross cost at New Mills was estimated at £540,625 and at Chapel £188,604.

It was in 1959 that the Education Committee adopted a policy for reorganisation of secondary education on comprehensive lines. The proposed plan arose from local further discussions and consultations. The development plan pointed out that beyond 1969 further progress would depend on the availability of financial resources for new buildings and for the modification and extension of the existing schools. The plan assumes that the statutory leaving age will be raised to sixteen years in 1970/71 and takes into account increases in the school population arising from projected housing development based on information from the county planning officer.

September 1966 saw the arrival of several new members of staff, and these included David Woods and Alan Leech, both of whom like Robert Wilson earlier, later went on to reach the top of their profession having had the support and encouragement to help them to do so from their time at New Mills Grammar School.

David Woods, forty five years after beginning at New Mills writes 'I started as New Mills Grammar School in September 1966 as one of a group of new young teachers that P.H.V. had I suspect deliberately recruited to balance the many older and 'traditional' staff. Indeed looking back one of his great talents was to appoint teachers with great potential as many of them became Headteachers or senior education figures. I left the school in April 1972 after he had already left.

My memories of P.H.V. are as follows. He was tremendously energetic and determined as he faced the task of modernising a grammar school whilst preparing to make it a comprehensive school. To a young teacher he was very supportive but sometimes very challenging in his desire to drive the school forward. He had absolute commitment to the school and its pupils and was impatient to see quicker progress. I remember some 'dramatic' staff meetings which I'm sure P.H.V. enjoyed enormously as he thrived upon robust debate and discussion. He loved directing the annual Shakespeare productions which were great successes although there was always some friction as he pulled students out of class in the Autumn Term!

I have been Chief Adviser at Birmingham Schools and now London Schools and I am often called upon to discuss school leadership. There are of course, many styles of leadership and I would always describe P.H.V. as a 'charismatic' leader, who led with passion, energy, enthusiasm and hope always extending the vision of what was possible for the school and its community.

I have a memory of him signing off personal letters in the style 'Do well and be well', something which I have occasionally copied. I have very fond memories of him and still sometimes tell affectionate stories about my time with him at New Mills, so he clearly had a conscious impact upon me'. (Professor David Woods. CBE., Chief Adviser for London Schools. Teacher, New Mills Grammar School 1966 to 1972).

Alan Leech, who was a teacher at New Mills Grammar School from 1966 to 1969, and who later became Headteacher at Bohunt School in Hampshire from 1978 to 1997 writes, 'Philip Vennis or P.H.V. as he was generally known amongst the school staff, was a major figure in the history of New Mills Grammar School. He was responsible for transforming a small town grammar school in a not very affluent area of Derbyshire into a highly successful and flourishing institution.

I worked with him for the three years 1966-9 and offer my opinions and recollections more than forty years later, following my own career in education which some time later saw me Head of a comprehensive school in Hampshire. He was a restless, aspirational, determined and forceful Headteacher. He was able and well read. He had a vision, in the days before 'blue skies' thinking and mission statements, of the kind of school it was possible to bring to the inhabitants of the small nineteenth century textile towns and villages scattered along the deep river valleys of the Rivers Goyt and Sett. He didn't set out this vision, or call it such, but it was implicit in all he did. This vision was focused upon the sixth form and the encouragement of, if possible, all the fifth year pupils (about 100 each year) to stay on at the school and study A levels. Hence, it was important to try to get the best O level results from the youngsters and have an extensive tailored suite of A levels available to them. The other part of the vision was to then ensure that as many as possible of the A level students went on to university, teacher training college or other higher educational institution.

As a result, P.H.V., in those pre developed financial management days, persuaded the Local Authority to give him additional staff teaching posts so that he could offer more A level subjects. Hence, the school offered not only the normal range of subjects, but also the relatively new Economics and British Constitution alongside French, German, Spanish, Russian, Latin, Greek, Ancient History, Further Maths, Technical Drawing and the normal range of other subjects. In order to ensure a good take up for the wide range of subjects, he created a 'fast track' O level class composed of the top set of three in a year group who would take their examinations at the end of their fourth year. Since these people had already assumed they were to remain at school until sixteen years (though the law had not yet been changed) this group invariably formed the bed rock of the Sixth Form. Drawing from this group it was also possible to seek to persuade them to stay for a third year in the Sixth Form and try for an Oxbridge university place.

The numbers within the Sixth Form were high (150 to 200) and it was a dominant force for good within the school, leading 'Houses' and sports activities. University and higher education entry was high. Comparatively it is impossible to assess the school in league table terms, since such measures did not exist. However, it is clear to me that by comparison with similar neighbourhoods within the North West, such as the one I was raised in Lancashire, the school did extremely well. Many youngsters went from New Mills to receive a higher education as a consequence of the endeavours of P.H.V. and the staff at the school. These were not only the sons and daughters of some of the professional parents who commuted to highly paid jobs in Manchester, but also those from working class homes in the more industrially based New Mills Urban District.

He encouraged staff to be 'form tutors' and to seek to relate to their own group, though placement was changed each year, an action which could disrupt the relationship. He wanted all staff to undertake additional things, for example running House Drama evenings, assisting with the annual school dramatic production (often a Shakespearean play) or sport. For instance, apart from my teaching of Economics, Geography and General Studies, I was School Librarian and given a budget for the purchase of books, and assistance from several Sixth formers as Librarians. The school ran sports teams in hockey, rounders, tennis, football and cricket and competed against other schools. We had a major Sports day.

Teaching did not receive the kind of scrutiny of today and there was little 'monitoring' of classrooms, but then neither did other schools. But P.H.V. encouraged departments to prepare schemes of work, though they were heavily geared to the prevailing O or A level syllabus of the day. A number of the teachers were extremely good and very inspirational for the pupils. The school was unquestionably aided in this respect by the number of A level teaching opportunities which were available. The school was, therefore, attractive to the new wave of younger teachers who began to leave university departments in the 60s as higher education expansion was implemented.

It was a stimulating and exciting place to be, even though the accommodation was, by today's standards, relatively poor, with the buildings carrying many more students than the place was built for and possessing a number of so called temporary classrooms. The excitement of the place often owed something to P.H.V.s character and dynamism. He was restless, often overworked and sometimes had more ideas about change and the operation of the school that the staff as a whole could cope with. For instance, he taught a proportion of the timetabled week, did not have enough secretarial support, but insisted on being the Producer/Director of the annual Shakespearean play (with an enormous cast in excess of 100) at the same time as he was writing every single university reference for what could be as many as 100 students. Therefore, he became tired and sometimes said things which upset staff or students and which he usually regretted. Hence, at the weekly social gathering of about twelve highly committed teachers at the Mason's Arms, in New Mills, each Friday evening, life at school and exciting, irritating and exhilarating things surrounding P.H.V. during the previous week were a major topic of conversation. This was the forum where a plan was hatched to try to persuade him to scrap the 'fast track' O level class, on the grounds that a number of the pupils, especially the boys, were not mature enough to cope. He resisted pressure to change this policy for several years, but not before much debate and a number of clashes.

Always trying to further the learning opportunities for the pupils he often did highly unusual but creative things. For instance, Harold Wilson's government took a decision to formally devalue the pound against the dollar and P.H.V. thought the Sixth form should seek to understand this decision and its consequences. Hence, he asked me to assemble all Sixth Form classes in the hall and give an explanatory talk about this. Another example which had consequences for me was when he decided to stop teaching Religious Education for one hour and ten minutes per week for one of the incoming fifth year classes because the experience of the previous year had been particularly unsuccessful.

Instead I was drafted in to teach them a Certificate in Secondary Education (CSE) course in Social Studies for the year. He once surprised those gathered at a school assembly by asking everyone to pray for a successful evening for Manchester United during their European Cup against a major continental European side. I think they won!

The school was an industrious place to be. The pupils were orderly and enjoyed the atmosphere, which I think they found stimulating. There was no corporal punishment and I cannot recall anyone being suspended. P.H.V. had an important approach to leadership in that he was amazing in his capacity to name and congratulate pupils and staff for their contributions and achievements. Naming House captains and vice House captains, sports captains, major acting roles in 'Antony and Cleopatra' or debaters in competitions was a major feature of the school. As, too, was the naming of people in the annual Speech day remarks by the headteacher. With Staff he was particularly good at sending them a letter at the time of their leaving, and in making a speech about their achievements and work for the school at the final staff meeting of the year. He did the latter in a most professional manner, irrespective of how co-operative or un co-operative the person had been.

He was a campaigner on behalf of the school to seek to recruit the best staff possible, offer the widest range of subject options, combined with the creation of a stimulating learning environment which would for the vast majority instil a quest for knowledge and a desire to move on to higher education. In that he was particularly successful.'

The whole of the Autumn Term 1966 saw rehearsals and performances of 'Antony and Cleopatra'. Shakespeare's tragedy had a cast of over one hundred in it. Philip's production received immense support and his philosophy that children's personalities develop through drama was very evident. He said at the following years Speech day, 'It seems clear to me yet again, when I think of the large number of rehearsals and the tremendous talent and effort that went, via the children, into the production of 'Antony and Cleopatra' that we could see clearly a boy or girl gaining very great self discipline and knowledge of how to move, how to react and how to be involved in a great tragedy of this kind and how to be disciplined enough to listen in detail, and to remember in detail, very minutely rehearsed moves. Discipline at rehearsals and at the actual performances was very great and many commented upon it and I think this was one of the great gains to the girls and boys concerned and I am sure they will never forget it.

Philip rehearsing Cleopatra for the production of
Antony and Cleopatra staged in December 1966.

When you think of the costumes, the makeup, the scenery building, the lighting, the sound and the many other ways in which children helped; there being a total of just over 200 of the 600 children in the school involved in this production - this was a great team effort. As so often in school life, those who did most gained most, and those who did most had the best examination results anyway. Perhaps part of the play's success really arose because we were overcoming so many difficulties. One of these difficulties was caused by having to build a large set in a cramped school hall – and visualise just what it would look like in the Art Theatre.

"Bravest at the last. She levell'd at our purposes, and, being royal,
Took her own way. The manner of their deaths?
I do not see them bleed.:

Antony and Cleopatra, produced 1966.

But this is not a reason for not having a school hall with a decent stage to mount our plays and operas on, and I do hope that this will be included in the first phase of buildings at New Mills. 'Antony and Cleopatra' was the high watermark in the school's year; we were pleased to be so well reported in the Times Educational Supplement in the review of the play in 30 December 1966, 'Antony and Cleopatra'must both be an enticement and a threat. It is crammed with opportunities for a large cast and beset with pitfalls for most of them. At New Mills Grammar School in Derbyshire the enticement was yielded to and the threat defied.

In an imaginatively significant permanent setting the action was continuous, and, with allowance for some dramatic pauses, speedy. With stage crowds one difficulty is to strike a balance between lack of involvement and complete absorption in the concerns and conversation of principals. No doubt in a laudable resolve to induce everyone on the generally populous stage to pull full weight, Mr. Philip Vennis had allowed mass attention and much vocal reaction to matters personal and confidential. In its movement, however, including vigorous though formalised fighting, this was a finally disciplined production.

Mature interpretation of character and emotion one could not look to have, not really sensitive speaking of the verse, but both Antony and Cleopatra ended more convincingly than they began. Enobarbus was more consistently in character than anyone else.'

A rather more humorous report of the production was written in the School Magazine under the name of 'Euphronius', the article being entitled 'You'll have me in tears in a minute', which was one of Philip's catchphrases.

'It started quite mildly – "Anyone wanting a part in 'Antony and Cleopatra' please come to the library at ten to one." However, as time went by, we progressed to "All the Sixth Form please come to the library..." and finally as enthusiasm was aroused, "Anyone wishing to drop out of 'Antony and Cleopatra' please come..."

Right from the start the play seemed to be jinxed. The boredom of one rehearsal was enlightened by the decline and fall of part of the Roman Empire, from the top of the six foot high set; the early rehearsals of the battle scenes were accomplished by an epidemic of lacerated fingers; on various occasions members of the cast, and others, just managed to avoid injury from flying drumsticks, exploding amplifiers, collapsing scenery, protruding screws under the platform, toppling tea cups, and, most frequently, the, err...helpful suggestions of the producer.

"Pity me,...do not speak to me". W. Shakespeare

Every Friday night a marathon rehearsal was held, the most popular part of which was the four o'clock tea break. The 'shop on the corner' and the 'chippy' became very prosperous, whilst the Prefect's room was cunningly transformed into a night club, with an a-la-carte menu of cheese and onion pie and coffee (black or black). Attempts by a well known chef to introduce a new menu (dry bread and tepid tomato soup) were not received with universal acclaim, although, in general, a good time was had by all.

"We'll feast each other 'ere we part" W. Shakespeare

With amazing haste, the great day approached; at times the producer could be seen pacing anxiously, looking at the clock and muttering "two weeks, three days, two hours, thirty minutes, twenty seconds...two weeks, three days, two hours, thirty minutes, ten seconds,...two- " The mental strain caused many tempers to become frayed, together with the insulation on part of the sound amplification. Both these effects produced some rather shocking scenes...

A week to go; a sense of urgency pervaded the cast – well, some of it anyway – and we concentrated on perfecting various professional touches. Particularly memorable was a discussion of the intricacies of the stage 'burp' – a thoroughly enjoyable afternoon.

"Tomorrow, the last of many battles I mean to fight." W.Shakespeare

Then came the marathon rehearsal to end all marathon rehearsals; twelve hours. By lunch time on this vital day the cast was ravenous (i.e. hungry) and the author of this literary masterpiece was dispatched by a legion of threatening Roman Soldiers to scour the town for a meat pie. His return with the nearest available approximation (corned beef sandwiches) was not entirely appreciated, but I am digressing: back to the plot.

Then 'the night' came. First night nerves were calmed by a somewhat fractured choral rendering of a medley of Christmas carols, and the consumption of enormous numbers of sandwiches. During the actual performances various dubious theatrical 'firsts' were claimed, such as the first person to appear on stage carrying a bag of chips, the first Roman armour to reach eight inches above the knee, and other even more illegal practices which I had better not mention since the headmaster is one of our regular readers.

"The time of universal peace is near." W.Shakespeare

However, all went well and the production was acclaimed as a great success.' Family life for Philip became more demanding with the arrival of his third child, a boy, in May 1967. The arrival of this second son completed his family and he always felt very lucky with his loving children and wife. He now had three children under five years of age, and although he was busy with school life he would always make time for his children and education of them was always top priority. He thoroughly enjoyed these early years of married life with his young children living in Marple. Apart from being the family breadwinner, one of Philip's greatest contribution to the family was his enthusiasm for organising family holidays. Because of the experience of organizing the scout camps at Dulwich College and East Ham Grammar School, a family holiday was of a much smaller challenge. However, holidays abroad continued throughout family

17. *The main entrance of Ounsdale School, built in 1956 as a Secondary Modern, becoming Comprehensive in 1958 and later changing to its current status as Ounsdale High School.*

18. *In the foreground is part of the separate block that was built for the teaching of practical subjects and in the background of the picture is part of the three storey block built for the academic teaching.*

19. A view from Spring Bank looking towards Union Roada and the hills beyond.

20. Part of the route that had to be travelled between the lower school buildingsat Spring Bank and the Upper school buildings at the main site of the Comprehensive School in Church Lane in 1970.

21. Front elevation, New Mills School, designed by George Widdows with the foundation stone being laid in December 1912. It is now a grade 2 listed building and is of distinctive architectural quality and displays the well-crafted use of locally won grit stone.

22. A view of the Grammar School across the valley, showing the octagonal hall and the Anglican Church in the background.

23. The River Sett in New Mills. The town is built around the confluence of the River Goyt and the River Sett.

24. The front elevation of Itchen Sixth Form College.

25. Itchen Sixth Form College, main entrance.

The foundation stone for this building was laid in December 1925.

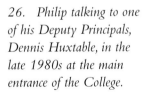

26. Philip talking to one of his Deputy Principals, Dennis Huxtable, in the late 1980s at the main entrance of the College.

27. *Itchen celebrating its twentieth year as a Sixth Form College at the Speech Day in November 1987.*

28. *College Assembly in the 1980s with the Chairperson of the Governors present.*

29. A formal Staff photograph in June 1988.

30. An informal Staff photograph in June 1988.

HAPPY RETIREMENT PHV

31.

31 and 32.
As part of a 'thank
you' to Philip the
Governors decided to
rename the library as
'The Philip Vennis
library'. Philip was
most touched and
honoured by this
gesture.

life and the experiences gained by the children were invaluable. Philip enjoyed planning the route to be taken (with his children when they were old enough to do so). Always a great adventurer nothing was too mundane. Camping, travelling, mapping and an enthusiasm to show his young family all the sights he himself had seen in post war Europe led to enjoyable and interesting holidays. He said that 'family life is the best life, watching the children growing up and daily changing. Days when children are growing up are the best days.'

Another young man who started his teaching career at New Mills Grammar School in September 1967 was Ian Stuart, who after leaving New Mills, became Head of Department at Parrs Wood High School in Manchester in 1973, and some years later Head of English at an Isle of Man Comprehensive School – Castle Rushen High School. Ian was appointed by Philip on the strength of his drama background as he had done a lot of acting and directing in school and university. He recollects that 'To be entirely honest, I found P.H.V. terrifying at first. It wasn't that he had a short fuse – he had no fuse at all. So I spent my first two years trying hard not to be noticed. However, being in charge of the annual play – as well as inter house drama competitions, I had to stick my head over the parapet on a fairly regular basis. I did a modern dress "Macbeth" first and this was followed by "As You Like It", and "Hansel and Gretel". After that was a production of "The Crucible" and so on every year. P.H.V. was not one for chamber theatre – he demanded that everything was on an epic scale. He only let me do "As You Like It" on the condition that I brought in more characters – so I was forced to write a cod–Shakespearian scene with foresters and wrestlers and heaven knows what.

Most of the plays were put on in New Mills Art Theatre, a real theatre, demanding theatrical skills from the whole company. P.H.V. always gave me total backing for each production. I was able to pull company members out of lessons – THE PLAY was always top priority. I was not always popular with my colleagues. Philip believed (rightly) that putting on a play is an immensely educative enterprise, demanding social skills, and commitment. Pupils who were not particularly sporty could shine as actors, costume makers or lighting technicians. Somehow or other we always created a "company feeling". After the end of one performance we were clearing up and one boy – Lester Cooper - he was the SM came up and said "What are we doing next then, sir?" I knew then I was on a winner. Interestingly, P.H.V. often came into rehearsal, and never said a word, didn't break in at all. At first I thought he was saving his ire for later. But he let me get on with it. We did a blisteringly good "Oh What a Lovely War" – and took it on tour as well. There was a real tradition of good theatre at NMGS. It helped young people grow.

As it was my probationary year, P.H.V. came into quite a few lessons, sat at the back, and never said a word. No praise – but no blame either. I was a form tutor – and loved it. P.H.V. was red hot with form tutors. You had to know your kids – what their strengths and weaknesses were – what their options and career prospects were likely to be. After the summer examinations there were endless staff meetings about options – you had to have all the details at your finger tips – and if you didn't – then you got torn apart in public. And he was right to do that. Teachers can be lazy… It slowly dawned on me that P.H.V. was simply concerned with the children under his care. That was his entire concern. Nothing else mattered at all. Our personal relations were always wary. And yet he gave me a superb reference for my next job – and tried to poach me as Head of Drama when he went to Southampton. Looking back, I wonder if all the blustering and shouting was a cover for shyness. His weakness was that he lacked finesse or subtlety; his enormous strength was an unwavering, unstoppable urge to help young people in the awkward process of growing up. That was his whole professional life.'

Philip in his speech given in November 1967, long before schools were involved with 'league tables of results' stated that 'he had no desire for the school to be judged on examination results.' He went on to say that 'results were good and I have no doubt they'll continue to be so, but a good school is not one in which the children are made ready for examinations, but one in which they are made ready to be citizens of our community. And this can only be done by developing their personalities, allowing them to take part in sports and drama and debate of all kinds, training them for public speaking etc., as we are trying to do. There has never been any evidence in English school life that those who withdraw from school life do better in the examinations. However, teenagers today, especially the older ones, find it extremely difficult to settle down to academic work for a full evening. The distractions are very many and grow more numerous. Television is only the most obvious one, but all kind of other distractions occur. The result is, in fact, that Sixth formers don't work anything like as hard as they ought to. Even when they think they are working, they are not working hard enough or in the right way – they must be encouraged to concentrate and do an hour or two hours' work on one subject at one time and not peck at it in the modern kind of dilettante way, otherwise results will be good but never as good as they could be and, in particular, able children will not gain the high grades that they ought to gain. It is obvious from the results that those who do most for the school, do best in exams. It is important to remind Sixth formers that these days universities and colleges want to know about all their activities in the Sixth form and about their minority time.'

Another area Philip voiced concern about were the problems which secondary schools faced and which had been recently summed up in 'The Guardian' in a series of articles on 'the permissive society'. 'How is the school to face this vast change in the attitudes of young people and attitudes to them by parents and social workers? Are they schoolboys and schoolgirls still or are they students in the American manner? How are we to line up the need for a boy or girl to become a true academic and have true learning in the Sixth Form and still be allowed the kind of permissiveness which society seems to want? Are we, in fact, tearing them apart? Is it possible to have the demands fulfilled the we make upon them for A level and as a school in so many other ways, and still allow this permissiveness? The Lacey Report came out for full legal rights at eighteen. Has anybody stopped to think what results this might have in a school where 80 or so of its pupils are over the age of eighteen? There are very great new or nearly new problems here, and if they are not new, they are new in relation to numbers. The size of the Sixth form now dictates the whole policy of the school. It's more than a quarter of a not very large school. Everything we do or largely so is either about it or connected with children when they will be one day in it. How can we act otherwise? The eighteen plus competition dominates us all.

But schools are not permissive societies; they are, and they will always remain non-permissive; to some extent they will always remain authoritarian. They have to know best; they have to protect their young people, they have to direct them and discipline them, and, at the same time, to bring them up to be good citizens of the society into which they will move; they have somehow to allow them a liberal atmosphere, to allow them choice and to allow them responsibilities and power. Last year, for the first time, we held a vote for the Head Boy and Girl etc. This is good but everybody in school teaching, in my view, knows, if they know anything about it, that youngsters profit from discipline and we'll not confuse discipline with punishment; and yet, if the permissive society and not least its commercial backers treats them as though they are adults in every kind of way, and wants to sell them the kind of adult products, or clothing or even problems, then how on earth is the school to do its job? We are co-educational and that's fine and healthy and I believe that boys and girls are far better off in a co-educational atmosphere especially in a Sixth form than in a single sex school. We have to give a lead; but we must not give in; this is not in the school's line. We must be sceptical, we must question, and we must point out that fashions will change. We, perhaps, need to be at any one time ten years behind; we need to drag our feet and to wonder out loud about 1967 and its tastes to our Sixth and fifth formers and continually remind them, which is so really true that there is nothing new under the sun, that even their Love-Ins and their Flower shirts and so on are only the usual youthful revolt.

This is alright. Let them revolt, but we must keep it within some perspective and sometimes say 'No'; but, above all, we must be certain, in school life, that we say 'yes' to some important things – to the creative side of life – producing good citizens with a sense of self-discipline.

This is the revolution that is affecting secondary school life. This is the revolution about which we should be most caring. We must not fritter away our time on the comprehensive problem and not notice the very much greater problem that is occurring in our midst. We must spend time and energy on sex education, on marriage guidance, on the question of girls careers in an early marrying age, on getting ready girls who will return later to professions after they have been married for some time, on the whole question of the upbringing of boys in the kind of society that perpetually titillates them, on the whole question of why they are hippies or flower children and what they mean and how sincere their peace feelings are. The school has to line itself up with what's best in these things. That is why we are devoting our concert to the idea of 'Peace'. We want to point out to our young people that peace is a pretty old idea and that, throughout literature, and history, men have been attached to it, and that it isn't new and that it's always been attractive and that the best minds have always wanted it.

I want the school's motto to be "As Far as Who Goes Farthest". It's self-discipline in a teenager that matters most. We shall help them to have self-discipline and to go as far as who goes farthest – if they will let us, but they must, of course, let us. They must allow us to advise them and guide them and discipline them, until mentally and physically they are the kind of young people who have enough self-discipline to cope with life in a contented, full and fulfilled way and then, indeed they will make good citizens. It is actually from 'Julius Caesar', and we might read the whole quotation as follows: - Casca, who is speaking, has decided to join in a great undertaking and give it his full support, and he replies to the invitation to join that undertaking – as any child may think on joining us.

> "You speak to Casca,
> And to such a man that is no fleering tell tale,
> Hold my hand; be factious for redress of all these griefs
> And I shall set this foot of mine as far as who goes farthest."

Of course, much of the 1967 speech referred to going comprehensive and Philip again expressed his worries and his hopes for the future. 'Of course, it's right and proper that at some stage, the school should become comprehensive. One has two very important views about going comprehensive; one is that, unless you are prepared to sacrifice the interests of the abler children within the community, you must see that enough of them are in one place for all their options to continue and for them to have competition with one another. Speaking as the Headmaster of the Chapel, Whaley Bridge and New Mills Grammar School, it seems to me quite impossible to suppose we shall do other than harm at the moment, or in the next few years, if we split the children who come to the grammar school in any kind of way. With this in mind any kind of comprehensive school in New Mills must, for the moment, be a compromise. It will have to be some kind of grammar comprehensive, not unknown elsewhere in the County and quite common in other parts of England, until such time as there are enough above average children to supply the options and the competition at two schools. I am not happy about the split school idea between the buildings of the grammar school and those at Spring Bank.

Our kind of school as we know it is dying. We know that institutions must grow and change as a nation does. The 1902 Act State Grammar Schools, of which ours is a fine example, have in fact, to quote Othello "done the state some service" and it would be a brave man, in the state of England at the moment, who in any sense spoilt them and wrecked them unless he were absolutely certain that what he was getting in their place was very much better; how can any of us be certain? We can only make intelligent guesses and judge by experience elsewhere. The evidence, in my view, points in favour of comprehensive schools. They do so much for flexibility and for those children who currently get so disappointed by not coming to the grammar school. But nevertheless our kind of school produced the people who were the leaders of our war effort in two wars, and many of our technologists and our new skilled men and economists are from them in our own time. Our grammar school, like many others is a going concern.'

The comprehensive question was still very open, but it seemed probable that the County's plans of erecting a first phase of buildings at the grammar school site in order to become comprehensive with Spring Bank in the early seventies would go ahead. This plan would mean a partial use of Spring Bank building during the first years of the comprehensive. Philip did not feel that this was ideal but he did say that 'schools do not overwhelmingly depend on buildings and I have no doubt that the spirit of the school will not largely alter'. The grammar school was in disparate buildings and was very crowded. 1968 heralded the beginnings of raising money to build a swimming pool, by the end of the summer the school was promised £2,500 (half the cost) by the Education Committee and already the PTA had raised over £2,000. The plans for the swimming pool were completed, digging commenced in the spring of 1969. The swimming pool was to be a permanent structure with a clear span roof enabling children to learn to swim on site instead of travelling to Marple swimming pool.

In September 1968, Phyllis Dale joined the staff as the new Senior mistress of the school. She was Senior mistress at Henry Cavendish Technical High School in Derby for ten years, before joining New Mills. The post of Senior mistress was an onerous one in the school and she often acted as a co-deputy head, in charge of girls' welfare and discipline. Phyllis Dale was not afraid to give a lead and as a senior woman in education she was an excellent role model to the girls and an example to them as how to achieve in their chosen professions. January 1969 saw the Deputy Head teacher Bert Read go over to Spring Bank as Acting headmaster until the two schools finally came together. It was right and proper that the most senior person in the Grammar School after Philip, should be the one to have detailed knowledge of Spring Bank, which would be so necessary when the two schools come together. With this move of Mr. Read to Spring Bank, Phyllis Dale became Acting Deputy headmistress.

The school at the beginning of the academic year in 1968 had 653 pupils with 175 of these in the Sixth form. Accommodation was still a huge problem, with teaching taking place in many small rooms throughout the school and there being no spare rooms whatsoever. A complicated timetable was in operation with over 1,200 lessons a week being taught, there being 25 A levels and 27 O levels and 15 CSE subjects on the timetable.

Again, at the Speech Day in November 1968, going comprehensive was presented to the audience. Philip tried to allay fears for the school and its standards when it goes comprehensive. He said that in the first phase, the new school would be a semi-comprehensive or semi-grammar, with a large selected intake still, as had become common in many parts of the country where comprehensives had come in phases. I think it right and proper that this school should not have been broken up in any circumstances. I therefore think the scheme not an unreasonable one. I am sure the school would continue to cooperate, as it had done for a long time with Mr. D. Northall, headmaster of Chapel en le Frith County Secondary School, and we hope to have his ex-fifth formers in increasing numbers in our Sixth form. It is very important, of course, that we should be seen to be doing this and it is important to say in public that boys and girls at Chapel are welcome into the Sixth Form to do A level work with three Os or three CSE grade ones or a mixture of these – and into the Sixth Form to continue with their fifth form work and to do some Sixth Form work with fewer than that. This will always be true. In addition, there will still be the fact of the thirteen - limited but still there where absolutely necessary.'

New Mills Grammar School staff in 1969. Philip in the middle (eighth from the left and the right), with Phyllis Dale to the left and Bert Read to the right.

Speaking of the school's union with Spring Bank County Secondary School under the merger, Philip went on to say 'Unfortunately, we still have to use, for a part of the first phase, a remodelled Spring Bank building. But over £20,000 maybe £25,000, will be spent on the building, and there will be a very complete remodelling and restructuring, so that parents need not fear that facilities won't be proper and modern, including indoor toilets, and more than adequate for first and second formers. All first and second formers will be taught there for a large part of the week, though they will come up to the main building to the gymnasium and for some crafts. We shall be running a kind of semi-grammar school and we hope to take the best from both schools, and then build on that best. But it would be unfair of me if I didn't say that I hoped that the Grammar School's work will continue much as it was, with a greatly added flexibility of staff and subjects, with an additional mixing among the boys and girls, and with much increased and finer buildings. For these reasons I think the Grammar Schools' work will go on, and in fact, be much enhanced. We have no doubt at all that the Sixth form will grow, particularly after the leaving age rises in 1972; I have no doubt, too, that we shall have fifth forms over a very wide range of ability, working at a high level. But we shall not neglect either that part of our work, which is currently only done at Spring Bank; all I think will flourish together and learn from one another. We shall be no extreme kind of comprehensive school; we shall only have mixed ability where mixed ability has proved to work in certain limited subjects and certain limited age groups; we may have what is known as broad banding in part of our timetable, so that people can mix together within a reasonable range of ability. Some would say that we have mixed ability in our big Sixth form groups. It will be hard work for boys and girls and harder work for the staff; modern methods and modern schools are harder work for staff, though they may be more interesting. We can look forward, therefore, most certainly to the continued growth and life of New Mills Grammar School as we have known it within the new New Mills School. We need have no fear for our school or its standards'.

Philip continued to talk about the State Grammar School. 'State Grammar Schools have contributed a very great deal to the history of education in England. Ours, like so many other 1902 Act Grammar Schools, has contributed its share during these sixty six years. In the introduction of new methods and new subjects, in providing a way out for many working class boys and girls, in providing leadership in two wars, and in setting up a kind of great class of people who feel proud of having been to the Grammar School, not through any snobbery, but from the skills that they learned there and the pleasure of having been there and the kind of staffs and loyalties to staffs that they met there. The Sixth form has always been its crowning glory; it still is a very English institution.

For all these reasons we can feel proud, at the end of the day, of what the State Grammar School has done; this is no time, in my view, as is so fashionable in some circles, to be denying and decrying the work that we have done and the work we are doing. Neither is it the time to criticise the grammar schools as though they were still circa 1950. They distinctly are not; they have long since modernised their timetables, introduced a great many new subjects, as we, ourselves, have so greatly done and most certainly in the last years in teaching methods. It isn't true to say, as part on an attack on a grammar school, that they are out of date; quite the contrary in my view. It is easy, of course, to deny the use of examinations – they have been inflicted on us by others, in any case others imitate us. But it is true of a good grammar school that we don't worry about examinations, we would not be doing three blocks of four periods each of minority time in the Sixth form if we were over-worrying about A level, nor indeed would we be doing 'Macbeth' next month, nor would we do all the drama, and sport and music, nor would we have this very hard work for Speech Day. How can the people say that grammar schools exist merely to take examinations? It is simply quite untrue and quite unfair. A good grammar, and I hope New Mills is one, like any other school, tries to keep its youngsters at the stage that they should be at, in aptitude, age and ability, and we, for our part, in the thirds and below try very hard not to worry about the obtaining of O levels and CSE, and I have every confidence that the best of all of this, and that is most of it, will continue as a proper tradition in the new New Mills School which will start in September 1970 or September 1971.'

The final section of Philip's 1968 Speech Day speech looks again, continuing from last year's Speech Day, at the permissive society alongside authority, discipline and responsibility. 'It is important now to turn to the problems that beset schools in our time and community. There is the whole question of the school and the so called permissive society. A school as I have said before at previous Speech Days is, by nature, a place of authority; it is not authoritarian – that is quite different; it has authority, which derives from London, and, through the Chairman of the Education Committee at Matlock, through the Director and the Divisional Executive and the Divisional Education Officer to the Headmaster and, through him, to the school. This devolving of authority leaves, in every case, great areas of decisions to be made by the next man or woman or boy or girl so that, in a good school, even the first former has his area of decision- making; this is right and proper. The question is whether the school is to be a narrowing oasis of discipline in the best sense, a framework in which young people can happily grow up, or whether it is to give in and make its peace with that permissiveness. As is well known I take the first view. I think we have to stand out for reasonable authority and reasonable discipline and a reasonable framework in which young people may grow up, until such time as those tides will turn, as turn they surely will. There is fashion in permissiveness, as there is surely fashion in dress. It isn't of interest to the school that long hair is normal outside, or short skirts normal outside. What is of interest is what is best for that youngster to wear at any one time in relation to the others in his or her community. The effect of all upon each is the most important thing to be learned in a school community and, if it is not learned there with reference to joining the world outside, then it will never be learned. In our Sixth form of course, we quite clearly have semi-student status and we have long had this; at New Mills I hope we have had it these past years. They have great privileges – the chief one, may I remind them and their parents, is of course, the pleasure and delight of doing A level work, of meeting the minds of the staff in discussion at A level, of being exposed to minority-time, and of the pleasure of meeting one another. In relation to school life, parents have to decide whether they are going to back the authority of the school in every way; we stick to the minutiae of school life because they are our framework; we assemble because it shows that we depend upon each other at the beginning of each day; it shows, too, I hope, that belief in God is still something that unites most of us and for those for whom this is no union, then we must hope that they will gain something from the social nature of prayers said and hymns sung. We have to stick to punctuality, to lines in corridors, to silence while teaching, to some forms of punishment, if that is necessary to support discipline, but only if it is necessary. We have to ask parents to send their children to school on time and clean and in uniform; we have to have our rules about lunch observed; if they are going home that is well – if they are not, they are in our care and we have to be allowed to make the decisions; even in regard to Sixth formers parents should realise, as indeed later in regard to students, that they still have a responsibility, not only because of the law but because of the responsibility of parents towards their young people of whatever age.

We all know that young people mature earlier; we really do not need to be told this; but maturity must bring responsibility, not irresponsibility, and I suppose the largest signs of maturity will be the ability to take responsibility in a community such as a school and to use it properly. All depend upon each other. We cannot, in all conscience, send young people forward as students unless we feel that they have become, while at school, responsible, and mature young adults. This is our greatest single problem and we must not lose sight of this absolutely major and central and crucial problem in education – the one in fact that will surely continue to grow and grow until, in the end, unless we are very careful, it may overwhelm us. The question I pose again to end is "Are schools to produce responsible young people through a framework of authority – by making them more and more responsible in the literal sense, i.e. answerable – as they grow older – or are they, with the community at large, to say no authority is needed, to allow this framework to go by the board and to allow permissiveness in ever sector to reign; in all this we shall have to include sexual permissiveness, or permissiveness connected to drug taking" when put like that everybody will see quite how laughable it is to allow the latter to happen. Now can we have permissiveness in sex, in discipline, in work, or indeed in anything? Permissiveness no doubt in the sense originally of 'permission being granted' was in order. But it can be much bettered by saying 'this amount of responsibility is yours; see how you can do with it', then come back for more as you grow older, as you grow more responsible, as you grow mature, and we shall give you more.

Our aim, now and in the future, is to bring up and bring forth mature young people who are completely responsible. If our school motto is 'As Far As Who Goes Farthest' – then it is to be taken to mean that people can go on along the road of education throughout their lives, learning as they go, keeping up with the best as far as they can, coming out of the race at the right moment for each to suit his or her own personality and contentment, and, all the time, growing more responsible and more able to bear true responsibility. I believe our young people are fine young people, I believe they have to be given room to try for themselves, and I believe that they hold out great hopes for the future of our land because of their frankness, their zest, their intelligence and their idealism.'

One of the pupils, John Robinson, at the School during its going comprehensive from 1966 to 1972, illustrates some of the discipline and authoritarian manner of the school when he remembers 'I can recall that Mr. Vennis took me for Latin. He terrified me at times but that made me work harder. He used to ask each of us questions and if we got it wrong, we had to stand up. Depending on his mood, which probably reflected how well we were doing, he would give us more chances to sit down. Otherwise we were given 'impots' (impositions) when we had to translate a piece of Latin. Other times we would start the lesson standing up and get to sit down when we answered a question correctly.

Whilst he was a strict disciplinarian, and used the cane, particularly on one of my brothers it seems – but never on me or my two sisters (who both went on to become teachers) we subsequently rated him as a headmaster forward looking for his time. When I was in the Sixth form, and should have been doing private study, I was playing football with some fellow students. Mr. Vennis caught us and simply said "you will need a shower now that you have finished". It was very clear to us what he meant and we never played football again in study time.

School was tough because I came from a Council estate. That meant dodging people from Spring Bank Secondary School on my way to and from

223

school – with my cap for the first two years – and competing with those who had more money. I don't regret my childhood, I had two loving parents, great brothers and sisters and a generally safe school environment free of bullying thanks to Mr. Vennis. He never treated children differently because of their background. He was one of the first to accept equality of opportunity and this is one of the reasons many students came to realise he was ahead of his time.

I can still sing 'I vow to thee my country', 'Fight the good fight' and 'Jerusalem', which we learned for the annual speech day at Ferodo. When I sing them to myself, I think of the school and Mr. Vennis stood on that Ferodo's stage. I can still picture him leading assembly in that great hall at New Mills.

I think I lived most of life at school in fear; whilst I never really had many bad times I cannot remember many happy times. I do attribute much of my subsequent success in life from having the discipline I learned at school. I now employ about a thousand staff in the Civil Service and I wish more of them had had the same discipline.'

By Speech Day 1969 it was just under a year before the school was to finally go comprehensive and Philip spent time at the Speech Day looking to the past and the future, he was optimistically looking to the future with 'this great experiment in education as it affects the New Mills area'. He began by saying that 'The school has seen many changes since its foundation when, under Mr. Nichols, the secondary boys and girls moved across the valley in 1912; it altered during and after the First World War years; after the 1944 Act it greatly altered. Since the fifties the grammar school altered to be more selective and since the sixties, in my view, it's altered a second time to become the place where modern minds gather. In the sixties it has faced up to new challenges; and out of each change the school has carried forward renewed strength from older traditions; each time these have left behind a considerable residue of what is best in them, while the new growth points have brought added value to the school's life. Every kind of modern method is now housed under one roof – in Languages, in Classics, in Mathematics, in the Sciences. If our particular Grammar is not doing them all it is grammars that are doing them. The State grammar school need not bury its head because it's being buried. Of course it is a clear truth that it has no friends at any court. There are those who care about the public school and those who care about the Direct Grants and those who love secondary moderns, and clearly a lot of people who love Comprehensives. To find a defender of the State grammar you have to go very far indeed and yet it remains a truth, as Churchill once said, that it was this kind of school that has produced the leadership of the country these last fifty years. We need not worry moving forward, the best of what we have done will go on – it will go on because it is good. So here again is a new challenge and a new change, but only one of many the school has seen –

a moment perhaps of immediate and greater growth, but one through which the school will learn a great deal that is valuable. In particular, it will be pleasing for the school to be reunited with the school at Spring Bank from which it was artificially divided 60 years ago and to which it will be reunited, at first across the town but eventually on this one Grammar School site. It is we who enter comprehensives from a position of strength. Comprehensives have partly become – I say partly – out of envy of what we are and it is right and proper we should share the good things that we have so we need not be afraid for, if we are afraid, we must be distrusting our own abilities and what we can do. It is my view that all will share and that, in a proper comprehensive, the able child will gain by mixing with his fellows, by better buildings and facilities, by a bigger staff which is more flexible and by a greater flexibility of courses. If we have had a fault it is in pretending that academic work can be done by people far down the ability range and very often our third and fourth streams have suffered accordingly. At New Mills, I think, we have tried very hard to fit less academic courses for these less able people and they, within the grammar school range, now at the bottom, will most gain among those at the grammar school from the comprehensive set up and those, too, at the top of the secondary modern. But we have to be certain that the two extremes will gain – the 'high flyers' of the grammar and the true grammar school people in our middle form and the bottom people of the secondary modern. All this has to be arranged and will be. Now at New Mills, to start with, we shall have a semi-comprehensive and we shall go on, in fact, being New Mills Grammar School for a lot of our entry. Parents need have no fears if boys and girls come to us selected from the Whaley and Chapel areas, then we shall know they are selected and they will be in our examination band. Children will be banded, not streamed, within – as it were - grouped abilities of the exam group and the non-exam group and possibly others. I repeat the point that, if their address is in Whaley or Chapel they will quite clearly be in the exam group and that is where they will stay through their school careers. We must, I think, give parents this assurance. They will, in fact, still be selected for New Mills Grammar School. However, those who would be, or would have been, at the grammar school will gain greatly from a much extended and new building, for example, we are currently 700 on the site, but next year will perhaps be only 650 on the same site with a much extended building. For once we shall not be queuing up to move along the corridors. We do remarkably well at the moment in a complex timetable. We shall have a new gymnasium, new engineering shop, metal shops and crafts rooms of all kinds for arts and crafts, a new laboratory, a new kitchen and a kind of hall area for some of our drama and music.

The first and second formers will be at what is now the Spring Bank building which is being renovated and will be a fine modern building. It is a great disadvantage to have split buildings and some people use the word 'botched up' about comprehensives. I don't know about that. I do think it is a pity but we must be determined to see we have one school with one spirit and that the boys and girls at Spring Bank are part of the main school.

On the other hand there is a clear advantage for them to be a little separate as young children and not too much involved in the older teenage area. None of us want them to grow up too soon and here we shall be able to see them in their own little unit with the Head of the Lower School in charge and yet with the whole school staff teaching them. These things cause difficulties of transport for the staff and this is certainly an essential difficulty. Other difficulties are certainly that those children will have to come up to the main site to use the swimming pool, which is for them mainly and the gymnasium but all these things will be arranged.

Of course comprehensive schools are now a political issue and that is a great pity. It seems certain to me, that they are right and proper if properly started and properly staffed with proper buildings and I put the buildings last. Children, parents, governors matter more than buildings and the Authority. Children come first of those things. You have to have the right spread of ability.

Above all, first before all these, comes the right staff. Nothing matters besides that. If you have the right staff you can do the job. Buildings come last. They matter. The less abler the child, the more they matter. Nevertheless they don't supremely matter because a good staff will overcome – as we have always shown here – great difficulties. We have to be in a position to attract the right staff. I think we shall, being on the edge of the Manchester conurbation, where not all staff are happy, where it is pleasant to come out to teach from the Manchester suburbs and where people want to live. We have pleasant children for them to teach, good parental support and good governor and Authority support. I think Derbyshire is well known for this – we shall continue to attract, I am quite sure, with our large Sixth, good staff.

It is important that the Sixth stay large. Sixth forms today are not big at our size. A recent report shows that something like 250 is needed realistically for it to be completely viable in all A level subjects and, if we are going in for non A level courses, it will need to be 350 or so. That I have no doubt it will become, but, of course, we must never allow any day when the able A level Sixth former is split so that we can run less groups for them and less subjects and where they have less competition.

I think it will be a good school. Able children will still have competition with one another, will gain in the buildings, gain in the staffing, gain in flexibility and truthfully gain socially from meeting other kinds of children whom they have not seen since their primary school days.

The pity of it is that we are in the middle of this struggle between the Government, who are now making it compulsory, and those who may be the Government will undo this. This will not of course affect us here in Derbyshire or at New Mills since going comprehensive is not in question. It does seem to me right, it does seem to me a pity that we are in split buildings and we cannot have a complete building but on the other hand we have great advantages of having the first and seconds together separately, of a big sixth, of the grammar school element going on. These are all good things and all I think will gain, not least those selected to come to what will now be apparently a partly comprehensive school.

It is very important in the midst of the struggle and the Black Paper and the doubts that are being put upon, not to confuse too many issues. There may be debate over teaching methods, though I think it is right that we should currently try to change – though gradually – to those now in use in modern Mathematics and the Languages. There may be debate over how to go comprehensive and in what order, but I do not believe there really is a debate about the fact that the 11-plus does not quite work properly, that it is, in case, too early to select, and that we must have a school where all can come at 11-plus and that must clearly be a comprehensive school. There is really no debate over this – we may debate selection at thirteen and, in a sense, within the school, having banded it at eleven we shall select again at thirteen and clearly finally select, so to speak, via O level and CSE for the Sixth form at sixteen years. This is right and proper for life must have selection. It is selective and teenagers have to learn this at some time. The debate is over then.

We must enter this great experiment feeling confident that it will work and quite optimistic at New Mills that the best of the Grammar School will go on. We will feel a little sad that New Mills Grammar is undergoing a change but we will see that, what comes out of it at the end, will only be a change – perhaps for the better – we will not withhold the good things we have from others but share them out and, in the process, do our own characters and our own work great good. I like 'As Far As Who Goes Farthest', I think it suits the kind of feeling we want within the comprehensive that each boy or girl can go far and I would also like to offer as another school motto – one which may be sympathetic to some and that is from Shakespeare's 'Henry IV' "Shadow will Serve..." by which I mean that this poor soldier whom Falstaff is recruiting still has, in Shakespeare's view, some quality which can be developed, that he will do – as it were – and something can be done for him. This, I think, might apply to every child in the comprehensive and perhaps 'Shadow' will serve to sum up and may well do us as a more compassionate or a newly compassionate school motto.'

Philip was invited to address the last Speech Day to be held in Spring Bank

County Secondary School in May 1970, and he tried to wind up, as it were, on some aspects of education and to look forward with Spring Bank, to the coming metamorphosis of going comprehensive. He began by talking about the history of schools in New Mills by saying 'There was first, in New Mills a British School at Providence in 1864 and Mr. Nicholls remarkably was Headmaster there for one year 1878-9. The present Spring Bank building, as a result of the 1870 Act opened in 1879. Mr. Nichols was Head of the Board School and of the Science School. In 1908 he gave up one post and became Head only of the Science School. Through the 1902 Act separate secondary State schools were called for and New Mills Secondary School to become New Mills Grammar was begun on the Grammar School site in 1914. Mr. Nichols then brought across the valley older children, leaving 350 on the Spring Bank premises and taking about 200 across the valley.

Let us all register, then, in the town and around that sixty years or so ago we were one unit and we are becoming one again although as a split school, which is unlucky, the younger children will be left this side of the valley and the older boys and girls will, again, be across the other side. Sixty years has seen separate ways. In the last few years there has been a coming together in the Sixth form and at thirteen plus, and during the last year, in preparation for the comprehensive, large numbers of children coming across – staff committees, staff getting to know one another and boys and girls so we all shall not be new to one another in September by any means. We shall be reuniting across the town into one school. We should have liked to have welcomed everybody onto the main site just as everybody started on the Spring Bank site, but it is not to be, not for some time anyway. We shall function in split buildings. We won't pretend it is not a disadvantage, but it is one that we intend to overcome and one we intend, in fact, to turn into an advantage.

The last year has been a unique year for Spring Bank, a school which has being running in a building which is being radically altered around everyone. Spring Bank comes into the comprehensive with a feeling that it has survived all the disruptions and it therefore has courage ready for the new situation with a feeling of pride and unity'

Philip went on to talk about the future of the combined new school. Again he said that 'there is nothing to fear, we move into a position of great strength; we need not worry, but only flattered if there is any envy of us; we need not doubt that the general standard of work will improve; we need not have any doubt that for both the grammar school pupils and those from Spring Bank will benefit from the flexibility of courses, the number of staff (over 70) and above all the number of subjects. It is time therefore, to pin one's flag – my flag – firmly to the comprehensive mast. There cannot be any doubt that what we are doing is right. Some say you should not form comprehensives until you have a building purpose built and certainly I thought so and, in some ways, think so. But when I think that might have been eight years – and we should have eight years more of the present division and separateness – then I cannot believe that this would have been right and I think it worth going ahead – even in split buildings – because I know we are going to do so much for so many.'

He went on to outline how the school would be run - the Lower School Department at Spring Bank with eight first forms and eight second forms. There is to be two bands of children, mixed ability with four first streams and then three streams in the second band and then a remedial group. All can move up or down, there will be complete flexibility. In the third year all children will come to the main site, where they have been coming for P.E., games and swimming from the Lower School, so they will know it, know us and prefects will have been with them in the Lower School from the Sixth forms so they will know the Sixth.

While they are in the lower school they will have assembled once a fortnight in the main gymnasium so that all can meet as a school and we can build esprit there. We avoid the extreme of absolute mixed ability groups across the whole system but we shall have mixed ability within a band. And yet we allow for anyone to come right through to the Upper Sixth if they want to, even though they may start in the first form remedial. Whatever the system in the Lower School, in the third year everybody will have a chance, and will have the background to proceed onto a course in the third year, which is partially like the Lower School and partially like exam work and from that they will proceed to exam courses in the fourth year.

The Middle School consists of third, fourth and fifth Formers on the main site. Hopefully all children who are now in the second year will make good use of the fact that they must stay until sixteen.

There will be the Sixth Form School, still taking boys and girls from Chapel Secondary School, which will include new courses for Sixth formers who will not be just taking A levels but could be taking a combination of A Level work, repeating CSEs or O level, Advanced CSE work, which is going to come, other kind of exams or non-exam courses, new courses or one year Sixth form courses. There is something for everyone.

The school will be divided for subject work into seven main subject areas – English, Mathematics, Science, Languages, Environmental Studies, Creative Studies and Physical Education. There will in addition be a Remedial department, and a Careers and Counselling Department.

Buildings are being refurbished and constructed. We are really proud of our new swimming pool which has just been completed and a new gymnasium soon to be completed, which is something I have always wanted. Playing fields are not as good as we had hoped for; we shall still have to go on using the Youth Club, Derby Road, and Watford Bridge. We are getting the playing fields ready in Marsh Lane, which is not too far from the main school. The red grade hard playing area will soon be ready and then there will be facilities for soccer, rugby, hockey, netball, hard play areas, jumping pits, running tracks, cricket square, practice golf and a £10,000 pavilion in the near future. Also in the near future we shall have our new hall and the first part of the Sixth form suite.

All this could not have come about if it had not been for the generosity of Derbyshire County Education Authority. The teaching staffing is generous; the secretarial and ancillary staffing is generous. There is £10,000 for the pavilion, £32,000 for the playing fields, £2,000 having been put on to the main buildings and £35,000 has been spent on the restructuring of the Lower School at Spring Bank. The new main buildings on the main site at the grammar school will have cost over £130,000 and we have another £60,000 to be spent there. We have had substantial sums of money for the furniture, apparatus and equipment. The swimming pool was given £2,500 from the County whilst the PTA raised a further £2,500.

In September there will be over 1,200 pupils in this new school. In my belief we are going to have a great and strong school in New Mills academically and in practical things, in drama, in music, aesthetically in every way. The unified school may be one of the strongest, should be one of the strongest in Derbyshire. Finally I say to parents, do not let your boys and girls give in. Take advantage of anything I have spoken about of the facilities, of the staffing, of the courses, of the work, of taking exams, of getting the right jobs, of pushing on to their ability road. Above all, of enjoying the school, in gaining every day from it some new feeling that life is worthwhile, some new windows been opened in each new lesson every day, eight times a day, something new, something joyous and fine, and something which will make them mature more easily into better adults, whose personalities have developed and fulfilled on all fronts. Now I say to you boys and girls what is important for you is to use the facilities, don't spoil them, don't neglect them, become a leader of some aspect of school life, push on with your work, take advantage of what we offer and come and ask us questions as many and as often as you like. Don't feel, even if you have only two terms to go in the new school that it is not there for you – it is. We have something for you, something to help you, something to give you more fun, a better career and it is a remarkable experiment.

Life at school is based on two main educational principles: Every child has the right to be himself and to grow into the kind of person that he has it within him to become and that no child can reach maturity without learning to live fully and happily with his fellows. Let us aim for these; and you boys and girls come along and aim with us.'

And so in September 1970 as the High Peak Reporter said in its headline on the 11 September 1970 'A bit of local history is made - All in school opens.' It reported that 'New Mills School opened on Tuesday, absorbing 1,120 pupils from the former grammar and secondary modern schools, and the eleven year pupils who, since the first time since the 1944 Act were not segregated by the 11-plus examination.

Although the children from the New Mills and Hayfield area took the 11-plus examination as a safety precaution – in case everything was not ready for the turn over – the results were not made known and all the children have entered the new school, formerly Spring Bank County Secondary School, together.

Children from Whaley Bridge and Chapel en le Frith will, however, still enter New Mills School on a selective basis, until the emergence of a comprehensive school at Chapel in the near future.'

Georgina Hutber was the first 'Head of School' for this the New Mills School. She transferred to New Mills Grammar School in 1968 and recalls some forty years later 'I was not sure what had hit me on the day I arrived at New Mills Grammar School. Fresh from a fairly small girls' grammar school, I was overwhelmed by the size of the school and the smallness of its headmaster. Bombastic, ginger and freckled, P.H.V. whirled round the school making everyone tremble at the speed of his coming and going. His ideas seemed revolutionary to me – encourage the brightest and best to take GCE O levels a year early and spend three years in the Sixth form, take the Oxbridge entry exams in the third year Sixth while pursuing a range of studies in subjects other than one's chosen subjects...In fact, looking back, 'minority time' was probably one of his greatest ideas, studying another language (in my case Russian), Current Affairs, Music, Sport, English Literature, Drama, modern Maths, etc., for three half days a week – turning his Sixth Form into well-rounded individuals.

As pupils, we were not sure whether to love him or hate him, but we could not deny his energy in shaping the school in his image of good education.'

New Mills School's first Speech Day was held in November 1970; just two months after the comprehensive school came into existence. The then Chair Person of the Governing body Mrs. Weston, said that a lot of hard work had been put into the comprehensive school scheme, particularly by the steering committee, set up to go into the question of reorganisation in detail and especially by Mr. Vennis – all helping the changeover to go smoothly. Mrs Weston went on to say 'Last year when we met, we were in a period of doubt and anticipation. Doubt as to how the plans would work out, and about the change to comprehensive, and anticipation because, in spite of all the difficulties we saw what the possibilities were in a comprehensive school.' One of the greatest difficulties had been the working out of a timetable, with 74 members of staff and over one thousand children. Philip said 'If it is not quite a child based timetable in single terms, it very nearly is so. I do not think that very much more time or work could possibly have been put into it. The other major problem for the new school to face was that of the split building. Although boys and girls in the lower school were happy enough, enjoying the best of both worlds, the problem was for the staff. We must be the most travelled staff in terms in numbers of journeys and the number of people making them, in the country. (Colour photograph 20.) However they are enjoying it and the staff are marvellous in their willingness to lend their cars for the County's purposes. The usual number of journeys in a week between schools is 223. In addition there are special buses bringing boys and girls from the lower school to the main building for physical education.'

One of Philip's main messages in his speech was the difficult task of making Sixth formers work hard. He said that A level results were quite good, but quite clearly not good enough. I have said for many years that the young people in the Sixth form find it cosy and comfortable and that is good. They seem to enjoy coming and in a way they come almost too easily and comfortably. Whether that is our fault or not I do not know. It may be a national feeling that this should be so. They have their own unit and this is good. In the middle of this, however, we do find it more and more difficult to make them work, with any persistence and tenacity for A level, except the very ablest, quite able people are getting grades much lower than they could do, and some not getting A levels at all, who clearly could do. It is partly the result of the entry system, in which they know they can gain an entry with lower grades or perhaps no grades or that the grades signified by University or College are not going to be stuck to in the event. Perhaps however this is good. I do not wish to say that nobody works, I do not want to say that the A level results weren't good in places, but they were patchy and we do want, from parents and Sixth Formers, a much greater effort this year, a belief that it matters that you get the A levels worthy of your ability and that to set off on a course, even though you had got in with A levels lower than you might have gained had you worked hard, is not good for work in the future at College or University or for your career. We want a considerable effort here.'

At the end of what was to be his last Speech Day at New Mills Philip said 'We decided to have a Speech Day as a new school, to show some *esprit* and union, it is not a Speech Day in the old sense I hope, though the best things from the Grammar School continue in every kind of way, especially a love of proper learning, but in addition we hope to see a further flowering in music and speech and drama, and we hope to see a situation where every boy and girl can hope, quite easily, to draw on a prize for something. Competition is not bad, in my belief, if it is truthfully open to all in each ability and age group and in each interest group. We want to run an open, free, co-operative school where discipline is self-discipline and rests on each child separately, different in a way from the old style Grammar School in its attitude to pupils, as I hope New Mills Grammar School had grown to be. This is our idea, where there is no fear of punishment, though that may sometimes be needed, where the things work because people want it to work and enjoy working it, where co-operation reigns and where the only form of punishment is the attitude or nod of ones fellows and where some kind of self-discipline slowly emerges for each boy and girl at each of their stages of puberty and each of their stages of growth. This is our aim, where all shall mix together.'

Philip began applying for other jobs at the beginning of the academic year of 1970. His main referee was the Associate Director of Derbyshire Education Committee, W.K. Fowler who wrote of Philip 'He is not the easiest of people from the point of view of an Assistant Director for Secondary Education because he cares a very great deal about his school and does not easily take no for an answer. So far as he is concerned this is rightly the most important secondary school in the County. He has considerable abilities, he is a very good schoolmaster, he is aware of the changes in young people and the social trends that affect them; he cares a great deal about every boy and girl in his school. He has shown himself to be a man of some educational vision with considerable powers of leadership. At his present school he has widened very considerably the curriculum opportunities both in academic and technical subjects. The size of the Sixth form has markedly increased from 82 to 200 during his headship and the range of options in the Sixth form which is now being offered is quite notable, for a school of this size. Mr. Vennis has, until recently, personally directed the work in Drama in the school and under his guidance it has become outstanding. A very sensitive production of 'Romeo and Juliet' was taken to Alsfeld in Germany as part of the twinning scheme, in which the school has been very active.

Mr. Vennis is keenly alive to general trends in education and whilst insistent on maintaining the high academic standards which have for so long been the prerogative of the grammar schools, he has been equally anxious to direct the activities of the Sixth formers in particular into worthwhile and helpful community projects. His vitality and leadership show themselves in every aspect of school life. His relationships with his staff, a high proportion of whom are quite young, are good, and he believes in consulting his staff about new ideas.

With regard to his relationships with parents, Mr. Vennis has reorganised and strengthened the Parent Teacher Association and they appear to give great co-operation and show considerable interest in the work of the school. There is no doubt in my mind that his school, in all its activities, is extremely vigorous and lively. Mr. Vennis' resourcefulness and determination are evident in everything that he does.

The beginning of 1971 saw Philip appointed Principal of Itchen Sixth Form College in Southampton. But before his departure from New Mills School he was to sort out the consequences of an arson attack on the new buildings on the main site. The school's gymnasium and most of the equipment were virtually destroyed and changing rooms were badly damaged. The engineering workshop was put out of action, machinery in the laundrette was damaged and 500 towels were destroyed. At the time of the attack in March 1971 Philip said 'We have over one thousand pupils and all will be affected by the closure of the new wing.'

In the School magazine two articles written by Philip were published on his leaving New Mills. The first article titled 'As Far As Who Goes Farthest' sums up his time in New Mills and some of the achievements of his eight and a half year tenure ship. The second article is some of his personal memories and is titled 'Cor; What Larks, eh, Pip! both articles are reproduced here.

'But education is a rather serious business. I am for the comprehensive school, and was when I came – and had been for some time. My experience dates back now to when I became Deputy head of a Comprehensive in Staffordshire in 1958 – four years there as Deputy Head, eight years as the Headmaster of a rural Grammar that became a Comprehensive. I feel old in the tooth and in the game as I go to run a Sixth Form College in Southampton.

There are no final answers in education. All ways must be tried as we move forward. The Sixth Form College may prove to be one of the answers to some of our prime dilemmas in comprehensive education.

But it is of course a central myth that schools really differ very much from one another. There are good and bad grammars, secondary moderns, comprehensives and no doubt Sixth Form Colleges. It's the staff and the pupils and the parents and the governors and the Authority in some kind of working partnership that matters, and the Headmaster is the lynch pin of that set up. His style, his originality, his ideas, matter most in keeping the whole thing moving as a unit. We've had our struggles here, we've had our problems. I've sat through innumerable serious meetings on I don't know how many plans of how to go comprehensive in this area. We've had grinding disappointments and endured savage and bitter attacks during the years from this quarter or that – and at this meeting and that.

This area is vexed by its geographical makeup much more, I would think, than most areas in England. It feels no unity as an area; it is in fact a curiosity

234

that it's not divided, middle and working class, or rural and town, so much as township against township and this has ground several good plans into the dust, in my time here.

However, with what good will we could, we accepted the split school and the fact that the Grammar School would in the end be divided, but we won an area Sixth Form – in my view a great victory. We fought a long long delaying battle until the ground was sure and we could form a comprehensive properly; we had therefore the time (essential in my view) to build up a staff in the Grammar School who were to be great leaders of the combined school, and who were not afraid of putting new ideas forward and new methods into action. As I said so often, we owe a great deal in England to the State Grammar School and we must try to carry through what is best of that. I also said that we had nothing to fear, that we were strong in ability, in unity and in ideas and these things would carry us on. So I believe it has happened; we've had great help from specialist staff from Spring Bank and new staff too, eager to accept our new educational revolutions in ideas and methods.

In trying to erect a truly educational timetable which would push our opportunities in all directions, we have uncovered an unlooked for array of unusual talents and interests. The timetable is the servant of the school, and it should, in my belief, stand on its head if necessary to make 'Abyssinian' so to say, available for the one pupil that wants to study it. But it does take time and patience and a belief that such a timetable matters, and it makes one remember one's office as a place whose walls contracted as the night wore on, until making such a timetable seemed a long long nightmare of a fight against time.

It is worth saying too how much I remember having to soothe this girl or that boy over results and over waiting for entry of having no entry to this or that University or College; and how I remember feeling personally hurt by the immense savagery of our system which makes so apparently much depend upon Certificates – when the results come out - and some have some and some have none – the late twentieth century version of the 'haves' and 'have nots'. Yet there are great successes here, persuasions by phone, persuasions of Sixth formers to go on, making more ambitious the less ambitious – on the whole a story of many successes.

To me, the Sixth form and their work and their fun remain the teenagers I most enjoy – sharp minds getting sharper, being sharpened against one's own - 'diamond cut diamond' all day through.

Now here we are, in an obviously unified school where each, I hope, feels he or she is 'somebody', where new ideas are current but not rampant, where great new ventures, like the Creative Studies, or the Engineering Science, or the Nuffield Classics, or our new modern language methods, or our modern Maths, or our Environmental Studies or Local Studies or Social Studies are being ventured and adventured every day. Some – what seemed new, like Minority Time, is now 'old hat!' Some that seemed progressive, like a Prefect's Council, is passé. That is as it should be; a decade has passed; there are new styles, new ideas, new modes: we move on and so we should – to new paths in communication, consultation, participation – aiming always for a more educated general citizenry as well for high-flying leaders. Nevertheless schools in my view must be a shade sceptical of the newness and rawness of the time in which they live. Perhaps they should average at two to five years behind the times in some ways – certainly I believe in terms of fashion. During my time here I've lived through, as it were, the life and death of the Beatle Empire. At the time I was known for saying that 'Yea, Yea, Yea' would also pass, and pass it has. Schools must cast an extremely sceptical eye on the passing show and stand for what truly matters and what is most likely to be lasting.

They must, with D.H. Lawrence 'stand for life and creation amid all this death and destruction' and they must stand always for man as a private being, as the tolerant animal, and for a belief in Burn's dictum that 'A man's a man, for all that'. And so he is and so he shall be.

And rightly, from time to time I've stressed in assembly, the whole question of racial problems, and how boys and girls growing up ought to view others with a liberal, tolerant eye, trying to see each person as a person; they should take forward, as I've always said at leavers' services, no loyalty to the school as an institution, only a belief that some of what we have said may be worth remembering in their coming relations with their fellow-men.

Now new moves are with us – women's liberation – right in so many ways, new forms of mixed ability, new ideas for running comprehensives – all this is good. Permissiveness too, good where it leads to liberty but not where it leads to licence. I have tried to see that the single means, as I know it, by which personality may be developed in school life most quickly – that is Drama – has had a proper and strong place on and off the timetable. We were among the first grammar schools to put it in that place and I hope it will always remain there – not only the great school play which is like the great First Xl at Soccer or Hockey, but drama on the timetable for all.

And so now, I wish every boy and girl, past, present and future, but of course particularly present, all proper success in life; by which I mean a life long contentment and a completion of each one's personality; this may come partly by using the school to its uttermost. I hope you all grow up to be citizens who care for one another and for every other citizen, no matter who he or she may be or from where or of what colour or race or religion or creed, he or she may come. It does not matter. If you belong to a club and that club makes you divisive whether it be Christianity or any other, that is negative. As I understand it, the great Christian message is for love, and for love in a family, and I believe us all to be of one family. I hope too you will grow up to be sceptical and questioning and participating and as unlike sheep as possible.

With Martin Luther King, so tragically murdered and for whom we had such moving assemblies, I say 'I have a dream' and that dream is one where boys and girls shall grow up to believe in a unifying love of each for all – which will be based on an overwhelming tolerance for one another's faults; for these we have

"As far as who goes farthest" indeed, but more importantly
"Goodwill subdues Violence as Water Quenches Fire"
"And Farewells goes out sighing."

The second article contains many memories and begins with the quotation "Cor, What Larks, eh, Pip!" 'This quotation from Dickens' "Dear Joe the Blacksmith, when he writes to his Pip in London, is absolutely apt for one view of my nearly nine years here; it has been "Great Expectations" indeed. We have had, my colleagues, the Sixth form, and I, endless, indeed endless, streams of laughter. We have seen the joke at every turn and it is difficult now to recall however, the many committee meetings and other kinds of meetings and assemblies, private and public, where we have laughed at the various fantastic situations in which we have found ourselves. I remember with great pleasure a great many light-hearted moments through all the years. The many and extraordinary funny things that happen on the way to going comprehensive belie description.

I remember too those lovely but funny things that happened in "Romeo and Juliet" with "a rose (nylon) by any other name" floating down in the Alsfeld night, that the music would not work and the tape went backwards behind the stage at Alsfeld. I remember the contrived non-balcony for the performance going, and I remember too the breathtakingly moving moments in the play, especially between Marjorie Morton as the Nurse and Helen Miller as Juliet, it's a play, it always has been and it always will be, for the young in heart, and blessed are they; it's for tears, and some laughter too. Who of those involved, and I alone am left, on staff or in the school, can forget quelling that audience in a German beer house on a rainy night - or the absolute magic of the last performance as Juliet's body was carried out to Favre's Pavane and then at the end

"A glooming peace this morning with it brings;
The Sun, for sorrow, will not show his head:
Go hence, to have more talk of these sad things;
Some shall be pardon'd, and some, punished:
For never was a Story of more woe
Than this of Juliet and her Romeo."

And we played then from "West Side Story" – "Somewhere a place for us" – in 45 or so productions in school life I cannot remember a more gloriously apt or indeed sadder moment indeed.

Two years later came 'Antony and Cleopatra' and the frightful and frightening chaos of the monument in the hall, of the falls and the marchings and the fights and the armies, of Pompey's Pirates and Roman swords and great battles and Hibbert's voice and that fine performance from Christopher Clarke as Enobarbus, and moving moments like Jean Vernon's weeping Octavia, and Caesar's (Derrick Martin) "He calls me boy". Roger Garlick's mountain of a voice and mountain of a death were wonderful things and Mary Rimington closing the evening with her dream of the perfect man –

> "I dream'd there was an Emperor Antony:
> O, such another sleep, that I might see
> But such another man!
> His face was as the heavens; and therein stuck
> A sun and moon, which kept their course, and lighted
> The little O, the earth."

Shakespeare in school life points a little finger towards perfection, towards an achievement, towards creation, towards knowing one of the great dramatic works of art. He remains for me the best school play because on so many levels he can be enjoyed and understood and so many people can gain something from so many rehearsals. But what a business Drama at New Mills has been, with its final lurch to the Art Theatre the extraordinary business of putting up a set somewhere, assembling around it, moving in the last week to another place with one rehearsal only, and who remembers now that funny but fine outing in the snow with 'Macbeth' – 60 in all – to St. Helena's Girls School at Chesterfield? They certainly wondered at us!

I remember that at New Mills, among some things to remember, have been the Grammar School's assemblies in our funny hall as it was, with so many gathered to breathe in and out – some fine moments, even when they were round an Egyptian monument. We always achieved the impossible. I remember weeks connected with Churchill's death, and other moving assemblies – connected I hope with our world now. Speech Day concerts too – I savoured – again on Churchill or Love or getting to the moon, all moving for me.

The whole pleasure of school life is inextricably woven with its concomitant sadness; it is the passing scene and people come and go and staff come and go and yet the underlying growth goes on. The school is never weakened by its losses; new blood is always on the way in.

I remember amusing evenings with colleagues in pubs and the long, long staff meetings about entries – difficult decisions arrived at about who should take what. I remember with pleasure a long list of Heads of School and Head Girls and Boys and Prefects Councillors all – those attempting to lead the Grammar School as it grew to be a Grammar Tech and then grew again to be Comprehensive. And now that last year before we changed when hard work on the Steering Committee and even to midnight or 1 a.m. was gained amid good laughter, good colleagues and a timetable made in an atmosphere of work but also of hope and fun. And so to two terms in a Comprehensive that I believe to be well on its way to being a true success story.

We had P.T.A. forums and Sixth Form forums, we had wine and cheese evenings, we had fantastic sponsored walks and efforts for the swimming pool – wanted for so long and finally achieved after so much effort by so few. We had long music and verse evenings and some very fine language evenings and wonderfully remembered first and second form Drama – and certainly fine moments in Sixth form Drama from Jean Vernon as Antigone to Jane Barnsley as Blanche. We had additions to the school which caused us fun and fury like the language laboratory and the numerous terrapins and what seemed so funny at first and which we have grown so used to, the quite frightful if not frightening so-called Sixth Form House, and its furnishing by the P.T.A. There was growth in all directions as suited England in the sixties. I hope we met each year with the right decisions for that year the right growth at the right time: I know we met it with worry. I know we met it with hard work, I remember too we met it with some fun.

Schools are sometimes inclined to think too seriously of themselves. We at any rate had various school mottos. I am still rather for "As far as who goes farthest" but I quite like "It's your laughter we're after" and all have seen the joke in "There's always Monday," – and "you will have me in tears in a minute!"

There will be no more Mondays I'm afraid for me.' Of course, there were many compliments and tributes paid to Philip at various leaving events at the end of the Spring Term in April 1971. One of the longest and most heartfelt tributes came from Mr .A.E. Read, who was Deputy headmaster under Philip and was appointed Headmaster when Philip left for Southampton. 'Mr. Vennis came to the Headmastership of New Mills Grammar School in September, 1962, the fourth of a distinguished line of Headmasters, and though the change of Head is always a most important event in the life of any school, this particular change was to prove a most significant one.

A new Headmaster should bring to a school some fresh contribution in his philosophy of school life, whilst, at the same time, recognising the traditions of his school and the need for some degree of continuity. He must, therefore, have regard for past, present and future, and this was particularly true of a Grammar School of the early Sixties.

I do not often look backwards – but, of course, this is one moment when it is fitting to do so. New Mills Grammar School had already established a fine reputation for itself, and had already faced something of the need for some degree of development and expansion in the construction of the new Science Block and in some reconstruction schemes within the Main Block.

The arrival of Mr. Vennis soon saw the mark of further changes directed especially towards the life of the pupils in the school, in the extension of the House system, and in the setting up of a School Parliament and a Prefects' Council, both with the general aim of creating a wider and more democratic field of school government, involving more of the pupils themselves. Yet those were comparatively minor changes, though they reflected something of the nature of things to come.

The headmaster of an English Secondary School still has a tremendous influence on the life of the school in his charge, and rightly so. The things which happen in his school are, on the whole, the things he wishes to happen. Consequently, by his personal drive, enthusiasm, and sense of conviction of the rightness of his far reaching aims, Mr. Vennis has been able to put into effect the remarkable change to a Comprehensive system of education in New Mills and district.

As I look back over the past eight and a half years, the following points come especially to my mind. First, the widening of the scope of the Sixth form to include not only those pupils who would by nature assume the responsibilities of leadership in the life of the community at large, but also those of somewhat less academic ability who have since been able to look back with pleasure and satisfaction on their years in the Sixth Form. This development has, I am glad to say, continued to the extent that there are now in the Sixth Form those who have something to gain just by being there in the Sixth form atmosphere of school life. We have now reached the stage of assuming that the majority of fifth formers will regard themselves as potential Sixth formers, not only for the academic advantages to be gained, but also for what they will gain as people. All this does not mean of course that members of the Sixth are spared the pressures brought to bear on them to make them see the need for hard work. That too is part of a headmaster's job.

The second major contribution to the general life of the school has been in the field of drama, not only by the encouragement of drama as a school subject in the curriculum, but by the productions under Mr. Vennis' direction given by members of the school. The production of "Romeo and Juliet" both in New Mills and Alsfeld, must surely rank high in the field of school drama and the reputation of this was upheld in that of "Antony and Cleopatra". For those who took part in these productions, they were, I am sure, never to be forgotten, emotional experiences. Perhaps even more important however was Mr. Vennis' readiness to hand on to other members of staff the possibilities of achievements of this kind. This is, in a way, one of the penalties of being a Head; one cannot always follow one's own interests – there is no time – and one must encourage others to do this in their general contribution to the success of the school.

Certainly, by a tremendous effort, P.H.V. has helped many to gain their ends, and all U.C.C.A. candidates (and other eighteen plus pupils) will know how much time has been spent on testimonials and on interviewing techniques. The same time consuming energy has been spent also on members of staff who have been encouraged to move on when it has been in their interests to do so. Thus, many members of staff have owed a great deal to this kind of unselfishness which has resulted in their personal promotion, even at the expense of the school itself. At the same time, newly appointed staff have brought to us their own personal contributions to the school, and we now have a fine staff in a staffroom which in outlook is both alive and progressive. All this is part of the Headmaster's achievement.

Above all, however, has been the tremendous achievement of the establishing of our Comprehensive School in New Mills, as the result of an enormous amount of work, foresight and careful planning. Mr. Vennis has been the driving force behind all the preliminary work, and, though he would be the first to acknowledge the value of the help of others in this mammoth task, the credit is mainly his.

There are, therefore, certain personal qualities for which we express our gratitude. Mr. Vennis has always shown a spirit of generosity in so many ways – generosity in 'things' and generosity of spirit. His own home has been so often open to so many people connected with the school; the 'van' has so often escorted many people home at a late hour. Then too has been his obvious sense of humour without which I believe a school cannot really function happily. The Head's room has still remained, on occasion, a place of judgement – but more often it has been an 'open house' for meeting and repartee in the wider sense of the school. Above all, in these personal qualities, has been his deep sense of understanding of personal matters of a domestic nature in the lives of both the staff and pupils. He has always realised that even comparatively trivial matters may suddenly loom large as crises in a person's life – and these have always been treated with respect and sympathetic understanding. In matters in general Mr. Vennis always has a liberal outlook, especially with regard to such matters as education, religion, and such explosive matters as that of colour and racial prejudice. But I believe that those in the teaching profession must be idealists even at the risk of being thought impractical and unrealistic. We must give a lead in these matters – if we do not do so, we fail in our prime duty.

We shall miss all these things, and I know that Mr. Vennis will miss us, particularly the younger elements in the life of New Mills School. But that is how life goes. There comes a time in life when one must accept the challenge of a new venture. All experiences add up to the final assessment.

Mr. Vennis goes to Southampton with our very best wishes for his future success as Head of a Sixth Form College, with its challenge and opportunity. The same good wishes are extended from us all to Mrs. Vennis, who so generously entertained many of us at their home and who has been such inner strength to Mr. Vennis in his work. We think too of their delightful children who will, we hope, remember something of us in the years to come.

Shall we hear still those catch phrases 'You will have me in tears in a minute' or 'There's always Monday morning'. No I fear not. They will become part of a past phase in the development of educational life in New Mills, but to us, who shared that time, they will be a personal memory.'

CHAPTER 8

Itchen Sixth Form College Southampton

Itchen College lies to the east of the City of Southampton in Bitterne. Southampton City has a history dating back to Roman beginnings. About 70 AD the Romans built a town on the bend in the River Itchen where Bitterne now stands. This sheltered position on the Itchen with double tides made it an ideal port. In Roman times it was a major port capable of accommodating ocean going vessels. By 450 AD, Clausentum, the name given to the town by the Romans, was enduring attacks from Jutes and Saxons, after unsuccessfully extending the fortifications, the Romans were defeated and retreated from Clausentum.

The Saxon King, Ine established Hamwic on the other side of the river Itchen between 690-850 AD, in the area where St.Mary's Church stands today. Saxon Southampton was a large and important port with a population between 4,000 – 5,000 people. Many were cratfts people engaged in pottery making, weaving and bone working and some were merchants. Women weavers made woollen cloth and the main export from the port was wool. Trade took place between Southampton and France, the Netherlands, Scandinavia and the Rhine Valley.

In the ninth and tenth centuries Saxon Southampton suffered raids from 840 AD onwards by the Vikings and Hamwic began to decline. Later in the century King Alfred (King of Wessex from 871 – 899) defended the town by creating burghs (later termed boroughs) against the Danes. It was however, thought that these Danish raids and the silting up of the River Itchen brought about the decline of tenth century Southampton. Many people moved to a new settlement on higher ground beside the River Test, called Hamtun. The name changed from Hamtun to Hampton, the Ham in Hampshire is taken from Hampton, with the county once being called Hamtunshire.

Following the Norman Conquest in 1066, Frenchmen came to live in Southampton which by now was on the east bank of the River Test. Many of these Normans settled around French Street and Bugle Street and worshipped in St.Michael's Church, which was founded in 1070 and is the oldest building still in use in modern Southampton. Southampton again became a major port, involved with the import of French and Spanish wine in exchange for wool and cloth. Southampton was prosperous, unlike many other parts of the country who suffered disruption and poverty under the Normans. Unfortunately the town was ransacked in 1338 by French, Genoese and Monegasque ships that landed near St.Michael's Square. They killed many women and children who were sheltering in St.Michael's church, although many inhabitants fled to the countryside. Many houses were burnt down, but the following morning the English counterattacked and killed about three hundred of the invaders. The Hundred Years War was nearly two years old when Southampton suffered these raids. However, the Hundred Years War of 1337 – 1453 also helped Southampton's prosperity, as ships were built for the Navy in Southampton and the town was the main port for the departing Army, which brought business to local food providers.

By the end of the fourteenth century such medieval customs as the feudal system had begun to decline, with the Black Death, the plague of 1348 resulting in a shortage of labour and thereby helping this decline.

Wool was England's main export at this time, and this contributed to Southampton's increased prosperity. The area in which Itchen College now stands, would have been grazed by sheep, as was the rest of Bitterne, Sholing and Thornhill. Southampton was the third busiest port in England after London and Bristol.

Trade was beginning to decline in the late fifteenth and early sixteenth century and Southampton ceased to be an important port by 1600, as other ports were allowed to import wine, which had previously been the town's prerogative. Southampton did however, have coastal trade, and many goods were transported along the coast. Decline also affected the town buildings and some houses became dilapidated.

Southampton recovered with the help from the influx of Huguenot craftsmen who fled religious persecution in Belgium and settled in the town. The Huguenots were skilled weavers and introduced the manufacture of serge cloth into England and were an important part in the revival of the town's fortunes. In 1620, Southampton was the departing port for the Pilgrim Fathers aboard 'The Mayflower'. The Pilgrim Fathers chartered 'The Mayflower' to sail to the New World in order to escape religious oppression in England. It was a good stout ocean going ship of 180 tons and sailed from London with about seventy people on board and arrived in Southampton at the end of July 1620. The Mayflower departed on 15 August sailing to Plymouth where it finally departed England with a total of one hundred and two passengers on board on 6 September 1620. The English Civil War, 1642 – 46 saw a Parliamentary Garrison move into Southampton. In Bitterne, the troops plundered the small population for food as they passed through the village. On the whole the seventeenth century for the town of Southampton was one of decline, with some areas of the town falling into neglect. This was partly due to the Great Plague of 1665 as about one eighth of the town's population had died, it took almost a year for life to return to normality. By the mid eighteenth century Southampton's fortunes were on the rise as the town became a fashionable spa and resort. After successive royal visits by Frederick, Prince of Wales (1707-1751) the town's business improved, hotels were renovated and the town expanded. Local farming communities like Bitterne reaped the benefit for the need for more produce. As a result some of the wealthy visitors decided to live in Southampton and began to build houses in areas such as Bitterne, which gave them views across the River Itchen and beyond. These homes of the gentry then needed servants and tradesmen to help support their homes, so cottages and shops were then built. Improvements in communications further stimulated the growth of Bitterne village.

Visitor numbers declined after Southampton lost favour as a Spa resort to the town of Brighton, and by 1820 it faced a very different future. Its fortunes as a port had begun to recover as trade began to revive. Southampton had been a port of embarkation for armies fighting overseas. Soldiers passing through during the Napoleonic Wars (1803-1815) brought prosperity to the area. The port expanded with timber, grain, building stone, slate and coal as well as wine and fresh fruit. A new dock was built in 1838-42 to cope with this increase of trade. In 1841 the Ordnance Survey Department was transferred from the Tower of London to Southampton, thus providing employment for many local people. The town continued to expand and grow. Henry Robinson Hartley left a bequest of £103,887 for the establishment of an educational institute, for the study of sciences and classical and oriental literature. The first building was in the lower High Street and was known as the Hartley Institute, before moving to new buildings in Highfield in 1919, where the beginnings of the University of Southampton were established, becoming a full university just over one hundred years after the bequest in 1952.

Fom the 1880s the North Atlantic trade had increased and White Star moved their Trans Atlantic liners to Southampton in 1907. The docks were further expanded in 1890-1911. One of Southampton's tragedies was the sinking of the RMS Titanic, in 1912, which had sailed from the port and four out of every five crew on board were from the town, with about one third of those who died also coming from the town. Cunard was based in Southampton from 1919, with their Blue Riband liners RMS Queen Mary and RMS Queen Elizabeth.

Southampton was an important staging post for the military in the First World War, with over eight million troops passing through on their way to the front, as well as 800,000 horses and mules, 177,000 vehicles and 14,000 guns.

Southampton lost more than two thousand men in the conflict.

Following the First World War, Southampton continued to grow and develop, in the thirties passenger traffic expanded with about seventy five thousand people passing through the port in 1938. Major imports still included fruit, potatoes, grain, timber and wool, with the exporting of many manufactured goods as well. Southampton Civic Centre was built between 1932 and 1939.

Southampton suffered very badly during the Second World War, because of its strategic importance as a major commercial port, with six hundred and thirty one residents losing their lives in the bombing. Southampton once again became the main embarkation and supply port for the war. Over three million service men and women passed through the town from D-Day until the end of the war in 1945. One of the heaviest bombing raids took place in September 1940 in which the Spitfire factory was destroyed as well as neighbouring houses, workers and civilians were killed. More than four thousand houses were destroyed throughout the town and eleven thousand seriously damaged. Almost all of the old town and shopping centre had been destroyed. .

Rapid post war development took place following the Second World War since there was an acute housing shortage. With all of this development the Council found it necessary to build thirty two new schools in Southampton between 1950 and 1964. The centre of the town's layout was altered, with some of the ruined shops being replaced in the High Street and Above Bar in 1956. In the fifties and sixties Southampton remained the foremost passenger port in Britain, with over half a million passengers passing through the port in 1963. About four per cent of the national imports arrived at the port in the 1960s. Southampton was given City status in 1964. In the seventies containerisation became much more important and this meant that some of the old docks were no longer needed and as air travel became cheaper in the sixties, the number of passengers passing through the port declined and in eighties some of the old docks were converted into shops, offices and marinas.

Shipbuilding and heavy engineering continued in the Old Docks and along the banks of the River Itchen in the fifties and sixties, and small industries began to come to the area. But from the eighties jobs in the manufacturing industries started to decline with more jobs opening up in banking, insurance and finance. Tourism became an increasingly important industry with places like the thirteenth century 'Merchants House' being opened as a museum in 1988. Southampton has always benefitted and been influenced by the sea and rivers. The city is at the northern tip of the Southampton Water, a deep water estuary, which is a ria, formed at the end of the last Ice Age. The River Test converges with the River Itchen and continues to the sea as Southampton Water, which flows into the Solent. The River Test, which has salt marshes that make it ideal for salmon fishing, runs along the western edge of the City, whilst the River Itchen splits Southampton in two – the east, where Bitterne and Itchen College are to be found and the west, with the City centre being located between the two rivers. Southampton Water has the benefit of a double high tide with two peaks. This unusual phenomenon is not caused by the two entrances to the Solent or to the Isle of Wight as is commonly believed, but it is due to the manifestation of the Shallow Water Tide. This tide is a distortional effect upon the astronomically generated tide caused by shallow waters and begins somewhere of Start Point, and manifests itself as a Double Low Water at Portland and then becomes a Double High Water at Southampton.

A history of Itchen Grammar School 1906 to 1971

'The changes that took place in the School were considerable, but they bore little relation to the even greater, more numerous and far reaching changes in education which were yet to come'. (P.H.V. 1962)

Itchen Grammar School's early history reflects the development of secondary education in the Itchen area from its earliest beginnings – a pupil teacher centre, which came about as a direct result of the 1902 Education Act. In 1902, the Itchen area was under the administration of Hampshire County Council, who directed that an investigation into the condition of Higher Education in the county be undertaken. This was completed between 1904- 05 and the report regarding 'The civil Parish of Itchen' read 'The needs of this populous district present one of the chief difficulties which I (Mr.M.R. Sadler, late Director of Special Inquiries of the Board of Education) have encountered in the course of my enquiry. From an educational point of view, I am persuaded that what the district needs is a really good higher grade school. I realise however, that the district is already very highly rated. I hope, however, that at some early date, if not at present, it may be found possible to give this district the benefit of a higher grade school. It should not be necessary to attach to such a high grade school a Pupil Teacher Centre. The girls and boys from the Parish of Itchen who may desire to become elementary school teachers ought to go into a Pupil Teacher Centre at Southampton.' However, Hampshire County Council were swayed by the financial conditions and by November 1905 a council minute records 'The Director of Education reported that he had made arrangements for the hire of a room at the Oddfellows Hall, Bridge Road, Woolston, at fourteen shillings per week, for the Pupil Teacher Centre'. As a result of this decision, Secondary education in the Itchen area began. The Pupil Teacher Centre allowed pupils at the age of thirteen years to enter and after a two year course, take the Cambridge Junior Local Examination. The Centre was co-educational, and, if successful, the boy or girl would be indentured as a pupil teacher, spending two days at the Woolston Centre and three days a week in elementary schools, learning to be a teacher. Pupil teachers might begin by marking books and work, but if the teacher were to be absent, often the pupil teacher would take the class of fifty or sixty children possibly at the age of fifteen. After completion at the Pupil Teacher Centre, leaving with the Preliminary Teachers Certificate a successful pupil teacher would continue his or her training at a

Teacher's Training College such as King Alfred's in Winchester or at the training department of Hartley University College (now part of Southampton University).

The first permanent Principal of the Pupil Teaching Centre was appointed in October 1906, a Miss Edith North, who was a woman of character and determination. Prior to her appointment, Mrs. Frank Burt ran the Centre. Miss North recalled in a diamond jubilee article in 1956 "All I know is that when I was appointed at Itchen, the Director of Education, Mr. Cowan, said I was the first Principal. I began on 6 October 1906, and was there until 26th October 1916. I began with an assistant – a Miss Ward – and she came daily from Cosham where she ran a similar institution".

By May 1907, it was necessary for the Board of Education to hire a second room, and another assistant, Miss Rowlands.

From 1908 onwards the Board of Education were urging the County Education Committee to provide better Secondary education for Itchen, but unfortunately financial difficulties again stopped any progress and the Board threatened to withdraw recognition of the Centre, which would mean the withdrawal of the grant.

In October 1910, The Director of Education produced a report headed "Woolston New Secondary School" which included the following statement, "Briefly, it is recommended that there should be a secondary school of a somewhat new type, with a strong manual and technical bias, which shall appeal to the artisan population of the Itchen district as a preparation for apprenticeship, and also include provision for the training of Pupil Teachers. Workshops for wood and metal work, with some accommodation for elementary school children, would be erected separately, adjacent; and similarly, there should be class rooms for domestic subjects." The school was to accommodate 170 children; at this time the Pupil Teacher Centre numbered 47 pupils.

Progress for this new initiative was slow. In 1912, the seven acres of land in Middle Road, on which the present Sixth Form College stands, was purchased and plans for the building were drawn up. The land purchased was rough, unfenced with an abundance of gorse, bracken and blackberry bushes.

Between the buying of the land and the building of a new school, the Pupil Teacher Centre continued to grow and in 1913 Oswald Lodge in Portsmouth Road, another building owned by the Oddfellows, was rented, and two additional members of staff Miss Twitchen and Miss Weston were appointed. The Centre demonstrated the need for secondary education in the area and throughout its existence proved its worth. This achievement was mainly due to the first Principal, Miss North, who was a determined and able leader who found no difficulty in controlling and disciplining young pupils in not so ideal working conditions.

At the outbreak of the First World War in 1914 the Centre was strong with the promise of promotion to a 'Technical school', but this only remained a promise during the war years. Miss North retired in 1916 and Miss G.V. Cook succeeded her, moving premises from Oddfellows buildings to the first floor of the Portchester Road Elementary School, (which later became Woolston Secondary School for Boys). Miss Cook was an imaginative and capable headteacher, but she only remained in charge until December 1918, when she moved for promotion to a larger school in East London.

After the end of the war, the pre-war plans were reconsidered. The County Education Committee appointed a temporary headteacher, Mrs. Macrae–Gibson, with a view to appointing a Headmaster for the new Technical School. The standards and traditions set up by Miss North were maintained and were ready to be absorbed by the Secondary School.

In May 1919, the County Education Committee advertised for the services of a Headmaster "with experience in both Secondary and Technical school work". Mr.F.J. Hemmings was appointed the first Headmaster of Itchen County School. Mr.Hemmings was Principal of the Weymouth Technical and Engineering school, at the time of his appointment. He took up his duties at Itchen on 1 August 1919. This was the beginning of the School's existence on a grammar school basis. It remained for two more years as a Pupil Teachers' Centre, with the last Pupil Teacher leaving in July 1921. The Centre's task had completely finished in one sense, but in another sense it was enlarged, and a new organisation was needed to enhance the pupils' opportunities.

Upon opening, in September 1919, Itchen County School had major accommodation problems. When war broke out in 1914, the proposed new buildings for the 'Technical School' were shelved. After the war new plans for temporary accommodation for 160 pupils were brought forward and approved by the Board of Education. These new buildings should have been ready for occupation in September 1919 on the site of the present Sixth Form College. They were not ready, and the County school continued to use the first floor of Porchester Road Elementary School.

However, with a surge in the demand for Secondary education and a residue of ninety four pupils from the Pupil Teachers' Centre, by the end of the Autumn Term in 1919 there were 156 pupils on roll. By October 1920, numbers increased to 228 pupils. With this increase in numbers, the proposed temporary accommodation was to be inadequate within two terms. The slow completion of these temporary structures meant that the main body of the school could not be transferred to the Middle Road site until June 1921. The delay was partly due to the transfer of the whole Itchen area from Hampshire County to the Borough of Southampton, and so the County Education Committee would not spend further money on a school which they were not going to own. School numbers grew, but not the buildings. Southampton took control of the school in November 1920. Temporary premises known as 'the huts' were erected, but these would only accommodate 160 pupils. With 250 pupils on roll, further accommodation for at least 300 to 350 pupils was deemed necessary by the Southampton Education Committee. The secretary, Mr. Williams reported in late 1920 that 'much work remains to be done and a considerable amount of money will probably have to be expended to complete the very limited accommodation provided. Under the best conditions the organisation and supervision of a Co-Educational Secondary School is a far more complicated problem than that which has to be dealt with in the case of a school for boys or girls only. The present makeshift arrangements, especially as they necessitate frequent journeys on the part of the staff and pupils between two buildings far apart, create many difficulties, and from the point of discipline are to be deprecated. If the present dual nature of the school is to continue, effort should be made to bring the whole school under one roof. The development of the school may ultimately necessitate the division into one school for boys and one for girls, but for a year or two this separation is not an urgent requirement. The urgency lies in the direction of bringing all pupils into one building, or at least of bringing the whole school onto one site. Bearing in mind the fact that the Board of Education has for some time past been pressing the County Authority to vacate the new elementary school building now occupied by the Secondary school, I consider it would be wise to utilise the present site to a greater extent and as early as it can be done. The site has the disadvantage of being on the outskirts of the district but new houses are being erected and ultimately the site will be quite central.'

A second report written by Mr .Hemmings to Southampton Education Committee, as a response to Mr. William's report, summarised the past development of the school and then went on to say 'Mr. Williams' sympathetic appreciation of the enormous difficulties under which the school is now working has already brightened the outlook'. Mr. Hemmings concluded that 'The whole problem therefore, is extremely difficult. The limited accommodation is capable of development, and the Secretary has already suggested a course which, if adopted, will meet the needs of the next few years without entailing heavy capital expenditure. I hope that his suggestion will meet with the Committee's immediate consideration. Luxurious and costly buildings are not required. The whole district is likely to develop very considerably during the next few years and the erection of buildings capable of easy adaptation to changing conditions will be the most suitable.

In the meantime I wish to ask the Committee to take the necessary steps towards the completion of these temporary premises. Drains have to be laid, railings erected; furniture provided, cycle sheds built, and paths prepared. Much of this work could be done in readiness for occupation next term.'

The transfer of most of the pupils to the Middle Road site took place in June 1921, 'the huts' provided six form rooms, one science laboratory, a workshop, a housecraft room, a large assembly room (used also for Art and Physical Activities) together with the Headmaster's room, secretary's room and two staff rooms. Four rooms were kept in use at the Porchester Road School; as the buildings in Middle Road were insufficient to accommodate the whole school. This necessitated a journey of some difficulty of one and a half miles from one section of the school to the other.

One effect of the transfer of the school to Southampton from Hampshire County highlighted the fact that in the Borough the whole of the Technical Education was concentrated in Evening Institutes and at the University College; so the original scheme of a Secondary Technical School had to be abandoned, and the whole of its organisation concentrated on the development of a normal secondary school, which after the Butler Act in 1944 became known as a grammar school.

Mr. Hemmings was a headmaster who possessed great enthusiasm and energy and cultivated within the rapidly growing 'Itchen Secondary School' a corporate spirit. The main period of growth was the year 1921, although prior to this in 1919, school functions such as the first official 'Prize Distribution' or 'Speech Day' was held in July 1919. Other traditions such as Sports Day and the Christmas Social/Party also began in 1919. 1921 saw the establishment of a prefect system and house system, which became especially influential in the life of the school. The school colour – maroon – was taken from the Pupil Teachers' Centre football colour and in 1921 the distinctive school cap of maroon with a white ring was introduced. Within the school there was enthusiasm for all games, with cricket and football having been started at the Pupil Teachers' Centre. A general inspection of Itchen Secondary School took place in March 1924 and at the end of the year Mr. Hemmings was transferred to Taunton's School, also in the Borough of Southampton. The Inspector's Report paid tribute to Mr.Hemmings' achievement in setting the Secondary School on the right path. His energy, persuasiveness and determination were fully used in his first Headship. For most of his headship the school was housed in two buildings, yet he passed on to the next headmaster a school with a distinctive tradition and one which was becoming a vital part in the educational system of Southampton.

The new headmaster, appointed in January 1925, was Mr. E. Coteman, who held a degree from Christ's College, Cambridge and who had taught in several Public Schools and at the time of his appointment to Itchen was Science Master at Rossall School. Again, like Mr. Hemmings, much of Mr. Coteman's time at Itchen was concerned with problems of accommodation. In Mr. Hemming's time at Itchen, January 1922, complete plans for a permanent building to house 470 pupils and provide all the laboratories and practical rooms had been submitted to the Education Committee. The Board of Education, however, insisted that 'the provision of new buildings for Itchen Secondary School should be postponed for the present, pending the erection of Taunton's School.' A delegation from Southampton travelled to London to meet with officials of the Board, but achieved little, except that the Board agreed that it would not be practical to send the boys from the Itchen area to the rebuilt Taunton's School – (which was a boy only school). Plans were later amended and approved by the Board in June 1924. These plans were to provide classrooms for 325 pupils and the huts were to be converted for use as laboratories and practical rooms.

In autumn 1925, work began on the new buildings, with the foundation stone being laid on 17 December 1925 by the Mayor of Southampton Councillor, J.E. Silverman. (Colour photograph 24.) A sealed bottle with a copy of the 'Southern Daily Echo', the Times, current coins and a document stating the foundation stone was laid that day, was placed in a recess in the stone. The buildings were expected to be completed within a year and would have accommodation for 350 pupils. (Colour photographs 24. & 25.)

In September 1926, the first floor was ready for occupation, but the ground floor was still incomplete and so teaching had to be undertaken with the noise from the ground floor. The whole school was now accommodated on one site. The huts were adapted, but the completion of some parts of the building dragged on until 1939.

The buildings were to have been completed in two stages, and in December 1928, the Secretary to the Education Committee wrote to the Board inquiring whether the Board would consider the completion of the permanent buildings. The letter described the state of the huts and the ensuing difficulties.

'1. The temporary buildings now in use for laboratories, practical rooms etc., consist of army huts which were purchased and erected by the County of Southampton Education Authority shortly after the War at a cost of approximately £3,800. The huts are constructed in the usual flimsy manner of temporary army huts and they are showing very serious signs of wear. In recent storms so much rain came through the roof in the Domestic Science room, in the Art room and in the Woodwork room that the pupils had to move continually from place to place and in the afternoon lessons had to be discontinued there. Pools of water also collected in the assembly hall and in the masters' staff room. The school is in a very exposed position and though every effort is made to maintain the roofs of the huts in water tight condition, their state is such that some more permanent material than felting is required. The huts, however, are not in a state to carry any heavy roofing material without considerable expense being incurred on the strengthening of the walls. Most of the huts have now been in position since 1919 and in the opinion of my Authority the time has come for them to be replaced by permanent buildings.

2. Apart altogether from the question of the deterioration of the fabric, sustained effort is impossible in the art room which adjoins the assembly hall because the latter room is used for physical training and for singing, and in inclement weather the girls have to pass through the Art room to the hall. The vibration of the floor when drill (and games associated with the drill) are taking place in the hall makes fine work impossible, and the noise of commands, movements, singing etc. continually interrupt lessons and makes it difficult for the pupils to concentrate on their work. Furthermore the Art room is much too small for a class of 35 for object drawing and painting and no other room is available for the purpose.'

It was not until May 1929, that the Board replied saying that they 'were prepared to consider the question of the completion of the permanent buildings'. Plans were drawn up and submitted to the Board and in January 1931, the Southampton Education Committee received a letter from the Board approving the expenditure of £51,598. Before the plans were approved by the Board, on 8 December 1930, the Assembly Hall burnt down in a spectacular way. Fire engines were hindered by the foggy December night and when they arrived the whole building was a mass of flames. The fire brigade saved the remainder of the huts, but the Hall and Art Room were completely destroyed. At the time it was ironically regarded by many that the preservation of the remaining huts by the Fire Brigade and not the destruction of the Assembly Hall was the disaster!

Immediately after the fire, Mr. Coteman conducted Assembly by standing on a box in the centre of the corridor, but the Education Committee quickly replaced the hall with a temporary building.

A national financial emergency in 1931 faced the Education Committee in their deliberations over the expenditure necessary to complete the buildings and they decided that the scheme could not go forward. It was a difficult situation for the school, with only the building which housed handicraft rooms and the form rooms usable and these being able to accommodate only 335 pupils of the 431 on the roll.

By 1933 the situation was desperate, and the conditions under which the school was working were officially described 'as deplorable in so far as the use of the hutments is concerned, especially for the winter months, when it is impossible to exclude the rain'. Southampton Education Committee not only had to contend with difficulties at Itchen, they were also concerned at the same time that King Edward V1 School was growing rapidly and had a most inconvenient site and that the Girls' Grammar School was housed in a former pupil teacher centre with three annexes. The Authority felt these two schools must be given priority because their teaching rooms were so unsatisfactory compared to the more satisfactory ones at Itchen. Mr. Coteman was very disappointed that the Committee's decision went against him, but by September 1934 Itchen had four additional classrooms added to the permanent building and the huts were replaced by a temporary – permanent structure which lasted over three decades. The handicraft block returned to its intended usage.

However, in 1935 Mr. Coteman, with support from His Majesty's Inspectors, demanded a gymnasium. In 1936, the Higher Education Committee agreed to the completion of the East Wing, the erection of an Assembly Hall, a Gymnasium, a dining room and a kitchen. Approval from the Board of Education was received in June 1937 and building began immediately, and by September 1938 there had been added to these buildings an Art room, a Craft room, a Prefect's room, a Library and a Senior Mistress's room. The hall also included a well equipped stage. The gymnasium and dining hall were completed and ready for use in September 1939. For Mr. Coteman, the battles he faced in achieving these new buildings only to have to leave them at the outbreak of war must have been a bitter blow. The new buildings Itchen finally gained were far beyond the original plans, but though good in their day, could not have accommodated the growth of the school and the necessity to meet modern demands.

When the Second World War broke out, Itchen had been a Secondary school for twenty years and was acknowledged as a respected part of Southampton's educational provision. Mr. Hemming's early foundations, built upon by Mr.Coteman stood the test of time; but a greater test was yet to come. This was the evacuation of Itchen to Andover Grammar School. 1 September 1939 saw the Government's plans for children to be evacuated from danger areas to other safer parts of the country. The scheme was voluntary and so in fact when Itchen moved to Andover Grammar School, although there were 520 children on the roll, only about half of the pupils went to Andover. Itchen remained at Andover for sixteen terms.

Upon arrival at Andover, staff and senior boys from both schools dug air-raid shelters. Soon, however, the schools settled down to what could be a normal education for the children in the circumstances. Andover Grammar School worked in the mornings and Itchen from 13.30 to 17.30 with alternate Saturday afternoons off school. The afternoon sessions in the winter for Itchen was particularly trying, pupils had to enter a school full of stale air and as evening approached the gas lamps were lit and the blackout put up. Finding accommodation for the children to be billeted in took up a lot of staff time, especially having to encourage hostesses to take in children and smooth out any troubles. Some pupils complained of being unhappy, some hostesses wished to discard their billetees for various reasons and new billets had to be found. Andover became a very full town when refugee families from London arrived to add to the accommodation pressure.

Throughout Itchen's stay in Andover, the host school always did its best for Itchen in difficult circumstances. Staff from both schools had extra duties such as fire watching to undertake. Each year, throughout the war, Speech day was held, to which the Mayor and Mayoress of Southampton together with members of the Education committee would always attend. They did not wish for Itchen to be a forgotten part of Southampton but still to remain a vital part of the Borough's educational provision.

The school buildings in Southampton were initially used by the A.R.P. Medical Services where they set up a casualty station, but later the Medical Officer of Health took over the gymnasium as a clinic and the Ministry of Food established a British Restaurant in the dining hall. In June 1940, French troops evacuated from across the Channel received tea and sandwiches provided by the Women's Voluntary Service from the Domestic Science window. The buildings escaped any serious damage, although one bomb which did not explode fell through the dining room roof and then through the gymnasium floor. Itchen's evacuation to Andover ended in December 1944.

The school had changed considerably during the War, many staff had left or retired, some buildings were still occupied by the people who had been there during the war; the Clinic remained in the gymnasium until February 1948 and the British restaurant remained in the dining room sometime after that.

Mr. Coteman had many problems to deal with, there was a rapid influx of children in 1946 – the number of pupils doubled and this was exacerbated by the Butler Act which abolished fees in grammar schools and provided secondary education for all. The school's name was changed to Itchen Grammar School. Many grammar schools had to adjust to the disappearance of fee payers and the sometimes different character of the entrants at the age of eleven. The strong tradition built up at Itchen helped them to assimilate these problems and the familiar routine of standards of work returned.

The exterior of the school had suffered during the war, the field and cricket pitch had been damaged and all attempts made by the school to re-turf the square and the field was often in vain, because all the metal railings had been removed as scrap-iron for the war effort, and after school hours many people would enter the field and trample the new turf. The field, however, was eventually returned to its pre-war state.

After twenty five years at Itchen Mr. Coteman retired in April 1950. He had served the school during troublesome times, but he left the school as a Grammar School with established strengths of tradition. Ironically, just prior to his retirement a proposed re-organisation of schools within the town, wanted Itchen to be converted into a Girl's School. Protest at this proposal was strong and widespread and in no uncertain terms the Itchen area let it be known that Itchen Grammar School, the only co-educational schools within the Borough, was an institution that formed an integral part of the local community.

An important aspect in the development of Itchen Grammar School was the formation of an Old Students' Association. This was formed after the First World War, when Mr. Hemmings took over the school. The Old Students' Association, took on the name of Old Issonians when the 'Itchen County School' transferred to the Borough of Southampton and became known as Itchen Secondary School – 'I.S.S. – hence Old Issonians. However, little real progress with the Old Issonians was made until after Mr. Coteman's arrival and then the Association began to move. The main aim of the Association was 'to foster and maintain the spirit of fellowship begun in the School and to render to the School such assistance as may from time to time be possible'. By 1939 membership had reached over a hundred members, but following the Second World War in 1945 the Association had to begin afresh. Slowly the Association reached over three hundred members, giving valuable support to the newly named Itchen Grammar School. The Old Issonians formed successful sub-associations running hockey, football, dramatics and social events. After the Jubilee celebrations in 1956, membership grew to six hundred, but as the school changed into a College subscriptions to the Association fell. By 1980, sadly, the Association only had one hundred paid up members, but the aims of the Association remained the same. The Old Issonians were largely responsible for the successful protests when Itchen was planned to become a Girls' School and when it was to lose its Sixth Form to become a Comprehensive School.   In September 1950, Mr. Charles Thompson, who prior to his appointment at Itchen, had been headteacher at Ilfracombe Grammar School, also co-educational, took up office. Like Mr. Coteman, Charles Thompson had been educated at Christ's College, Cambridge.

Mr. Thompson's main problem on arrival at Itchen was of how to approach the new General Certificate of Education, and changes within the school came about thus giving greater flexibility to the organisation of the school.   During Mr. Thompson's headship, the school celebrated its first fifty years of existence in 1956 and in the magazine to celebrate this event it is written 'The School's greatest source of strength is to be found in the fact that it is co-educational. From the earliest days of the Secondary School, when co-education was far less common than it is now, social activities involving both boys and girls were a readily accepted feature of the school, and this aspect of the school can largely be attributed to the happy friendly atmosphere that has always been felt both among the staff and in the School as a whole.' Mr. Thompson, in the 1956 magazine wrote ' In the life of many schools in this country fifty years is but a short span of time and the building up of standards and traditions is a process that requires much patience. Yet though the history of Itchen has impressed me by its evidence of solid achievement in so short a time, the School can still add to its success and newly formed traditions. Moreover the challenge and the opportunity lie close at hand, for it is situated in a rapidly growing part of Southampton, close to modern industries. Those who read the history of Itchen will have no doubt as to Itchen's answer to the challenge and its future growth.'

Mr. Thompson's appointment in 1950 up to his retirement in 1971 saw many developments at Itchen and the twenty one years of his headship and the following years under Philip Vennis marked the beginning of a fruitful period in the life of the school/college. Charles Thompson was well respected by his staff and some of the reforms he carried out in his Headship included the banning of the use of the cane, the amalgamation of the single sex staff rooms, the building of the swimming pool and observatory and the replacement of 'the huts'. The swimming pool was built from money raised in the summer of the Jubilee Celebrations in 1956 and it was officially opened two years later in June 1958. It was the first school swimming pool to be built in Southampton and for many years it was used for teaching junior children. The huts were demolished in 1963 and in September 1964, the long struggle to gain proper laboratories became a reality and made life much easier for the scientists. The completion of the long awaited major extensions and improvements brought Itchen Grammar School up to current standards and represented another landmark in the school' s history and in post war school building in Southampton.

The Architects for this extension were Messr Richard Sheppard, Robson and Partners of London who have been responsible for several post war schools in Southampton. At Itchen in the new block all the teaching rooms were planned on the first and second floors. The ground floor was almost entirely open and stepped down to the playing fields. The extensions were linked to the main school building at first floor level by a group of staffrooms also overlooking the playing fields. On the first floor there was provided two Biology laboratories and rooms for needlework and housecraft, and on the second floor there were three laboratories for Physics and Chemistry, plus a Geography room with a terrace and access to the observatory on the roof. This accommodation was a far cry from the temporary huts erected in the twenties.

The debate over comprehensive education and Sixth Form Colleges as an option was taking place throughout the country, there were supporters of the idea and opponents and so in 1966 the National Union of Teachers set out a discussion paper 'National Union of Teachers, Secondary Reorganisation, Sixth Form Colleges 1966'. Eric Macfarlane in his book 'Sixth Form Colleges summarises this document and the pros and cons for the provision of Sixth Form Colleges as follows:

'Considerations favouring Sixth Form Colleges:

1. The growth of a distinctive teenage culture, coupled with the earlier physical and emotional development of young people, has led to pupils of sixteen and over finding it irksome to conform to the uniform standards of behaviour that are commonly imposed on a school as a whole. There would be opportunities for a mature relationship between staff and pupils in a Sixth Form College. Rules regarding dress, smoking, relations between the sexes and matters of discipline generally could be relaxed, thereby removing one of the reasons for early leaving.

2. A large number of young people find the transition from school to university too sharp; a Sixth Form College would find it easier than a school to employ methods of individual and group tuition and therefore would afford a more gradual introduction to the self-directed work of a university.

3. A Sixth Form College, drawing pupils from several secondary schools, would be able to offer a greater variety of courses for the sixteen plus age group than a Comprehensive School. Provision of laboratory and workshop facilities, including technicians, would be specific to courses at this level.

4. A sixteen plus college would attract well qualified staff and use them more economically. It was most unlikely that there would be adequate well qualified staff, particularly in Mathematics and Science, to meet the needs of the Sixth Forms in a system of eleven to eighteen schools.

5. Existing schools could be adapted more readily to a system of eleven to sixteen schools and sixteen plus colleges than to other forms of reorganization: Sixth Form Colleges therefore offered a better practical solution to the immediate problems of reorganisation.

Arguments against the formation of Sixth Form Colleges:

1. With the raising of the school leaving age pupils would be required to transfer to a Sixth Form College at the very time when the opportunity to leave school first presented itself: there was a likelihood in this situation that many pupils who would have continued in school where they felt at home would not make the effort to transfer to another institution.

2. Many of the reforms put forward as attractive features of Sixth Form Colleges could be – and indeed in some areas had been – introduced to schools. It was not necessary to separate sixth formers from younger pupils in order to relax the rules regulating their behaviour or to create an

opportunity for mature relationships between pupils and staff. Good schools already gave their sixth formers a degree of responsibility for organising their own work which prepared them for the situation they would meet at university.

3. The concept of a well integrated secondary school course followed by a separate two or three years in the Sixth form can be carried too far. At the moment opportunities exist for some pupils to start advanced level study after four years in the secondary school and for others to repeat a fifth year type course in the Sixth form. This flexibility would disappear if pupils had to transfer to another establishment after the fifth year.

4. There would be a loss for both teachers and pupils in a system that precluded Sixth Form staff from teaching younger classes. A difference in prestige and probably in levels of salary would emerge between the eleven to sixteen schools and the sixteen plus colleges which would make it difficult for the schools to recruit staff of comparable calibre to those in the colleges.

5. The segregation of the sixteen to nineteen age group from the younger pupils would bring to an end the much valued tradition in secondary schools of older pupils assuming important leadership roles. Younger children and senior pupils alike have benefitted from the qualities and relationships associated with this tradition.'

In the same year (1966) as this debate was being discussed Southampton Education Committee, under the leadership of Sir James Matthews, decided that Southampton should go comprehensive and so a working party of teachers was formed to advise the Committee. The brief was unclear, but the Committee favoured the formation of Sixth Form Colleges. Support from the working party to this idea was strong but some Secondary Modern Heads were opposed to any change in the conviction that the increasing number of transfers to the Sixth Forms would not provide full opportunities for any pupil wishing to stay at school up to the age of eighteen. Much discussion ensued but the working party was told that the Comprehensive system was to be based on the formation of Colleges. It was then agreed that there should be no academic bar to entry to a College, although no one knew of the numbers of students who were likely to attend them. The Committee submitted a proposal to the Department of Education that Taunton's and The Girls' Grammar School be converted to Sixth Form Colleges by allowing no further entry at the age of eleven, whilst Itchen was to receive a comprehensive entry until it became clear that a third city College would be required. Again a strong protest was lodged on behalf of Itchen stating that there would be no proper provision for Sixth Form education in the east of Southampton, where forty per cent of the population of Southampton lived and that there ought to be a co-educational college. Reconsideration of the plans took place and in April 1967, it was announced that there would be three colleges, that the 11-plus entry to the former grammar schools would cease in September of the same year and that Taunton's and The Girls' Grammar School ought, in due course, to become co-educational. Itchen was a very popular Grammar School in the sixties and this reflected the mood that co-education was right for this age group, but Mr. Thompson faced problems in the transition from Grammar School to Sixth Form College.

Southampton was a small county borough but they were the pioneers of the 'Open Access Sixth Form College'. The borough's concept of the comprehensive college quickened its rate of reorganisation after the 10/65 government circular (which requested Local Education Authorities to begin converting their secondary schools to the comprehensive system). Local circumstances in the city of Southampton were very much in favour of the Sixth Form College form of reorganisation. The three maintained grammar schools, Itchen Grammar (co-educational), Richard Taunton's Grammar School (Boys) and the Girls' Grammar School were legally established as 'open access secondary colleges' in 1967, taking in at sixteen almost everyone who wished to continue their studies. The Girls' Grammar School, under the headship of Miss Louise Vail, had since 1964 stopped requiring the usual academic qualifications for entry into its Sixth Form and thereby showed a strong commitment to the open access concept in the Sixth Form. This commitment to the open access policy of Southampton Education Authority under the leadership of the Chief Education Officer, Dr. P.J. Browning, MA, CBE, was not to be swayed, despite there being disagreement over the alternative ways in which reorganisation should be adopted. Southampton was the first Local Education Authority where reorganisation plans departed from the idea of the Sixth Form. Itchen Grammar School became a co-educational College whilst Taunton's Grammar School and the Girls Grammar School were respectively a college for boys and one for girls. For ten years these two Colleges remained the only single sex Sixth Form Colleges in the country, late in the seventies they became co-educational, with the Girls' College renamed as Hill College. Over the years, all three Colleges steadily grew, especially as the city of Southampton had a good record in staying on after the school leaving age of sixteen, and, when Philip took over Itchen College in 1971, two thirds of all fifteen/sixteen year olds were staying on. The Colleges continued to demonstrate consistent improvement in the qualifications on entry to the Colleges from 1971 to 1976.

Nationally, the main interest in Southampton's scheme was the working of the open access entry. Dr. Peter Browning argues strongly for the case in a memorandum to the Education Committee in July 1971, just after Philip's arrival at Itchen, saying that he was against an imposition of any formal entry requirements. He went on to state that 'the position is that pupils can transfer from neighbourhood comprehensives without any formal requirements, the only condition being that the student himself wishes to pursue full time education beyond sixteen and is prepared to apply himself; what matters is the degree of motivation on the part of the students; this is of the greatest importance for future success, and more so than any measure of intelligence or academic attainment, whether eleven plus or sixteen plus'. Support for these open access principles came from the Joint Four (the Grammar School organisation), the local National Union of Teachers, and the Heads and Staff of the three Colleges. For Philip it was his lifetime's ambition to bring education to all, especially poor and working class children, as he himself once had been. The principle of open access was held as Dr.Browning goes on to say as 'educationally sound and vital to the continued development of comprehensive education in Southampton, in the interests of pupils of all abilities at all stages of the educational system.' The system of comprehensive secondary education and open access colleges became fully operational in Southampton in September 1972, when the first comprehensive intake of 1967 reached sixteen plus and provided all the new students to the Sixth Form Colleges. So thereby, Itchen and the other two secondary colleges, Tauntons and the Girls' Grammar, had the last intake of pupils who joined the then Grammar Schools in 1965, to work their way through the college. One such pupil, at Itchen College, P.J. Saunders, remembers, 'The most obvious and unique difference was that we were always the youngest year in the school and it was not until reaching the second year sixth that we had a junior year below us.'

One reason, in the view of Dr. Browning, for open access Colleges is that if access were limited in terms of examination qualifications as he argues 'There would be strong pressures on secondary schools to ensure that pupils achieved the prescribed number of examination passes, with dangers of "cramming" and restrictive influences on the curriculum and non-examination activities of the secondary schools i.e. creating a 'sixteen plus' situation in these schools comparable to the "eleven plus" limitations on the primary schools.' Benn and Simon in 'Half Way There' state that 'In developing genuinely open access, Southampton is in line with the parallel development of the 'open sixth' in Comprehensive schools generally.'

Sixth Form Colleges also believe in all round education and so offer an amazing range of enrichment opportunities and activities and pastoral support that is specialised for the age range. Attending a Sixth Form College can provide a life changing opportunity and student's progress from them with the work and personal skills they need for higher education and employment. Sixth Form Colleges provide a very effective bridge between the school environment and the adult world of higher education and employment, treating their students as adults but with the support and pastoral care needed for sixteen to eighteen year olds. At least seventy-eight per cent of the level three cohort in the Sixth Form College sector are known to progress to higher education.

The idea of an 'Open Sixth Form College' was never discussed by the working party and in 1967 since no such institution existed. Each college was left to work out its own salvation and it did not take too long before major problems were to emerge. A College of students, 'all over sixteen years old' needed a different, less restrictive approach as compared to a school, such as the relaxing of the wearing of a school uniform. But there was also the question of what to do with the remaining grammar school children below the Sixth Form who would always be the youngest within the school. Itchen tried and succeeded in avoiding mistakes by giving these pupils the attention they deserved, for example, school rules became more relaxed as they entered the fifth form.

The change at Itchen was reflected in two ways – the formation of a College Council and the establishment of a Sixth formers Common Room, for which the Sixth formers had to accept responsibility for its proper use, tidiness and cleanliness.

For Mr. Thompson, the major organisational problem was how to get so many newcomers to settle quickly on a suitable subject course. The numbers dealt with between 1967 to 1971 were small compared to the years that were to follow, but it was important to get all students started on their timetable as soon as possible on entry. Entrants came from all seventeen secondary schools within the City, plus other schools. The Secondary Heads' co-operation was paramount to the success of the transfer of the pupils. Southampton Education Committee was generous with the staff ratios at Itchen in these early days, and all the groups were of a traditional Sixth form size. More teaching space was needed and some existing rooms were divided.

Mr. Thompson, thus began the early days of Itchen Sixth Form College, he wrote some years later 'I find it impossible to convey the feeling of starting absolutely from the beginning with no guiding principles or experience to help us and I do not think anyone who was not in this situation can ever fully understand it. The four years from 1967 to my retirement were very mixed. Some of the staff strongly disliked the change, but some, as one would expect from good members of the profession, never allowed this feeling to affect their contribution to the new College. There was continual formal and informal discussion; we did our best to anticipate the problems we would face, but we could not always succeed. I was personally concerned at having to attempt to establish a new and untried institution so late in my career; but looking back, I am glad that I had to face the challenge and I am confident that, with the willing and effective help of the Staff, Itchen College made a good start in those four years on this the latest stage of its history.'

Mr. Thompson reached retirement just before the grammar school entry had worked its way through, leaving the new Head, now called Principal, Mr. Philip Vennis with two years of the old grammar school intake combing happily with ever growing numbers from the comprehensive schools.

The Times Educational Supplement reported Philip's appointment at Itchen in December 1970 in the following article. 'Heading for change – Itchen College – one of Southampton's trio of brave new secondary colleges for the sixteen to nineteen – is to have a new Headmaster. He is Mr. Philip Vennis; Head of the New Mills School in Stockport, which recently went comprehensive, and his experience there should stand him in very good stead in his new post.

For one thing the changeover at New Mills was from grammar to comprehensive – Itchen College, too, has had to cope with a run down of its grammar course in the past four years. For another, New Mills has a Sixth Form on nearly 200 which for some years now has been open access. And Itchen College, in common with its sister secondary colleges, works on the open access principle. What this has meant to Itchen is a phenomenal increase in the intake each year. Figures for all three colleges' show that last year's transfers at sixteen plus represented an increase of twenty-seven per cent on the 1968 figure – which itself showed an increase of fifty per cent on the previous year's total. Mr. Vennis will clearly have a lot of eager customers on his hands.

Mr. Vennis (Dulwich College and Peterhouse, Cambridge) is 45, and married with three young children. He has many dealings with the sixteen to nineteen age group, and has a special interest in drama.'

'From Headmaster to College Principal' 1971 to 1988

"Education is a serious business. I am for the Comprehensive School and the Open Access Sixth Form College. There are no final answers in Education. All ways must be tried as we move forward. The Sixth Form College may prove to be one of the answers to some of our prime dilemmas in comprehensive education. Schools really don't differ very much from one another. There are good and bad Grammars, Secondary Moderns, Comprehensives and Sixth Form Colleges. It's the staff and the pupils and the parents and the governors and the Authority in some kind of working partnership that matters, and the Headmaster is the lynch pin of that set-up. His style, his originality, his ideas, matter most in keeping the whole thing as a unit." (P.H.V. 1971)

Philip applied for the headship of Itchen College in September 1970, and it is evident that at this early stage of his relationship with the College that he had his own philosophy of how he wished to run such a College. He states in his letter of application that 'I would enjoy the challenge of such a College built into a Grammar School Sixth, where the College would have every chance of keeping and building the right kind of atmosphere and *esprit*. Comprehensive education must continue to give the ablest children the right opportunities and teaching in an atmosphere of true learning, the somewhat less able a flexibility of course and choice, which will open new windows for them and the least able a chance to mature in as atmosphere of loving care. Every student must be well looked after by some teacher or teachers throughout his or her time at the College. If the latter is so then we can be optimistic that this vast experiment in education will turn out to be in the best interests of all our pupils. Clearly we must use every means to see that we are 'levelling up'.

I feel that decentralisation will be the key to the organisation of a Sixth Form College. I see, perhaps, seven main departments – Science (with Engineering), Creative subjects, which could be the Arts and Crafts, Mathematics (including Statistics), English (including Drama), P.E. (including all outdoor activities), Environmental Studies (the middle subjects – History, Geography, Economics, Politics, British Government, Religious Knowledge, Geology) and Languages (including Classical Languages and Ancient History). I think we should need a Director of Drama and a Director of Music and certainly we should look to having a modern outlook in all kinds of ways in relation to dramatic movement and mime, and modern drama, and to musical performances of both modern and classical works. We the College in every kind of way want

265

to to make him or her feel that this is his or her College, that he or she has a say in running it with the staff and headmaster, and that every effort will be made to listen to any reasonable request. On the other hand permissiveness must not go so far that authority will be lacking or over – questioned. A '*via media*' is essential in these matters and in my experience nearly all Sixth Formers like to have some authority, some final decision (provided it isn't too immediate) and to know where to draw the line and what that line is. It is a question of information and communication and being sure that lines of communication are open; it is a question, above all, of the Headmaster – while being flexible and moderate – not giving ground where he should not, quite definitely (while listening to his staff and Sixth form) realising that his is the responsibility for the running of the College and letting it be known, therefore, clearly, but firmly, what lines of behaviour there are where authority may be questioned and where it quite definitely may not. This, to me, seems to be essential in the new situation of the seventies into which we are moving. Above all, it will certainly be necessary to meet, with moderation and flexibility, and even perhaps with compassion, the problems of the new Sixth Former in his or her student status.

Undoubtedly a Sixth Form College is going to turn out to be one of the ways of solving the staffing problems in comprehensives. In addition, it may help to solve the discipline problem connected with this age group. It will certainly be necessary to proceed one step at a time and to feel one's way forward. It will be necessary, too, to keep up high academic standards and a true love of learning on one wing while extending courses and curricula to ensure that all of this age group can gain by at least one year at the College. My own preference would be for a three year course – fifteen to eighteen for the ablest – sixteen to nineteen for the average and less able Sixth former. I feel in three years one would know them well enough to make sure that their courses in further education, or their careers, were suited to their desires, characters and abilities. A two year course is likely to be the norm, but it will certainly be necessary to have good reports from 'feeder' comprehensives about the Sixth Former concerned, and it will be necessary to get to know him or her with speed and settle him or her in the College quickly. One might hope that some of the 'feeder' schools would run four year courses to O level so that the ablest can have three years in the Sixth before eighteen, and, thus pave the way for a good third year Sixth.

I look forward to facing the very great challenge of this new adventure in education and of enjoying the company of staff and Sixth formers while individually sorting out their academic and career problems in a pastoral way. It would be with optimism that this kind of Junior College should face up to the seventies using its very newness and experimental nature as the basis for a forward-looking experimental attitude, while absorbing, from the past, and from the great Sixth Form tradition of our grammar schools, all that was best (and that was a very great deal) in that tradition. From being the crown and glory of one school, as it has always been, and rightly, the Sixth form, in its new College, would now become a shared crown and glory for several schools, serving its whole area in every kind of cultural, academic, creative, athletic, practical, dramatic, musical and aesthetic way.

The specialist rooms must be continually used, it must maintain its university entry, both to Oxbridge and to elsewhere, and, not least, the balance of subjects in that entry for our main business is quite clearly with Engineering and the Sciences; the Arts man, perhaps, must see his job more as helping the scientist and persuading him that the Arts will be of importance in his life. Interesting work in music, choral and orchestral, must continue and I personally would be very interested in attempting, myself, some modern work in drama, as well as perhaps some modern interpretations of Shakespeare with very considerable Sixth Form casts – again with an especial interest in having Science boys in them. The games tradition and athletics must also continue as well as the many clubs and societies.

There is a dual task here for a time. The Sixth Form College which is arising from the Grammar School must continue its traditions and make them grow further among the very many new educational ideas of the seventies. At the same time the utmost co-operation in work and leisure must be sought with the local Technical College in order to begin to make sixteen plus educations a unity.'

Arrival at Itchen College, April 1971.

267

Philip was appointed to Itchen from 1 April 1971 and this is what Jo Dunford remembers 'There was a momentous change in 1971 for Itchen College. Earlier it had fought off a proposal to turn it into an all girls' school, possibly comprehensive. Then came the proposal to give Southampton Sixth Form Colleges with a suggestion there should be just two, ignoring Itchen and creating Colleges from Taunton's School and the Girls' Grammar School. Fortunately a sufficiently strong case was made for Itchen to be the first mixed Sixth Form College in the City and to be open access. Mr. Thompson had decided to retire and Mr. P.H. Vennis succeeded him with the challenge of dealing with the new situation.

Heads of Departments from the existing staff met Mr. Vennis at the spring weekend conference (March 1971) in Bournemouth organised by Hampshire County Council to present the ideals of a Sixth Form College in the school year preceding the September start. A fundamental great change then became obvious when the appointed new Principal summoned a staff meeting the first evening after dinner when various staff roles were assigned to different of staff. Mr Vennis had certainly been busy vetting staff CVs and had new ideas as to who should do what – especially creating the post of Student Counsellor. Faced with these arbitrary ideas certain Heads of Department were left wondering what the future would be like as no discussion with the relevant members of staff had been held.

When the term began the first staff meeting contained Mr. Vennis's decision that the three roomed staff room set up had to be changed with the inclusion of the men's only room to be absorbed into the central room and the ladies room to be open to all, keeping the refreshment facilities. Certain feathers were ruffled by the men losing their privacy and their smoking area.' (Jo Dunford, who joined Itchen Grammar School in 1958, and in 1962 became Head of the Sixth Form Arts and then as the Grammar School became a Sixth Form College she became Head of Careers).

Jo continues by saying 'Mr. Vennis or P.H.V. as he wished to be known had definitely come to put his own stamp on the school/college with his over-riding aim of putting Itchen College on the map which he proceeded to do with tremendous energy and determination and by visiting not only all the local comprehensives but also those very much on the periphery giving out the message of the breadth, depth and strength of Itchen's curriculum and College ethos. Good appointments in music and drama led to continued high standards in both. Much excellent and innovative work in both, as well as in art, design, pottery, fashion and technology was put on public view. Some paintings were chosen to be put on the walls of the Industrial Tribunal Office. Itchen became recognised as an open access College of high academic standards whilst also working hard with those who came in with no or very low qualifications. City and Guilds examinations could be taken and later National Vocational Qualifications. The relationship between staff and students took on a more relaxed nature although mutual respect for one another was maintained. A Student Council was elected and given responsibilities. Proper emphasis was given to careers and higher education advice with the opportunity to meet with a wide ranging number of professional people in all walks of life as well as much time allowed for individuals to have discussions on their own needs and ways to fulfil them as well as how to grow in maturity to be able to play a useful part in society. Tutors played an important role in this, work experience was also arranged. The curriculum was continually being re-assessed with new subjects being offered. P.H.V. was determined to oversee the timetable of every student on entry. His own love of the Classics and his belief in the advantage of having studied A level mathematics, regardless of the perhaps low GCSE base, sometimes had to be challenged as not appropriate to the aims and ability of every student.

Relationships with staff were generally good until any voices were raised against new developments close to P.H.V.'s heart – this could lead to P.H.V. taking a stroll round the field! However, P.H.V. was extraordinarily kind, compassionate and considerate when members of staff/students or members of their family had health or serious other problems. Arrangements would be made to ease the situation as much as possible. Relationships with ex-students were also good, with excellent support too for the Old Issonians' Association.' Jo Dunford helped with the running of the Old Issonians for many years but unfortunately this Association folded in 2003 as ex-students kept contact via online facilities. In her role as Head of Careers Jo says that 'P.H.V. gave me a generous time allowance to produce a detailed careers programme giving up to twenty plus choices for one period every week – compulsory attendance for students! He also gave me time for lengthy interviews with each student; this was the envy of most of my colleagues in careers work elsewhere.'

As Jo Dunford mentioned there were momentous changes taking place at Itchen, some of which some staff were not happy about. This early dissatisfaction of how the new headmaster was handling changes came to a head when two members of staff, who remained anonymous to Philip, went to see the Chief Education Officer, Peter Browning. This all took place in the September term in 1971, Philip having been at the College for one term. His response to this difficult beginning culminated in the following address to staff in an attempt to finish the matter and to give the staff his perspective on the events that had taken place. 'On Thursday last, two members of this staff saw the Chief Education Officer for some time. I believe they had previously written a letter to him implying that the matter would be personal business. He, therefore, agreed to see them. He agreed to be confidential and rightly has kept this confidence, so I do not know who they are.

Apparently the matter rapidly ceased to be personal and became instead a question of personalities. In addition, they implied that the staff were discontented, thus half appearing to represent the staff, and that there was a possibility of Union action and this, of course, upset Mr, Browning. I heard about this first last Thursday and again Friday but the Chief Education Officer was unable to see me until Monday morning.

The party at my house, therefore, which I was very pleased to give, and which my wife and I enjoyed, nevertheless had a cloud over it. Perhaps this was part of the savage intentions of those involved. Perhaps they intended to do the College good – scarcely the result. Perhaps they thought I would go – not the result either. Perhaps they thought the Chief Education Officer would not support me – wrong again.

Most of us would, I hope, tear up anonymous letters and not receive anonymous telephone calls. I am not sure that anonymous interviews are any different. The matter is probably unprofessional and I have not yet decided what action to take.

It was a savage attack in a way and perhaps even intended to cause the discontent it talked about. Certainly it has caused mistrust amongst us. Which colleague here can now be certain that there will not be an anonymous report on him, or her, to the Chief Education Officer – trust is essential in running a place. My conscience is clear. I have no secrets and everybody can know and hear what I am saying about them.

Was the intention, as the Chief Education Officer put it, "to flash an amber light?" I had thought this term that there was no discontent and that things were going well.

I can only suggest two palliatives now. One is that the staff write a letter that I can take to the Chief Education Officer when I see him again, either signed by Mr. Lewis (Deputy Headmaster) for all, or signed by all who want to, which implies briefly that people are content and that things are going well and possibly that they support the Headmaster and his policies. Two, that we invite (I know he would come) the Chief Education Officer to lunch and coffee afterwards in the Staffroom when he can talk to people and he could find out how content they are.'

Later in the same term, Philip spoke at a large County conference about his philosophy of the Sixth Form College/Comprehensive College as he saw it. He began with a little history by saying 'The 1902 Education Act produced the kind of grammar school of which I was Head in Derbyshire for eight years before going comprehensive, and of which Itchen Grammar was another example.

Both were co-ed and were the kind of grammar school (run by the State and the Local Authority) which did so much for England during these sixty plus years and did it well and nobly in and out of war, producing a class of citizen who served the State and the community and his/her fellows well. Its particular crown and splendour was of course the Sixth form. For a time that was small but gradually it grew both in numbers and in subjects and more recently still it began to take in from other schools and in some cases to be open access, even while serving as the Sixth form of a Grammar School. It became generally ready to adapt itself to absorb all kinds of teenagers in this age group and all kinds of subjects and work. But it still kept those basic traditions which we have inherited and which we in turn must keep. These were quite clearly an *esprit*, a love of special knowledge, a proper care for academic learning and a feeling that hard work and study in depth has its own reward. A kind of self-disciplined community expressed via academic work and via sport, drama, music, clubs, dance, etc. These things we inherit, these things we have, and all these things we shall continue to hold and to adapt for all and for all the future. Of course, such an adaptation brings problems. It is not easy to adapt a nearly A level idea to an open access College. We have O levels, we have CSE, we are going to have the Certificate of Extended Education, we have Secretarial Courses, we are going to have people on non-exam courses of any kind. To each of these we must adapt the ideas of self-discipline, of hard work, of a feeling for the College, of some love of some special knowledge in depth. We must see those sides of the Grammar School Sixth which developed personality and were its unique hallmark – that is to say the combination of the academic, the practical and manipulative, the athletic and the aesthetic – that these things remain with us.

We shall move forward together in this kind of way making sure that we know one another's problems and that we care about each, that each separately is known well to someone, and that problems are fully discussed whether of work or of a social or human nature. I believe in the future of this kind of secondary college. We cannot fail to be successful, how can we? There is clearly a rising tide or even flood of young people of all abilities who want to continue their education full time to eighteen. The raising of the school leaving age will almost certainly make that tide rise even faster and deeper. We have to have a situation ready to receive these youngsters, throughout the range of work from three or more A levels to some craft and practical and vocational one year courses. We have to have our options open, ready, and above all we must be adaptable and flexible, ready to help and serve each and every teenager who turns up. To quote Churchill about more serious matters we must 'never give in' about any teenager's future nor allow him or her to give in; this is clearly important.

People want to come to Itchen and other Sixth Form Colleges for much the same reasons they wanted to come into the Sixth form. These reasons were always very mixed and they still are. Some want to go to University, some to College, some into other careers, some want a cosy two years, some want a finishing school, some want to get some more O levels, some want to retake a year, some just don't know what they want and some want a resting place en route and in life. There is nothing wrong with any of these reasons. For each, or all, of these reasons, people might come to a Sixth Form College. We wanted to be truly open access but we must make sure that we have the right courses for the right person. We can say that the two year College to which all the first year students will have come at sixteen in September this year, is no easy matter to organise or an easy place in which to get to know people. We have to look at the problems of loneliness, we have to look to the problem of *esprit*, we have to look to the problem of settling down, and we have to look to the problem of some courses being rather too short, we must look to a large number of people wanting to come for three years. Whether they come at fifteen plus or sixteen plus, whether they stay till eighteen or nineteen, for all these young people we have to present a proper and individual course. We know that the reasons students come are varied, but we have to make somehow a unified comprehensive College, where each develops according to his or her own ability and each takes the course right for him or her at that time. We must mix the students up somehow some of the time if we are to get any feeling and any unity. We must mix them socially and administratively, and we mustn't let problems of administration stand in our way. The administration which would be good (for example the appointment of a Bursar) must serve the academic and social nature of the College. We must make sure that each student matters separately and very much is someone and that the tutor base of 12 to 15 students remains the basic set-up. We have, of course, in each tutor group to see that there is a mixture of subjects, of levels of ability, and of the two sexes and to all of these separately we have to give equal emphasis. We have to belief that each sex, each subject group and each level of each subject – is equally important and we have in all this to try and believe that subjects are not particularly separate anymore, indeed, less and less so. The nature of pastoral care in the College is basic to it. We will need expertise on the modern problems of drugs, smoking and alcohol and we must not with our age group be without people on the staff who have a hold on these problems of our time or the problems connected with sex education, marriage guidance and human relationships, and race. Sixteen plus is the beginning of the adventure of adulthood and young people need our guidance and our care. Schools need a gradually diminishing framework, a gradually relaxing atmosphere. That framework may hold fairly well and strong until sixteen plus. One of the great advantages of a College like Itchen is that we do not have younger children who need a closed framework. We can relax this imposed framework gradually so that people here are using self-discipline and not depending too much on external discipline, even though they may appear to want it. We, in my belief, have to give a lead in relaxing that discipline. We have to know that young adults have gradually to be taught to use self-discipline and not to over rely on the discipline of a framework. We must do this so that they are ready when they leave us at eighteen plus to go forward to places where quite frankly the discipline can be very relaxed indeed. The word is 'civilised' for all our behaviour each to the other where we care about people. But it may be that at eighteen plus young people are going forward to other places where there is no kind of imposed external discipline and where they do have to rely completely on themselves. It is clearly part of our purpose and business to get them ready to use their whole personality and skills in terms of self-discipline.'

Like Jo Dunford, Jane Hale had been a member of staff at Itchen Grammar School during its transition into a Sixth Form College and she remembers Philip's start and subsequent years at Itchen. Jane says of Philip's arrival 'He made a dramatic impression on the College from the start. Although, up to this time, we had been taking students as sixteen plus from nearby schools, and were in the process of becoming a fully fledged Sixth Form College, our curriculum was still largely that of the former Grammar School. Mr. Vennis wanted the College to offer subjects at CSE as well as O level, and gradually the College began to offer a wider range of courses to suit an open access College. He encouraged the introduction of very successful CEE courses; a qualification specifically designed for Sixth Formers, as well as a range of new and innovative A level syllabuses throughout the 70s and 80s. He was enthusiastic for Itchen staff to be in the forefront of developing these courses, and several members of staff became senior examiners in these new syllabuses.

P.H.V. was more interested in people than bricks and mortar. He used to say 'I'm not interested in having a posh College,' and the fabric of the College did not change significantly during his eighteen years. He was more interested in academic achievement, in his words, looked for, 'that of God which is in every teenager'. He wanted students to aim high academically. He was known to fling open the door of a classroom to demand, "Who, in here, is aiming for Oxbridge?" Woe betide the class in which every hand did not shoot up! He would give coaching in interview technique and help students personally to get into Oxford and Cambridge. In addition, students were encouraged to take part in public speaking competitions such as, 'Youth Speaks', to produce College magazines and to learn a musical instrument.

The annual Speech Evening was seen as an opportunity to show the language skills of the College. For weeks beforehand, every lunch hour would be spent in the hall, practising the reading aloud of passages in every foreign language taught in the College. Audibility and pace were everything, and while not all students enjoyed the experience at the time, it gave invaluable experience in speaking in public.

In those days the College was small enough to hold full assemblies. These might be either inspirational or sometimes disciplinary, but usually memorable. The annual Remembrance Assembly was always quite an emotional affair. The Honours Boards, bearing the names of the former pupils of Itchen who had died in the First and Second World Wars were on either side of the stage, and P.H.V. would refer to these names and remind students of how like themselves these boys had once been. On stage would be two people with a personal connection to those named, providing a real sense of connection to the events of the past. Poems would be read, and Elgar's music played. On one occasion the 'Last Post' was played by a student. P.H.V. made no apology for the solemnity of these occasions. He was not in favour of war, but used to say that our fists were made to fight if necessary, as well as to knead bread.

In March, 1987, after the Zeebrugge ferry disaster, P.H.V. held a special assembly. My daughter, who was a student at Itchen at the time, recalls seeing with astonishment how his words, and the music which was played, reduced the biggest and toughest Southampton lads to tears. P.H.V. was not afraid to be emotional when he felt the occasion demanded it.

General Studies were known, typically for P.H.V., as Humane Studies, intended to broaden the learning experience of students. Absence from these lessons was taken seriously. On one notable occasion, those who had missed a lesson were detained in the hall to be admonished with the words, long remembered by ex-students, "This is not Butlins and my name is not Billy!" Over the years this became the stuff of Itchen folklore!

P.H.V. cared about his staff in a very personal way. Any family problem, such as the sickness of a child, was treated with great generosity, and we were encouraged to put family life first. I am sure that this made us all more conscientious teachers. He would go out of his way to help individual members of staff who had health problems. He encouraged staff as well as students to aim high, and it is no coincidence that, in his time, no fewer than three Itchen staff went on to become Principal of their own Sixth Form Colleges.

Of all P.H.V.'s achievements, the one for which the College undoubtedly owes him the greatest debt of gratitude, is its very existence. In the 1980s, there were strenuous moves to merge the Colleges in Southampton. No one could have fought harder that P.H.V. to keep Itchen College open as an individual institution. Without his efforts there would undoubtedly be no Sixth Form

College on the eastern side of the city – always the less fashionable side – and hundreds of students over the years would have been poorer for this.' (Jane Hale, Head of English, now retired from Itchen College, but still working as an Examiner for AQA in A level English). At the end of his first term at Itchen in July 1971, Philip held the first of what would turn out to be seventeen leavers' services, where he reviewed what students had undertaken whilst at College and looked forward to their new beginnings elsewhere. Much of what he said in the first service was similar to the address he had given his Sixth Form College Principals earlier in the term – an outline of the history of Grammar Schools/Sixth Form Colleges and the philosophy behind his beliefs in State education and Sixth Form Colleges in particular. He told those leaving that day in 1971 that 'It will be twenty years before we know whether a Sixth Form College works. Those leaving who have done two or three years here will have some of the answers. Those leaving next year who will have come right through the comprehensive system from the age of eleven will have more of the answers. To all those leaving now you can look back on being the last children of eleven to enter Itchen Grammar School and who have been the last and youngest members of the place all through – it is not too sentimental nor inappropriate to hope that you will carry on some pride in Itchen Grammar School and that you won't feel that the change has been for the worse, that you will feel maybe a little lucky to have managed your seven years of teenagedom here. Both you and those who have been here for two years who came at sixteen plus will I hope have some kind of love of scholarship, caught some feeling for some special knowledge from one of the staff or come to care in depth for some specialism, you will have had some windows opened on the joys of discovery in knowledge and learning. You will have met friends and you will keep them. You will have taken part in some drama or music or club which will be a happy memory. I need to say a little about what institutions like this are trying to do. People matter, not things, not bricks and mortar, not schools or colleges, not institutions and not countries. You will fall in love, as people say, and if you care about people you won't hurt them. Parents matter – you may be different from them but they have a right to their worries. Don't push them. The generation gap is not new – the generations have always differed. Do show them loving care – and other people. Friendships – these are love too – and children too when you have them – though perhaps that is the easiest love to see. For the moment the love you have will mostly be for your girl or boy friends. I think the best rule of thumb for behaviour is – to the young women to say "you will be treated as you appear to want to be treated" and to the young men – in some ways more importantly – to remind you that girls are full people and full individuals with full emotions and full minds, just as you are. You do yourself an injury whenever you treat a girl other than as a full complete individual – an object.

Will you care about coloured people and old people or the community or will you think it is just to be used and abused? Coming from this College you have a chance to lead and care more than most. There is in England, from time to time, an attempt to stir up a wave of racial prejudice but as research has shown me the British are really among the most tolerant of people, and you have to underline that tolerance by everything you do. It is, of course, that people are different, including the colour of their skins. That we are black or white is one of the great wonders – so don't get involved in any quite disgusting racial intolerances. No group thinking or acting. It may be said that our kind of organised society depends most and centrally on the transmission of memories and I hope that when you are thirty five you will want to be able to transmit to your children some happy memory of some day or hour in Itchen Sixth Form. Yet we must just not look back, these things must be basic for looking forward and for optimism. We must have, however giant the problems around us, some hope that British Society is one we will want to live in to which we will want to contribute and to which we will be able to offer some useful service based upon something we have done, learned, or been through, someone we have befriended or who befriended us during these teenage years. I have to declare myself an optimist about the set up. I have to believe, I do believe, that this system can be made to work and that we shall have a liberal, rational but still sentimentally based College and that those virtues of the old Grammar School which I value very dearly can continue – love of learning, well based good fun, and strong friendships. We wish you all that you want for yourself as you leave us'. The leaving of these students, many of whom had been in the Grammar School for all of their Secondary education, marked the real beginning of the Sixth Form College as it is known today. The following year, December 1972, Philip addressed a conference in Woking (where a changeover to Sixth Form Colleges was to take place) entitled 'The Sixth Form in Action' at which again he talked about his philosophy and thoughts, eighteen months after his appointment at Itchen. He began by saying that 'I have five hundred and twenty five students attending the College for a variety of reasons. Some of the girl students come to be 'cosy' since they were not ready to go forward into the world yet, and the College was regarded by some as a 'finishing' school. This is alright since we do valuable things for them and with them. Unemployment is another reason why young people come to the College, in some cases students had left school, gone out to work for a while and then decided to continue with their studies. The Sixth Form College is not a rival to the established Technical Colleges, it complements it, not rivals it. The Sixth Form College is unable to compete with the Technical College as far as equipment goes. It is 'nonsense' to think that the boy who is not academically gifted is automatically good with his hands. There is a large area of research needed for the less able boy. One of the biggest problems in the running of a Sixth Form College is getting to know the students in the short space of two years. We would really like a three year College – from sixteen to nineteen years old; and there are signs that this is coming. English education is always in a rush; people thought that one ought to have A levels by the age of eighteen and a degree by twenty one. I think a look at America might convince us it is not necessary to be in such a hurry. The Sixth Form College ought not be too big, I suggest the new College for Woking ought to be a reasonable size and should have a generous staff to student ratio. The ideal to press for would be one member of staff for each nine students. The students at Itchen are 'frank' and not rebellious, they take their work very seriously and many of the less able do too much homework. The College gives its students a general education in the widest sense and covers many aspects including careers advice and sex education. Students are given contraceptive advice since every time a girl becomes pregnant it is not just a social tragedy but a failure of the education system. Itchen College timetables a double period for general studies courses and these emphasise areas of knowledge which are important for an understanding of ourselves as individuals, and of the society and world we live in. I conclude by saying that the Sixth Form College has advantages and disadvantages, but it does give the opportunity to many young people a student life that they had been denied for years in England.'

Canon Ronald Milner was appointed as Chairperson of Itchen College Governing Body in 1972 and he remained the Chairperson until he moved away from the area in 1983. He was always very supportive of Philip and committed to the College. Some forty years later he has recalled some of his memories of working with Philip and Itchen College. Ronald begins 'Philip Vennis was tailor made for the development of sixteen to eighteen Secondary Colleges in Southampton following the 1967 reorganisation of education in the city which transformed the Grammar Schools into open access comprehensive schools and secondary colleges. The process of change took five years to complete so Philip took up his appointment as Principal during the last year of the implementation of the change in 1971. Prior to this reorganisation Itchen College had been a co-educational Grammar School taking pupils who qualified for entry by passing the 11-plus examination. Philip's approach to education was 'comprehensive' in the fullest sense of the word. He was totally dedicated to the concept if 'open access' which allowed young people of all abilities to continue their education within a College community which provided resources and encouragement to develop their ability to the fullest extent. The Itchen prospectus was designed so that students were challenged to explore their potential not only in academic subjects but in cultural activities and practical everyday social skills. The more curriculum spread there was the happier Philip would be! So alongside Mathematics, Biology, Chemistry, English literature and the like, there were strong departments in music, drama and art and investment in home economics and a wide range of sports activities. A major installation in the Principal's office was a large board on which was displayed the timetable of the College activities. This was a complex display allowing Philip to see exactly what subjects were being taught, where they were being taught and who was teaching them! It was the College in action at a glance; an all embracing picture encapsulating the very being of Itchen. It was also typical of Philip's determination to keep the College focussed on its comprehensive purpose. This could have slipped into oppressive control but he had a deftness of touch which made blunt confrontation of problems acceptable to staff who needed checking and students whose activities were disruptive and threatened the reputation of the College. No one was in any doubt about Philip's total enthusiasm for building a thriving, creative and caring College community. It was his clear commitment to the College community which convinced staff and students that the firm demands of his leadership were not driven by a personal power complex.

The College Speech Day was a major event in the college calendar. This was the occasion when Philip focussed what had been happening during the previous twelve months and related it to the overall aim of the College. He gave a great deal of time to the preparation of his Presentation, revising it and honing it until he was satisfied it reflected the whole range of what was going on and made clear its comprehensive purpose. Inevitably there was an account of academic achievements in all the subjects covered by the curriculum. There was also an account of activities which contributed to the cultural richness of the college. Among these were music, Drama and Art, Home Economics, social action in the local community and, of course, sports activities. Philip's own special interest was literature and the Arts so you always detected a note of enthusiasm as he recounted the contribution of the college Drama department and the concerts performed by the various college music ensembles, not to mention the exhibitions put on by the Art Department. Speech Day was the occasion when the College opened its doors to the local community and the city. The Mayor was always invited as was the Chief Executive, the Director of Education, the local M.P. and City Councillors. Philip was acutely aware of the place of the College in the life of the city and jealous for its reputation. There was always an edge of rivalry with the other two Secondary Colleges and their Principals!'

Canon Milner goes on with his memories by recalling activities of some of the College Departments, he begins with the Music Department of which he says that 'Under the leadership of Jonathan Palmer Itchen music was thriving in the seventies and early eighties. The department's reputation attracted students with musical ability and entering the rooms accommodating the department involved walking carefully through a spread of music stands, drum kits, double basses and assorted clarinets, violins and the whole gamut of music making. There was an air of excitement about the music at Itchen! Concerts were a regular part of college life featuring chamber orchestras, a regular Big Band sound and jazz events, not to mention a strong choral contribution enabled by Miss Cynthia Jolly, a member of staff and an ex-opera singer. One outstanding achievement was the appearance of a College orchestra at the Royal Albert Hall, London, playing music composed by students at the College. It was indeed a golden age of music making strongly encouraged by Philip.' Canon Milner continues with his reflections on the Drama Department by saying that 'Philip had a particular interest in English Literature and was well experienced in the production of plays. Shakespeare was his favourite and much quoted! The College had a Drama studio for small-scale productions while larger productions were staged in the College hall. Memorable among these were Kapek's 'Insect Play' and Ben Johnson's 'Bartholomew's Fair' produced by Mr. Gray, one of the three Deputy Principals. The latter play caused a moment of tension when Mr. Gray allowed an actor to utter the words "shit in the chair", claiming that they were the words used in the original seventeenth century production. Philip, however, deemed them inappropriate for an Itchen production and requested that they be altered to "sit in the chair". The outcome of this clash of the purists is not recorded!

During Philip's reign at Itchen the Art Department produced several excellent exhibitions of student's work. Just as the Music Department was a litter of instruments so the Art Department was festooned with canvases of students' portrait painting, still life and landscapes. The emphasis was on originality and an adventurous use of colour. The feel of the Department was free and exploratory! One development which Philip encouraged was the use of photography as an art medium. This allowed students who had limited ability with paint, brush and pencil to capture images on film and develop them in the College 'dark room'. In every way possible Itchen was widening the range of opportunities it offered to students encouraging them to discover for themselves and explore their potential.'

As Jane Hale mentioned in her recollections the reading of foreign languages and Literature readings were a central part of the Itchen Speech Day, Canon Milner reiterates this in his passage on the Language Departments. He says 'One regular feature of Speech Day was student reading of passages of literature in a wide variety of languages, including lesser known languages like Russian. This encouragement of language learning was part of the College commitment to widening horizons and encouraging international understanding. During Philips time at the College a link was established with Atlantic College founded in 1962 in Wales. This College was the brain child of Kurt Hahn who believed that a peaceful world could be made more possible if students from many different nations were encouraged to live, work and learn together. Air Marshall Lawrence Darvall who was instrumental in founding Atlantic College took up the idea. It is easy to see how this vision of peaceful co-existence through mutual understanding was inviting to Philip with his attachment to the Quaker community, being an Attender at Southampton Quaker Meetings.

Another feature of Speech Day and other occasions when the College opened its doors to the wider community was the contribution of the Home Economics Department, under the leadership of Mrs. Rose, preparing and serving refreshments to large numbers of guests. The Department included a small flat fully furnished as a venue to entertain a small number of guests. In this flat the students were able to learn the basics of hospitality. On one occasion the Principal, his wife and the Chairman of Governors and his wife entertained the American Ambassador and his wife at a dinner served in the flat by the students.

If Speech Days were for public display of the life of the College Community, Assemblies were internal gatherings for the strengthening of College life. The Hall was the venue for these College student gatherings. Philip was always the conductor of assemblies, though guests were invited to address students from time to time. In a way assemblies were a sort of anchorage of college corporate life and an occasion when Philip's Quaker beliefs were on display. He frequently used the phrase 'That of God in every man' and it was a salutary experience to be there when he led several hundred students in a period of silent reflection for two or three minutes. There was never any disturbance or restlessness that I recall. A special occasion was the Remembrance Day Assembly each November. I have a vague recollection that members of Itchen Grammar School who gave their lives in the First and Second World Wars were remembered by name but I clearly recollect the regular reading of a poem by John Pudney 'For Johnny' lamenting the death of an airman –

Do not despair
For Johnny head in air;
He sleeps as sound
As Johnny underground.

Fetch out no shroud
For Johnny in the cloud;
And keep your tears
For him in after years:

280

Better by far
For Johnny-the-bright-star,
To keep your head,
And see his children fed.

Canon Milner concludes his recollections and memories with the following passage. 'In the years following the seventies education has been increasingly seen as the avenue by which the national economy is fed. Its function has been more narrowly defined as a tool to strengthen the capacity of the state to generate wealth. The curriculum is pruned to save money; language studies and humanities are subordinated to more commercially relevant subjects like science and engineering. The windows of education are being closed and the curtains drawn. For Philip this would have been an alien educational world. Itchen College was in the business of opening windows, pulling the curtains open and encouraging students of every sort of ability to explore what excited them, whether it was maths or chemistry, Russian or Music, Drama or Art, Cooking and Baking, Basketball or learning to drive a car. Education was about self discovery and widening horizons, becoming a more rounded and able person, equipped to contribute to the general good and earn a living. Philip's guiding light was 'That of God in every man' which could be translated 'That which is creative in everyone'. Itchen was about creativity. It was a place where hope was stirred and opportunity embraced. In large measure the inspiration which made that work was Philip and the staff he assembled and led.'

Throughout his time at Itchen College Philip spent much of his time visiting the feeder Secondary Schools, to which he was often invited as guest speaker on the occasion of their Speech Days or to talk to the pupils who would be leaving their Secondary School at the end of the year. He would provide information and inspiration for their future. Open Days held at Itchen for incoming students always included an address from the Principal, as attracting students to the College and selling the College to these pupils was vitally important for the future of Itchen. The information he gave at these events covered much of College life and he talked about open access, courses available, organisation of the College, pastoral care within the College, general studies curriculum, careers support and programme, A levels, O levels, CEE, methods of teaching, the student council, social clubs and activities and often summed up by saying "Use the College, enjoy it, for those who do not go on it is a chance to be a student for the first and possibly the last time. It is a liberal regime, permission is given but there is no permissiveness – we will not put up with it. It is a chance to learn to be a student whilst still being at home with home control and support. There is not constant supervision, but you have to move to a definite goal as set out in your timetable and with your Tutor. Learn to be yourself and be disciplined by your inner self; be self-disciplined and work with determination; we have rules on behaviour and work but there are no rules on dress excepting that it should be reasonable and not provocative. We will listen to the student voice, you are free to be yourself and one of the central achievements of the open access college is that there is a student's life for all abilities. We will help you but do not come if you do not want to work. Itchen is devoted to being a happy place to grow up in – a community of caring individuals where individuality may best be shown in caring for others less lucky. Our overall intention is to produce contented and fulfilled adults who may well question our society and wish to reform it but not to destroy it – who will cling to the centre and will distrust those with extreme notions and nostrums who would only produce chaos in which all would suffer. Girls in particular have a larger place in carrying forward a civilised torch – what kind of homes and wives and mothers and children will they provide? Girls have to look forward (such is the dual and more difficult nature of girls' education) to being married and to being thirty plus, when young children are at school – and then needing to use their trained career from thirty to sixty – the returner's career. We must have no more untrained widows, divorcees etc who are among the new poor. Our assembly here is of a religious nature, sometimes there is a silence. The all important Christian virtues of humility, forgiveness, repentance and love must shine through in the life of each teenager taken separately here, and therefore the College's life. So come and enjoy two years with us – examinations, other work, leisure time, social life – the real education from sixteen to nineteen – the drawing out of each through late adolescence to full adulthood.'

When Philip was guest speaker at a Secondary School Speech Day the emphasis of what he said to the assembled audience would vary, for example when he addressed a boys' Secondary School such as Merry Oak he would include not only information about Itchen and Further Education and careers but he would ask such questions as "What kind of young man will you be? What will your attitudes to girls and women, marriage and parenthood, your employer and society be? " He then proceeded to answer some of these thought provoking questions. "These are the things by which you will be measured. Treating girls and women as your complete equals, finding the right partner, distinguishing sex from love but remembering that they are best in unity and unified, the family unit – remembering what you owe by way of hard work. You may not owe society anything but you want to take part in it – maybe reform it, but nevertheless nurture it – you yourself will be the sufferer if it falls apart. Civilisation may be on very thin ice – don't attack it unless you have something better to offer and you are certain of it. Be wary of all those who have extreme notions on how to alter things. The end product may be worse than the one you have. Ask questions, yes, but human societies need pattern, structure and organisation or all suffer; chaos brings unhappiness.'

At Sholing Girls' School Speech Day Philip tailored some of his speech to include the following. 'Co-education is a preparation for life, it goes on until death. I believe that marriage and parenthood can be fulfilment for women and we do not have to feel that being a housewife is not anything. What greater fulfilment perhaps for many women? Nevertheless men's death in middle age is a mark of our society and girls would be silly if they were not educated as far as they can be for an independent career.'

Recruitment of students was a fiercely contended issue between the three Sixth Form Colleges in Southampton and institutions beyond the city boundary. The prospectus of each College was an important part of the promotion of each individual college. In his book 'Sixth Form Colleges' (1978), Eric Macfarlane uses part of Itchen's as an example of courses available. He writes 'It is not usually difficult to see either an exceptionally gifted or an exceptionally backward student as an individual with particular needs and problems. The Sixth Form has traditionally made special arrangements for the very able student, allowing him to take extra subjects and special papers and giving him individual or small group tuition in preparation for the Oxbridge scholarship examinations. The comprehensive college, like the comprehensive school, will also naturally attempt to give the same sort of consideration to the student with severe learning difficulties. It is the great majority of students, those who fall somewhere between the two extremes, that are in danger of losing their identity and being categorised. The first and probably the most important stage in avoiding this is to establish a curriculum that attempts to provide the exact combination of studies that each individual requires. Such a curriculum will not only offer different levels of work but will allow a student who so wishes to choose a course that combines work at various levels. It should enable him to specialise or, alternatively, to keep his options open. It will not package its subjects into administratively convenient combinations such as arts or science groupings. The Itchen College prospectus, for example, offers 44 General Certificate of Education courses at A level, 26 two year and 30 one year O levels, 15 Certificate of Extended Education and 6 CSE (sixth form) options. In addition, students are able to prepare for the examinations of the Institute of Linguists, the Royal Society of Arts, the London Chamber of Commerce, the Pitman Examinations Institute, the Guildhall School of Music and Drama and the Music examinations of the Associated Board. There is a range of 24 non-examination courses which occupy all students for four periods of the week and a recreational activities programme, also followed by all students, consisting of 30 options.

A curriculum of this kind bears little resemblance to that of the traditional sixth form. It includes a host of new subjects, both within the GCE range and in addition to it, which provide for previously neglected attitudes, interests and career aspirations. Furthermore, not only does it greatly extend the levels, and combination of level, at which students are able to work, but it introduces alternative syllabuses and approaches within a subject to cater for different interests at the same level. It is, for example, particularly pleasing to see the comprehensive colleges introducing the syllabuses of the Institute of Linguists alongside the GCE O and A level language courses.' In another section of his book Mr. Macfarlane quotes a different part of Itchen College's prospectus as an example of a totally different philosophy for the open access sixth to that of the sixth form of the past. This quotation is taken from Itchen College's prospectus of 1975, 'What is most important for each student separately is that he or she will have pursued his or her potential to the utmost while at the college and will look back on two or three years with pleasure and happiness.

The College hopes to make its students happier, more contented and more fulfilled adults – as married young people, and as parents – in their work and in their play. These are some of its aims. All are welcome at the College – no matter whether they have a number of O levels or none, a number of CSE 1's or none, a number of other grades at CSE or none. It is open-access.'

Mr. Macfarlane then comments 'It takes some courage to justify an educational establishment for the post statutory school-leaving age in terms of student happiness and fulfilment, particularly at a time of pragmatism, when objectives are more fashionable than aims, and accountability a more acceptable concept than idealism. Moreover, we Englishmen are easily embarrassed by words like 'happy' and 'fulfilment', especially if we encounter them as a declaration of intent. Perhaps we feel it a weakness to acknowledge human desire for such a state of wellbeing, or fear that to admit to higher feelings and the existence of values beyond the definable and measurable is too open an invitation to the criticism of the sceptic and the ridicule of the cynic. Yet, if it is not to become a servant of its own system and daily routine, a school or college must have ideals in the form of general aims.

Mrs. Jan Feber was a part-time member of the English Department staff, and she writes the following recollection of her time at Itchen College. 'Philip was headmaster/Principal during most of the eighteen years I spent teaching English part-time at Itchen College. I saw in him a person of enormous energy and determination, volatile and irascible at times but always enthusiastic for the good of the College. No one could doubt that he put the students first in planning and consideration. He cared deeply about their well-being and tried to develop the potential in every individual.

My husband was a Head of Department when Philip arrived and worked under him for two years. Both being men of strong character and ideals, they did not always see eye to eye but each, I think, developed a respect and liking for the other and they remained friends for life. When my husband left to become Vice-Principal of another College we continued, with our growing families of a similar age, to share friendship and interests. Perhaps for this reason my memories of Philip are more concerned with him as a family man than as a Principal. While he demanded allegiance and high standards at all times he was ready to listen to my needs as a mother, even when I pushed him to the limit in my requests for suitable working hours! I leave comments on the vicissitudes of his personality and success as a Principal to those who knew him better in that capacity.

The episode which stands out in my memory illustrates Philip's intuitive kindness, especially where the family was concerned. It was my small daughter's sixth birthday and she was laid aside with a nasty bout of 'flu. Unfortunately, it was a teaching day for me so I had to leave her in the care of the cleaning lady, who also did emergency child-minding. She was not happy! As I went into afternoon lessons I happened to meet Philip who asked after the family, as he always did. I told him of my daughter's illness and asked, as I had a free period at the end of the afternoon, if I might go home early. I shall never forget his reaction and the warm concern in his voice.

"You can't leave a six-year-old at home on her birthday," he exclaimed. "Go home to her now. I'll cover your classes for you". And he sent me off then and there. It was a kindness typical of Philip Vennis which, far from betraying any laxity of discipline, promoted a strong work ethic since he so clearly valued his staff and sought to alleviate their personal needs. I and my family will always remember him as a kind, supportive boss and a good friend.'

Despite running a large college and all the commitments linked to it, Philip often was invited to talk at conferences and on more than one occasion was asked to take part in Church Services. One such instance was when he talked about 'Teenagers' at a Unitarian service in March 1974. Philip was always keen on raising Itchen's profile and status within the City of Southampton. The following passage includes some of his thoughts on teenagers. 'It is unhappily true that not everybody seeing the modern teenager sees "that of God in every man". Hackles still rise regularly – long hair, patched jeans and an apparent general air of anything goes or permissiveness. What I want to do is to try and see through the new "uniform" (so to speak) to the young people beneath. To try not to write them off or to judge them in a group. If you judge people in gangs they will get into gangs. That each is different, that each human being is different – God's individual – is something that we Christians know and agree with. Why then do we find it so difficult to make individual judgements, each of us separately, about each of them? Teenagers to my knowledge and experience are more different from each other than children who are younger, that must seem obvious, or adults who are older. Adolescence is the age of divergence and diversity.

Each of them as they grow through puberty have to entertain the vexing problems of adult life, the emotional, and the sexual, financial problems of decision making. How ready do we get them for all this? How much sympathy? How much of an ear do we extend? How quick are we to write them off? Is all this new? It is not of course, as Juliet (who was fourteen in Shakespeare's play) knew too well; the girl, fearful yet loving, trying to decide what is right and not right in a family where father and mother are demanding actions that she can no longer carry out. Where to turn, who to ask, what to do – the resort to the quick marriage. All this we can see any day around us; in the overwhelming emotions of the moment. "Give me my Romeo, and when he shall die, take him and cut him out in little stars, and he will make the face of heaven so fine, that all the world will be in love with night, and pay no worship to the garish sun". That's how she and many since have felt. The play like its modern counterpart 'West Side Story' is a whole text book in some ways of teenage behaviour under highly emotional stress. We know it to be with us, we have seen it in Southampton.

Nevertheless what is new is the deliberate or almost deliberate attempt for the sake of money to dangle before teenagers too early – hopes of adult life, behaviour patterns and decisions. Schools cannot solve what parents cannot do, what society imposes. The media, does it help or hinder? It is curious that we ask teenagers often to adopt an old age pensioner for example, perhaps it is time to reverse, and can old age pensioners adopt a teenager? We have to learn to listen, to advise a little restraint, hesitation, prevarication and above all to assure them of a loving kindness derived for us at any rate from a belief that we are all in one family through God the Father and that members of a family help one another. It is the Friar in 'Romeo and Juliet' to whom Shakespeare gives those wise words "wisely and slowly; they stumble that run fast". Good advice I think for many teenagers in connection with their emotions.

But of course there is the generation gap; we may be written off, we may not understand, they think our emotions like our bodies may in their eyes have slowed up. They do sometimes move in a flock – but most are not sheep. If fewer are leaders then fewer are followers. Separately, individually you will find them courteous and kind and loving, and almost over willing to help society in many ways. Indeed such is the call on their good will for so many charities and sponsored goings-on of all kinds, that there is a danger of their becoming slaves to a society that depends more on charity than on justice.

"Leave them alone and they will come home", as the nursery rhyme goes, may be quite apt for us towards them. Teenagers want a just society and they must be allowed their say. They will always be, have always been a ginger group, as it were, in society, and now we have caused them to be mature earlier and educated longer. We have imposed very great problems which very few adults could solve. Juliet could behave, at least, naturally and marry at fourteen, but now she would have to worry about O and A levels, not to say education, perhaps till the age of twenty one and Romeo would have to become financially and economically viable before marriage. So that if we want them to observe what we rightly think is a proper Christian and moral code, we have to remember that we make this increasingly difficult over an increasing period of time through the monies they have or earn, the society they are in, the earlier maturity they have, the longer education imposed and a great complex of difficulties like housing and so on.

As I go about my business daily, I really sometimes am surprised that we get as few problems as we do, not as many. I have always thought that "blessed are the young in heart" is so to speak, the missing Beatitude. Certainly it is one which society needs to remember. They are not wrong but only different. To be young and urgent and impetuous, and emotional and above all idealist – let's not decry all that or them. I will finish by reciting "God who touches earth with beauty", written by Mary S. Edgar, a Canadian author in 1925 and to me it represents the optimism of youth.

God who touchest earth with beauty,
Make me lovely too;
With thy spirit re-create me,
Make my heart anew.

Like Thy springs and running waters,
Make me crystal pure;
Like Thy rocks of towering grandeur,
Make me strong and sure.

Like Thy dancing waves in sunlight,
Make me glad and free;
Like the straightness of the pine-trees,
Let me upright be.

Like the arching of the heavens,
Lift my thoughts above;
Turn my dreams to noble action –
Ministries of love.

God who touchest earth with beauty,
Make me lovely too;
Keep me ever, by Thy Spirit,
Pure and strong and true.

A contemplative moment in the grounds of Itchen. 1975

A completely different audience at the Gurney Dixon Centre listened to Philip in 1975 (and on other occasions) talk about Sixth Form Colleges and their links with feeder schools. His audience was of fellow Principals, Headteachers of Secondary Schools and officials and Advisers from Hampshire and Southampton Education. He gives an overview and insight of the running of a large College. He begins with an introduction about the City Schools. 'Itchen is open-access and fed by seventeen City Comprehensives (10 co-educational, 4 boys and 3 girls). In addition a number come from the fifth forms of St.Mary's Catholic College, King Edward V1th Grammar School and private schools in and around the City, or sometimes from further afield. The County Careers Service will have been involved at an early stage in the secondary child's life, and over options in the third and fourth years. The boy or girl will spend, of course, only four years in a Southampton Comprehensive (twelve to sixteen).

In the early part of their fifth year, meetings will be arranged at which the Heads of the Sixth Form Colleges and the Technical or Careers staff of the Colleges will meet pupils and parents to give information about their courses etc. The Area Office issues a number of brochures for various ages which sum up the various possibilities at sixteen to nineteen. In a sense, since the whole City has access to all the Colleges, they are in competition with one another, which is not always helpful to decision making.

Each College runs an Open Evening and/or Day in January to which large numbers of fifth formers and their parents come. After that, from Itchen, the Deputy Headmistress makes arrangements to interview – at the School or at the College – individual fifth formers who have expressed a desire to come to Itchen. She starts at about half term in the Lent term and goes on until after Whitsun. The schools will have been issued with large sets of the College brochure/prospectus and individual contacts made with the careers staff. The careers staff at Itchen will have been closely involved. During the year, in addition, there are subject or Faculty meetings between the staff of the feeding schools, especially the nearer ones, at Itchen, with the staff of the subject or Faculty here. The Advisory Body is also involved. Thus there are a great many ways in which information about the College is fed into the Comprehensive schools.

Finally the College holds an Induction Week after O level and CSE in early July. The Deputy Headmistress who is Head of the intake year and in charge of the access arrangements, arranges a week based on the second year timetable in which all prospective students can taste any subjects of their choice at A, O, CSE, and CEE levels, and in addition get to know the schemes for General Studies (Humane Studies), Recreational Activities, Tutorships, Student Council, Assemblies etc. After a week or so of this all prospective students will feel, we hope, more certain that they wish to come to Itchen – and more important, more certain of the subjects they wish to study. In the case of the less able who come (CSE 4s down), it should be possible to finalise their timetable, and this is true also of the most able – those who are certain to get seven O Levels or more.

In September the Headmaster interviews all of the new intake, some very quickly, some more slowly, with the Deputy Headmistress, Director of Careers Guidance and the City Careers Officers present. He has to make sure that sets don't grow too large, that the right rooms are being used for the right size of set, that a new group is formed if absolutely necessary, and that students have put before them a wide range of options to which they may not have given great thought. It is part of the philosophy of the College that every student shall have quite forcibly put before them the advantages of going on with Mathematics or starting it again, of doing some Science for nearly every career, of looking open eyed at the careers possible, to, if necessary, bring students down to earth who are very greatly over-ambitious, to point out multiplicity of courses so that their education may include all sides of their personality, they must look at the possibility of Creative subjects, the need to consider going on with a language – or starting one, the new Modes 3 at CEE, new attitudes to old subjects, - new A Levels like Psychology or Russian or Engineering Science or Drama or Design Technology or Computing Science – to give a few examples.

With the compulsory General Studies Scheme which all students follow in rota within their mixed ability tutor groups, and with the compulsory Recreational Activities afternoons, the philosophy is carried through of seeing that all students undertake some Spiritual, Manipulative, Academic, Aesthetic and Athletic education during their two or possible three years here. It seems essential that we should not think that during these key years in their lives any of those sides of education should disappear. We have to stand up and be counted in my view on this issue.

We pride ourselves on turning away no one for whom there is a reasonable course unless (and this is very rare) a headteacher has been absolutely opposed to the student coming on for certain good reasons. In terms of a trial for half a term or so, or in terms of finding or inventing a course to suit, we are unlikely to stop people coming. Not laziness nor results nor teenage faults connected with sex, alcohol or even drugs would necessarily stop us having a student, nor would previous trouble with the Police. In fact in September 1974, 60 to 70 students came who had an average CSE 4 or less or had not taken CSE at all. This coming year we might expect rather more of these students, perhaps because of the economic crisis and perhaps because of the teenage employment position. Some come after trying a job for half a term or so, some leave after half a term or so.

About half the entry will do three A Levels (chosen out of 50 or so), perhaps

50+ do two, and the same again do one. Of the least able who come, some will do a Typing/Speedwriting sub-secretarial course, some may do a Link course with the Technical College, some will repeat CSE or do a mixture of CSE Modes 3 and CEEs, and some do try O Levels. Perhaps the College is seeing three levels of work, the two and three A leveller, the one A and A/O leveller, the CEE student. For this purpose CEE for us is for the least academic and can clearly be seen to be so. It will not be so useful if it is mainly used by A levellers in non-specialist subjects or as an equal to A/O. At sixteen plus it seems unfair to the less able to have mixed ability (except in non-exam work like General Studies), and they need their target and their ticket, and CEE in my view should be that.

Now we are absolutely open-access and that is how it must remain. We pin our flag which is still new and bright and burnished to just this philosophy; there is no going back; only to name the possibilities is to see them to be impossibilities. How can we revert to a four O level entry and why should we revert to four or three or two or one? Long since, some of us (when we ran grammar schools) ran open-access sixths. So can we now call a bar at 4 CSE 2s or three CSE 3s or even one CSE grade 3? All lines and barriers of this kind are inconsequential, ridiculous, invariably carry exceptions and are a nonsense when you consider them in detail. It is my belief that students are getting better and better Os and CSEs in the fifth forms because they do not have to have a certain number to gain entry to the Sixth Form. If they want to come, then we must let them. We are a retake fifth form, and what is wrong with that? Quite a number of young people do one year courses and they may well increase, leaving at seventeen plus (not eighteen plus) having improved their CSE 5s to CEE 3s. With what possible reasoning could we deny them that chance? In an all through school no one would ask them to leave; they would probably be encouraged to return to the fifth form and take their CSEs again. For some local employment and some technically based courses, a CSE 3 in Mathematics or a CSE 2 in English is becoming an important ingredient. Those are new levels and new responsibilities; some of those who stay one year gain O level and CSE 1s and leave or then they start on a two year course at A level. Some come in at seventeen having done a year's work; some come for half a term and leave when they find it too hard. A few (ROSLA) are already here who would have left at fifteen had the law not changed and made them stay until sixteen, and they have said if sixteen, why not seventeen? We have to de-fantasize some. That's sometimes unpleasant, but part of the job. They want to be doctors, engineers – often a career Maths based – and never will be. They must now at sixteen plus be told, and we must tell them. Some leave when they find it's hard work, and some are asked to leave – we do not hesitate too long. Two or three you could say are truly remedial; a number need careful attention to their English work. The Certificate of Extended Education is with us. I believe it to be very good. We already have sixty candidates for the pilot project in English. It is good because it is modular. Students take two or three modules in the first year and they will leave with those certificated. If they are back in the second year, they can do modules three to five and have those certificated separately. Its middle grade has to be an O level equivalent; its higher grades will be a starting point for A level. These are good things.

The first group of young people to have gone into the Southampton comprehensives in 1967 took their A levels and left Itchen in Summer 1974. Their results are there for you to see. I am going to read to you an article in 'The Guardian' on 5 November 1974. "With more and more Sixth formers and further education College students taking A levels there have been a few mutterings about the standard dropping. It is easy to say that an A level is not what it was, but hard to prove or disprove, or so it was thought. The great difficulty is the general absence of the actual scripts – the answers written by the A level candidates of yesteryear. Most G.C.E. examination boards, once the appeals have been sorted out, put the year's scripts through the shredder or pulper. They just do not have the storage space to file them all away. Possibly the only exception is the Joint Matriculation Board. When the Department of Education (then under Mrs. Thatcher's guidance) wanted to see whether or not A level standards were falling, the JMB came up with ten years' scripts. With Department of Education money and Schools Council guidance, a team has sat down and re-marked all of them, first using the marking guidance used at the time, and then the current system. Either way the results came out much the same as from the contemporary markers. There were variations, but generally work that would have earned a particular grade in 1963, would have received the same grade ten years later. More, it seems, just means more of the same quality".

It was a marvellous example of foresight for the then Southampton Local Education Authority to make this change, and those figures closely involved can feel very content indeed that all has gone so well. Only someone not wishing to look facts in the face can possibly think that those (and many of these came here) who might have gone to grammar school at eleven plus would, at eighteen plus, have been in some way better off had they gone to the grammar schools in the town (and we were one) rather than come through this system. Then we must remember those who would not have gone to the grammar schools; they have very many A levels too. At whatever level you look, and in whatever way you judge them – results, character, personality, interests, university entrance, jobs, numbers, variety of subjects – you are bound to feel that this new system has served them well, and in many cases better than any older system might have done. I renew my faith in this system on the evidence of three years' entry from the comprehensives to us.

Results at sixteen are better than ever this year. We ought to congratulate the twelve to sixteen schools on their immensely encouraging first three years of results. And it is early days yet and results are only one part of their success. Let us have a look at numbers. Of 330 or so who have come in this year 144 have over five O levels or CSE 1s, that is good and shows a rise again over last year, forty six per cent of our entry against forty two per cent for last year.

Itchen functions on reason and reasoning. The place at times is a marvellous melee of seven hundred disparate young people going easily and reasonably about their business to their work without physical or mental pushing or shoving. There are no unnecessary rules, but we do expect work. They do their work in working gear, and they are not provocative. I ask them to be reasonable, responsible, answerable for themselves, and so each separately largely is. Their sports teams are good, their drama and music too. Their elections are sensible, their common room (although it does not always win my personal approval) is their business and run efficiently. They are responsible for their own monies and Bank account and behave in a mature manner. They are young adults but still need our guidance, that is sure. They need our skills and their respect for us depends upon our being skilled; but we do not ask automatic respect for some name or title unless and until skills are shown. I include myself. My room is available and I am available and unless I can show them skills in timetabling, in advice, in general know how and experience in running the College, then I would not expect them particularly to respect me because of the word Headmaster on the door. These are our new generation and these are the lines of our and their feelings in these matters. It is all open. Most go about their business properly and work very hard here. All mingle in their mixed ability tutor groups in the recreational activities and tutor group for General Studies. In other words there is an area of the College which involves mixed ability teaching - not for any examination – and in which the tutor group is a unit where friendships across ability and background may be permanently made. This tutor group travels together with its tutor through its College time, although they have to separate for their A, O or CEE work.

All this with the administration and the one to one interviewing is expensive on staffing, but it also brings great pressures on staff. The quantity as well as quality of effort is high. New methods, new styles or examinations, new subjects and subject matters all bring very great pressure. These open-access colleges are not easy to run. There are very great central difficulties in going over subject registers and keeping track of that minority of students who choose to be bored by or fed up by that, or who continually want to change their courses. This causes senior staff to have a very heavy work load. Then there is the question of the sheer weight and number of testimonials to be written – and the not easy business of getting the necessary information via the Tutor groups. Like so much else in education, it works because a dedicated staff make it work.

But what is the purpose of all this? The fear must be that without continual effort on our part we shall become an examination shop. We must not make that fear real. Itchen has to be a good place to grow up in; where in two or three years, at sixteen to nineteen, in my view we will have to try still to assemble – to have some quietest moment – indeed some reverence, if not worship. We have to see ourselves as eight hundred (that number includes the staff) individuals working together and growing up together – with no loyalty to any institution as such – but with the feeling for one another that comes from working together and a proper loyalty to people here, a feeling too for many less lucky – not least in the community in our half of Southampton. We must move towards the community college ideal.

I defy, as I always do, visitors to the college to tell whether in the pel mel melee of the break bun-fight who is for Oxbridge, who is for the typing pool, who is for the Forces, who is for a practical apprenticeship or who is for Polytechnic, who is for three A levels at A/B and who is for four CSEs at 2/3. Their generation (and we can instance the generation gap) has more and more in common (in Pop, in clothes, in attitudes). Is there not in this sixteen to nineteen age group here, a natural swing towards comprehensiveness among them which will force our hands if we delay? So who are we to divide artificially those who are so naturally united? Education, I think, must not be, cannot afford to be, divisive. But that is not to say that each must not seek his or her own level in work and life, own natural interests and proper width and depth of learning. Each must separately go, as Itchen's words say, "as far as who goes farthest". We must be proud of A grades at A level and not proud of those who might have got them and did not, and we must be proud of our grade 3s at CSE if that is the farthest for them – proud of the student who has gone to be a Nursery Nurse, and proud of those who have gone to Honours Degrees, of the student who has gone to be a fisherman and of the student who is reading Physics and so on and on and on. We must do it all, we shall – the cadet, the mechanic, the manager and the shopman – all. Our *raison d'être* will be that we include both sexes – as is absolutely the norm, and so good for proper human and humane relationships – all classes, all abilities and all parental experiences. We are not right to exclude from our student life, if we think as we do that this is a moment in life which is wonderful because of its friendships, its lack as yet of parental and family and job (not to say mortgages) responsibilities – if it is so wonderful, and it is - we have no right to deny it to anyone who can take advantage of it. But we have to watch too, in a time of great financial stringency, the cost of running the place. The bargain at Itchen is that you come here, you follow your timetable (exam and non-exam) you do your work, otherwise you leave. Outside the bargain we are interested in other matters only when they affect work or when they are brought to our attention. We adopt from the generation we teach their own phrase 'play it cool'. We have our pastoral, tutorial responsibilities, we have our Counsellor, Deputies in charge of your groups, careers system, tutors, subject teachers who listen and help. The counselling is private; but we do not pry and we shall not be prurient about student life. They have their business and we have ours. Ours remains largely a teaching skill. We put it at their disposal. We cannot solve all their or their parents' problems; we haven't the time or the energy, nor the skills. We are just one more agency and a small one in this business.

We then here want to give the above average in ability, the average, and the something less than average teenager two years of student life. We have to stop allowing to be students only those of certain abilities or from fixed classes, or largely so. We are pleased to be agents of a great change in the makeup of who's who in a sixth form and I hope we shall continue to be so. That I hope is what Itchen is about, open access, often first generation student life, for hard-working, not an examination shop – where each matters separately.'

Two of the hard working staff that Philip mentioned in his speech at Gurney Dixon were Robin Corbin, who was Head of Art and Design and Norman Savage who was Head of Classics and later one of the Deputy Principals. The following passages illustrate their roles whilst at Itchen under Philip's Principalship. Robin Corbin begins 'I joined Itchen College in 1974 and I learnt that the staff had run a book on my being appointed as I was the only candidate Philip could look down to! I immediately took to this red haired freckle faced man and wondered at the time if he had the character traits generally associated with ginger hair. I soon discovered that he had. As a leader of one of the first sixth form colleges in the country he was fearless in standing up to the Authority and he demanded if not bullied them on several occasions to achieve his vision.

P.H.V. (as he was universally known) was unique in that he interviewed all incoming students. In the early days the student body numbered six hundred plus, so this was no mean task when one considers that in these days (2012) of over twelve hundred students, interviews cover two weeks and are carried out by a team. One recalls that some students came out from Philip's office with a programme of subjects entirely different from the ones they had planned to take. Whether this was Philip's instinct and insight into what suited the student or what suited the class numbers in time table planning we will never know! Meeting every student and feeling that they were part of his college extended to his staff. I have never worked under a Principal who valued the family so much. Time off for family matters was instantly granted, sometimes without an explanation being required, and few if any abused this trust and understanding.

A complex and talented man, Philip didn't suffer fools gladly. When he felt he needed to castigate a member of staff and they had the temerity to defy him he could erupt. The level of noise exuding from his office indicated the stage of proceedings. The next day Philip could often be seen walking with the aggrieved recipient around the college field where Philip would apologize for losing his rag but not conceding the point. Though I rarely disagreed with him, one incident comes to mind when I displayed a series of drawings of male nudes in the college foyer. These had been produced by art students on their weekly trip to the local art college for a life drawing session. The well endowed male model, so well drawn by my students, was a source of distraction for the female cleaners and Philip summoned me to his office. The conversation began by my being called by my Christian name Robin, which progressed to Mr. Corbin and concluded with Corbin. Needless to say after a short period of time, allowing for artistic integrity, the pictures were removed and the cleaners completed their chores on time. Philip was a great supporter of the visual and performing arts and during his reign, the Art, Music and Drama departments were particularly strong resulting in several annual plays and concerts. In his time loyalty and camaraderie were far stronger than they are today (2012) and staff get togethers were well supported and attended by the Principal. Philip always left a little early knowing that the staff needed to let their hair down. He had the foresight to know that the presence of the Principal can be a little daunting for new and young colleagues. I remember decorating one party with hanging Father Christmases which were done in Philip's image. I was moved to know that he kept several for years as a memento. I was also privileged to take a series of family portraits for him, and in the tranquillity of his home with his nearest and dearest the true Philip shone through.

Every year at Itchen we had annual Speech Days and Philip would choose the theme under the title of "An Evening of Music and the Spoken Word". The following topics were featured: Sir Winston Churchill, The Victorians, The American Bi-centenary (1776-1976), The Silver Jubilee, The Twenties, The International Year of the Child, The Twentieth Century, The Year of the Disabled, The Sea, Memories, 1914 – A Perspective, Education and Industry, U.N.O. 40 years old and Itchen at Twenty.

For me these epitomise what Philip was all about in trying to maintain a morality and discipline which nowadays are sometimes hard to perceive.

Apart from maintaining my original post as Head of Art and Design, I undertook many roles at Itchen College and was part of Philip's management team.

Nobody gets it all right but I had the pleasure of sharing important years with a man whose heart was truly in the right place.' Norman Savage reiterates some of what other members of Itchen College staff have recalled and says of Philip that 'he was a redoubtable champion of co-education. He fought and mostly won – battles on behalf of Itchen College in a way that showed how loyal he was to his principles and staff.

I am always deeply grateful to Philip for appointing me as a Deputy Principal.

He was a very humane person, always quick to assess the impact of an accident, illness or bereavement on any of his colleagues, even the non teaching staff, and to offer sympathy and express his concern, even to the point of ensuring that he/she could take time off, if necessary. I well remember how very upset he was about Betty Smith's hospitalisation and eventual death. Years later when he and I had both retired and he could no longer drive, he asked me to take him to Betty's grave at Kingsclere.

Though I worked under his authority for quite a few years, I was one of the very few members of staff who had authority over him in that I was his Head of Department. He was of course a dedicated teacher of Classics, particularly Greek. He saw to it that Classics maintained a place in the curriculum of the college. He drew rank in insisting that he be allowed to teach any first year students of GCSE Greek, and right up to the end made it very clear that he preferred the older style text books rather than the 'Reading Greek' course that I insisted we use. Not infrequently he made use of his clever timetabling: as far as possible he ensured that I had a free period whenever he was due to teach Greek, so that, if he had to miss a lesson because of a meeting, I could deputise for him. But I must say whatever he taught was well and truly drummed into his students; when I took them over for the second year of their course, they knew all the grammar and vocabulary that he had covered with them.

On a lighter note, colleagues used to dread being taken for a walk on the field by P.H.V. The staff room has a panoramic view through the window overlooking the field; so P.H.V. and any companion could easily be seen taking/being taken for a walk there; usually it meant that that person was in trouble or at least being urged to change any views of theirs, which happened to be opposed to P.H.V.'s own.'

In 1979, Philip found himself addressing colleagues at the Gurney Dixon Centre again, this time reporting on the progress and changes at the College since his last speech five years ago. His presentation gives a clear picture of the open-access nature of Itchen and how it arose and how it was then working. 'Since its foundation twelve years ago in 1967, Itchen College has been proud to be completely open-access in the widest and deepest sense. Indeed it has some claims to being the first open-access co-educational Sixth Form College.

At the beginning, as in other institutions, Itchen welcomed students to take only two and then later one A level, (as well as the normal three A leveller), of course the college also welcomed students to do a two year O level course or later a one year O level course. These were well established by 1972 as courses in the college. But the big change in open access came through the first beginning of CEE courses in which the college was much involved with the local CSE Board (S.R.E.B.) in 1973 and 1974. Alongside this move came the pressures for less academic youngsters to come to the college from comprehensive school fifth forms.

One of the reasons for this pressure represents in itself a success story for the comprehensives in Southampton – namely that less academic youngsters in fifth forms tended to follow the big group of more academic youngsters who automatically felt it right to come to the college.

CEE therefore from the middle seventies became an increasingly important part of the College's programme, first in English and then in Mathematics, also large groups were entered and had great success. The students who entered all held a CSE 3, 4, 5 or U (or would not have taken CSE at all) in one or more subjects. They would almost certainly not hold a single grade 2. Sometimes they would have been Easter leavers; sometimes they would have come back from some dead end job.

A grade 3 level at CEE. (i.e. CSE grade 1 equivalent) has been obtained by very many youngsters from a very low CSE base indeed and particularly in Mathematics startling numbers of students have gained an O level equivalent by this means. Fifteen or so other subjects have also been taken over several years with good results, but it is in English and Mathematics that the greatest benefits have been seen – for the very unacademic youngsters who held very low grades or no CSE grades. This success has no doubt been largely because the examination is modular and because course work has been assessed throughout. The whole business of course work has given very, very much more work to the staff, but many have been dedicated to its success. It has suited many students who have feared the 'one examination on the day' kind of course and it has re-interested many students in a number of subjects, especially in Mathematics, but also in Health Science, the Sciences, and History; the two year CEEs are almost certainly taken along side some O levels or with one A level. It is no use pretending that examinations grow less important, they do not. The more first generation and less able students we have, the more it could be said examinations matter. The CEE has shown us that examinations need not be so narrowing, so structured, so 'on the day', and the very word 'examination' itself therefore has to be qualified before use. A Sixth former doing four CEEs cannot be said to be following a narrow examination syllabus. We are the great adaptors of the time and we make a virtue out of necessity in almost every way by adapting to what seems most useful from new examinations.

CEE courses seemed excellent, but the College felt the need to move into a sub-vocational world and in 1978, after a great deal of preliminary work and many preliminary meetings, we started some City and Guilds Foundation courses. We were beginning to receive a number of special needs students as well as many from comprehensive school remedial fifths. Unemployment seemed to be making this matter more urgent. We did not believe that there should be any students on completely non-examined courses and we thought the examinations should be publicly accepted. City and Guilds were most agreeable to this kind of experiment. Last academic year we had therefore City and Guilds Engineering, Commercial Studies and Distributive Trades – all Foundation courses. Within them students took CEE English, CSE Arithmetic, CSE Engineering Science, Office Practice or Commerce. We have managed to extend this this year by running City and Guilds Community Care courses which involve a whole day out for the students on the course in Local Authority homes etc as work experience.

The results last year were excellent – not so much in CEE/CSE as in the City and Guilds itself pass rate – a number gaining Distinctions and Credits as well as passes. This experiment has proved most useful and most encouraging to the students themselves who averaged CSE grade 5 on arrival at Itchen. The value of a general Foundation Certificate from City and Guilds of a semi-vocational kind is very great and I consider this the most important step we have taken for some years in the open-access direction.

This is a rough picture therefore of the courses and subjects we use for the least academic students. Of course they are in the normal Tutor Groups of the College and do the General Studies programme of the College on the mixed ability tutor group base. They also take part with all the others in the two period a week Recreational Activities programme, attend college assemblies etc. but they do have their own careers programme. Of course CEE and City and Guilds courses have increased very greatly the number of one year students at the college. The total intake of students for this year is 430.

In combination therefore CEE. subjects and City and Guild Foundation courses have between them provided us with a most successful set of outlets for the less academic student to try; they have been enjoyed both by the students and the staff and have had considerable success. Through them Itchen has become increasingly open-access until with the advent of a group in 1978 from the local E.S.N. school that open-access has become complete. There are few sixth forms in E.S.N. schools and so therefore we have provided such provisions they might need – protection and maturity, the joining in of College life and the necessary teaching to increase their literacy and numeracy. Indeed the College is more comprehensive than the 'feeder' comprehensive schools (who do not have E.S.N. pupils) while most students still pursue three or two A levels; the sub A level area (and in particular CEE and City and Guilds – 45 students this academic year) has increased greatly and is now a major part of the college's work. The number of students who follow these less academic courses may in the future become an increasing percentage of the whole college.

However a true open-access comprehensive college will want to maintain a good 'mix' such as Itchen now has, between one, two and three year students and between four (a few), three, two and one A levellers as well as two year and one year O levellers, two and one year CEE students, two year and one year secretarial students and City and Guilds Foundation course students. In the midst of all these changes we have to keep high standards and do, especially for the more able. There is growth and change all the time, each part of it has to be measured and seen to be fruitful and not undertaken lightly. But we suit the times. It is my belief that every timetable should have a change or addition every year in some way; otherwise I do not believe we meet the changing needs of the students.

The College celebrated the diamond jubilee of the Grammar School/College in 1980 and this was cause for a review of the years before Philip's arrival at the College, and, for Philip to review his, so far nine years, as Principal as part of the celebration. 'Up to two years ago the College was fed by the whole City of Southampton's comprehensive schools – seventeen in total, because the other two Colleges (Richard Taunton and the Girls, now Hill) were single sex. When in September 1978 they became co-educational; each College was allotted a number of feeder schools so that meaningful connections and contact about syllabuses could grow between the schools and the College. This scheme is working well. Itchen schools are Sholing, Merry Oak, Woolston, Hightown, Moorhill and the two Weston Parks. In addition we share Hamble School with Barton Peveril College. Some pupils still come from Bitterne Park and from schools west of the Itchen. A number also come from Wildern School at Hedge End, and we have a useful connection with Brookfield School at Sarisbury. In addition pupils come from St.Mary's College, the Atherley School, King Edward V1 School and a number of other Independent School fifth forms.

The College has continued to grow in size and strength throughout the seventies. The roll in September 1979, when 433 new students entered the College, was over 720, of whom about 140 were on one year courses; and all the others were doing largely two or three A levels. Some start A levels after one year. A level results are good, as are other results. The numbers going on to Higher Education each year are growing and could reach one hundred and fifty of whom about half go on to the older kind of University. The rest go on to the newer Degree courses at Polytechnics, Colleges of Higher Education, Music and

Drama Colleges, to the new B.Ed's for Teacher training and to other kinds of post eighteen training. Many, of course, go directly into two A level type jobs at eighteen plus or O level type jobs at seventeen plus.

They do this from a curriculum which offers forty six A level subjects and a large number of O level subjects; the Certificate of Extended Education where grade three equals an O level has been a particular mark of the College's adventurousness in curriculum development for the least academically able and there has been particular success in CEE English and Mathematics for these young people. In the last two years five City and Guilds Foundation Courses have been developed – Distribution, Commerce, Residential Care, Science Industries and Engineering. Students who do not hold an O level equivalent pass in English or Mathematics have to take them at the College at O or CEE level. A levels in new subjects and combinations of subjects like Theatre Studies, two A levels in Music, Sociology, Geology, Law, Physical Science, Engineering Science, Design Technology, Electronic Systems and very many have been developed. There has been a particular growth in the Art and Craft side at all levels of the College life.' As Robin Corbin writes about the growth in the Arts and Crafts he says that 'the last six years have seen the consolidation of the work begun by previous staff and the broadening of our work in terms of facilities and the range of courses offered. Lithography and Photo Silk Screen processes are now available and Art Dress and Photography are flourishing. The newest course is the City and Guilds Distribution, dealing with display and advertising in the retail trade. Art History at O level and A level complements the work of some practical Art students, whilst providing an academic insight into visual problems for others. Pottery facilities have been updated with the addition of a new kiln and the implementation of the Factory Safety Act. Our problems now are happy ones – we need more space, and with more space and equipment we will attract more students. Approximately fifty per cent of our A level students move on for further Art Training and are well received by our local Art Colleges.

The Department involves itself in Community work and to a small extent in commercial graphics arts projects. It continues the tradition of supporting College events and productions with tickets, posters, costumes, set designs etc.'

Jonathan Palmer, who was Director of Music at the time of the diamond jubilee writes of the music at Itchen that 'Over the last ten years the Music Department at Itchen has always been fortunate in having substantial numbers of students both as specialists at A level and as performers; and at present there are twenty two studying A level in both years. Inevitably the opportunities for performance have been many and varied and all stem from the combination of ensembles that are possible having viewed the annual influx of students. Without doubt the principal musical event that has dominated every year has been the concert given as part of the 'Evening of Music and the Spoken Word'. There has been a different theme every year to which music has contributed. In each of these, it has been customary to invite ex-Issonians back to take part in the music.

In addition to the above events, a whole host of concerts have been presented over the years from Purcell's 'Dido and Aeneas' in 1973 and the 'Beggar's Opera' in 1974 to what was a highlight; 'La Creation du Monde' by Milhard in 1975. This was a twentieth century ballet which was created by the Music, Art and Dance Departments. Other achievements that shine out from the past must include Itchen's involvement with the National Festival of Music for Youth in Croydon. In 1975 and 1976 two groups played in the first two Schools' Proms in the Albert Hall.

On a lighter note, popular music groups have managed to run alongside classical ensembles. In 1977 the Big Band went to Le Havre for the weekend; in 1978 there was an evening of Musical Nostalgia.

Staff changes included Miss Cynthia Jolly joining us in 1974, thus enabling students to study singing within the timetable. Since that time her contribution to music development has been of great significance. Initially, it was thought that singing would only be useful as a second study due to the short period of time which students stay at Itchen. However, over the years, many students found that it became their principal study, or at least, on equal terms with their main instrument. The department is thriving and looks as if it will continue to do so'.

Philip continues 'To cope with this growth the staff at one stage reached seventy, although this has been lately reduced. Academic work is divided among six faculties: Communications, Languages, Mathematics, Social Studies, Science and Creative Studies, which in turn contain a number of departments. There are three assemblies a week, one long and two short, which are for information, congratulations and discipline and end with a worshipping silence.

All students take part in the Recreational Activities programme which has about fifty options and a General Studies programme (called Humane Studies) of four lessons which includes two practicals or making periods (Technology, Cookery, Furnishings, Art, Pottery, Drama, Dance, Computing, etc.) and two discussion programmes (Economics, Rights and Privileges, Conservation, Sex Education and Marriage Guidance, Environmental Science, etc.) There is one Careers lesson a week which gives students an option of nearly three hundred choices in the year. Mrs. Dunford herself, and now Mr. Huxtable, have been responsible for this regionally famous scheme of introducing up to ten people from business and industry, etc. each Tuesday morning to talk to students.

Drama at the College includes many plays produced by students for their courses. Since 1973 Itchen has had a drama department led by Mr. Ben Bradnack, to some extent independent of the English Department. A level

Theatre Studies and CEE drama contain large practical elements. Mr.Bradnack remembers with particular pleasure 'Bartholomew Fair', 'Wryzeck' and more recently 'Three Sisters' and 'In the heart of the British Museum'. One of the most satisfying to him was performed by three CEE students who had never done drama, for an audience of about ten. It was about looking for work; it wasn't about the polish, razzmatazz of a performance, for Mr.Bradnack drama's value lies in the mastery of experience through the medium of drama and the shaping of personal experience.

Resources have improved a little. The old student common room has been converted to a new Drama room, though still sadly underequipped.

Every second Friday in November the original Speech Day has developed into "An Evening of Music and the Spoken Word" which, apart from my own Address has had 'a theme of the year' with music and speeches (in English and foreign languages) connected with that theme. Taken all in all Itchen can be proud of its growth and success during the seventies. It truly was the first co-educational, open access Sixth Form College in the country in 1967 when my predecessor Charles Thompson began the change from the Grammar School and set the College going on such a sound basis.

We have continued to be leaders of curriculum development, of open access and of good disciplined learning in an atmosphere of liberty (not licence) – where young people can continue growing up from sixteen to nineteen in an atmosphere that suits their age group in the last part of this century, on a semi-student basis – home based but during the day with a student life of their own.

Above all Itchen can point to a silent contentment – partly inherited – which promises well for the future, and of which we are very proud. Disciplined work, good results, good eighteen plus entry and good careers are parts of the success story and that success story itself is based on the way in which students have responded to an atmosphere of calm happiness for 'We look for that of God in every teenager'.

At the end of the academic year which saw the College celebrate its diamond jubilee, the Director of Music, Jonathan Palmer, left the College. His last concert was held in July 1980 and Canon Milner and Philip addressed the audience at the beginning of the second half of the concert. Philip and Ronald Milner always had a good rapport, and before Philip's speech he had asked Ronald to say a few words before him. Ronald begins 'The Principal would like to say a few words; he had said to me before the concert that the audience "would be in the clouds from the sensational music". Can you bring them down to earth?" Philip requested of him. Ronald quipped 'that's not the usual direction, but if you insist, here I am!'

At this farewell concert many dignitaries and Education officials attended in order to show their appreciation of Jonathan Palmer's wonderful music making at Itchen over the last eight years. Philip began 'We all want to wish Jonathan Palmer well in his future. I am sad, but it has been a very happy evening, a marvellous concert with happy students. In my experience in education Jonathan Palmer is a "gigantic" person to have around. He has provided and organised many fine musical programmes, he has had wonderful support from students, ex-students and staff in singing and playing in many of them, as they have done so tonight. This evening was a sensational one of light music, but the audience will want to be reminded that Jonathan has also been involved with three operas, concerts of chamber music at the Turner Simms hall, twice in the School Proms, twice at Fairfields Hall, as well as the unique mixture of jazz, the big band, pop and saxophone quartets in the College. He has also been a figure in the City of Southampton, conducting the youth choir at the European Choirs Festival in the Loire Valley. The Director of Education, Mr. Aldam is unable to be here tonight and sends his regrets but offers his high appreciation of the splendid service that Mr. Palmer has given to Hampshire County in music making.

We are gathered here to say thank you, it may be corny but "thanks for the memory" and "We will (no doubt) meet again", which I will not dare to sing, although inwardly I want to! Of Jonathan Palmer I can say that "I wear him in my true heart's core" Thank you Jonathan.'

Some thirty years later Jonathan writes a reflective passage on working with Philip and his musical memories of his eight years at 'When you are in the early part of your career, you may be forgiven if you come over as ambitious and determined to 'move up the ladder'. In 1972, at the age of twenty-seven, I had already held the post of Assistant Director of Music at Brockenhurst Sixth Form College for three years, and was beginning to feel the need to look for my first Head of Department post. My wife and I had just bought our first house, and were taking countless photographs of our first child.

When I told some of my colleagues at school that I had an interview for the post of Director of Music at Itchen Sixth Form College in Southampton, the response was mixed. Instead of hearing words of encouragement, I found myself having to listen to advice. What was an open-access Sixth Form College? Brockenhurst College used to be a Grammar School, and was phasing out its junior classes. Had I not heard of the fiery Head from New Mills, whose reputation had gone before him? "You could be letting yourself in for all sorts of problems; after all, the Head is the one person with whom you have to be able to work". And, apparently he was a redhead, like me!

Needless to say, I found myself at interview; the panel included the Music Advisor, Peter Davies who had been brought in as a specialist. Before I knew it, I had been offered the job, and Philip was showing me around the campus. I was in a state of shock and excitement, when he nudged my elbow and said: "I do hope you have a sense of humour!" Later in the year, a month or two into the job, I was offered some advice by a more senior member of the staff. "At any meeting with him, it is not unusual for there to be some confrontation; you have to decide how strongly you feel about any ideas you have and be prepared for a noisy argument to achieve agreement. He will probably pace around the room in an angry state, his face puce, eventually storming out of the door. Within a few minutes, he will be back, with an apology, and approval for your proposal". It wasn't long until I found myself re-enacting this same scenario. Whatever my suggestion was at the time, I was confident and I knew I was right. My heart pumped fast; had I gone too far? It was my first victory! Although there were to be other occasions like this, our relationship seemed to be evolving with mutual respect. We did work well together, even if I didn't manage to establish a CSE course in music, or one in bad piano-playing. Philip was convinced the world was 'full of bad pianists'!

The Music Advisor decided to send his daughter Andrea to Itchen. She was a highly talented 'cellist, and it wasn't long until other young talent from the Youth Orchestra followed her example. By 1975, there was a glittering generation of instrumental players, all of whom were receptive to new opportunities. A wind quintet was formed that appeared in the first Schools Prom in the Royal Albert Hall. Philip immediately recognised the potential, and his support was never-ending. It must have been good because I stayed in that post for eight lively years.

There was only one large teaching room, with a walk-in store room, and no practice rooms; yet, we seemed to manage somehow. Instrumental lessons were given in all sorts of unexpected places; no one complained. It was at this time that I began to realise that the success of institutions is largely due to the people that work in them, rather than due any special, purpose-built facilities. The main hall was the only place to hold a concert, and there seemed to be plenty of seating.

At the end of my first term, I organised the first of many "Christmas Extravaganzas", in which the programme not only consisted of choirs, orchestra and solos. Audience participation was an essential element as well, with wassail songs that had to be learnt at short notice. Philip was clearly proud of these events and had a long list of VIPs, including all the top brass from within the Education Authority. It was common for all the three front rows of seats to be reserved for them, so the parents and friends had to sit behind, and every event concluded with an appreciative speech from the Principal. Although this practice did become routine procedure, it did represent a level of community support that was exclusive to Itchen College.

This can now be more easily appreciated in a retrospective way, having moved on to new situations and different communities.

In contrast with today, the timetable was not dominated by A level lessons. There were other non-academic sessions called 'Humane Studies' that all students were obliged to attend. Quite large groups would arrive in the Music room for a 'taster' session in music. For most of them it was their first visit to the Music Department; they were often curious, and I found the classes challenging. There were no instruments or studios, so I frequently presented an eclectic mix of music that might lent itself to lively discussion. 'General Studies' gradually disappeared as my career took me into the independent sector, where its value for the non-academic did not seem to be recognised.

I was given free rein to devise whatever musical event I felt appropriate at the time.

In 1973, I discovered that one of my 'A' Level music students (Tim Caesar) also played in a pop group called "Alco" outside College. I suggested to him that his band took part in a concert alongside the College Orchestra that were scheduled to be playing Beethoven's 5th Symphony. Such a juxtaposition of styles/genre seemed rather radical at the time, and probably raised some eyebrows. To this day though, I have always enjoyed contrasting musical styles within programmes.

It made sense to attempt a real collaboration, with the band and orchestra playing together in a special new piece. Tim chose three of his songs, I composed some extra material and orchestrations, and "Threads of Life" was born. The first performance was a sensation, but no one had thought of recording it. Within a short space of time, we booked the mobile recording unit from the University of Surrey, organised a weekend recording day, and decided to make our own Long Playing record. Debi Coombs produced a striking sleeve cover, and the Barbershop Group even contributed some songs to fill out the album. Around 200 copies were made, and today, nearly 40 years later, it has been become collectable, a copy apparently having been sold on Ebay for a four figure sum!

Another collaboration took place in 1976: a project to recreate the 1927 production of the jazz ballet "La Creation du Monde" by Darius Milhaud. Paul Gruitt from the Art Department carried out some serious research into the original set and costume design by Fernand Léger, and we worked closely together with Madeleine Chapman, the choreographer. The programme also included other music from the same period: works by Debussy, Satie, Stravinsky, Stravinsky and Ibert.

Alongside all this activity, the success of Itchen College Wind Quintet in the Schools Prom of 1975 provided the impetus to explore those areas of music that other schools seemed to be neglecting. In 1976, I assembled the best and most motivated group of instrumentalists I could find to form a group called "Itchen College Contemporary Music Ensemble". Many of these students ended up

306

going on to pursue their studies at Music College or University, intent on following a career in music. (It was at this time that there had to be two A level music groups due to the numbers of students who were studying music).

In the library of the University of Southampton I discovered a piece called "Round The Star and Back" by the distinguished composer Jonathan Harvey. It was one of those contemporary pieces written in a semi-graphic way, in the form of a circle on a large sheet of card; any number of players could be chosen. The composer himself, a lecturer in the university music department, came to Itchen College on a number of occasions to sit in on our rehearsals and make observations and constructive criticism. For the second time, we went up to London to appear at the 1976 Schools Prom in the Royal Albert Hall. What experiences! What it was to be a young teacher in the 1970s: energetic, courageous and full of ideas, all stimulated by a number of intakes of outstandingly musical students. Philip, like any head, recognised the potential for promotional publicity and took every opportunity to use it to the full. However, unlike every head, he gave complete, unhesitating support to the work of the music department. He would bring visitors into classes and music rehearsals with obvious pride. He always gave the benefit of the doubt to those he described as having vision and imagination, and attended every musical event I produced without fail. It was certainly one of the most exciting, formative periods of my whole career - a time when I was fascinated by the process of discovering musicianship in the individual, a time to interpret the College motto as it was then: "as far as who goes farthest". (Jonathan Palmer. Director of Music at Itchen College (1972 – 1980).

George Heller was appointed to Hampshire Local Education Authority as Deputy Area Education Officer to Southampton in 1978. He was one of the Authority's Officers who had most dealings with Philip and Itchen College. George frequently played in the College's Orchestra in the violin section, under Jonathan Palmer's direction. George left Southampton to become Area Education Officer in Havant in 1986, and so therefore he had continuous contact with Itchen for eight years. Southampton was one of the eight areas in which the county was divided for administrative purposes. This is how he remembers some of those contacts. 'Philip was an educational leader in East Southampton. In other words, he took the initiative on many educational initiatives in Southampton as a whole because he had the sort of personality which enabled him to do that on behalf of the City's educational community. He was passionate about pupils' life chances and saw schools and colleges as the way out of the circumstances which could constrain opportunity. He believed in Local Education Authorities and the political processes. He had no problem with Councillors making decisions about schools/colleges but was at pains to ensure that they were well briefed before they took decisions about the future of schools. He was never afraid to make his views known even if that irritated people; after all students were at the heart of what he wanted to do.

Philip used every opportunity to point out that Itchen was the first co-educational open-access Sixth Form College, whether this was in Hampshire or nationally was never clear but the point is that open-access was his mantra. In other words, the college was there to respond to anyone who felt that carrying on at sixteen would serve to help them in their future careers. No one was excluded so it was very comprehensive i.e. encompassing those who would go to the top universities as well as those who'd failed in schools or who themselves been failed by the schools. So it was a real mix of students and the better for it.

Philip took a close interest in all students whatever their background or academic aspirations. He knew them all and constantly walked the job. He used to take me around the College and I could tell that he knew so many as individuals. They were all valued; that was the point. Philip always had a teaching timetable; that's pretty rare for a College Head nowadays.

In many ways Itchen was the forerunner of what colleges are like now though the range of courses, both vocational and academic, is now much greater. However, Itchen did offer a range of subjects/courses which were offered to respond to the range of student needs in an area which was socially very mixed.'

One of Philip's Deputy Principals, who he appointed in his early days at Itchen College, was Mrs. Joyce Winterbottom, and this is how she remembers him (written in 1999). 'Philip's working life was full of achievement and he will always be remembered as a pioneer of Sixth Form College education: a person with vision and energy. What Philip started remains the bed-rock of post sixteen education. Philip was welcoming, hospitable and kind and always found time to show compassion to those in need.'   Lisa McCarthy was another member of staff in the seventies, and she says of Philip that she has 'vivid memories of Philip from his time at the College. He was a dynamic figure who unselfishly dedicated himself to promoting the educational needs of the students. He had a great warmth and understanding: qualities that were also evident in his relationship with staff. Although he was Principal he always understood the challenges of teaching in the classroom. Sometimes it seemed that he yearned for the days when he taught Classics at East Ham. He was a very generous leader who had a global view of everything that happened at the College. Personally I am grateful for his support and encouragement, and his belief in my ability gave me the confidence to build a career. Teachers were important to him and it is a lasting testament to him that so many staff who now hold eminent educational posts were nurtured under his guidance. Philip's tenure at Itchen was clearly an important time in the history of Itchen College. He was a tireless fighter for the

College. Its current standing within the community can be traced back to those days. I recall a very warm ebullient figure who loved conversation and had a real love of the College.'

Someone else who shared Lisa McCarthy's sentiments about Philip was Terri Stelling, who taught girls' physical education at Itchen in the seventies, she says of Philip that 'Philip was a great boss to me at Itchen College and provided every opportunity and encouragement for my professional development – as he did for many others on his staff. I remember him for many reasons but perhaps most for his optimism regarding the most humble of his students and his firm belief that a good education would provide them with the basis to do well in life. He truly believed in equal opportunities and I admired this aspect of his leadership.'

The highlight of Itchen's annual calendar was, as some of the contributors have already mentioned, the Evening of Music and the Spoken Word. For each of these evenings a theme was followed by the spoken word and music, and Philip would give an address to the assembled audience on a current educational topic in the hope that the profile of some of the plights of education would be raised, since the audience often included the local Member of Parliament, Education Officers from Southampton and Winchester and the local Mayor and some Councillors. The first of these annual Speech Days did not take place in November 1971, but in March 1972 and then again, the pattern of holding them on the Second Friday in November, began in November 1972. So two Speech Days for 1972!

The 1972 speech was comparatively short compared to the later speeches. Philip had been very used to delivering speeches at a fairly rapid pace and tried to keep them to about twenty to thirty minutes long in order to give plenty of time for the music and spoken word. Having been in Southampton one year he spoke of his optimism for the future of the college, he hoped 'that the number of pupils next year would top the five hundred mark and many new subjects and courses would be introduced. Because of the College's age group it was in their interests for teachers to relax discipline to help students take on the role of being self-disciplined. At sixteen the adventure of adulthood began, and one of the great advantages the College now enjoyed was that they did not have younger pupils who needed a closed framework. We can relax the framework so that people here are using self-discipline and not depending too much on external discipline, even though they may appear to want it. Young adults have to be taught self-discipline so that when they are ready to leave us they can go places where the discipline is quite relaxed'.

The Mayor Alderman John Barr used the occasion of the Speech Day to comment on Southampton's educational decisions. He said 'I have become conscious, since becoming Mayor that Southampton has led the country in so many fields, and education is one of them. I think it is fair to say the rest of the educational world is looking at what we are doing, and I believe what we are going to do will be very successful. In their reorganisation of secondary colleges along comprehensive lines, Southampton had not established mammoth schools as in London with over 2,000 pupils, which brought dangers of impersonality, anti-social behaviour by pupils, and chaos in administration and difficulties for teachers. Most of Southampton's schools catering for twelve to sixteen year old pupils had about eight hundred children. I am delighted that Heads and their colleagues are doing everything they can do to cement the partnership between home and school by developing their schools on neighbourhood lines so that each school is becoming a community focus for the locality. The increasing attraction of the co-educational Itchen College for students was pronounced and it may well be that if the strong preference for such a college continued, they would have to take this into account in their plans for the development of secondary colleges in the future.'

In January 1973, the local Southern Evening Echo gave a whole side of its edition to Itchen College, the article written by Patrick Piper gives an overview of the college with the heading of 'Co-ed to the full'. This is some of his findings which very much reflect the era. 'Itchen College must be one of the most unisex Sixth Form Colleges for miles around. It is co-educational in the fullest sense. Nothing wrong with that, either. The days when men could not cook an egg or sew on a button should be long gone, except for the odd relic of male chauvinism remaining here and there. But Itchen is pushing the frontiers a little further. All the courses are open to boys and girls, so you will find the boys learning to cook, sew and make their own clothes, while the girls get on with a solid bit of metalwork or boatbuilding.

"Everything is co-ed here except the loos!" commented the Head Mr. Philip Vennis, with some accuracy. '"When the students go home, father is surprised that his daughter has managed to make a pair of cuff links and mother is delighted her son can at last cook for himself."

One of the best courses is in bedsit cookery, covering those old problems all mums worry about when their children leave home – basic nutrition, finding decent digs, costing and budgeting, and how to cook a quick but nourishing meal on one ring.

The lads on the dress design course are turning their new skills to advantage, running up trendy tee shirts for themselves – and saving a lot of money. And if you want to play some sport – anyone for mixed hockey.'

The report goes on to comment on the freedom in the College. 'The freedom of experiencing student life while still a Sixth former is one of Itchen's great attractions. Even if students do not go on to higher education, at least they get a taste of the independence they would find there and learn from it the value of self-discipline. They wear pretty well what clothes they like and the boys seem to have their hair as long as they want. Somewhere the balance between self-expression and self-discipline finds its own level in each student. Said the Head, "It is a liberal place here and they are given enough freedom to grow up in. I try to let them find their own feet and not to make the College too much of an exam factory. We teach them to be adults, to learn to look after themselves. The only external discipline I maintain is that the whole college should assemble three times a week, if only for a brief silence together. Those that do go on with further education are, I think, more mature than other students and better prepared."

About forty went to University last year and thirty to teacher training colleges. Itchen has a student council, elected twice a year, and the student chairman is allowed to be a member of the governing body. "We take the Council and its views seriously", said the Head. Another area the Echo reported on was careers and this is what Patrick Piper wrote 'Most schools deal with the difficult and vital dilemma of choosing a career, but not many look to the time when a girl has married, had children who have grown up and then looks around for a job. Itchen College tries to prepare its girl students for this phase of their lives. Said Head Mr. Vennis "The girls today are much more aware that they will need a job to fill in the gap when their children leave home – or even before. I think they have a difficult dual role which the boys do not have to face." A lot of time is given to careers generally, so important with our present high unemployment. A level students get a chance to hear about more than three hundred careers and other students are able to go round factories, hospitals, the docks and elsewhere to help them decide their future. Special individual visits are also arranged. If students still cannot make their mind up by the time they leave Itchen, at least they have seen a good deal of the varied working life of Southampton.'

The last area of the College's life that Patrick Piper covered in this article was the art department. He says 'there in the corner of the Art Department stood a loo with two arms emerging as some poor lad apparently struggled to get out. But a closer look showed it was just an offbeat idea for a piece of modern art by a student I was told had now left. As I looked around Itchen College and walked along the corridors, with the walls hung with excellent paintings, it seemed that art really matters here and that the College is trying to impress on students that art ought to be all around us every day.

The range of work that Itchen covers is exceptional, including pottery, printing, sculpture, experimental photography, lithography and plastics and glass fibre works. There is also a technology shop where students can make canoes, boats, jewellery and so on and learn about enamelling, engraving, welding and engineering metal work. Talking of boats the College built a model hydrofoil and a two seater hovercraft last year, winning second prize in the Southern Science and Technology Forum with the hydrofoil. The hovercraft, a hefty monster that took months of hard work, was a great challenge to the students who built it.'

In the seventeen speeches that Philip presented to the audience at the Annual Speech Evening he covered many aspects of educational thinking and College ideas and philosophy. These included such things as the 'horrific rat race' by describing how the College provides an academic link between school and the 'horrific rat race of modern living'. He said, 'the Sixth Form College is not just about University places, careers and examinations. It is a question of what kind of adults will they be who have been to Itchen, what kind of wives and husbands, what kind of parents, what kind of citizens? The place is a kind of two year oasis where you may sit and ponder a little before the world engulfs you, before the horrific rat race of modern living finally sucks you in. It is a link between school and life. It has to be a good place to finish growing up in; it has to be a happy place. It has to open windows; it has to raise eyes far and high on distant horizons. College should be a place where permission is given for a wide range of activities, without being permissive. There has to be a framework of discipline which diminishes as time goes by. We must not become an exam shop – a clear danger in a two year College. We have to worry about the number of internal examinations and the amount of reporting and other paperwork a hard pressed staff must deal with when teaching must remain their priority.'

In the Queen's Silver Jubilee year of 1977, in the presence not only of the Mayor of Southampton but also in the Queen's representative Sir Hugh Smiley, Vice Lord Lieutenant of Hampshire, Philip reviewed the ten years since the College's formation. He said that 'in the ten years since the College's formation five thousand students have passed through the doors and I have seen no sign of the 'permissive society' among them. In my long experience of Sixth forms, both as Head and Deputy Head going back twenty years, I see little changes, if any, in sexual morality, in attitudes to pornography; very little towards attitudes in drink and very little in connection with drugs. Teenagers always fell in love and still do. Students who come here are certainly career minded. They want certificates. But they are private persons, and we are not prurient. As a comprehensive College, Itchen has pupils with I.Qs of 140 plus, and others with a reading age of seven, and some of ten years. But all must be taught to their own tune, to their own ability level. All must be drawn along the road to having their particular dream fulfilled. And for those who have no dream – we must offer one.'

A year later Philip publically acknowledged that he supported the idea of grants for sixth formers. He endorsed this by saying 'I would like to see at least forty per cent of seventeen year-olds in full time education and I hope that the authorities would consider giving grants for the sixteen to eighteen year old student. We would have to see that they work well and do not waste their time or grant. It would not be money wasted; only invested. For human talent is what English teenagers have and at the moment we are wasting much of it. These young people have "tremendous guts", they give up unemployment benefit to come back to College, but there is a worrying number of students, capable of taking A levels, who go into dead end jobs because of financial problems.' This theme also was revisited by Philip in the 1981 speech where he reiterated that 'Lack of money is the major reason why a considerable minority of students give up during their course for a job of any kind or for unemployment benefit. It seems ridiculous to pay them to be unemployed and not to pay them to work at College. Students should be paid either Social Security, grants or unemployment benefit. It is clearly better to have young people at College rather than on the streets.'

Two years later in 1983 the topic re-emerged, but on this occasion Philip spoke paying a "youth wage" to students. He said to the assembled audience in 1983 that 'The Government should pay a 'youth wage' to teenagers wishing to continue their education. Many girl students come to me on the verge of tears because of financial pressure on their families while they are completing their studies. They felt that they should be helping. What is the point of paying those who won't or don't work and not paying those who will work? It is a very upside down situation and now overwhelmingly urgent. Many students are being driven to abandon studying to seek some work for themselves, or they are joining the dole queue or a Youth Training Scheme. We encourage them to get part-time jobs, which are good and useful, but part-time jobs are few and far between and are grossly underpaid. It is time to look, both locally and nationally at this gigantic problem. So I am putting in a public plea for a wage at sixteen plus. Cash is in short supply in many families in east Southampton; many of my students have both parents unemployed. Those from single parent homes are hard put to sort out their personal conscience, their loyalty to their mother and their studies, as home pressures mount for them to quit. Teenagers are struggling with themselves, trying to weigh the sacrifices of their families, against the loyalty of their families – that is their families persuading them to stay on at College when things at home are obviously tight. In consequence, the College has lost two hundred students in two years and with decreasing enrolments it has recently faced a cut of nine from its staff.' By 1979, Philip's speech was about the cash restraints that were affecting the college. In the audience that evening were leading figures in the County Education Authority who listened to his

313

account of life under stress at the College. 'Teachers nearing exhaustion, classes too large and ill-equipped, student interest being sacrificed ...the everyday story of a school facing cash cuts. Staff levels are now unacceptably low; we are beginning to reach the edge of exhaustion for senior teachers. The furnishings and equipment are poor and there has not been a furniture or room-change programme or a buildings programme of any kind since the place became a Sixth Form College twelve years ago. I appeal to the Education Authority to retain our best standard of service for all teenagers of every ability who wish to come here, many for one year only. We cannot betray them. This College shows a truly productive way ahead. This College really is making productive citizens and that is a true investment of resources. These young people are all our futures...they are our feed-corn. If we neglected them, it would be at our country's peril.'

The theme continued in 1980, 'Cutting the 'fat' of educational expenditure has gone through the "lean" and is now into the "bone". I am not pretending that reductions in expenditure have affected Itchen College too deeply, as yet, as we have had a good year. But with our staff reduced to a 1 to 13 pupil teacher ratio, we are into the "bone". A safe level is one to ten.'

The 1982 speech was one which looked forward into the twenty first century. 'I wonder what the careers of the sixteen plus youngsters will be in 2025. We do not know what kind of England that will be. It is absolutely essential and no longer an 'extra' to look at leisure time education of many kinds. A year here which could have some vocational training with some generalist education may well be what is most needed now. Itchen has a capacity for change to meet the eighties but one has to be sure that the change is for the better. Looking just a short way ahead the College may lose students to the new Government Youth Training Scheme. Has the Sixth Form College already outlived its usefulness? Will it disappear into Further Education under the so called 'Tertiary' hat?

In April 1983 Philip was elected Chairman of the Hampshire County Secondary Headmasters' Conference. The Conference draws its membership from the county's 115 Secondary Schools and Sixth Form Colleges, and Philip was the first Southampton Headmaster to hold the appointment since the city's education role was taken over by Hampshire in 1974. Barri Hurford-Jones, Headmaster of Bitterne Park School said of Philip 'The effect of his personality upon Itchen has been profound. But it is in the company of his Headteacher/Principal colleagues that Philip has made an equally huge contribution. We saw him grow in stature as Chairman of the Secondary Heads Conference, proving from 'out front' in our considerable battles with the Education Office that if 'education begins a gentleman then continuation completes him'. Doris Mastermann, a Headteacher from neighbouring Portsmouth commented, 'Philip has fought such a valiant fight for so long and he has fought for his beliefs in all he has undertaken. I shall never forget the way in which he enlivened many a dull gathering and was always ready with a cheery word and an apologetic disagreement. It was such a pleasure to have him as a colleague.' Mavis Kingston was Principal of one of the Sixth Form Colleges on the western side of Southampton and had much contact with Philip says of him 'Philip was always such a supportive colleague and I knew that I could contact him in time of worry and get a positive and helpful response. He was always full of energy and challenge. He was such a vital person, appreciating both the ironies and the delights of life.' Philip's last major educational topic was about teachers' pay in 1986 when he pleaded for the country to pay teachers more. He said 'I have a man on my staff in Scale 2 whose children get free milk. Teachers' standard of living relies upon husbands and wives both working, and extra paid work being undertaken. They are grossly and crassly underpaid. If the country wants nearly half a million teachers to be best, then it has to pay up. It is all coming to a halt. The local education authorities were originally mean, but throughout most of the year it has been the Secretary of State who has been extremely obstinate. Meanness will never pay off. Teachers must be able look doctors and lawyers straight in the eye from similar salary levels. So the Chancellor must find some money – or we will stagger from crisis to crisis.' Philip then returned to a topic he had spoken about several times; he said 'Unemployment is particularly bad in Southampton. When eighteen year olds are looking for a job I advise them to go to Eastleigh or Fareham. There is a new Government pre-vocational education scheme which offers CPEV certificates to the seventeen plus age group. These include secretarial services, business services, engineering, technology and services to people. Anyone who completes a course will be guaranteed a certificate and a profile of their abilities. However, support for this scheme is undermined by educational cuts and staffing levels. England's future looks bleak compared to other countries. Young seventeen to eighteen year olds in France studying in further education averaged thirty-four per cent, in Italy and Australia forty-three per cent, West Germany fifty-five per cent, Sweden eighty-five per cent, U.S.A. eighty-six per cent, Japan ninety-four per cent....in the United Kingdom eighteen per cent.

The 1987 Speech Evening was Philip's last one, and it was on this occasion (and on several more later in 1988) tributes were paid to his leadership. Rt.Rev. Ronald Milner, who was now the Bishop of Burnley, returned to Itchen as Guest of Honour at the Speech Evening and he paid tribute to Mr. Vennis's part in the development of Itchen over the last seventeen years, to his energy, determination and flamboyance in promoting Itchen as a worthy Sixth Form open-access College. A very sincere thank you was given to Mrs. Vennis for her loyal support during the ups and downs of this period. No-one can deny that these last years have been particularly trying for anyone in a position of responsibility in education.' said Bishop Milner.

Roy Jones arrived in the last three years of Philip's tenureship at Itchen. He was Southampton's Area Education Officer and Assistant County Education Officer from 1985 to 1995, and this is his perspective on Philip and Itchen College. 'I was appointed Area Education Officer for Southampton in September 1985, taking up the position in December. The appointing panel comprised the three party leaders on Hampshire County Council and, as they offered me the job, they told me that my first task would be 'to bring some order' to the sixth form provision in Southampton by merging two of the three Sixth Form Colleges in the city. Suddenly I felt as if I was being handed the poison chalice! I arrived in the city on 1 December with some trepidation; in those days sixth form college Principals were like barons straining at the LEA leash and I knew I would have my work cut out. It wasn't helped when, a couple of days later, I went to my first meeting with secondary school Heads and college Principals at the Southampton Teachers' Centre and managed to lock myself out of my car. I remember that Philip was one of those who came to my rescue: to this day I do not know where he got the wire coat hanger that did the trick!

In that small act of kindness was the man. He was welcoming whatever the circumstances and always prepared to take that extra bit of trouble to sort out an issue, no matter how large or trivial. In the event, geography largely dictated that Philip's institution, Itchen College, should remain open and it would have to be the two colleges west of the Itchen that would merge. Nevertheless Philip did not retreat into Bastion Itchen as lesser men might have done; he remained involved and positive in the project without interfering in the affairs of the other two colleges. In the end, after some inevitable trials and tribulations, Southampton was left with two strong and prestigious sixth form colleges, one of which was Itchen.

Only three years before the Great Education Reform Act of 1988, education officers were not always the flavour of the month in schools and colleges. However, Philip, with his roots firmly in the development and spirit of public sector education, managed for the local community by the local community, was a great supporter of the local education authority. He was always ready to tell us where we had gone wrong and where we could improve, but when the 'chips were down' we could always rely on his support and good will. Most education officers had a few institutions where they knew they could relax for a brief while with a good cup of coffee and always receive a warm welcome: Itchen College under Philip Vennis was one of those.

First and foremost Philip was a 'students' man'. Their needs were always at the top of his agenda. Sometimes a little eccentric and no doubt occasionally a little irritating to his staff, he ensured that the college was organised and managed around the student interest. His good humour and wit, from time to time sharpened by an acerbic tongue, gained their respect and in many cases their devotion. He was not a soulless bureaucrat worried about the all important bottom line, as so many college Principals are today, but a larger than life man of character and energy who gave one hundred percent and expected one hundred per cent.

Times have changed immeasurably in education since the early nineties. Academics, incorporated colleges, free schools, all litter the education landscape and make it impossible to see a coherent structure. Despite the rhetoric of successive governments, local accountability seems to have been replaced by local interest. But for Itchen College in the eighties, he was undoubtedly the 'right man in the right place.' David Bothwell, Senior Advisory officer (Secondary) for Hampshire endorses some of the sentiments felt about Philip by saying that 'Before Philip took up his post at Itchen College, he had formed a vision of how the new open-access sixth form colleges should develop.

With astonishing energy and single mindedness he set about translating his vision into practice as soon as he took up his post. Itchen College welcomed students of all levels of ability, those whose academic achievements on paper were negligible as well as those destined from the start for university places. He was especially concerned that those from poorer backgrounds were as well provided for as the others.

The needs and welfare of students came first, above all else. If a student wanted to study a combination of Chinese, Psychology and Nuffield Physics, Itchen was the place to go. Ignoring all objections based on money and staff availability Philip would just get on with it and enable it to happen.

If a sixteen year old aspired to attend a co-educational college with a relaxed and friendly adult atmosphere, Itchen was the first choice. Hundreds of people, with successful jobs living happy lives, owe a debt to Itchen College under Philip's leadership.

Many feathers were ruffled in the process. Philip's energies were fired by a short fuse: he could be insufferably rude as well as persuasive and gentle. If any of us had been at the receiving end of his tongue during the day the chances were that the telephone would ring in the evening – Philip saying 'Sorry, my friend, I shouldn't have spoken like that. I'm sure we can come to some arrangement'.

Philip was always a rapid talker: if you didn't listen carefully you might miss some passing witticism – Philip had a great sense of humour, sometimes quite a wicked one! Were Philip's essential humanity, and his vulnerability, hidden from many? I'm not sure, but these are the many qualities that I will remember and cherish above all.

I feel privileged to have known Philip; the memories of his enthusiasm, his intellect, his energy, his humour, his humanity will always be remembered. The actor Jeremy Irons once said "I've always believed that the afterlife is what you leave behind in other people." Another Advisory Officer from Southampton Local Education Authority is Bill Eastman who recollects his contact with Itchen and in Philip in particular in the following words. 'Philip Vennis was appointed Principal of Itchen College in 1971. He retired in 1988 having served the college – staff and students – with devotion and care during those years. I was at the time, Advisor for Modern Languages and duly received an invitation to the College. The Modern Languages Department functioned well and needed little support from me. Consequently, I was able, when required, to support Philip as a member of an interview team for the appointment of new staff. It was from this position that I came to respect and to reflect upon his ideas and ideals. There were a number of things that I came to admire about Philip, in particular his unstinting support for the students from underprivileged backgrounds, his 'working class students' as he called them. He recognised those who needed his support and knew the parents and families. There are many who must be grateful to Philip and his staff for what they achieved on their behalves.

He was quick to react very strongly to matters with which he strongly disagreed. However, misunderstandings were soon mended with a walk round the College grounds or on the telephone. Thus I became, not only a colleague, but within time a good friend. We had much in common. For example, we both loved music. Music was an important and very successful part of the College life. My wife and I were invited to a number of splendid evenings at the College. We both loved travel, France and the United States in particular. For several years I ran the exchange with Central Michigan University which sent their education students to teach in our schools, at all levels. Philip became very involved in this programme and students came to Itchen College to gain valuable teaching experience in an English college, with considerable success. With our wives we were able to forge friendships with the C M U staff, contacts which endure even today.

When Philip retired he continued to build up a large and impressive collection of CDs which we often listened to together. I often feel that music was a powerful antidote to the illness from which he suffered so much. It was during this sad time that I saw Philip rather more than before. In spite of his suffering he never lost his sense of humour. He always enjoyed my jokes, particularly the political ones. Our lunches in a favourite pub in Lee-on-

Solent were part of a friendship that I miss even today. I remain grateful for that friendship.'

By June 1988 celebrations for Philip's retirement were taking place. As the Evening Echo said 'Itchen College's retiring Principal faces a round of farewell parties next month. Mr. Vennis, who has headed the College for seventeen years, will start with ex students on 9 July followed by current students on 14 July. Two days later staff and former staff will attend another goodbye party.' On Friday 15 July Philip addressed his staff for the last time. He begins 'I had some aims when I came here, two have clearly not been achieved, there have been too few girls undertaking physics and too few first generation working class students. But many of my other aims have been achieved and those are, of course, with you and I owe everything to you. For example, we have grown hugely the number of A levels and the kinds of A levels and the number of students doing practical A levels and we have hung on to minority A levels or let them grow. We have gone to the east of the City, and Hamble and Brookfield have a continually growing area. Indeed although at the moment Brookfield matters most, if Hamble were to come completely over to this College, and I think that likely, then they would be very, very important to you. We have a marvellous staff and remarkably among modern institutions in Education, we have had a stable staff largely speaking, teaching and non-teaching. We have grown a reasonable sense of humour amid the myriad worries, changes and bureaucracy of our time. We have let the Area Office and the LEA know that we do have independent minds here. We have kept our independence and autonomy within the Authority. The teaching Unions and Associations have been very, very fair to me and to us and I do thank their leaders here. We have had very good supportive governors. When we have had a crisis, they have been a support and have not been just grumbling at us. We have really had very nice students and, nearly all the problematic students, we have been able to deal with by talking to them and advising them with only a few exceptions. I must have expelled in seventeen and a half years about one dozen students.

Not many of you will know that when I was a boy I wanted to be a comedian and my Dad said that I had to be a schoolmaster. It was not that he thought that was the next best thing but I think it fairly clearly is! If you cannot have a laugh with those you are teaching, your lesson may go astray.

I was very lucky to have a marvellous first Head who allowed me to write my own first testimonial but that does not work now — if you let people write their own now, they are all worse than those you write. After nine years on the old scale 3 for English for the Science Sixth, Classics, the School Play, Scouts, I gained the Deputy headship of one of Conservative Staffordshire's new Comprehensives in 1958. The job for the Deputy was to convert a Secondary

319

Modern to a Comprehensive, to see to the academic work, to launch a Sixth form, to see to the boys' discipline and do some drama with the illiterate. For those interested in the last item I still have a tape of the scene from 'The Dream'. The boys and girls learned the parts by listening to the tapes. It was a very funny performance.

Four years later I was lucky to gain the headship of a good Grammar School, New Mills. Like my second job I was appointed because of snobbery – Dulwich, Cambridge, Classics. That is how the English system works and I learned to play it. Derbyshire at that time was equally Labour and Tory and there was a big interviewing body. I was there nine years and I turned it into a Comprehensive in thirteen different buildings. My greatest achievement was getting indoor toilets in the 1867 Secondary Modern, a fight I can tell you with nearly all evening meetings. I could not face a Comprehensive in so many buildings and was really more interested in sixteen plus anyway. The Sixth had grown hugely – an early 'umbrella' Grammar School plus two Secondary Moderns. I was dictating letters in a car going around the buildings.

I then got the job here, Peter Browning really liked me. Very many of you know the history from here. I think I have saved the College from closing; I think I saved it from going Tertiary and I mean saved. I am not an F.E. kind of man. I believe that Heads (and I am still one) should meet the students they teach. I saved the College from staff re-deployment for years and years and refused to countenance it and fought against it, in the end we have had very little redeployment. I feel I have always stood up for the staff and protected you all. I really cannot say more than that but there were fights and fights in the late seventies and early eighties. The place needs a fighter and no doubt that will continue. You cannot run these places unless you are prepared to fight for them.

Progressive teachers really, though great idealists, have to face the sad fact that nearly every battle they have won may have turned out worse in the end for comprehensive schools – except the major one. But the extraordinary fact is that the situation is recognised as normal and Sholing Girls' or Weston Park Boys' or even Woodlands are set as Secondary Comprehensive Schools and nobody expects Grammars or Secondary Moderns in areas like this anymore.

From my point of view the smaller comprehensives do not look so good but I realise the staff and parents see it now as an established kind of school and we who have been teaching longer that twenty years must shut up. On the whole I think the change was right and has done more good than ill but I was for streaming Comprehensives and for large ones – on the whole – an eight form entry. I am for the break at sixteen plus whatever the drawbacks, and I think these places are right; probably Tertiaries have to come and are coming of course. Figures show that the number of Sixth Form Colleges is stationery –

under one hundred and twenty and that the Tertiaries are growing now to perhaps nearly fifty.

Still it has been a good Local Education Authority to work for. So there it is. Look to the future. It is simply marvellous at Itchen. I would cling to the timetable, even the peg board. I give you Picasso; I gave the painting when I arrived. Have a look at Guernica whenever you feel depressed about minor things.

Historians will know the sad history of Disraeli. When he finally became Prime Minister after long, long striving, he said to the Queen "Maam, I have climbed to the top of the greasy pole" There is no evidence anywhere that he ever gave advice about or found out how to climb down again. He died not too long after he stopped being Prime Minister. Gladstone was then Prime Minister. He was doing the washing up one day, when a messenger came in and gave him a note. He turned to his wife and said "Dizzy's dead then" and continued with the washing up. I hope this is not for me!' On the following evening 16 July a large farewell celebration party was held in the College hall. Here tributes were heaped upon Philip with over two hundred and fifty people in attendance including Itchen M.P. Christopher Chope, chairman of the governors Betty Martin, governors, staff and former teachers, students and friends. Among those who spoke of their memories of Philip were County Education Officer, Richard Clarke; Colin Davis, Head of a Farnborough Comprehensive school, who was taught by Philip at East Ham Grammar School; Dr. Alan Leech, Head of Bohunt Comprehensive School in Liphook, who was introduced to teaching by Philip when he was Head at New Mills Grammar School, and one of Itchen's Deputy Principals, Dennis Huxtable. As part of a thank you to Philip the Governors decided to rename the library as the 'Philip Vennis Library'. Philip was most touched and honoured with this gesture.

Philip 's final address as Principal of Itchen College was given to the student leavers' assembly on 30 July. 'Churchill once said in a speech to the Sixth at Harrow School – he was very fond of the idea of forty years on and loved the song and indeed many of you will have seen the play – his attitudes and the sort of school, of course, are dated now yet some things from these traditions ought to remain, he said "Eighteen to twenty four, those are the years of adventure, experience and romance, those should be the years of fellowship and good cheer. I tell you all to make them so – eighteen to twenty four those are the years."

You are eighteen and I am nearly sixty three, you are beginning and I am ending. In September 1948 I addressed my first Sixth Form as a school master. You are my fortieth Second year sixth. It is of course, and properly so, a lifetime. Many do not live as long. I do not know how many thousands of late teenagers

I have known. I am not sad merely tired. I have stayed here a little too long. Certainly it was a different world in 1948 and yet things have changed less than many might think. The splendour of academic work continues. Many traditions of Sixth Form life continue. Many of the jokes are the same jokes but with small variations. The spread of ability in this Sixth form is much greater but that does not make people very different from their predecessors and your predecessors had the same fears, loves, romances, desires, objectives and worries, above all worries that you have. We had won a great war and defeated a terrible enemy and we were in the middle of tremendous social experiments under the Labour Government. Today, we are experimenting in the opposite way but it is probably right that the British should experiment. Churchill's words have not dated and this season of your lives eighteen to twenty four remains as he said.

I hope you have made friends at Itchen. I hope you will live happily and sensibly as citizens. I dare to hope you will make happy and sensible marriages and be happy and sensible parents. Naturally I hope your exams have gone well, that your Higher Education will be good and useful and desires met in every way possible so though we are both leaving we do not want to be sad.

Teaching is a sad scene. It always has been. It is, of course, but it is also goodbye just when you know people. I hope to meet you, Itchen hopes to see you. If you want to see the staff because you like them and you feel you owe them something, as you do, then come back but we do not want loyalty to institutions as such, we want it to people so I bid you farewell from my colleagues and myself. You represent I hope a last part of forty years' achievement, what little good I have done is represented in you. Now listen to one of our pre-eminent metaphysical poets of the seventeenth century, John Donne in this extract from his Meditation 17. ' No man is an island, entire of itself; every man is a piece of the continent, a part of the main; if a clod be washed away by the sea, Europe is the less, as well as if a promontory were, as well as if a manor of thy friend's or of thine own were; any man's death diminishes me, because I am involved in mankind, and therefore never send to know for whom the bell tolls; it tolls for thee.' And now lastly Shakespeare's farewell to the Theatre. Was he ailing? Was he old? Was he giving up London and going back to Stratford on Avon? This poem was put into The Tempest (Act 4 Scene 1) after the play was written.

"Our revels now are ended. These our actors,
As I foretold you, were all spirits and
Are melted into air, into thin air:
And, like the baseless fabric of this vision,
The cloud-capp'd towers, the gorgeous palaces,
The solemn temples, the great globe itself,

Yea, all which it inherit, shall dissolve
And, like this insubstantial pageant faded,
Leave not a rack behind. We are such stuff
As dreams are made on, and our little life
Is rounded with a sleep.

Peter Church became the new Principal of Itchen College in September 1988, and this is what he writes about his predecessor. 'Philip was a hard act to follow. He was a charismatic and mercurial presence who left an indelible mark on the College and also left behind a horde of Philip stories which I heard at various times throughout my years as Principal. Some may have been true, some almost certainly hugely exaggerated but all of them great fun!

I remember he came in during the appointment process as a whirlwind, hovered as a rather anxious zephyr during my pre-talks with staff and once on my own left me with the huge and totemic College timetable in his study – all bits of coloured card and pegs which I never got round to understanding. However it was the Timetable which was his instrument of control and when I abandoned the peg-board and left timetable construction to the computer geeks the College was never the same again! Philip loved Itchen College – as all of us did. He was remembered with great affection and with some awe, as a very influential Principal of the college and an active educationalist on the wider stage of Hampshire education. The staff he appointed to the college have in their own right gone to spread the ideals Philip believed in to many other colleges up and down the country. In fact, Philip must have appointed more future Principals than most. Certainly several thousand students gained life chances at Itchen over his years as Principal.

By his sheer force of personality he turned a selective grammar school into a comprehensive post-sixteen College which was to act as a pattern and example for many later Sixth Form College reorganisations throughout the country.

He remained an incredibly enthusiastic and supportive Friend of The College – and me - until his untimely death at a relatively early age. Hundreds of students from Southampton and around owe their success in life to his inspiration.'

Philip did not find retirement easy. Following the farewells and accolades at Itchen he immediately took a holiday to the U.S.A. with Diana. The holiday proved to be rather longer than he had planned. Within a few days of arriving at Phoenix Arizona, he suffered a minor stroke, which initially affected his eyesight, but luckily this later returned to near normal. He did, however, have to spend three weeks in the 'Frank Sinatra' hospital (one of Philip's favourite singers!) in Palm Springs and then three weeks convalescing before he could fly home.

Something like this stroke was predictable, he had been so energetic and on such a high in his final weeks at Itchen that something had to give. He had envisaged his retirement of being able to teach Latin and Greek once more and he had already been offered a part-time job to teach these subjects at Portsmouth High School for Girls. Because of the stroke this did not happen, although he did continue to teach Greek on a one to one basis in his own home.

To Philip, the main purpose of his life had gone and adjusting to the quietness of retirement was always going to be difficult. He was so enthusiastic and engaged with the education of young people that once this had finished he was lost and without an aim or focus. However, he did enjoy the eleven years he had in retirement. He continued to read and be informed about current education thinking, he spent many hours listening to and reading about classical music, in which he was very knowledgeable, he travelled abroad several times and spent time walking and enjoying the beautiful scenery of the Solent and South Downs.

Unbeknown to him that at the end of his life he would lose his voice, he had the foresight before this happened to make a tape of some of his personal and private thoughts. This is a little of what he recorded for Diana: 'I want you to hear my voice after I am gone. My wishes are for a Quaker funeral in the Friends Meeting House in Southampton and to be buried in the Quaker Burial ground, and I wish for you, Diana, when your time comes to be buried with me. I want the funeral to be held in the spirit of quiet peace and hope that you will be comforted and strengthened by those who mourn my passing. Southampton Meeting is my spiritual home, since I am a man of many words, the hours silence gives me a chance to nourish and refresh the spirit within me. Do not forget me, I think of my own dear father and the risk is that I will be forgotten. I loved my father truly, my mother outlived her time, she did not understand.

Diana, I have loved you and every minute I have always wanted to be with you. I am a man of wilful spirit and a man of ideas. You and I have grown old together and loved one another always. We have done wonderful things together. Life has no meaning unless it is with someone you love. We don't need to explain it, we can't explain.

Let me not to the marriage of true minds
Admit impediments. Love is not love
Which alters when it alteration finds,
Or bends with the remover to remove:
O no! it is an ever-fixed mark
That looks on tempests and is never shaken;
It is the star to every wandering bark,
Whose worth's unknown, although his height be taken.

Love's not Time's fool, though rosy lips and cheeks
Within his bending sickle's compass come:
Love alters not with his brief hours and weeks,
But bears it out even to the edge of doom.
　　　If this be error and upon me proved,
　　　I never writ, nor no man ever loved.
(William Shakespeare's Sonnet 116)

In a happy marriage 'the wife provides the climate, the husband the landscape',
'love makes the world go round' and that's been true for me. I believe in God,
and we will meet again'.

As the poet John Clare (1793 to 1864) says in his poem 'Love lives beyond the
Tomb.

Love lives beyond
The tomb, the earth, which fades like dew –
I love the fond,
The faithful, and the true.
Love lies in sleep,
The happiness of healthy dreams,
Eve's dews may weep,
But love delightful seems.
'Tis seen in flowers,
And in the even's pearly dew
On earth's green hours,
And in the heaven's eternal blue.

'Tis heard in Spring
When light and sunbeams, warm and kind,
On angels wing
Bring love and music to the wind.
And where is voice
So young, so beautiful, so sweet
As nature's choice,
Where Spring and lovers meet?
Love lies beyond
The tomb, the earth, the flowers, and dew.
I love the fond,
The faithful, young, and true.

Philip continues 'Family life is the best life, watching the children growing up and daily changing. Each age has its own wonderful payment for the age we are. I would like to see grandchildren and help educate them into intelligent young people with a love of literature and poetry – poetry is so important. I wrote these two poems (as well as many others) in 1949 and as my life draws to a close the first one always reminds me of you and your beautiful eyes; whilst the second one is about my leaving you and going to the 'prison', that is death.'

<u>Bright eyes</u>
Hello, bright eyes – look at me.
Say with me the poem
For two, written by all men.
Lovely lady of the gleaming
Look, listen gladly...
And the bright-eyed goddess
Athene answered, saying
"O that you were a goodly man for loving me."
So Homer was there too.
Come then, bright eyes.

<u>Disappointment</u>
My heart inside me wept,
But not with grief; with
Love again. I was late
But the phantom would take over,
Farewell, my love, for this day;

I know you and yet, not to know
These thoughts. A return
From exile, into prison, and
I think to love you still,
And will.

In July 1999, Philip was diagnosed with cancer of the thyroid, this was a terrible illness for him, since very early on he lost his power of speech and for a man who had depended on his voice for the whole of his life, this was worse than the amputation of a limb. Philip's voice was a large part of his formidable character – it was smooth and powerful, and could make you pay attention, comfort you or frighten you. The agony of losing one's voice for ever is horrendous – never being able to talk again and the loss of connection with others was devastating –

he had lost his 'self'. It cut Philip off from society, although he communicated by written word. He bravely faced the ravages of the illness and two months before he died he presided at his daughter's wedding – organising the service and the readings to make it a memorable day for her. He still had the wish, the ability and the skills to do this, and of course, the ceremony was most moving. One month before his death, one of his closest friends, Gordon Ward, who was English Advisor for Hampshire, wrote the following poem

Philip dear friend
Do not end, do not end
Ending is anguish
For you, and for us.

Philip dear friend
Try to mend, try to mend
Mending's a miracle
For you, and for us.

Philip dear friend
Whether you end, or whether you mend
Makes a world of difference
For you, and for us.
Philip, dear friend, dear friend, dear friend.

On 21 December 1999, Philip lost consciousness, and earlier on the same day his first grandchild came out of hospital. He was brought that evening into Philip's house, two hours before Philip died. The scene, something reminiscent of a Greek Tragedy – Billy, the new born baby being brought into the home in his mother's arms and Philip in a coffin being taken out by the undertakers.

ACKNOWLEDGEMENTS

The family have given their permission for the use of personal writings, private letters, and public speeches of Philip Vennis.

All the photographs reproduced in this book are from the author's own collection.

Every reasonable attempt has been made to contact copyright holders of passages reproduced in this book. If any passages have been inadvertently overlooked the author and the publisher would be pleased to hear from them and make good any errors of omission, which are brought to their attention, in any future editions.

I am most grateful to everyone who has helped or contributed in the production of this book. I am especially grateful to the following:

London Metropolitan Archives.
Dulwich College Archives and Archivist Calista Lucy.
Garth Davidson. Peter Edgley. Alan Gregory. Hector McLean.
Bletchley Park Archives and Archivist Stephan Ovens.
Royal Navy – Navy Command, Disclosure Cell Section.
Mark Cornwall-Jones. Myfanwy Cornwall-Jones.
Peterhouse Archives and Archivist Dr. Richard Lovatt.
Margrith Mistry. Professor Soli Mistry.

East Ham Grammar School, Old Esthameian Magazines.
Stratford Express.
Ronald Aldridge. Colin Curds. Colin Davies. John Edwards. Sir Christopher France. Bill Hubert. Ronald Impey. Donald Martin. John Moore. Tony Prince. Martin Rooke-Matthews. Peter Watkins. Brian Wright.
Ounsdale Omnibus Magazines.
William Salt Library, Stafford. Staffordshire Record Office.
Professor Colin Appleby. Philip Bodley. Jennifer Cornes (nee Piper). Linda Fletcher (nee Hoyle). Geoff Morris. Tony Unwin.

New Mills Old Millonian Magazines.

New Mill Historical Society, Dr.Bryant.

High Peak Reporter.

New Mills School headteacher, Jesse Elms, bursar Jane Crowton.

Derbyshire Records Office.

Christine Ely (nee Worthington). Heather Govier (nee Swinburn). Geoff Heath. Georgina Hutber. Dr.Alan Leech. John Robinson. Alan Sheldon. Elaine Stratton (nee Robinson). Ian Stuart. Robert Wilson. Professor David Woods. CBE. Dr. John Worthington.

Southampton City Archives.

Old Issonian Magazines.

Bitterne Local History Society.

Southern Evening Echo.

David Bothwell. Peter Church. Robin Corbin. Jo Dunford. Bill Eastman. Jan Feber. Jane Hale. George Heller. Barri Hurford-Jones. Dennis Huxtable. Roy Jones. Lisa McCarthy. Bishop Ronald Milner. Jonathan Palmer. Steve Perkins. Norman Savage. Terri Stelling. Gordon Ward.